Holy Places

Holy Places

How Pilgrimage Changed the World

KATHRYN HURLOCK

Profile Books

First published in Great Britain in 2025 by
Profile Books Ltd
29 Cloth Fair
London
EC1A 7JQ
www.profilebooks.com

1 3 5 7 9 10 8 6 4 2

Typeset in Garamond by MacGuru Ltd
Printed and bound in Great Britain by
CPI Group (UK) Ltd, Croydon CR0 4YY

Illustrations reproduced by kind permission of Alamy on pages 11, 18, 92, 117, 150, 162, 179, 186, 204, 255, 270, 280, 289, 294 and 309; by the Art Institute of Chicago on page 109; by the Rijksmuseum on pages 33 and 67; by the Wellcome Collection on pages 29, 82, 127, 142, 221 and 234; and from Wikimedia Commons on pages 46, 59, 192 and 264.

A CIP catalogue record for this book is available from the British Library.

ISBN 978 1 80081 743 2
eISBN 978 1 80081 745 6

MIX
Paper | Supporting responsible forestry
FSC® C171272

Contents

Introduction: A World of Pilgrimage 1
1. Tai Shan, China 10
2. The Ganges, India 27
3. Delphi, Greece 45
4. Jerusalem, Israel/Palestine 63
5. Mecca, Saudi Arabia 86
6. Rome, Italy 105
7. Istanbul, Turkey 124
8. Iona, Scotland 145
9. Karbala, Iraq 160
10. Chichén Itzá, Mexico 176
11. Muxima, Angola 190
12. Bear Butte, South Dakota, USA 202
13. Amritsar, Punjab, India 217
14. Lourdes, France 233
15. Saintes-Maries-de-la-Mer, France 252
16. Rātana Pā, New Zealand 267
17. Buenos Aires, Argentina 279
18. Shikoku, Japan 292
19. Santiago de Compostela, Spain 308

Notes 329
Acknowledgements 386
Bibliography 387
Index 437

INTRODUCTION: A WORLD OF PILGRIMAGE

In the winter of 1171, King Henry II of England was travelling through Wales on his way to Ireland when he decided to embark on a short pilgrimage. His Irish journey was purely political, as several of his Norman lords based in Wales had recently conquered parts of Ireland, and Henry needed to see them in person to stamp his authority on their actions. There was little other reason for the king to visit remote Pembrokeshire, but now that he was there it was the perfect opportunity to complete a pilgrimage to the country's most important religious site, the small cathedral of St David's. Fifty years before, the pope had declared that two pilgrimages to St David's had the same spiritual value as one to Rome, so it was an attractive proposition. And as Henry was about to embark on a winter crossing of the Irish Sea, it was also wise to pray for a safe passage, something he had done on previous occasions when sailing to his lands in France. While he was there, he also made a gift to the cathedral of two choral capes and some silver – just to ensure that his appeal was heard. His pilgrimage may have had a third motive: the king had recently quarrelled with the Welsh prince of the area, Rhys ap Gruffydd, and a pilgrimage was a sign that he intended peace, something the king needed the local ruler to believe while he was away overseas.

The following year, Henry returned from Ireland and landed at St Justinian's Bay just under two miles west of the cathedral.

This time he came 'dressed as a pilgrim, on foot and leaning on a staff', and went to St David's to pray. This visit was more overtly pious than his outward pilgrimage, as he came without his household (they had been sent on ahead to the more southerly port of Milford Haven), and the king timed it so that he would be there just after Easter. When Henry arrived he was warmly welcomed by the cathedral's canons (though not by a local woman who prophesied his death) and went into the cathedral to pray, thereby earning the spiritual reward that came with completing his second pilgrimage. He may have felt he needed it. In December 1170 his former friend and archbishop Thomas Becket had been martyred in Canterbury cathedral, allegedly at his instigation, so the need for absolution may have been very much on Henry's mind.[1] The small scale and remoteness of St David's cathedral belied its significance. As a pilgrimage destination, the king believed it had the potential to aid with his safety at sea, his relationships with other rulers and his immortal soul. Even simply reaching it was a sign of his power, as South Wales was not always welcoming to English kings.

Across the world and for millennia, people have taken to the road on pilgrimage to seek the help of their gods, saints and spirits when they needed protection, wanted to ease their troubled souls, sought cures or gave thanks, or wished to make some sort of political statement. For some, this meant undertaking a journey of thousands of miles over months, if not years, to reach a holy site. For most, it probably meant a local pilgrimage which could be completed perhaps in a day. Many pilgrims, like Henry II, went on pilgrimage time and again, visiting places with varying motives in mind as each holy place had something different to offer.

As a religious practice undertaken within most of the world's faiths, pilgrimage has always reflected contemporary events whether conducted by adherents of major religions, small sects or no set faith. For a Muslim who is able to do so, visiting Mecca at least once in their lifetime is an obligation. For Christians, pilgrimages are a voluntary but much-practised expression of faith. Hindus and Buddhists are encouraged to go on pilgrimage, while for the Native Americans of the Plains or the Romani people of Europe it is a major milestone and an integral part of their lives. But the hows, whens and whys have varied over time, and from place to place, affected by everything from warfare to the weather. In turn, pilgrimages have been undertaken for all manner of reasons, from personal healing and spiritual growth to seeking approval for political decisions or gaining support for imperial rule. Today, pilgrimages are primarily seen as opportunities for contemplation or to promote faith or well-being, but many of the oldest mixed the spiritual and the earthly in ways that could not be separated. The ancient Greeks regularly consulted oracles for advice on politics and war; the ancient Chinese sought the sanction of the gods of folk religion for dynastic change; medieval kings sought out spiritual support for their wars and gave thanks when they were victorious at pilgrimage sites. How might history have been different if pilgrimage had not been part of the political world? And on a personal level, pilgrimages were equally important. In the days before mass medicine, what would the thousands of pilgrims who sought cures at shrines and wells or international cult centres have done? Where would they have turned in desperate times?

Some pilgrimage places have endured for thousands of years, like the mountains revered in China, or the rivers and wells venerated all around the world. Others have come and gone, perhaps due to competition, as new centres promote their attractions and outclass them. More miracles, more powerful gods and larger buildings all sway pilgrims to adopt new holy places, while those sidelined struggle to survive the loss of income from the decline in traffic. Some pilgrimages died out because the places that attracted pilgrims in the first place fell into decay, or simply disappeared. Throughout history, the shrines and tombs of saints have been destroyed by natural events, hostile rulers or invading forces. It is sometimes simply that they are collateral damage, but when pilgrimage sites are central to the sovereignty of a place, attacks may be targeted and political. Political concerns drove the destruction of Sufi and 'Alid shrines in Iran and central Asia in the Middle Ages, and the temples of India during the era of colonial rule. Changing beliefs and ideologies have destroyed pilgrimage sites and even banned pilgrimage itself. The Reformation in Europe swept away shrines in Britain and the Netherlands; thousands of buildings were locked up, statues, reliquaries and images were broken up or melted down, and pilgrimage was effectively criminalised as Catholicism was suppressed.

New destinations are created too, as we'll see. Everything from caves to sacred groves, the bodies of saints to paintings have been adopted by people seeking a closer connection to the divine. Emerging religions have developed pilgrimage places, using sites associated with their founders and their lives to build new centres of faith in the same way that established religions have. The Church of the Latter-Day Saints, or Mormons, a nineteenth-century religion born out of American Christian revivalism, does not include pilgrimage as part of its official doctrine, yet that hasn't stopped its members from joining in with the growing enthusiasm for pilgrimage. Sites associated with Mormonism's founder, John Smith, like the temple where he had his first vision and the places he and his followers stopped on their three-month trek to Utah, are increasingly drawing the devout. Similar developments can be found around the world, the reasons for their creation as diverse as the new beliefs that underpin them.

Older religions, transported around the world through trade, colonisation or conversion, have always constructed new churches and shrines so that they have somewhere to go close at hand. This is what happened in Goa when Jesuit missionaries from Portugal built a church to house the remains of their founder, St Francis Xavier, who had died on his way to China in 1552. This beautiful church, the basilica of Bom Jesus, sits in the heart of the Portuguese district in Old Goa and is one of the seven wonders of the Portuguese colonial world. It is a testament to how missionaries and colonisers spread pilgrimage and religion by creating new focal points, but it is also just one of the hundreds of places around the world where the creation of new pilgrimage places was used by people of all faiths to settle, convert and make new communities. Where important sites grew, so too did wider networks of other pilgrimage places, and these were all incorporated into a place's local if not national identity.

Access to pilgrimage places has also been subject to change, and the global history of pilgrimage is also one of political and population control. During the Second World War, for example, pilgrimages were harder to take part in because of the disruption to everyday life and travel, but this was also a time when many people sought the comfort of faith, so pilgrims found ways to carry on, one way or another. Pilgrimages were used, unsurprisingly, to pray for peace and for help against the enemy, while access to pilgrimage places was blocked by occupying forces as a way to strip the conquered of their identity and deprive them of the comfort brought by the communal nature of pilgrimage. The German occupiers of the district around the

Black Madonna's shrine in Częstochowa, known as the Queen of Poland, renamed the road approaching the shrine usually thronging with pilgrims Adolf Hitler Allee to give the area a more Germanic feel.[2] More recently, pilgrimages have been used to exert political and secular control in times of peace. In late 2020 the Chinese authorities introduced a ban on 'personal' pilgrimages to Mecca by Uyghur Muslims. The London *Times* carried the headline CHINA BANS HAJ FOR MUSLIMS WHO FAIL PATRIOTISM TEST, as plans were unveiled to subject potential pilgrims to a programme of education and testing before allowing them on an accompanied journey to Saudi Arabia.[3]

Over the past century, pilgrimage has increasingly been used as a term to cover all kinds of journeys which are considered to have some sort of meaning: protest marches over unemployment or demanding the vote; holidays to the homes of famous figures like Elvis; journeys of remembrance and mourning to the Western Front or the Second World War internment camps created by Japan. The relationship between pilgrimage and tourism, something which has always existed and always been contentious, is pushed to the fore with 'pilgrimage' being used as a term to market escapes from the pressures of modern life, time spent in nature or opportunities to be together as a family. This seems like a story of secularisation, but religious pilgrimage continues to go from strength to strength too. In a world where many of the driving forces for pilgrimage appear to have changed, it is sometimes surprising to see that so much of what drives pilgrims to travel remains, and that it continues to have an impact on the world today.

This book explores the global history of pilgrimage through nineteen places, examining their role in world history and looking at how the activity of pilgrimage and the sites themselves have shaped society, culture and politics from the ancient world to the present day. It starts in the east with two of the world's great natural pilgrimage sites in the ancient cradles of civilisation, Tai Shan in China and the Ganges of India, before moving west to Delphi, home of the oracle that advised politicians and generals in the ancient Greek world. Then come four cities at the heart of several of the world's greatest pilgrimage traditions: Jerusalem, a place of pilgrimage for three of the world's major religions; Mecca, Islam's holiest site; Rome, the seat of Catholicism; and Istanbul, a city that has been under the control of Catholics, Orthodox Christians and now Muslims.

From there we move on to two places which reflect more local and personal pilgrimage traditions, albeit in different ways. Iona, a small island off the west coast of Scotland, was originally a medieval pilgrimage site important to the Kings of the Isles but is now a place of ecumenical faith and the international home for the members of the Iona Community. Karbala, by contrast, is the site of the largest Muslim pilgrimage in the world, but has the same intimate feel as Iona in that it is a pilgrimage of family and community.

From there we move to Chichén Itzá in Mexico and Bear Butte in the USA, both Native American religious sites with practices alien to the Europeans who encountered them. In contrast the invaders and colonisers were responsible for the foundation of Muxima in Angola, where they set up a church where enslaved people were forcibly baptised, a legacy which is problematic and hard to reconcile with the site's message of peaceful pilgrimage. Around the same time in northern India, a new pilgrimage centre was developed in Amritsar, not through enforced settlement and colonisation, but through the purchase of land to create a holy space for pilgrims.

The last six chapters cover a range of pilgrimages – from the internationally famous to the obscure and arguably profane. What ties them together is that they reflect modern ideas of what pilgrimage is and the variety of forms it can take. Lourdes and Saintes-Maries-de-la-Mer are two shrines dedicated to women in the south of France, but they could not be more different. The first is dedicated to the Virgin Mary and is the epitome of orthodox Catholic pilgrimage, the sick supported by priests, nuns and volunteers in an act of faith; the other is where Roma and Gypsy pilgrims meet to play music and celebrate into the night in ways that shock their more orthodox counterparts in Lourdes, and to revere Black Sara, a figure not recognised by Rome. The next two pilgrimages, to Rātana Pā in New Zealand and Buenos Aires in Argentina, celebrate twentieth-century figures revered both during their lifetimes and after their deaths who, despite considerable controversy, have continued to attract pilgrims. These pilgrimages are intimately entwined with the politics of their respective countries, participation being both a way to gain political support and to make a statement of resistance. The final chapters cover two of the world's great pilgrim routes: the 750-mile circular Shikoku pilgrimage in Japan and the 490-mile Camino Francés (French Way) to Santiago de Compostela in northern Spain. Though both are set routes, they are undertaken in different ways, the relative importance of walking, riding, cycling or driving a continual part of the debate over what it even means to be a pilgrim.

I could easily have chosen one hundred sites in one country alone and still been tortured by the ones I had left out. Hundreds of small churches, tiny springs and wells or remote mountain-top shrines are vitally important to those who live in their immediate vicinity, but have little impact beyond that. For every Mecca or Lourdes that draws pilgrims in their millions from around the globe, there are thousands of obscure sites dedicated to people you will never hear about, but which are reliably visited by a clutch of pilgrims each year. For them, they are incredibly important; for us, they are mere curiosities. Equally, there are important sites with global reach which I have omitted as they tell similar stories to the places I have picked. Those are perhaps for another book. In this I have chosen sites based on what they tell us about the role of pilgrimage in global history – how it can make or break regimes, inspire millions to pray for healing, unite and create communities, inspire the construction of global infrastructure or embody the identity of a people. Many of them will no doubt be familiar – Rome, Jerusalem, Santiago, Shikoku – while others are less known yet still important to understanding the myriad ways in which people have performed pilgrimage, and the impact it has had on them, their societies and the wider world.

1

TAI SHAN

China

When China's currency was reissued in 1999, one of the most striking changes was to the design of the banknotes. Where the old notes had shown images of a range of Chinese people, all new denominations carried a portrait of China's former leader Mao Zedong on one side, painted by the famous artist Liu Wenxi. For the other, the authorities chose places they considered culturally or historically significant to the Chinese: the hundred-yuan note showed the Great Hall of the People in Beijing, the seat of government; the Three Gorges of the Yangtze River, an area of outstanding beauty, was chosen for the reverse of the ten-yuan note. On the five-yuan note, they selected an image of Tai Shan (Mount Tai), the most revered of China's sacred mountains.[1] Lying 300 miles south of Beijing, and rising over 5,000 feet above the city of Tai, it is the highest mountain in Shandong province. The contrast between Mao's portrait and the image of this mountain could not be starker. The first depicts the founding father of Chinese communism, an anti-imperialist who rejected traditional paternal authority and reverence for ancestors, and who promoted loyalty to the communist people and state above all else. The other is the symbolic site of the imperial power that communism rejected, and of the

Five-yuan Chinese banknote, issued in 2005. The new notes featured sites of national importance in China such as Tai Shan, which was chosen for the most common banknote in circulation.

filial piety – ancestor worship – which communism largely suppressed but which has dominated Chinese culture and society for thousands of years.

China has five sacred mountains: Hua Shan in the west, Tai Shan in the east, two Heng Shans, one in the north and one in the south, and Song Shan in the centre. They are the representatives of the Five Elements (earth, water, wood, fire, metal) which are believed to make everything in the universe.[2] All five are places of pilgrimage, and several are bigger, but Tai Shan is the most important of them all because its position in the east means it is lit by the sun, bringer of life, before its fellow peaks. Indeed, ascending at night is a popular way to visit Tai Shan as this gives the pilgrim the opportunity to view the sunrise from its summit. It is probably the most climbed mountain in the world and has a history of worship dating back to the Neolithic era, though the earliest evidence of pilgrimage dates to 219 BCE when the first emperor went to the mountain's summit.[3]

In that time the mountain has attracted the greatest of China's leaders, its literati and philosophers, court officials, peasantry and the poorest of society. They come for myriad reasons determined by faith, philosophy and circumstance. For Taoists, Tai Shan is the home of a nature god, bringing much-needed rain, while its very size and presence are a reminder of stability in times of trouble.[4] For others, it is a source of life or a place where souls return, the god of Mount Tai overseeing life and death. Many deities are worshipped on Tai Shan, including the god of Mount Tai's daughter, Bixia Juanjun, but the mountain is also a god in itself, with great power over the fate of the people.[5] As a site of nature worship, a place where pilgrims seek help and where people go on pilgrimage to pray for children or the dead, Tai Shan has much in common with many places around the world. It has also attracted Chinese leaders for political reasons, including at least twelve emperors and over ninety of China's ancient kings.

Pilgrims reach the top by climbing around 6,700 steps from the North Gate to the summit, following a path dotted with small temples, shrines and sanctuaries, eleven gates and fourteen archways, past inscriptions commemorating the visits of previous pilgrims carved into the rock of the mountain itself. They have come from all over China, and from all of society's many levels. Writing in 1313, one official complained:

> nowadays gentlemen, farmers, artisans and merchants, and even runners, wrestlers, actors and whores ... will, for the purpose of praying for fortune and repaying their vows, neglect their businesses but bring together money and goods, gold and silver, vases and plates, saddles and horses, clothes and silks, and from far and near congregate from all directions; the crowd has to be counted in the tens of thousands and the hubbub lasts for days on end ... As there is such a crowd of simple and deluded people, there have to be cunning and evil fellows. It is not only bound to be a defilement of the divine intelligences, but also, we fear, will create all kinds of nuisance.[6]

The path up the mountainside was often packed with visitors, especially in the warmer months, a swarm so dense they have been likened to insects. Wang Shizhen, an official who visited three times in the 1550s, thought the lantern-carrying pilgrims who climbed this winding mountain path in the dark before dawn looked like 'a large collection of fireflies'.[7] The number of nameless pilgrims heading to the mountain summit was vast, and may have been as many as one million a year by the end of the century.[8]

Over time new sacred attractions have been added, like the beautifully named fifteenth-century temple of the Jade Maiden Pool, or the Han Dynasty cypress tree planted to commemorate the pilgrimage of Emperor Wudi (ruled 157–87). There are now so many that pilgrims are cautioned not to stop too often on the way up or they will never reach the top. Most pilgrims walk, though for centuries those who have been able to afford it have also paid to be carried by sedan chair or, at least since 1983 (and before the mountain's UNESCO status would have hindered such developments), go by bus and cable car.[9]

A thriving economy sprang up to cater for the great numbers of pilgrims to Tai Shan. The essayist and administrator Zhang Dai's seventeenth-century visit involved guides who organised accommodation, sedan-chair carriers, fees to access the mountain and, for those who wanted them, courtesans. Large banquets were laid on for pilgrims, accompanied by music and singing, which enabled the guides to profit considerably from the eight or nine thousand pilgrims Zhang Dai said came every day. In the space in front of the Tung-Yueh temple, seventeenth-century pilgrims could also enjoy cockfighting and wrestling, watch plays and listen to storytelling, or shop at the many stalls and stands.

Over the centuries the route up Tai Shan has acquired numerous hawkers and businesses catering to pilgrims.[10] Zhang Dai was particularly unimpressed by the poor who lined the route, begging for money, and by the inscriptions that covered the mountainside. 'The beggars exploited Mount Tai for money,' he moaned as he was carried by sedan chair past their outstretched arms, 'while the victors exploited Mount Tai for fame.'[11] The beggars were still there in great numbers when the American painter Mary Mullikin went on pilgrimage in the 1930s. One lived in a purpose-built bed at the side of the route, while another had a stuffed dummy of himself made to sit beside a begging bowl while he went about his other business. Sitting in the middle of the path, the beggars were impossible to ignore.[12]

What makes Tai Shan so important is what it symbolises. Mountains define pilgrimage in China. Unlike many other parts of the world, in China pilgrimage centres tend not to develop in cities but around natural sites. In fact, in Mandarin Chinese there is no equivalent to 'pilgrimage'. Instead, people refer to *chaoshan*, 'to have an audience with the mountain', or *jianxiang* (or *chin-hsiang*), 'to offer incense', a common devotional activity of mountain pilgrims.[13] Mountains were, and are, important in many of the faiths practised in China – Taoism, Buddhism, Confucianism, folk religions – as is the practice of offering incense to the gods, so much so that it is common to see incense burners for sale across China in the shape of mountain ranges or peaks. Though each faith might worship a different god or goddess in these places, or believe that they are responsible for varying aspects of their lives, what matters is the mountain itself. As the French historian Édouard Chavannes put it: 'The mountains are, in China, the divinities.'[14]

Pilgrimages of Duty

One of Chinese society's defining beliefs is the importance of filial piety, a key tenet of Confucianism and Taoist philosophy. Filial piety encompasses a wide range of acts and attitudes, but most enduring are reverence for, and obligation towards, one's ancestors, care of one's parents and providing male heirs to continue the family line. It is common to almost all Chinese beliefs and has been for several thousand years. So central has filial piety been in Chinese history that under the Tang dynasty (sixth to tenth century) it was illegal to abandon your parents or mourn insufficiently, while China's more recent one-child policy prompted cases of sex-selective abortion, infanticide and abandonment as parents desperately tried to have a longed-for son. Filial piety is about more than one's own family though. Loyalty to ancestors was considered synonymous with loyalty to the empire, so for much of China's imperial history filial piety was expressly promoted.[15]

Filial pilgrimages were so popular that they appeared in poems, plays and novels from the Middle Ages onwards, usually as cautionary tales about the importance of true filial observance. According to these beliefs, the living had a responsibility to honour their male ancestors through offerings and prayer, and in return the dead would help the living in times of need. Pilgrims could appeal to the dead at Tai Shan because the mountain was a gateway to them; the Chinese believed that the souls of the dead went to a small hill at the foot of the mountain, and there were judged by the god of the mountain. This made Tai Shan the perfect place for communicating with ancestors as they could be more easily reached there. Indeed, the mountain is so strongly associated with death and ancestry that some shaped the tombs of their dead like mountains. Little surprise that 'going to Tai Shan' became a euphemism for dying.[16]

An unbroken family line was necessary so that the living could pray for the dead and be safe in the knowledge that in years to come their descendants would in turn pray for them. This meant that a pilgrimage to Tai Shan was about both ancestors and descendants, as in addition to honouring the dead, men might also pray for a son to carry on family obligations after they no longer could. To fail to have a son was to fail one's ancestors.[17] From the thirteenth century onwards, women started to climb Tai in the belief that it would bring them and their family a male heir. Childless women had no real place in Chinese families, so the birth of a son was essential to give them a place in the family line and security within the home during their lifetimes. Royal princesses and imperial consorts appealed for a son on the mountain, asking Tai Shan to give them an heir 'to ensure the substantiality of the state'.[18] Elderly women with bound feet went to pray for male grandchildren and wives for sons, burning offerings in the hope they would be helped. They primarily prayed to Bixia Juanjun, daughter of the god of Mount Tai, who had (and still has) a particular role as a fertility goddess and a reputation for granting pregnancies to heirless couples.

Even though the influence of filial piety on Chinese society has diminished in the modern age, women still climb the hill in the hope that they or their children will conceive boys, burning paper money and incense as they have done for centuries.

Women pilgrims have long been regarded with some suspicion in China, perhaps because they have often used pilgrimage to escape from the strict and limiting confines of Chinese social mores. In the middle of the seventeenth century, a magistrate called Huang Liu-hong composed a popular guide for his fellow judges in which he claimed women used pilgrimages as a cover to travel and engage in decidedly irreligious activities, and warned that they 'seek liaisons with dissipated youths in secret passages of monasteries'.[19] He complained of orgies in Tai Shan's holy temples. Suspicion of women pilgrims is a common theme in the history of all kinds of faiths, and Huang Liu-hong's anger probably says more about him than about the actual behaviour of Chinese women on pilgrimage. Nevertheless, his accusations were widely accepted, and the Chinese were keen to enact laws that explicitly prohibited female pilgrimage, though these laws had little effect.[20]

Imperial Pilgrimage

The earliest recorded imperial pilgrimage to Tai Shan was conducted by China's first self-declared emperor, the brutal and tyrannical Qin Shi Huang (221–210 BCE).[21] He was making a clear statement: he had unified China to create an empire, and he ruled over it all without question. He is probably better known for the Great Wall of China, and for his burial in the mausoleum guarded by the 8000 soldiers of the Terracotta Army, but his assumption of the title 'emperor' when before China had only had kings was his real crowning glory. He was a

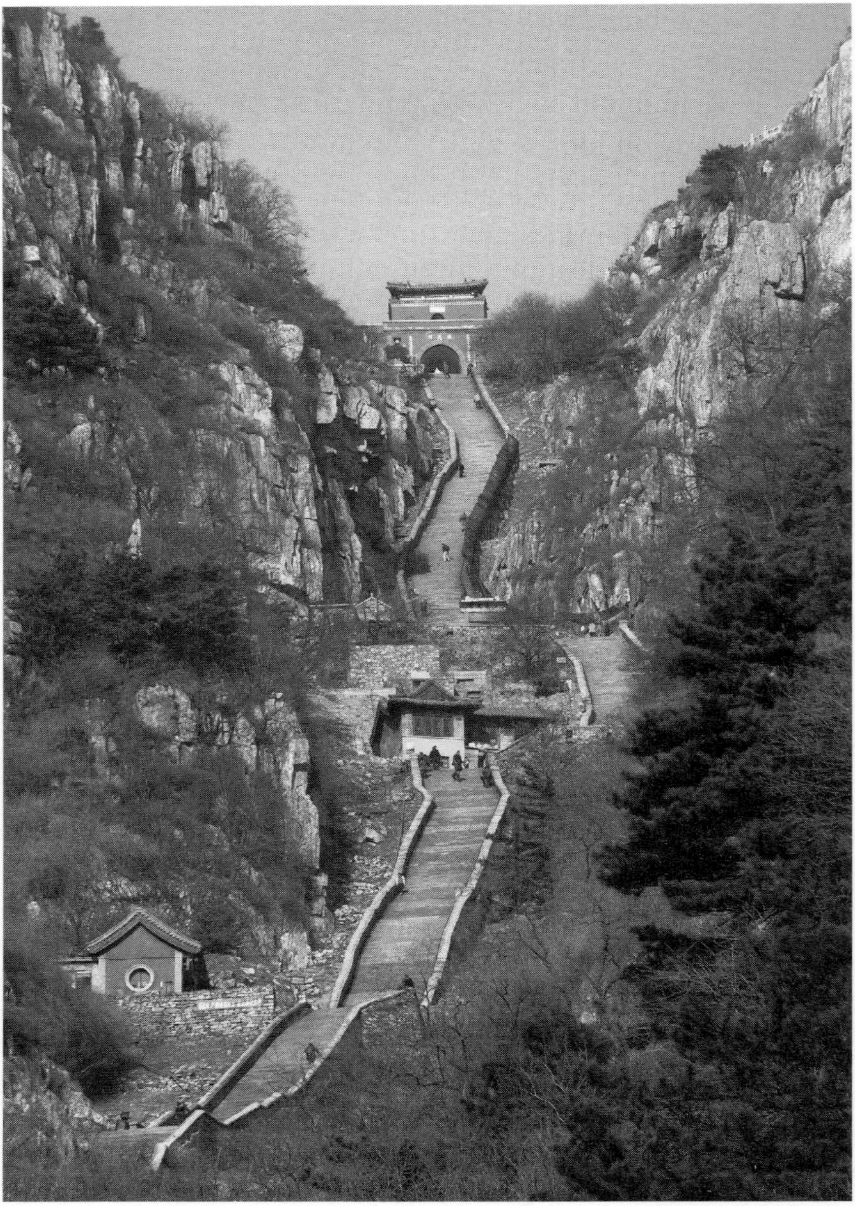

Reaching the top of Tai Shan involved climbing thousands of steps. Emperor Qin Shi Huang attempted the ascent in his chariot, while some modern pilgrims opt for the cable car.

man clearly at home with grand display, so it is little surprise that accounts of his pilgrimage describe him scandalising the scholars who advised him by completing his ascent of the mountain not reverently on foot, as they recommended, but racing up in the imperial chariot. His pride was punished, as the disrespected deity sent a storm as punishment which forced him to abandon his chariot on the downhill journey.[22]

While on pilgrimage Qin Shi Huang carried out the *feng* and *shan* sacrifices, rituals performed in honour of heaven and earth respectively.[23] The specifics of the ceremonies are unclear, but they involved making offerings to the god of Mount Tai at the foot of the mountain (the *shan* sacrifice), and then at the top (the *feng*), where emperors may have buried jade tablets inscribed with their successes, and burned offerings to the Jade Emperor in heaven, ruler of the world, whose grand temple stood nearby. Successful completion of *fengshan* was a sign that a ruler had received the mandate of heaven, a seal of approval on his reign as the Son of Heaven.

These were rituals shrouded in mystery. When Emperor Wu of the Han dynasty (ruled 141–87 BCE), the ruler responsible for opening the Silk Road to China, conducted *feng* in 110 BCE, he only took one other person with him to the top of the mountain. A few days later, that man was dead, leaving the emperor the only one who knew what had taken place. Historians have speculated that he believed the ritual would transfer a secret illness to his attendant, or that he was seeking the immortality that he believed was bestowed on emperors who were blessed by the gods.[24] This belief may have inspired some other imperial pilgrims. According to an inscription written some two hundred years later, 'If you climb Mount Tai, you may see immortal beings. They feed on the purest jade, they drink from the springs of manna. They yoke the scaly dragons to their carriage, they mount the floating clouds ... May you receive a never-ending span, long life that lasts for ten thousand years.'[25]

Pilgrimage to Tai Shan demonstrated imperial power and sacred approval of an emperor's rule. Guangwu (ruled 25–57 CE), the founder of China's Han dynasty, presumably waited so long after assuming power to complete his pilgrimage to Tai Shan because at the start of his reign he only ruled part of China.[26] It was only in 56 CE, after years of conquest and forcing local warlords to submit to his authority, that he could claim to rule the whole country and be worthy of completing the pilgrimage. At Tai Shan he would receive the mandate of heaven, a sign of favour and the legitimacy of his rule.[27]

The pilgrimage of Emperor Gaozong (ruled 649–83 CE) was about more than control over lands inside China's borders. By the 660s the emperor dominated his neighbours and was more powerful than his father, Taizong (ruled 626–49), had been. Taizong had never been to Tai Shan, despite the frequent urging of his courtiers, because he thought that 'his merits were not so glorious as to deserve the honor'.[28] The driving force behind Gaozong's pilgrimage was his wife, the much reviled but formidable Empress Wu. A former courtesan, Wu became Gaozong's second wife after his first proved childless. Wu was ruthless and ambitious, allegedly murdering her own daughter in an attempt to frame a love rival. From 660 onwards, following her husband's first stroke, she increasingly took control of the imperial court. She was quite literally the power behind the throne, sitting behind a pearl screen in council meetings so she could listen in and whisper instructions to her husband. She was the only woman in Chinese history to use the title 'emperor' – *huangdi* – in her own right, making this pilgrimage the only time a female emperor visited Tai Shan.[29]

Empress Wu came on the pilgrimage with her husband in

great style, the imperial couple accompanied by a train of followers sixty miles long made up of imperial princes and high officials of the court and military, soldiers and foreign dignitaries, as well as the hundreds of wagons carrying the food and tents the pilgrimage party needed. They set off in the closing weeks of 665 and arrived in Tai Shan the following year.[30]

Wu was interested in omens and symbols and knew how to use them to boost her power, demanding she be fully involved in the pilgrimage rituals. When the *fengshan* sacrifices were performed,[31] Empress Wu insisted that she be allowed to take part as a way of honouring previous empresses – filial piety being a good excuse – but also to show her power. Not only had she and her husband insisted on most of the court coming with them, they were also attended by representatives from Japan, India, Khmer, Khotan and three Korean kingdoms, and the exiled Persian court, whose leader served the emperor as one of his generals.[32] With an audience like that, not only did this pilgrimage show the dominance of the imperial family over China and its neighbours, it ensured the message of imperial strength would be carried across Asia.

Empress Wu's pilgrimage was about power, expansionism and her own status. The pilgrimage of the Song emperor Zhenzong (ruled 997–1022) in 997 was also a political act, but it appears to have inspired him to spread the wonders of Tai Shan to the people of China. His forty-seven-day pilgrimage, made in the first year of his reign, included the declaration of an amnesty and the announcement of a three-day bacchanal.[33] This was an interesting choice of celebration for a sacred journey, given that writers were highly critical of those who failed to undertake the pilgrimage with due solemnity, but then Zhenzong seems to have been a more generous and fun-loving emperor than many of his predecessors. Keen to promote Tai Shan and its spiritual importance to his people, thirteen years later the inhabitants of the northern province of Shanxi were given permission to build temples dedicated to the mountain closer to home as the real thing was too far away to reach easily.[34] This was the spiritual accompaniment to his politics, as this emperor's rule was defined by both the strengthening of his dynasty and the consolidation of its power in China, two developments he could claim were the result of his acceptance as the Son of Heaven at the start of his rule.[35]

Emperor Kangxi (1662–1722), of the Qing dynasty, was China's longest-ruling and perhaps greatest emperor. He was also widely travelled, reviving imperial touring in the aftermath of a damaging civil war. Coming to the throne at the tender age of eight, the protracted Revolt of the Three Feudatories hampered his attempts to gain control of the empire. However, he was politically astute and realised the need to bring together his heritage – he came from the Manchu people – and the wider Chinese people. He had used his youth and the years of war to study Chinese and realised that the country's scholars and elite Han literati needed to be brought on board if he was going to succeed. He also understood that many of his subjects were reluctant to accept the new dynasty (he was only the second Qing emperor to rule China proper), adhering by habit as much as anything else to the Ming dynasty that had come before. To get them on his side, Kangxi would have to show that he had the backing of a higher power and that he had been accepted as the Son of Heaven. This was important given that, when the Manchus took power, they claimed that their predecessors had been defeated because their incompetence had lost them heaven's approval. The result was his eastern tour and pilgrimage to Tai Shan in 1684.[36]

On arrival he ensured that he personally prayed so his

connection to the sacred mountain was not in doubt. Also important was the fact that he completed most of his ascent on foot, a sign of his respect for this holiest of Chinese places.[37] So far so simple, but there were other problems that Kangxi had to address on this pilgrimage. He had to keep the various ethnic groups within China happy, a tricky balancing act where it was easy to alienate whole sections of society with one ill-considered action, so Kangxi's pilgrimage wasn't quite like that of other emperors. Imperial pilgrimages were supposed to focus on worshipping the god of Mount Tai, but in 1684 Emperor Kangxi spent more time and energy praying to the goddess Bixia Juanjun.[38] This was probably designed to appeal to the general Chinese population. If going to Tai Shan satisfied the Han elite, and the preservation of Manchu cultural practices pleased his homeland, then praising Bixia, a goddess famed for her compassion to all, would be a popular move with the wider population of China.[39]

Compassionate rule was important to Kangxi, and he used his pilgrimage to show just how concerned he was for his people. He ensured that the revenue collected through the incense tax, instead of being sent to the central government, was reinvested in paying workmen to maintain the buildings on the mountain that the pilgrims had come to visit.[40] More important was his reaction to a site high up on Tai Shan that had long been known as Suicide Cliff, a place where some pilgrims jumped to their deaths at the end of their pilgrimages. They did this as an act of filial honour, perhaps giving their own lives for the return to health of a father or other relative. Previously, officials had tried to prevent this by renaming the place Love Life Cliff or Cliff for Loving Life, but the rebrand doesn't seem to have had much impact because it was still a suicide spot when the emperor visited.[41] The emperor was asked if he wanted to walk over to see the cliff, but he was angered by the suggestion, saying that people had a responsibility to honour the mothers and fathers who had given them their bodies by looking after themselves. He felt that suicide flew in the face of filial piety. 'If children have already killed themselves,' he raged, 'they cannot care for their parents. The act of suicide is not filial ... What would be the purpose of seeing such a place!?'[42]

In an interesting contrast to Zhenzong's desire for some Chinese to have a reminder of the mountain and its imperial associations closer to home, Emperor Kangxi wanted to symbolically take possession of Tai Shan so that he controlled it even when he was not physically present on the mountain. He commissioned a work known as the *Chart of Mount Tai*, a map commemorating the pilgrimage of 1684. What the map meant was that, even when the emperor was not physically on pilgrimage at the mountain, he had its representation locked away in the archives of the Forbidden City's imperial administration, where he was amassing the largest art collection in Chinese history.[43]

A few years later, the emperor commissioned a series of decorated scrolls depicting his southern tour, including the pilgrimage to Tai Shan. They showed Kangxi as the ideal classical Chinese ruler, a permanent reminder that he had gained the authority from his pilgrimage to rule all of China.[44] He also went one step further to demonstrate that, though he was Manchu, he could derive power from Tai Shan just like any other Chinese leader. He composed an essay claiming that Tai Shan, though an ancient Chinese site of worship, had its roots in his homeland in the Changbai Mountains, which divide Manchuria from the Korean peninsula. Tai Shan, he argued, was the head of a dragon, whose body lay beneath the land and sea controlled by China, its tail extending to form the Changbai. He cleverly used the Han Chinese principles of feng shui to make his point, claiming he had researched the facts thoroughly, demonstrating not just his connection to Tai Shan but his mastery of Chinese learning.[45]

Qianlong (ruled 1735–96), Kangxi's grandson and the last emperor to go on pilgrimage to Tai Shan, was very much following in the footsteps of his ancestor when he went there in 1748, the first of his nine pilgrimages to the mountain.[46] His was an imperial pilgrimage and an act of explicit filial piety in honour of his grandfather, whom he revered. When his longevity meant that his rule threatened to exceed that of his grandfather, Qianlong retired so that he would not eclipse Kangxi's reputation.

Qianlong had ruled China for a dozen years by the time he set out on his first pilgrimage, but he hadn't felt the need to visit Tai Shan before; the usual desire to cement a new rule by going on pilgrimage appears not to have been a concern. But 1748 was a particularly bad year for the emperor, who was in deep mourning following the death of his infant son Yongcong from smallpox, for which he blamed himself, and three months later of his wife the empress, the devout and virtuous Xiaoxianchun.[47] The emperor was subject to great rages, and in his grief he disinherited two of his sons for lack of respect and lashed out by punishing hundreds of officials he felt were not mourning his wife enough.[48] Some historians have seen these reactions as born of insecurity, and his subsequent public display of celebration at Tai Shan as a way to boost his self-esteem as he appealed to his imperial ancestors in his darkest hour, though there is no doubt that his grief over the death of his wife was real, as he composed over one hundred poems mourning her over the next four decades.[49] The deaths may also have been seen as signs of heaven's displeasure, the pilgrimage thus a way to reclaim divine favour.

Qianlong left his mark on the mountain by commissioning a twenty-metre-tall carving of a poem on a rectangle of light stone, visible high above the city of Tai, the only man-made addition to the mountain that can be seen from the south of the city.[50] This was done to mark his first pilgrimage, the poem written by the emperor himself in commemoration of the event. It was also a sign of ownership, marking the mountain in much the same way as he had the contents of the imperial art collection stamped. In all, he commissioned more carvings on Tai Shan than any other emperor.

After the death of Qianlong in 1799, there were no more imperial pilgrimages to Tai Shan. In part this could have been because the emperors no longer needed to go; despite occasional internal problems and threats from the West, China's territory grew and stabilised to become the country we see today, and the Qing dynasty endured until the revolution of 1911 without needing to perform the *feng* and *shan* sacrifices.[51] It is also tempting to think that there were no more imperial pilgrimages because China's greatest emperors had taken symbolic possession of the mountain, depicting pilgrimages on works kept in the Forbidden City and leaving a permanent and highly visible mark on the mountain itself. Instead, in line with the more compassionate rule they tried to demonstrate to their subjects, the emperors ruled in the Confucian style of fair governors, and Tai Shan and its pilgrimages could be given over to the everyday people of China.

2

THE GANGES

India

Ten thousand feet above sea level, high in the Himalayas, the twenty-mile-long Gangotri glacier slowly melts. The air up here is thin, the ground often covered in snow and ice. It is far from hospitable, yet people come here on pilgrimage because for many Hindus the glacier is the source of the Ganges, their holiest river, and because of a belief that the Himalayas are the home of the gods. Meltwater flows from Gomukh, the 'cow's mouth' of the glacier, and down through the foothills of Garhwal to the Gangetic plain, home to almost half a billion people. As the river passes through settlements which have themselves become major pilgrim sites because they are on the banks of the Ganges, it takes on more and more water from dozens of tributaries. After over 1,550 miles of meandering across northern India, the Ganges (or, as it passes through Bangladesh, the Padma) splits into channels criss-crossing the world's largest river delta, and discharges into the Bay of Bengal.

The River Ganges is the biggest and longest pilgrimage destination on earth. According to the *Upanishads*, an ancient Sanskrit text recounting the origins of the universe, the river was formed when one of Hinduism's principal gods, Shiva, calmed the power of the goddess Ganga by filtering her through his hair.

Where Ganga fell to earth, she was contained in the form of the river. As with most pilgrimage sites, the reasons for pilgrims to travel to the Ganges are myriad. Pilgrims visit the Ganges to absolve themselves from sin, believing the water is capable of washing it away. Some come to seek aid in business dealings or with a court case, to give thanks or to ask for healing, or for spiritual refreshment. As with many pilgrimage sites linked to death and rebirth, there is an old belief that a visit to the Ganges can help a woman conceive, and if she then meets with success, she has to offer her firstborn son to the river in return by throwing him into the water.[1]

The water of the Ganges gives knowledge, offers an entry point to the other world, holds the nectar of immortality and is still believed to be eternally pure. Its power extends well beyond the river itself. Rajendra the Great (1012–44), ruler of the Chola empire which covered southern India, was so determined to harness the sanctity of the Ganges that he sent his military commanders to collect jars of its water for him. After he conquered the lands around the Ganges, Rajendra built a tank in a temple dedicated to Shiva to hold Ganges water, and forced captives to bring water from the river. He called his capital city Gangaikondacolapuram, 'the city of the king who conquered the Ganges'.[2]

Akbar (ruled 1556–1605), one of the greatest of the Muslim Mughal emperors, insisted on having the river water brought to him wherever he was, as it was the only water he would drink and cook with.[3] This was popular among the Hindus he ruled over, so much so that both his son and grandson continued the practice. Three centuries later, the river water was used to swear on in court.[4] Water was diverted from the Ganges itself to create satellite pilgrimage centres, such as the tank at Manipura where well over a thousand years ago the river was channelled two miles to the so-called Gate of the Ganges, where pilgrims could bathe

The water of the Ganges was so spiritually potent that it was often transported across India by holy-water carriers or enslaved people. It was used in religious ceremonies, for washing, or to create bathing pools for pilgrimage and prayer.

and take advantage of the charity and free accommodation provided by the local rulers. More recently, at the annual Kanwar Mela festival in honour of Shiva, millions of pilgrims, most of them poor, take away containers of water from the Ganges to temples and homes all over India. This is seen as a way to reaffirm the link between the Hindu faith, India and the Ganges, and it has become more popular in recent decades in response to political changes and increasing consumerism as it continues to allow the poor to play an important role in Hindu society.[5]

Just one of the seven major Indian rivers that are considered goddesses, the Ganges is the most important and has been revered since sometime between 1700 and 1100 BCE. Evidence of pilgrimage in early Hindu tradition is thin to the point of non-existence, and it looks like it took a while to get established as a practice in the religion; bar mentions in some third- to fifth-century texts, it does not start to appear frequently in the traditional texts on Hindu law until the twelfth century.[6] About 300 years later pilgrimage to the Ganges was regular and important enough for regulation, as codes that were probably written earlier in the Middle Ages were revised several times over. These works set out laws and expectations on how a pilgrimage to the Ganges (as well as other places in India) should be conducted.

By the middle of the sixteenth century, pilgrim traffic had increased considerably. The stability provided by Mughal rule meant it was safer to travel long distances.[7] Writing in the third decade of the century, the English cleric Samuel Purchas claimed that the Jesuit priest Emanuel Pinner had witnessed 4,000 pilgrims going to the Ganges at Varanasi, one of the most important cities along the river's length, and was informed by the governor of Bengal 'that there came thither sometime three hundred thousand or foure hundred thousand Pilgrims'.[8] He was one of many outsiders who reported on pilgrimages to the Ganges. Jean de Thévenot, a Parisian explorer who travelled the country in 1666–7, claimed that he had witnessed pilgrims throwing themselves into the river naked.[9] Two centuries later another traveller (for travellers are some of our best witnesses), John Matheson, claimed he saw a pilgrim praying atop a pillar standing in the river at Varanasi.[10]

Pilgrimage Cities of the Ganges

All of the Ganges is sacred, but particular places are crossing places between this world and the world of the gods. They are considered holier than other sites at certain times of the year.

Haridwar (also called Mayapuri, Gangadwar or Kapila), Prayag (Allahabad or Prayagraj) and Varanasi (Avimukta, Kashi or Benares) are the most important, but there were lots of smaller places which had and in some cases still have their own allure. According to a travel guide written in the first decade of the twentieth century, pilgrims came to Bandukpur in the winter to pour water from the Ganges over an image of Jageshwar Mahadeo in thanks or to seek favours. Kakora, near but not on the Ganges, benefited from a fair held in the month of Kartik because pilgrims came to trade after they had bathed in the river.[11]

Two of the most sacred cities on the Ganges are where the great Kumbh Mela is held. This is a religious festival that probably celebrates the Kumbh, the vessel carrying the nectar of immortality taken from an ocean churned up in a war between gods and demons. Where the Kumbh spilt drops of its precious liquid or, in other versions of the legend, where the pot stopped on its journey to paradise (at Haridwar and Prayag on the Ganges, and Ujjain and Nashik on other rivers), Kumbh Melas are held every twelve years or thereabouts, in January and February – the timing of the festivals to coincide with the movement of the planets does not result in perfectly regular repetitions. Pilgrims come to get a touch of that immortality and to enter the Ganges at a *tirtha,* one of those crossing places that bring them closer to the divine, as the time of the Kumbh Mela is considered particularly auspicious for bathing. So strong is the attraction that it even tempts hundreds of sadhus, religious mendicants who are usually reclusive, to venture on pilgrimage. There are also smaller Melas at other intervals, and at other places, which also bring pilgrims to the banks of the river.

Travelling down the Ganges from the Himalayas, the first major riverside pilgrimage centre and site of the Kumbh Mela is the city of Haridwar, about a hundred miles from the river's source, where the Ganges meets the plains. One of the sites revered as a place where the gods spilt golden nectar, it is believed to be the doorway to the gods Vishnu or Shiva. Although often referred to as an ancient gathering, the origins of the Kumbh Mela at Haridwar are hard to discern. When Haridwar fell in 1399 to Timur the Lame (Shakespeare's *Tamerlane*) he massacred many pilgrims who may have conceivably been there for the Kumbh Mela, but the evidence isn't detailed enough to decide. The earliest certain reference to the festival in Haridwar is in the 1695 *Khalastatu-t-Tawarikh*, in which the city is called 'the greatest of all' the places on the river's banks and the fair held there is referred to as the Kumbh Mela.[12] This was certainly a large gathering, and it turned Haridwar from a small riverside settlement into a huge city, a thriving market which brought great riches through trade in salt and cloth, brass and ivory, looking glasses and weapons.[13] By the middle of the nineteenth century, Haridwar was 'a celebrated place of Hindu pilgrimage' where people came to bathe at one of the many ghats on the river's edge. These are large, wide flights of stone steps which lead down to the river, giving easy access to and from the water. The author of one guide of 1842 referred to the 'great fair' held there which attracted up to two million people and, crucially, the belief that the water was 'supposed to acquire additional sanctity every twelfth year; and the concourse of pilgrims is then always greatest'.[14]

Four hundred and twenty miles downriver as the crow flies is Prayag, known as *Tiritha Raja*, 'King of the Tirthas', a particularly sacred crossing place where the Ganges meets the Yamuna River. Just like the Ganges, the Yamuna is both a sacred river and the embodiment of a goddess. There is something elemental about the meeting of two rivers, and along the Ganges meeting places like these, *sangam*, are believed to be especially

Ghats are large flights of steps which give access to the water of the Ganges. Some are particularly holy to pilgrims, while others are popular sites for cremations and as a result often very crowded.

sacred. That at Prayag is most sacred of all because the Ganges and Yamuna are joined by a third river, the mythological and invisible Saraswati, and because it is the end point of an ancient all-India pilgrimage circuit. Because of its importance, another iteration of the Kumbh Mela is held here in the belief that, when it takes place, the three rivers flow with the nectar of immortality. The current form of the Kumbh Mela, formalised under the British, doesn't seem to be as old as the one at Haridwar but it is nevertheless ancient and was perhaps already long-established by the seventh century.

What Prayag's Kumbh Mela lacks in antiquity it more than makes up for in terms of scale. At the confluence of these three rivers over the course of about a month, tens of millions of pilgrims move into a twenty-square-mile pop-up megacity constructed in just two months. The Kumbh Mela held in 2013 lasted for fifty-five days and attracted somewhere between 70 and 120 million pilgrims. The temporary settlement is so large that images sent from the CartoSat2 satellite to the Indian Space Research Organisation in 2019 showed it could be easily seen from space. It is about the same size as Exeter in England or Rennes in France and is a marvel of modern urban planning and civic management, as the permanent city of about one million expands into the land on the undeveloped flood plain next to the junction of the rivers. This settlement needs not just tents to house the pilgrims and festival personnel, and temporary ghats to give them access to the Ganges, but the sort of services needed in permanent settlements like healthcare provision, fire stations, police and food shops.[15] Divided into fourteen districts, each is equipped with these necessities. The city straddles the river, which is crossed by eighteen temporary pontoon bridges.

Bringing together millions of people in one place for a short period brings its own headaches, but it also brings opportunities. Many of these are for the people in Prayag itself, who cater to the needs of the pilgrims and find it a lucrative time of year. But the movement of so many people from across the Indian subcontinent also means that the Kumbh Mela has an impact far beyond the Ganges, and the people who travel to and from it bring information back to their homes from hundreds, if not thousands, of miles away.

Surviving evidence suggests that Prayag's first Kumbh Mela was probably held in 1870. The British then in charge of the city were faced with some of the same organisational problems as their modern counterparts, albeit on a smaller scale. The historian Kama MacLean argues that the city's Hindu community claimed the great (possibly assumed) antiquity of their Kumbh

Mela to defend it from possible suppression by the British authorities.[16] By giving it greater status they not only protected this vast event, but also prompted the British to support the pilgrimage, specifically by providing organisation and logistics. Over the next few decades, there was some opposition to the British role in the pilgrimage, not least from Christian missionaries in India who were horrified by what they saw as government support for a pagan religion.

Pilgrimages to the Ganges brought benefits to pilgrims and hosts alike, but the growing numbers flocking to key sites could be fatal. This was a genuine concern for India's British rulers. Not long after the British crown took over direct rule of India in 1858, they started to research the role of these mass pilgrimages in the spread of cholera, and it became apparent that the Kumbh Melas created ideal conditions for the rapid spread of the disease.[17] The cholera outbreak of 1891–2 was probably exacerbated by a particularly large Ganges pilgrimage gathering at Haridwar.[18] The huge gathering prompted a very rapid spread of cholera that resulted in almost 170,000 deaths in the city alone and three quarters of a million across India as a whole. The mobility of pilgrims spread the disease beyond the country's borders, and in the following two years there were hundreds of thousands of additional deaths across Afghanistan, Persia and Russia.

Some of the accusations levelled at pilgrimages as super-spreaders should be treated with caution, given that the colonialists were often scathing of Hindu religious practices and critical of reverence for the Ganges, but it was undoubtedly the case that epidemics were facilitated by pilgrimage gatherings. Considerable effort was poured into tackling the threat, and eventually the British government in Bombay established a committee that reported on the 'menace which Haridwar is to public health'.[19]

Crowd control (or the lack of it) was another threat to life and limb. The ghats on the river were often too small to accommodate the numbers thronging to them. A stampede at the Haridwar Kumbh Mela in 1820 resulted in the death of almost 500 people, after which the ghat was enlarged. Almost a century and a half later in 1954, at Prayag, Indira Devi witnessed six million pilgrims arriving in the first two months of the year, probably because the Kumbh Mela was considered especially auspicious due to various alignments of the full moon with the days of the week. It was also the first Kumbh Mela since the smaller wartime festival of 1942, which had been limited by restrictions on travel and anti-Mela propaganda, and the first since India gained independence in 1947. The numbers in attendance put considerable strain on the infrastructure, and on 3 February this resulted in the death of 800 pilgrims. Giving evidence at an inquiry into events, one bereaved woman blamed the government for promising 'excellent arrangements' for all but only caring about the most important pilgrims. Eight of her family members died. On the day of the disaster, the crowds of pilgrims were so dense that people complained of being unable to breathe and of oppressive heat despite the cold of the morning. Though a tragedy, not everyone saw the fatalities of 1954 in the same way. Addressing the investigating committee, one pilgrim testified: 'If we are killed we shall attain salvation. If we escape death, we shall go home. We shall be gainers in either case. Those who die at such a sacred spot, at such an auspicious moment, would be very lucky! We wish to have the good fortune.'[20]

The most important of all pilgrimage cities on the Ganges is Varanasi, which lies about halfway between Delhi and Kolkata. Said to be one of the oldest permanently inhabited cities in the world, it overlooks a large sweeping bend of the river lined with eighty-eight ghats. The oldest is probably the fifth-century

Manikarnika Ghat but most were rebuilt in the eighteenth century. Varanasi is the home of Shiva, god of destruction and the deity who helped the goddess Ganga bring her river to earth, and is believed to be the centre of the world (specifically, the Manikarnika Ghat claims that honour), making it the one place among the thousands of pilgrimage sites in India that a Hindu really *must* visit at least once.

The city has thousands of temples, and even the surrounding area is considered sacred for many miles in each direction. Being a Ganges city enhanced its prestige, but it also helped that Varanasi was the site of an ancient ford and straddled the river, which not all towns and cities on the Ganges did. This meant it grew in importance, as did the sheer volume of people who lived in the city's hinterland. The area was more densely populated than anywhere in Europe by the nineteenth century, giving the city a steady supply of local pilgrims too.[21] By the time the American Robert Bowne Minturn wrote about his visit at the end of the 1850s, he felt able to call Varanasi the 'Holy City of India', a place where the wealthy chose to build large houses on the waterfront so they could live out their days next to the holy Ganges.[22]

Pilgrims to Varanasi had their needs catered to by *paryatak mitra,* traditionally men from the same family that had always helped them and their ancestors.[23] The same system operated at Prayag, and competition to secure the custom of new pilgrim families was so fierce that the *paryatak mitra* often sent agents across the country to secure new agreements before they even arrived.[24] Catering to the needs of pilgrimage was a highly competitive industry as the business sustained so many families along the Ganges. High-caste Brahmins (priests) guided pilgrims in the correct forms of devotion, advising them on when to shave and how to dress, important if the pilgrims wanted to avoid damnation. There were rules to stop Brahmins from accepting gifts, presumably to prevent bribery for things like access to better spots on the ghats. In the 1820s around a fifth of the population of Varanasi were Brahmins, a ratio suggestive of just how many pilgrims came to the city every year.

Varanasi's chief attraction for pilgrims was (and is) as *Mahashamshana*, 'the great cremation ground', a *tirtha* on the Ganges where the faithful could reach *moksha* and break free from the endless cycle of death and rebirth. As a city of death, it was not at all unusual for the elderly to ask family members to take them on one last pilgrimage to Varanasi. Five of the city's many ghats are considered particularly important places for cremation though there are other options available over a six-mile stretch of the river, so pilgrims and mourners must vie for the best spot. Chief among them is, unsurprisingly, the Manikarmika Ghat. Wherever cremations happen, the resulting ashes are scattered in the river.[25]

Previously cremation may well have followed death in the river itself, the proximity of the other world making the Ganges an attractive suicide option.[26] Some believe that those who drown themselves in the river will break the cycle of earthly rebirth and be reborn in heaven to enjoy happiness. Some also hope that a recently deceased person whose corpse is thrown into the Ganges will not fall into the evil states of existence in his next rebirth.[27] The earliest written record of pilgrimage to the Ganges, by the seventh-century Chinese Buddhist Xuanzang, tells us that he witnessed hundreds of men throwing themselves into the river at Prayag in an act of ritual self-sacrifice.[28] Seven centuries later, pilgrim suicides still seemed to happen. Ibn Battuta, a Muslim explorer from Morocco who spent three decades travelling in Africa and the East from the 1320s to the 1350s, referred to pilgrimage to the Ganges several times in his work. He claimed that those pilgrims who drowned themselves in the river proclaimed they did so to get closer to their god. 'He then drowns himself,' Ibn Battuta concluded of the Hindu pilgrim, 'and when he is dead they take him out and burn him and cast his ashes into the river.'[29]

Controlling Pilgrimage

When the first prime minister of independent India, Jawaharlal Nehru (1889–1964), wrote his last will and testament, he asked to be cremated, his ashes taken to Varanasi and a portion scattered in the Ganges. Nehru claimed he had no 'religious sentiment' but chose the river because it embodied the country he loved: 'The Ganges ... is the river of India, beloved by her people, round which are entwined her racial memories, her hopes and fears, her songs of triumph, her victories and defeats. She had been a symbol of India's age-long culture and civilization, ever changing, ever flowing, and yet ever the same Ganga.'[30]

The river was also considered a unifier across religious divides. In 1917 the political activist Sarojini Naidu made a speech to bring people together, in which she reminded her audience that 'when the first Islamic army came to India, they pitched their caravans on the banks of the sacred Ganges and tempered and cooled their swords in the sacred waters. It was the baptism of the Ganges that gave the first welcome to the Islamic invaders that became the children of India as generations went by.'[31] Given this strong emotional attachment to the Ganges, the river – the flow of its water, as well as access to its banks – was also a way to control India and her people, and authority over pilgrimages could be used to reward, cajole, tax or limit the spiritual sustenance alluded to by Nehru.

India had first come under British rule in the late 1750s when the East India Company defeated the nawab of Bengal in battle.

Perhaps in response, it seems that pilgrimage by India's Hindus to the Ganges grew over the century of the Company's rule. The Ganges was still unmistakably *India,* and pilgrimage to it was almost an act of defiance. The immensity of the task did not stop the Company from trying to control the river though, its most ambitious projects being the Bhim Ghoda Weir just outside Haridwar and the construction of the Ganges Canal, started in 1842 in response to a famine that killed 800,000 people, a tragedy that was probably not as worrying to the Company as the fact that they suffered significant financial losses. The Ganges Canal was supposed to stop this from happening again. Unsurprisingly, devout Hindus were distinctly uneasy about diverting their goddess in this way, and the priests at Haridwar were alarmed that the weir would inhibit the flow of the sacred river. The Company tackled these concerns in the way they did most problems, using their great wealth to buy acquiescence by financing the reconstruction of the ghats along the river.

Many of India's princely rulers were granted exemption from paying the pilgrim tax levied by the East India Company if it was in the Company's interest to do so. This meant exempting hundreds or even thousands of pilgrims, as the maharajas travelled with large retinues to show off their power. When Raja Bhakt Singh of Alwar set out on a pilgrimage to Prayag in 1813, he did so with five elephants and twenty-five camels in addition to over one thousand attendants and soldiers. The higher-status pilgrims were carried in one of the forty palanquins and twenty carriages. Given that his destination was right next to the British fort of Allahabad, the inclusion of the soldiers caused some concern. Bhakt Singh may have been using his pilgrimage train to remind the Company that he was still a powerful man. Another unnamed raja of the 1830s undertook a pilgrimage to the same place and seems to have used it at least partially for relationship-building and PR work. According to a somewhat unimpressed-sounding officer's wife, Hanriette Ashmore, on the morning of 13 February

> the encampment of a wealthy rajah presented itself: we understood that he is performing a pilgrimage from Bengal to Allahabad, there to wash in the sacred junction of the rivers Jumna and Ganges. Some of our party paid his camp a visit, and were treated with an exhibition of quail fighting. He had a great number of elephants in his train; one, only five months old, was a pretty little creature, and sucked a hand which was presented to it. In the evening, several of the rajah's caparisoned elephants came into our camp, and were mounted by those who had nothing better to amuse themselves with.[32]

In 1808 the Company waived the pilgrim tax for any Indian soldiers (sepoys) in their service who wanted to bathe in the Ganges at Prayag.[33] This was quite a concession, given that the bulk of its 250,000 soldiers were Indian, but deemed worth it to ensure their loyalty. Fanny Parks, who lived in Prayag for a time as she was married to a Company man, commented, 'Every man, even the veriest beggar, is obliged to give one rupee for the liberty to bathe in the holy spot; and if you consider that one rupee is sufficient to keep that man in comfort for one month, the tax is severe.'[34] Several decades later when Caleb Wright delivered a lecture to an American audience about his recent time researching in India, he told them 'a barrier or fence is to be seen extending from the Ganges to the Jumna [Yamuna]. Soldiers were stationed there, to prevent the pilgrims from passing it until they had purchased of the East India Company tickets granting permission to bathe.'[35]

Unsurprisingly, British control of access and the tax levied on those not granted an exemption was a cause of considerable anger and resentment among the Brahmins who had been in charge before the Company took over from them in 1801. The Brahmin priests at Prayag had a reputation for being greedy, and they were angered by the tax because if pilgrims spent all they had on access to the Ganges, what would be left for them? When the British abolished the tax, the Brahmins complained about that too. Discontent rumbled on into the middle of the century as the priests spread stories about supposed British plans for forced conversion to Christianity. Things came to a head in 1857, when those same priests joined in with the rebellion started by a mutiny of East India Company sepoys who believed the paper covers of the cartridges they were issued with, which had to be removed by mouth, were greased with pork and beef fat. This offended both Muslims and Hindus. The rebellion was eventually defeated, though enough Brahmins remained at Prayag to resume their activities when pilgrimages resumed.

One incidental benefit of British rule was to make pilgrim journeys to the Ganges quicker and easier. Rail construction began in 1853, and by 1901 the country could boast over 25,000 miles of track. India's rail network was constructed to support British mercantile interests – to access raw materials and transport manufactured goods – with the East India Company not initially seeing the railway as a passenger network for the simple reason that they believed there would be little call for it. To some extent they were right; many Indians saw the railway as an alien, colonial thing with no relevance to their lives. However, pilgrims started to use the railway in big numbers in the early twentieth century, despite some companies specifically stating that they would not carry pilgrims, especially during the busy Kumbh Mela season. They presumably didn't mind tourists travelling to pilgrimage cities by train; the 1907 *Travellers' Companion,* published by order of the Indian Railway Board, specifically described pilgrimage sites 'situated on or near existing railways'.[36]

The Dying Ganges?

By the time the crystal-clear water of the Gangotri glacier is discharged into the Bay of Bengal, it is utterly filthy. Once the water was clean; a Persian chronicle written in the closing years of the seventeenth century tells us that it was 'a most wonderful fact that if the water is kept in a pot even for a year, it does not acquire a bad smell or change its colour'.[37] Sadly, by the turn of the twentieth century people were acutely aware of how polluted the river was becoming. One angry correspondent to *The Lancet*, England's leading medical journal, called the Ganges 'a vast sewer receiving the sewage of all the sewered towns on its banks'. Much of the pollution came from Kanpur, where tanneries and textile mills pumped their waste directly into the river.[38]

Since then the volume of pollutants has only increased as the numbers of pilgrims, residents and businesses of all kinds have grown.[39] Untreated sewage (over eighteen billion litres of it each day), chemical waste, heavy metals from ash and run-off from agriculture that washes over six million tons of contaminant a year into the water combine in a toxic soup. Levels of coliform bacteria are dangerously high.[40] By the time it reaches Varanasi, the Ganges is effectively an open sewer. At that point up to 40,000 bodies, some of them only partially burned because people cannot afford the fuel for effective cremation, are put into the river each year.[41] All efforts to improve the situation have so far failed. Prime Minister Narendra Modi, whose parliamentary seat is at Varanasi, has promised to clean up the river.

When he came to power in 2014, Modi dramatically declared 'Ma Ganga has called me' to clean up her river. But given that scientists claim the retreat of the glacier that feeds the Ganges will eventually lead to a reduction in the volume of water, the concentration of pollutants will only get worse.

Among many Hindus there is a belief that the Ganges is itself a purifier and so can never really be polluted: the water will always be both spiritually and physically pure. This only adds to the problem of saving the Ganges. While beliefs about what is and is not pollution, and what is hygienic or unhygienic vary depending on whom you ask, the fact remains that no matter what the cultural norms of Ganges pilgrims are, the flora and the fauna of the river are in catastrophic decline. Many other Indians no longer bathe in or take water from the Ganges, concerned about the rising incidence of disease linked with it. What this means for the Ganges and its pilgrims is concerning. At the riverside city of Rishikesh in 2016 Swamsai Chidanand Saraswati contemplated the state of the river and the harm being done to the goddess considered a mother by many. He issued a stark warning: 'If Ganga dies, India dies.'[42] What will happen to the pilgrims then? As with other pilgrimage places central to community identity – Bear Butte for Native Americans, Amristar for Sikhs, Mecca for Muslims – threats to access for pilgrims could have repercussions far beyond the river itself.

3

DELPHI

Greece

Pilgrimage sites are not immune to the passage of time. While they might seem eternal, there is no guarantee that pilgrimages will persist indefinitely, or that the sacred qualities of a mountain, a river or a church will continue to be recognised. Places where people once flocked can fall into ruin, the details of their histories muddied or lost. Delphi, once paramount among pilgrimage sites in the ancient Greek world, suffered this fate.

Over two thousand miles north of Delphi the Altes Museum in Berlin boasts part of one of the world's most expansive collections of classical antiquities. Initially comprising sculptures looted from Warsaw by Friedrich Wilhelm of Prussia in the mid-seventeenth century, the collection was continually added to. Eventually, a decision was made to establish a new museum to grant public access to what had previously been a royal collection. The artefacts were arrayed inside newly built display cases across several rooms, the sculptures supplemented by acquisitions ranging from pottery and glassware to more statuary and all manner of archaeological finds.

Among these treasures lies an unassuming terracotta and black dish with two handles, depicting two distinct figures: a woman seated on a tall three-legged stool holding a dish and

Messages from the god Apollo were delivered by his oracle, the Pythia, in his temple at Delphi. The most important kings and the poorest farmers sought her advice for their problems.

a laurel sprig, and a man standing before her.[1] The woman is Themis, a daughter of Gaia, revered as the embodiment of the earth and custodian of the Delphic oracle situated on the slopes of Mount Parnassus in Greece. The man depicted is King Aigeus, a mythical Athenian king. Produced about two and a half thousand years ago, this small dish bears testament to the tradition of pilgrimage and consultation with Apollo's oracle at Delphi, once the pre-eminent destination for pilgrims in the ancient Greek world. Here kings and warriors sought counsel on crucial matters of state and their chances of success in war. However, just over a millennium later, the oracle's influence waned, and Delphi fell into ruins.

Origins

The origins of the pilgrimage to Delphi are obscure, such facts as can be ascertained mixed with mythical narratives. At some point, the goddess Themis relinquished her authority to Apollo, a god associated with, among other things, truth and prophecies. These were dispensed at Delphi through his high priestess, known as the Pythia. The Homeric hymn 'To Apollo', composed sometime between the late seventh and mid-sixth century BCE, recounts Apollo's search for a suitable place to build a temple in his honour, culminating in his selection of a place then called Crisa. Having found this perfect locale on the slopes of Mount Parnassus, Apollo assumed the guise of a dolphin (*delphis*) and attracted sailors from Crete to come and establish a new settlement. This was Delphi.[2]

In another version of the story, as recounted by the lyrical poet Alcaeus (died *c.*580 BCE), Apollo is portrayed as initially reluctant to establish the oracle, having been instructed to do so by his father Zeus, king of the gods. Only after a period of hesitation does Apollo comply with his father's order. A third work, the fifth-century BCE play *Eumenides,* follows the story alluded to on the Altes Museum dish. Here Gaia, the embodiment of the earth, passes the oracle to her offspring, the Titans Themis and Phoebe, after which it is given to Apollo. Regardless of the legendary narratives surrounding its origins, there is evidence which suggests Delphi may have been attracting pilgrims seeking advice from Apollo's oracle as early as the early eighth century BCE. To the ancient Greeks, Delphi had significant cultural importance as the *omphalos* (navel of the earth), and a carved stone was erected to mark the very centre of the world.[3]

Pilgrims either arrived by boat or via one of the overland routes linking Delphi with central Greece and the city of Corinth. Many opted for sea travel, especially if they were coming from Sparta across the Gulf of Corinth, landing at the ports of Kirra or Itea before ascending the steep hill to the temple complex. Pilgrims could take advantage of the transport networks used by visitors to the Pythian Games, held at Delphi every four years from about 582 BCE, one of the four Panhellenic games of ancient Greece and second only to those at Olympia.

When they came was constrained, as the window for consulting the oracle was limited. Delphi might close for the winter months when the seas were too rough for pilgrims to cross, or when Apollo was thought to be absent from Delphi.[4] When the oracle was open, pilgrims could only see the Pythia on certain days. The dates were well advertised to save wasted journeys, but they were rare occasions; indeed the oracle was only willing to dispense advice on an annual basis at certain points in Delphi's history. When the Pythia was unavailable, pilgrims had to explore alternative methods of obtaining Apollo's guidance. These included interpreting omens from a selection of objects and deciphering messages conveyed through the casting of dice.

Pilgrimages and requests to the oracle involved the completion of rituals. Pilgrims might first wash in the Castalian Spring, a hundred metres beyond the sanctuary walls. Then they would wind their way up the Sacred Way through the walled city of Delphi, past the many treasuries that testified to the citizens' wealth, to the Temple of Apollo, which dominated the site. In some cases a sacrifice would be made on the pilgrims' behalf by someone from Delphi, a *proxenos*. This was usually a goat, which was sprinkled with water to seek its assent; if it shuddered, it was a good day for a prophecy. A less expensive sacrifice involved burning a *pelanos*, a small cake made specially for the Delphic ritual which varied in cost depending on the status of the pilgrim. Even this wasn't exactly cheap, costing perhaps two days' pay for one Athenian pilgrim.[5]

When pilgrims reached the Pythia, they found a local woman, probably from a middling or lower-status family, sitting on a tripod. We know most about what sort of person she was thanks to Plutarch.

> She who serves the god here at Delphi was born of a lawful and honourable marriage ... and her life has been well ordered in all respects. But, because she grew up in the home of poor farmers, she carries with her nothing in the way of skill or expertise or ability when she goes down into the oracular shrine. On the contrary, just as Xenophon says that the bride should have seen and heard as little as possible before she goes to her husband's household, so also the Pythia goes to the god being inexperienced, unlearned about almost everything and truly virginal with respect to her soul.[6]

Someone of higher status, educated and worldly, might have ideas of her own, and Apollo wanted a simple vessel for his messages.

The Pythia was probably post-menopausal too, as Plutarch tells us the chosen women were usually over fifty and expected to hold the position for the remainder of their lives.[7] They were required to be celibate and might well be widows, but were dressed in the garb of a virgin in honour of the first priestess, who was abducted and raped. It was her fate that prompted the decision to appoint older women.[8] John Chrysostom, archbishop of Constantinople in the period following the eclipse of Delphi, claimed that the Pythia was the wife of Apollo and that she sat astride her tripod to 'receive' him. 'When the evil spirit rises from below,' he believed, 'and slips through her genitals, she is filled with madness. Letting down her hair, she raves about the future and foams at the mouth.'[9] This interpretation of what went on undoubtedly tells us more about the good archbishop than it does the Pythia.

No one knew how the oracle at Delphi received her visions. Some legends state that the Pythia's tripod sat over a chasm or fissure of some sort, or perhaps a cave; the claims vary. Theories about poisonous vapours seeping from a cleft in the ground are based on the works of several writers of the first and second centuries CE, but these have largely been dismissed because these were of the later Roman era in Delphi and because no such vapour-emitting chasm has ever been found.[10] However, there is seismic activity in the area, so it is not implausible that one did exist but has since closed up. On the other hand, in the 1990s geologists who looked at the site suggested that the limestone on which Delphi is built releases ethylene, a sweet-smelling gas that may account for the visions and a sort of sacred odour. That theory hasn't met with more success than any other alternative.

One story about the frenzy of the Pythia was recorded by the Roman poet Lucan (39–65 CE), who attributed it not to fumes or a sacred odour, but to possession by the god Apollo, which was, of course, the whole point of the oracle. Over a century earlier, in 48 BCE, Appius Claudius visited the oracle, who had been inactive for several years, to ask what would happen in the current civil war. When she offered a reasonable response, he didn't find it convincing. Threats followed. At that point, Apollo entered her and

> ... In maddened trance
> She whirled throughout the cave, her locks erect
> With horror ...

She knocked over the tripod, shaking her head, walking in circles and burning with anger. Appius thought this a much better show, and seemed satisfied with her pronouncement that he would play no part in the war.[11]

The Greek geographer Pausanias, who visited Delphi in the second century CE, believed the Pythia's inspiration came from drinking from a spring at Delphi, in which case fantastical stories of the frenzied Pythia in some sort of heightened state may be inaccurate, with consulting the oracle a far calmer and more straightforward affair. The problem is that most authors who describe the ritual of consultation never actually witnessed it themselves, let alone visited Delphi, so they were repeating second- or third-hand accounts at best. Plutarch, a priest at the Temple of Apollo in Delphi and thus the one witness you would expect to know, says nothing about noxious gasses and unintelligible messages at all. What he did write about was the *pneuma* (which could mean anything from wind to inspiration) that came from the earth and influenced the Pythia in much the same way as heavenly bodies influenced those who read the heavens. It seems likely that – boringly – the idea of a manic Pythia probably comes from a misreading of Plato's concept of *mania* and from other texts.[12] This was taken up so enthusiastically because a priestess high on fumes dispensing wild prophecies makes for a more impressive story than the reality of a middle-aged woman calmly delivering messages from Apollo.

The Big Questions

Delphi's fame rested on its reputation as the place to go for advice if you were a leader mulling over political decisions, constitutional questions, social problems, your chances in war, which gods to favour or perhaps because you needed to know how to respond to crises like plague and famine. Consulting the oracle was a sound move if a potentially unpopular decision was necessary, as the leader could point to Apollo's advice (assuming they found it acceptable) and the people would be less inclined to argue.

We know a reasonable amount about the sort of things people asked about as some six hundred of the Pythia's oracular responses have been recorded, some historical, others probably legendary. Those that relate to matters of war and other matters of state are particularly helpful in illuminating why Delphi was so famous and so fought over, and show us just how important consultative pilgrimages were to decisions with an impact well beyond this small place. Seeking the oracle's advice was fraught with problems though, as access was strictly controlled and depended on who you were and, most important, where you came from. First in the queue were people from Delphi; then came those from other cities they had granted this right to like Athens or Sparta, a right which could be removed or restored as political relationships shifted; next were delegations from other Greek city states; last were individuals with what were presumably considered lesser concerns. You have to wonder if those at the back all managed to get the advice that they had come perhaps a long way for in the time allotted.[13]

As access was hierarchical and the reputation of the oracle so great, leaders were keen to show that they had been on a pilgrimage to receive advice on policy or confirmation of decisions already made. The Athenians, to whom the Pythian Apollo was their ancestral god, regularly sent representatives on pilgrimage to Delphi, particularly when big decisions were necessary, while their enemies the Spartans claimed that their constitution came from the oracle at Delphi – an attempt at one-upmanship. City states also used the opportunity provided by pilgrimages to the oracle to secure praise from Apollo which they could brag about. Such hubris was risky. In about 700 BCE, representatives from Megara, a city on the coast west of Athens, asked the most important question of all: who were the best of all the Greeks? They assumed the answer would be themselves, of course (otherwise, why ask?) but received the rather humiliating answer that the Megarans were not even in the top ten.[14]

A safer question for pilgrims might be to ask which deity should be honoured to give them the best chance of success. Pilgrims from Thourioi in southern Italy asked which god they should worship as their founder, and Apollo's oracle unsurprisingly told them that Apollo was the god for the job. When Athens was ravaged by a catastrophic plague for four long years, the city authorities presumably dispatched pilgrims to Delphi because they erected a statue of Apollo Alexikakos (averter of evil) in the city either in the hope of warding off future plagues or to give thanks for Apollo's help.[15]

Visits to the oracle to consult on personal matters were undoubtedly more common though the advice given is rarely known. Should I marry? Will I have children? How can I recover my health? What, asked a priest called Jerakles from Phokis, should I do as I have broken my vows by getting drunk and having sex? Straddling the boundary between public and personal, the people of Delphi itself asked what they should do if Jason of Pherai, who was going to preside over the Pythian Games in 370 BCE, raided Delphi's treasury. He was ruler of a powerful Greek state and commanded a formidable force of mercenaries, so you can understand their nervousness. He was assassinated before the games, solving their problem.[16]

Often the question asked has been lost and only the response survives. One wonders what the citizens of Alea asked before 300 BCE to provoke the answer 'They should flog women at

Dionysus' festival'.[17] One of the most specific questions put to the oracle by pilgrims in the third century BCE was what to do about the hares that were overrunning the island of Astypalaia in the south-eastern Aegean Sea. The oracle advised buying hunting hounds, and the problem was soon solved, a solution you might have thought the pilgrims could have come up with themselves. Still, the fact that people could travel so far without fear to ask the most mundane questions showed how safe the eastern Mediterranean was at that time.

War

Political structures within the Greek world might change, but unfortunately conflict was a near constant – and therefore so were pilgrimages to ask about the likelihood of victory. From the seventh century BCE, when Greek city states began to embark on programmes of territorial expansion, their rulers frequently consulted the oracle at Delphi about the wisdom of their military plans. The earliest instance of a consultation and subsequent colonisation was probably that which led to the founding of Syracuse on Sicily in the 730s BCE, and plenty of others followed. Pilgrims asked whether to support the Greeks against the Persians in 480 BCE,[18] if it was wise for Gyges to seize the throne of Lydia, and how Agesipolis, king of Sparta, should conduct his campaign against Argos in 388 BCE.[19] According to the Athenian general and historian Thucydides (died *c.*400 BCE), the Spartans asked the Pythia before they declared war on Athens and consulted her before deciding to colonise Heraclea in Trachis.[20]

Many such consultations were actually about seeking Apollo's approval for decisions that had already been made. In other cases asking for advice and receiving an answer from the oracle was not the end of the matter. According to the 'Father of History' Herodotus, who knew Delphi well, when Grinnos, king of the island of Thera (modern-day Santorini), went to seek advice from Apollo in the late seventh century BCE, the oracle told him to establish a new city in Libya. Unfortunately, neither King Grinnos nor Battos, the man he tasked with the job because he (by his own admission) was too old and overweight, had a clue where Libya was. Failing in their task, the kingdom of Thera was afflicted with drought for seven hard years. Not knowing why, they sought advice from Delphi once more and were told that their failure to do as Apollo had instructed was the cause of the drought. So off Battos went again in an attempt to fulfil the oracle's instructions, this time visiting the island of Crete and asking directions, but he couldn't find Libya, landing on another island instead. Back to Delphi they went. It was a case of third time lucky: the oracle told them to seek out the Libyan mainland, and this time Battos succeeded, founding the city of Kyrene, near present-day Shahhat.[21] Until its eventual abandonment in the seventh century CE following military assault and several earthquakes, Kyrene was a powerful city and thus a testament to the wisdom of the advice given by Apollo's priestess.

Sometimes the oracle gave confusing and opaque answers that could be interpreted several ways, if at all. Most famous of all these was the prophecy given to the wealthy King Croesus of Lydia, who ruled from about 560 BCE. He revered the oracle and gave gifts to Delphi, including purple robes sent in honour of Apollo. Seeking advice on whether or not to attack the Persians, he sent messengers to seek answers from several oracles in Greece and Libya. Receiving the responses, Croesus read through them and ignored those he didn't like, choosing the one given to him by the oracle at Delphi because it agreed with the decision he had already made. The Delphic oracle told Croesus that if he crossed the Halys, the river marking the boundary line between his kingdom and the Persians, an empire would be destroyed. Buoyed by this, Croesus set out confident of victory and did destroy an empire. Unfortunately, it was his own.[22]

On another occasion the Athenians asked how they could defend themselves against the Persians. Trust in your wooden walls, the oracle advised them, sparking some debate about what this meant. Was the wood the palisade that surrounded the Acropolis in Athens or, as their leading general Themistocles argued, did the oracle mean the wooden-sided ships of the Athenian navy would be the salvation of the city and its people? The oracle was consulted again, and the Pythia's new answer prompted most Athenians to side with Themistocles. The Athenians subsequently triumphed at the naval Battle of Salamis (480 BCE), and both Themistocles and the oracle were vindicated.[23]

The ambiguity of the oracle's utterances generally left them open to interpretation, but during several conflicts Apollo and his priestess were accused of taking sides. During the Persian Wars (499–449 BCE) Delphi's advice was considered pro-Persian; when Sparta took on a league of states in the First Peloponnesian War (460–445 BCE), its enemies seemed to have Apollo's backing. When this sort of thing happened, pilgrims often headed to other oracles in the hope of getting different advice. The oracle of Zeus at Dodona in north-west Greece was one of the most notable, the Athenians tending to go there when their usual destination Delphi seemed biased against them. That seems to have been the wiser choice anyway, given that the advice the Delphic oracle gave – not to take on the Persians – turned out to be completely wrong.

The Sacred Wars

The importance of Apollo's oracle at Delphi in guiding political decision-making meant that access and control of the sanctuary were jealously protected and frequently fought over. Although on occasion one or other of the rival Greek city states did succeed in establishing control over the site this was generally seen as undesirable. The solution was to create a confederation with representatives drawn from across Greece, the Delphic Amphictyony (league of neighbours), to care for the fabric of Delphi.

In 595 BCE the Amphictyony launched a war against the city of Kirra. This nearby port had imposed a tax on travellers to Delphi which was reducing the income that the sanctuary earned from pilgrims. The Delphic Amphictyony was victorious, and the port was destroyed. About a century and a half later, the Second Sacred War began when the Phocians, the people inhabiting the area of central Greece which included Delphi, took over the sanctuary. The Spartans briefly removed them, but when they returned home the Phocians reappeared with Athenian backing. Nearly three decades later, access for all was eventually restored by the Peace of Nicias (421 BCE), a treaty agreed between Sparta and Athens, although Delphi would continue to be sacked, occupied and abused to pay for mercenary forces over the course of another three Sacred Wars.[24]

Finally, Apollo stepped in to protect his own. Under attack by Gauls from Western Europe in 279 BCE, the people of Delphi appealed directly to Apollo for help. He sent, so the legends say, a mighty force against the invaders. Rocks crashed down from Mount Parnassus, the earth shook, bitterly cold weather assailed the Gauls and ancient Greek heroes returned to save the shrine. Apollo and the Greeks triumphed, and the Gauls were defeated, but Delphi was already losing its importance.

Decline and Fall

The decline of Delphi as a sacred pilgrimage centre began around the time of the victory of King Philip II of Macedonia over Thebes and Athens at the Battle of Chaeronea in 338 BCE and the rule of his son and successor, Alexander the Great, who came to power in 336 BCE. Previously, Greek rulers and political entities had settled their disputes through war or by consulting the only overarching authority on which they could agree: the gods. As the most important oracle in ancient Greece, this gave the Pythia unparalleled power and influence. But Philip and Alexander did not recognise Delphi, and as Greece came under Macedonian control, authority passed to the king.[25] Alexander's relationship with Delphi was short-lived and brutal: he attempted to forcibly consult the Pythia and, when that did not go well, turned against the oracle. Having conquered Miletus in Asia Minor, he favoured Apollo's other oracle nearby at Didyma, at the heart of his empire, which seemed a more fitting site to seek advice from the gods.

Meanwhile the Delphic oracle was increasingly the focus of Roman attention. Apollo may have been a Greek god, but his absorption into the pantheon of Roman gods in the fifth century BCE meant he was a familiar and much-worshipped figure. Roman pilgrims asked for advice at Delphi in 216 BCE when Hannibal of Carthage invaded the Italian peninsula.[26] Twenty-five years later the Romans took control of Delphi, driving out the Aetolians, who had controlled it for a century or so, and Rome's leaders began to take an interest in it. Emperor Augustus, for example, resurrected the idea of the Amphictyony. The Greek geographer Strabo, writing on the cusp of the Common Era, said that in his day Delphi was still revered and famed because of its reputation for giving advice to some of the most important figures in Greek history and myth,

After the fourth century CE faith in the oracle was replaced by Christian beliefs. Delphi and the Temple of Apollo fell into ruin, and were not rediscovered until the late fifteenth century.

> because of the temple of the Pythian Apollo, and because of the oracle, which is ancient, since Agamemnon is said by the poet to have had an oracle given him from there; for the minstrel is introduced as singing 'the quarrel of Odysseus and Achilles, son of Peleus, how once they strove . . . and Agamemnon, lord of men, rejoiced at heart . . . for thus Phoebus Apollo, in giving response to him at Pytho, had told him that it should be'. Delphi, I say, is famous because of these things.[27]

There was a brief renaissance of visiting in the first century of the new millennium, but these could not be said to be pilgrimages. Emperor Nero did so in 67 CE for the Pythian Games: unsurprisingly, he won *everything* and carried off 500 of Delphi's 3,500 statues.[28] That does not mean that Delphi was forgotten, as gifts were made and rebuilding carried out, some of which was rather lavish, like the library and a new house for the Pythia.

What really did for Delphi was Christianity. Emperor Constantine (ruled 306–*c*.337 CE), the first Christian ruler of Rome, stole many of the statues that adorned Delphi to decorate his new palace in Constantinople. The last known piece of advice allegedly issued by Apollo's priestess at Delphi was delivered during the reign of Julian the Apostate (ruled 360–63), who dispatched his personal physician on a pilgrimage to ask if the paganism Julian was trying to reintroduce into the empire would succeed in pushing out the still relatively new religion of Christianity. The Pythia apparently advised him that the god Apollo had no 'prophetic laurel, nor a spring that speaks' any more.[29] The site was damaged by a massive earthquake a couple of years later, and less than twenty years after that, the Romans shut down the sanctuary at Delphi altogether. All the oracles in Greece were prohibited from divining the will of the gods in the final decades of the fourth century, and oracular pilgrimages appear to have stopped dead.[30] Rome now revered the Christian god, and if people no longer believed in Apollo, what was the use of going on pilgrimage to ask for advice from the Pythia? Not long after, the Temple of Apollo at Delphi was destroyed, and a thousand years of divination at Delphi came to an end.

Modern Oracles?

No one has walked or sailed to Delphi on pilgrimage since then, not least because there is no Pythia there to pass on a divine message. Delphi, lost for centuries as it fell further into ruin, was rediscovered by the Italian merchant Cyriacus of Ancona in 1486, who charted the ruins and examined the remaining inscriptions. Several centuries passed before members of the Society for Psychical Research, founded in Britain by, among others, Alfred Lord Tennyson and Lewis Carroll, called for an investigation into the oracle. This and archaeological interest in the site prompted long-running negotiations which finally resulted in investigations in the years either side of 1900. These found no evidence of a cleft emitting vapour, and thus could not explain the source of the Pythia's supposed visions.[31] Instead, other theories were advanced: the oracle was psychic or had telepathic powers, or the whole thing was a clever lie, the oracle prompted by hidden priests.[32] What did not happen was the revival of pilgrimages to Delphi. Across Europe, Christian pilgrims were increasingly on the march, but in Greece pilgrimages to the shrine of a pagan god attracted nobody.

Perhaps though, Delphi pilgrimages might resume, albeit in a different form. At other places – Rātana Pā in New Zealand, Buenos Aires in Argentina – pilgrimages to fringe or previously unrecognised sites have sprung up in the last century. In 2009 Loukas Tsoukalis met a group of 'thinkers and policy makers' at Delphi to discuss the state of the European Union and 'compare alternative policy directions'. He described the discussion they had and the information they gleaned as the result of consulting a sort of oracle. Quite who or what was consulted is as opaque in Tsoukalis' account as any ancient text, but he claims the group consulted a modern Pythia, who gave answers, sometimes via the internet, that were sometimes difficult to interpret, though others were 'crystal clear'. She apparently told them to change their way of thinking, that she had seen such trouble in Europe before and that Europe was well placed to adapt.

This isn't perhaps the most sensible way to manage the

complexities of international relations and multi-state collaboration, but given the state of much of the world's politics in the early decades of the twenty-first century, perhaps seeking advice through a pilgrimage to the oracle at Delphi isn't the worst either.

4

JERUSALEM

Israel/Palestine

In 1581 Heinrich Bünting of Magdeburg in Germany published a map of the world that would have been of no use at all to a traveller or to any other cartographer. Nor would it have helped sailors navigate the shores of even their own lands, let alone those of distant countries. Bünting would not have been remotely bothered by these shortcomings; his work was intended to accompany his *Itinerarium Sacrae Scripturae,* a guide for people reading the Bible. His world map or *mappa mundi* depicted the world in the form of a clover leaf, a symbol of the Trinity and of the city of his birth. Bünting explained that he had created 'the whole world in a clover leaf, which is the crest of the city of Hannover my beloved fatherland'. This world consisted of three leaf-shaped continents: a reddish Europe, warm yellow for Africa and fresh green for Asia. At the centre of it all, joining the lands together, was a city of red-roofed buildings, the focus for both viewers of the map and of Bünting's world: Jerusalem.

For the Jews, its first pilgrims, God resides in Jerusalem. For Christians, whose pilgrimages began not too long after Jesus died in 33 CE, it is the place where he lived and where the important events at the end of his life were played out: the Last Supper, his betrayal and arrest, his final journey along what became known as the Via Dolorosa, as well as his execution, entombment, resurrection and ascension to heaven. For Muslims, it is where the Prophet Muhammad ascended to visit heaven on the Night Journey in 621 CE, leaving behind the impression of his foot, and the place where the gate of paradise would open.[1] Never important enough to be an imperial city, not connected enough to be a useful administrative centre, and not resourced enough to be a key site for manufacturing, Jerusalem was built for and on religion. In turn, the city, both real and imagined, has had a reach right around the globe, drawing pilgrims in their thousands and then millions for centuries. Jerusalem is probably the most famous city in the world, and the most contested. For millennia, different faiths have fought over the right to settle and worship in the city, and for pilgrims to visit the holiest sites of their respective faiths.

The Birth of Pilgrimage

For Jews, the focus of pilgrimage to Jerusalem has always been the Temple. The First Temple was built by Solomon, son of the biblical King David, three millennia ago, and endured for four centuries before the city was besieged and the Temple burned down in about 586 BCE by the Babylonians. Most of the city's population then went into exile in Babylon and did not return until invited to rebuild the Temple half a century later. This Second Temple was dismantled and then rebuilt by the Jewish King Herod I (*c.*72–*c.*4 CE). Herod's motives were mercenary; he was actively trying to attract Jewish pilgrims for the revenue they would generate.

Herod's investment paid off. He transformed a cramped and unwelcoming city into somewhere attractive to pilgrims. Inns and hostels were built; aqueducts brought in water for ritual bathing, and everything from catering to the souvenir trade received a massive boost. The reconstructed Temple and its surrounding compound covered more than thirty-five acres, which made it the largest sanctuary in the world at the time.[2] Given that a few centuries before, the whole city had fitted inside an area smaller than that, this Second Temple must have dominated Jerusalem. We know pilgrimage to Jerusalem subsequently became wildly popular, and Jewish pilgrims from outside the country are mentioned for the first time in sources from Herod's time.

By the middle of the first century CE pilgrims were coming in such numbers that, when an invading Roman army arrived in Lydda in the year 66, they found it 'empty of men' because they had gone up to Jerusalem for the Feast of Tabernacles. The city allegedly welcomed three million Jewish pilgrims that year, a highly exaggerated figure that nevertheless gives a sense of how crowded the small city must have felt at the time.[3] The population could swell by up to half on the most important holy days, and all the pilgrims needed somewhere to stay, food to eat, and water to drink and bathe. At first, most facilities may have been temporary – tents, for example, or water taken from springs – but over time these were replaced with permanent buildings including cisterns to collect water.

Everything changed with the final destruction of the Second Temple in 70 CE by the Romans. They were so pleased with this achievement that, when they returned to Rome, they commemorated their victory by constructing the Arch of Titus next to the Forum and adorning it with images of their loot. The Temple was never rebuilt, and all Jewish pilgrims were left with was one part of the complex known as the Western Wall. Within sixty years they were deprived of even this remnant of their sacred past when the emperor Hadrian rebuilt Jerusalem as a Roman colony (Aelia Capitolina), introduced the cult of Jupiter and forbade Jews to enter the city. Most fled to the east or south in the scattering of the Jews known as the Diaspora. When they did return on pilgrimage, they did so primarily to mourn the loss of the Temple and the destruction of Jerusalem.

The decline of Jewish fortunes in Jerusalem coincided with the beginning of Christianity's relentless rise. The execution of Christ about three decades before the final destruction of the Second Temple did not immediately inspire waves of Christian pilgrims – the occupation of Jerusalem by the Romans was one barrier – but when the Tenth Roman Legion departed for Aela (modern Aqaba) on the northern tip of the Red Sea in the late third century CE things began to change. Not long after, the Roman empire got its first Christian ruler, Constantine the Great (ruled 306–*c.*337 CE), who refashioned Jerusalem to cater to pilgrims of his new faith. The most important addition was the Church of the Holy Sepulchre, built on the site of Christ's entombment. The anonymous Bordeaux Pilgrim, author of the earliest surviving Christian pilgrimage account that we have, came to Jerusalem in about 333. When they arrived, it was still a few years before building work was complete, but they provided a snapshot of the work in progress on this 'church of wondrous beauty', which became the focus of Christian pilgrimage in Jerusalem. Constantine passed an edict insisting on tolerance of Christians in the empire. Unfortunately, he was less tolerant of Jews, who he considered members of an 'abominable sect'. He continued the ban on them entering the city, although he gave Jewish pilgrims access to the Western Wall, all that remained of the destroyed Temple, once a year.

Constantine's building plans were just the start. Development took place across the small city and its hinterland, creating more and more for Christian pilgrims to see, which meant

The Church of the Holy Sepulchre, built over Christ's tomb, was the most important pilgrimage site in Jerusalem for Christians. This woodcut illustrated Bernhard von Briedenbach's pilgrimage account. Written in the 1480s, it was widely known in Europe.

staying for longer and spending more money. The emperor Justinian built the vast Nea (New) Church on Mount Zion, designed to accommodate large numbers of pilgrims.[4] It was reduced to ruins over a millennium ago, but a mosaic created in the sixth century to decorate the floor of a church in Jordan shows it was one of the most prominent buildings in the city. By the time the emperor Theodosius I came on pilgrimage in about 520, there were twenty-four churches on the Mount of Olives alone. Where pilgrims came, so too did Christians who wanted to settle in Jerusalem permanently. Monasteries and nunneries sprang up to accommodate communities of the faithful, many of which supported the growing pilgrimage industry. The anonymous man known as the Piacenza Pilgrim after his place of origin came towards the end of the sixth century and reported 'visiting many monasteries and places where miracles had been performed' around Jerusalem.[5]

Jewish and Christian pilgrimages to Jerusalem became more difficult after the Muslim conquest of Jerusalem in 638, six years after the death of the Prophet Muhammad. Islam was still a comparatively new religion, but the city had played an important role in the life of the Prophet and there were sites there sacred to Muslims. Texts were written – including the *Fada'il al-Quds*, or *Merits of Jerusalem* – which extolled the sanctity of the city and explained that Jerusalem had a role to play in the End of Days. Half a century later, Caliph Abd al-Malik (died 705), whose rival and enemy at the time, Caliph Ibn al-Zubayr (died 692), controlled the Muslim holy city of Mecca, changed the religious topography of Jerusalem by building the beautiful and eye-catching shrine called the Dome of the Rock on the Temple Mount (the site of the Second Temple) and the al-Asqa mosque. The Dome of the Rock was built over the stone considered to mark the place where God created the world. This was the same stone on which Jews believed Abraham had intended to sacrifice his son before God intervened. Muslims were encouraged to visit Jerusalem en route to Mecca. This integrated the city into Muslim pilgrimage traditions by promoting it as the third most important city in Islam and enabled Abd al-Malik to boost his claims to the caliphate over those of his rival Ibn al-Zubayr.

Muslim-dominated Jerusalem was a tricky place for non-Islamic pilgrims. Orthodox Coptic Christians, historically persecuted by Muslims when they refused to convert, stopped coming during the turbulence of the tenth and eleventh centuries. At various times there were specific bans on pilgrimage activity, like that imposed in 1008 by the Fatimid caliph al-Hakim (mad and tyrannical or divinely inspired, depending on who you believe) on pilgrims wanting to visit on Palm Sunday.[6] The situation reached a crisis point in September of the following year, when al-Hakim ordered the destruction of synagogues and churches and, most shocking of all, the Church of the Holy Sepulchre itself. It was razed to the ground, and according to a contemporary historian the rock tomb where Christ had lain was smashed causing 'all trace of it to disappear'.[7] Fortunately for Christian and Jewish pilgrims, al-Hakim seems to have been an outlier; the Holy Sepulchre was rebuilt by his son and soon after the city welcomed non-Muslim pilgrims once more.

The Persian writer and traveller Nasir Khusraw (1004–1072/88) noted, 'From the Byzantine realms and other places too come Christians and Jews to visit the churches and synagogues located there.'[8] But reaching Jerusalem was still fraught with danger as members of the Great German Pilgrimage of 1064 found to their cost. Depending on which estimates you are inclined to believe, it had up to 12,000 participants. The unarmed pilgrims were not met with open arms as they travelled across Europe and through Constantinople; instead, many were attacked, starved, imprisoned and deprived of water. Those who survived eventually reached Jerusalem, but their experiences showed how dangerous the journey had become. Seven years later Jerusalem fell to the Seljuk Turks and Christians weren't allowed in at all. It was the dangers of the journey and the capture of the city by the Seljuks that helped inspire the military expeditions to the Holy Land now known as the Crusades.

A safer journey and access to Jerusalem for Christian pilgrims were largely assured with the capture of the city by forces of the First Crusade in 1099. Taxes were levied on pilgrims and money lavished on the Christian sites by its new rulers: churches, damaged or dismantled under Islamic rule, were rebuilt and cemeteries established for those who died on pilgrimage. A new infrastructure of hospices and markets selling provisions and souvenirs was established too, allowing Jerusalem's merchants and residents to make a living from the pilgrimage business. This included Malquisinat, the road to the north of David Street founded by Melisende (died 1161), the first Christian queen of Jerusalem. This street specialised in providing ready-cooked food to passing pilgrims, which was what gave it its name, which translates as 'street of bad cooking'.[9]

To protect Christian pilgrims from attack (if not from the food), two orders of fighting monks were founded in Jerusalem during the eleventh and twelfth centuries: the Knights of St John of Jerusalem (otherwise known as the Hospitallers, which still survives and in Britain is known as St John Ambulance) and the Poor Fellow-Soldiers of Christ and the Temple of Solomon, known as the Knights Templar. Even so, a pilgrimage was fraught with danger as reaching Jerusalem meant crossing hostile lands or dangerous seas, and even when they managed to reach Jerusalem pilgrims were not always safe. According to a life written by her younger brother Thomas, when the feisty Margaret of Beverley went on pilgrimage back to the land of her birth (though English she had been born in Jerusalem) in the 1180s she became caught up in the siege and capture of the city by Saladin, which led to the Third Crusade (1189–92). Margaret apparently put a metal cooking pot on her head and got stuck in defending the walls, bringing the soldiers water until she was felled by a blow to the head.[10]

The turmoil in this period did not mean that non-Christian

pilgrimage stopped, with Jewish pilgrims from Western Europe taking advantage of better transport and communications with the Holy Land. Even though the conflict between the rival religions over control of Jerusalem was brutal and bloody, when it came to religious practice there was often a surprising degree of tolerance. Usama Ibn Munqidh (died 1188), a Syrian writer, went on pilgrimage on several occasions. Many of the religious sites sacred to Muslims had been converted by Christians for their own use, such as the Dome of the Rock and the al-Aqsa mosque, which had been turned into a church and the headquarters of the Knights Templar respectively. But Usama was welcomed and still able to practise his faith. 'Whenever I went to visit the holy sites of Jerusalem, I would go in and make my way up to the al-Aqsa Mosque, beside which stood a small mosque that the Franks had converted into a church. When I went into the al-Aqsa Mosque – where the Templars, who are my friends, were – they would clear out that little mosque so that I could pray in it.'[11] That said, there was still hostility from some Christians. On one occasion a man who had recently arrived in Jerusalem rushed into the mosque and tried to make him pray like a Christian, facing east. Usama was at least lucky enough to complete his pilgrimage in safety. Judah Halevi, a Jewish poet from Granada, arrived at the Muslim-controlled city in about 1216, but was probably killed by a crusader on his journey home.[12]

With Saladin in control from 1187, Muslim pilgrims returned to Jerusalem. The new regime was however open to pilgrimage and settlement by other religions, so pilgrimage access for Copts – banned by the crusaders as heretics – was restored, and Jews were allowed to settle in the city once more. The latter also continued to come on pilgrimage, like Rabbi Samuel Ben Samson in 1210, and Rabbi Jacob between 1238 and 1244.[13] Just as the crusaders had built or expanded Christian holy sites and dismantled or appropriated Muslim shrines, so Saladin and his successors did the opposite. St Mary's on Mount Zion, a possible site of the Last Supper, was largely demolished, and Jerusalem was reintegrated into the Islamic hierarchy of pilgrimage with Mecca and Medina. The city was also developed as a place of Muslim scholarship, a reaction to its years under crusader control, though it never attained the same status as cities like Damascus and Cairo.[14] After the fall of Acre, the last crusader stronghold in the Holy Land, in 1291, the region became more stable, and a rebuilding programme to promote Jerusalem as an Islamic city was set in motion. As a result pilgrimage increased once more.

The end of the age of Crusades and secure Islamic rule over the city led to a more balanced approach to pilgrimage in Jerusalem for its various faiths. That is not to say pilgrimage was easy, but for many the city was important enough for the risks involved. As the *Guide-Book to Jerusalem* of *c.*1350 put it:

> Jerusalem is the holy city of holy cities, the mistress of nations, the chief of provinces, called the City of the Great King, and placed in the midst of the earth, being as it were the centre of the universe, so that 'all nations might flow unto it'. The possession of patriarchs, the nurse of prophets, the teacher of apostles, the cradle of our salvation, the country of the Lord, the mother of faith, even as Rome is the mother of the faithful, chosen of God and sanctified, where stood the feet of the Lord, honoured by angels, frequented by every nation under heaven.[15]

Observing the cooperation between members of the different faiths at the time, the secretary of the Mamluk treasury in Jerusalem (the Mamluks had been in charge since 1260) commented, 'Noble Jerusalem is venerated among all Muslims, Jews, and Christians as a place of pious visitation for all of them, the difference among them being only in the sites of visitation within Jerusalem. We have only pointed this out because in it is a lesson in the mutual agreement as to its veneration and its status as a destination for visitation.'[16]

Christian visitors to the city had to rely on the Franciscans, who managed pilgrimages after 1342. The friars were careful not to upset the status quo, often guiding the pilgrims around the relevant sites at dawn to avoid clashes with Muslims.[17] Islamic law protected freedom of worship for Christians and Jews, whether resident or visiting temporarily, and in turn the pilgrims brought prosperity to the city through trade and the payment of taxes. This is why Rabbi Obadiah da Bertinoro from Italy, travelling in the last years of the 1480s, was able to report, 'The Jews are not persecuted by the Arabs in these parts. I have travelled through the country in its length and breadth, and none of them has put an obstacle in my way.'[18]

By the fifteenth century, the Jerusalem pilgrimage was seriously big business, especially if you were servicing the Christian and Jewish traffic out of Venice. European pilgrims tended to travel from the port, and in addition to needing to stay for several nights (or sometimes weeks, if the weather was against them) before sailing, they also needed to buy provisions (a mattress, a chicken in a coop, clothes, food), as well as passage on a ship. For those who could afford to, it was possible to go on pilgrimage more than once, which naturally meant repeated financial outlay. Developments in how fifteenth-century pilgrims reached Jerusalem have been seen as a precursor to modern tourism, as pilgrims increasingly paid for an organised trip and complained bitterly when they did not get what they expected. Felix Fabri, a Dominican from Ulm in present-day Switzerland who went on pilgrimage in the early 1480s, found his trip so unsatisfactory that he soon went again. He justified this to the readers of his entertaining account by explaining:

> I was by no means satisfied with my first pilgrimage, because it was exceedingly short and hurried, and we ran round the holy places without understanding and feeling what they were. Besides this, we were not permitted to visit some of the holy places, both within Jerusalem and without ... I seemed to myself to know less about all the holy places than I did before I visited them.[19]

Ottoman Jerusalem

After the Ottoman empire defeated the Mamluks and took control of Jerusalem in 1517, Sultan Suleiman the Magnificent paid considerable attention to the restoration of the city. He spent lavishly on the Islamic holy sites, restoring the Dome of the Rock and paying for its exterior to be adorned with tiles.[20] He also paid to overhaul Jerusalem's water system. Support for pilgrims was a family affair, as Suleiman's powerful Ukrainian wife Roxelana turned a former Mamluk palace into a pilgrim hospice and soup kitchen that comfortably fed five hundred poor people each day.[21]

Pilgrimage by Christians and Jews was permitted because the same practice was a religious obligation for Muslims, but non-Muslim pilgrims had to be discreet. That did not mean pilgrimage was as popular as it had once been. There was a belief among some in the West that the Ottoman Turks were degenerate, the holy places ruinous and the route to Jerusalem fraught with danger, although in reality the Turks probably did what they could to protect pilgrims. The city's garrison spent a not inconsiderable amount of time seeing off 'rebellious Bedouins' who prayed on the pilgrims as easy targets for robbery and kidnapping.[22] Aquilante Rocchetta, a Calabrian traveller in the last years of the sixteenth century, claimed that he had 'rarely heard of pilgrims being killed by Arab robbers or captured by Turks', and that those Turks they did encounter tended to offer aid.[23]

The European Reformation of the sixteenth century meant a reduction in the number of pilgrims coming from the West – Catholics because they were concentrating on prayer to reclaim those lost to Protestantism, and Protestants because they did not believe in the spiritual benefit of pilgrimages. This resulted in a decline in spending and revenue, and despite the rebuilding of the previous century in the seventeenth century Jerusalem fell into a state of decay. Jean Boucher, a Franciscan writing in the mid-1610s, attributed the desolation of the city to divine displeasure, blaming Christians' failure to recognise Christ's message and God's subsequent punishment.[24]

For those pilgrims who did reach Jerusalem, problems were as likely to come from the resident Christians as from the Muslim authorities. As the Ottoman empire declined, so too did its grip on the city. The different Christian denominations – Greek Orthodox, Armenian, Catholic – argued incessantly over all kinds of things and seized each other's properties.[25] Disputes over access to the Church of the Holy Sepulchre, restored from its ruinous state in 1719, meant that in 1757 an Ottoman edict known as the Status Quo divided custody of the shrine between six denominations. The edict was effective and continues in force, but the groups distrusted each other so much that the key to the church was given to a local Muslim family for safekeeping. They still look after it to keep the peace.[26]

Alongside the bickering Christians, pilgrims from Jewish communities across Europe supported by the city's Jews continued to visit Jerusalem. From the early 1730s, chartered ships began to arrive in the Holy Land carrying Jewish pilgrims, with Italy, the Balkans, Turkey, North Africa and eastern Europe furnishing the highest number of pilgrims. The Sephardic community in Istanbul chartered a boat every year, and guidebooks were produced for Jewish pilgrims to Jerusalem. In return, the Jewish quarter of the city gained a small income (most of what was spent went to the Muslim city authorities) and stayed connected to Jewish communities outside the Holy Land. Many Jewish pilgrims also settled in the city, enabling the ageing Jewish settlement, beset by high mortality and low birth rates, to survive.[27] In the following century, as the idea of creating a Jewish homeland emerged and then focused on Palestine, the fact that Jewish migration to Jerusalem was already taking place undoubtedly bolstered the Zionist cause.

In 1853 a minor dispute in Jerusalem between French-backed Catholic priests and Orthodox monks backed by Russia sparked the outbreak of the Crimean War between the Russian empire and an alliance of Britain, France, the Ottoman empire and Piedmont-Sardinia.[28] The impact on Jerusalem was devastating as financial support from Russia ceased and the regular stream of pilgrims dried up. The Jewish population, who relied on alms and income from pilgrims, were hard hit and had to rely on charity from the better-off Christians. The Russian bureaucrat Boris Pavlovich Mansurov (1828–1910), commissioned to produce a guidebook by the tsar's brother Grand Duke Constantine, was so horrified by the conditions he found for Russian pilgrims in Jerusalem that he wrote a report in 1857 instead, warning about the 'series of trials' pilgrims would meet as they entered the city.[29]

However, when it was safe to travel again, pilgrims returned to Jerusalem with a vengeance. Western Europeans took advantage of the rapidly expanding steamship routes, while Russian

Orthodox pilgrims made extensive use of the railway network spreading across the tsar's empire.[30] A road to Jerusalem with a metalled surface was opened from the coastal port of Jaffa in 1867, followed by a railway in 1892, and the city increasingly attracted Americans. Mark Twain sailed with pilgrims and tourists in 1867, a journey that inspired *The Innocents Abroad*, a novel which showed pilgrims as often less than religious.[31] Pilgrimage to Jerusalem increasingly mixed secular and sacred motives, as though visitors still came for religious reasons, many just wanted to see the historical sites of the city, record its antiquities and (in the case of some of the British) 'boldly assert' what they saw as their right to pass through Palestine to reach the British empire in India.[32]

In 1869, having cut his teeth on domestic ventures – trips to the Great Exhibition in 1851 in London, for example – the entrepreneurial travel agent Thomas Cook took a group of people through Palestine. He had thought of the idea as long ago as 1850, inspired by hearing of the Holy Land from a clergyman he met on one of his Highland Tours, but it took a while to work out the practicalities. One thing he wanted to ensure was that women could take part, which he did before he launched his first pilgrims' tour, making Jerusalem and its pilgrimage pivotal in the development of modern tourism.[33] Cook's company organised its first Catholic pilgrimage from the United States in 1889. This was a first-class travel package taking in places like Paris, Milan and Venice, as well as major sites in Rome, where participants visited various pilgrimage churches en route to Jerusalem. They stayed in some rather lavish places, like Le Grand Hôtel in Paris (despite popular perceptions, pilgrims have often sought to make their journeys more comfortable), but when they reached Jerusalem, their residence was the more austere (though now luxurious) Franciscan Casa Nova.[34]

Not all of Jerusalem's wealthier pilgrims were content to stay in a monastery (or were religiously suited for it). What was needed to accommodate these new kinds of affluent pilgrims were more modern, better-equipped hostels and hotels. Notre Dame de France, for example, was established in the mid-1880s by the Assumptionist Fathers as a guest house to accommodate French pilgrims, but has since morphed into the luxurious Vatican-owned Notre Dame of Jerusalem Center. Far from living the simple life of the devout pilgrim, early twenty-first-century pilgrims are encouraged to relax after a day of religious tourism with the finest imported cheeses and wine in the city in the rooftop restaurant, with views over the Old City.[35]

The need to provide for pilgrims has allowed various religious groups and nationalities to cement their position in Jerusalem. Country- and religion-specific communities, places of worship, hostels and hospices were founded in Jerusalem from the late Middle Ages onwards. For example, there are specialist establishments for Sufis, and monasteries and nunneries for the various Christian denominations – Greeks, Copts, Syrians, Nestorians and so on. When he visited in about 1730, Father Horn, from Thuringia in Germany, accused many such establishments of being avaricious rather than charitable, as they knew 'very well how to empty the purses of pilgrims'.[36]

Orthodox Russian pilgrims, who came on subsidised train tickets in numbers so vast that the annual influx was described as an invasion by a peasant army,[37] benefited from a dedicated district built for them in the wake of the Crimean War outside the city walls. This encompassed hostels and a new Russian cathedral, which was supported by the Russian consulate and founded with the tsar's approval.[38] This sounds like altruism, but the pilgrims were encouraged and supported because they gave

Russia a presence in Jerusalem at a time when it was still part of the Ottoman empire.[39]

Russia was not alone in wanting a political foothold in Jerusalem, and many countries established consulates, ostensibly to serve their pilgrims while visiting the city. They started to appear in the middle of the eighteenth century, but it was the opening of the British consulate in the late 1830s that marked the acceleration in international representation, and several other countries soon established presences in the city to promote their interests. This meant a certain amount of jostling for space. The French, for example, built their hostel between the city and the Russian compound (the first important foreign building project outside the Old City) on the Jaffa Road as a check on Orthodox expansion.[40] The building race was partly about keeping up with the neighbours, but also about keeping an eye on them.

Though foreign powers were able to use pilgrims and pilgrimages to gain some degree of influence in Jerusalem, for those not concerned with geopolitics a Jerusalem pilgrimage could still be an important status symbol at home. Greek Orthodox pilgrims, who started to come in large numbers in the nineteenth century, returned home to respect from their community for having been to the Holy City. From the sixteenth century onwards, an Orthodox Christian pilgrim to Jerusalem might be referred to in their home community as a hajji, using the term applied to a Muslim pilgrim to Mecca. This evolved into such an important marker of status that Jerusalem became a popular honeymoon destination, so a child could be conceived in the Holy City. If the child was born there, then the boy or girl would be a hajji too. The answer to why the Jerusalem pilgrimage was so important to this group undoubtedly lies in the historian Valentina Izmirlieva's contention that it was an attempt by Greek Orthodox individuals within the Islamic Ottoman empire to gain status by securing their pilgrimage the same degree of respect as the Muslim hajj to Mecca. But, as with so many things, the pilgrimage and the use of the title became so popular that both became commonplace and lost their appeal.[41]

Twentieth Century

Change came to Jerusalem during the First World War largely because the British prime minister of the day, Lloyd George, was facing growing public anger about devastating losses on the Western Front. What he needed was something to counteract negative newspaper headlines, a success that would cut through the horrors of the war and speak to something bigger, more universal, and be seen as a sign of hope. In a meeting Lloyd George told his assembled generals that he wanted to give the British people a Christmas present – Jerusalem.[42] Britain might be struggling in the European theatre of war, but it was still strong enough to take control of the holiest city in the world. General Edmund H. Allenby was dispatched to the Middle East, and following weeks of bloody conflict, the mayor of Jerusalem surrendered the city before bombing damaged its holiest places.

Dressed as a pilgrim, Allenby walked through the Jaffa Gate into the city on 11 December 1917 as the cameras rolled to capture the event, so those back at home could soon enjoy the spectacle of *General Allenby's Entry to Jerusalem* in their local cinema.[43] And so a pilgrimage to the Holy City was opened up to a new demographic – members of the army serving in the Middle East – and it soon became popular with the more devout. 'It was always one of the dreams of my life to see Jerusalem,' wrote Bede Camm, a Benedictine monk serving as a military chaplain, who joined one of the first military pilgrimages in 1918. 'But I never expected to see it as I did; Jerusalem delivered, delivered from the age-long tyranny of the Turk, with the Union Jack flying over her towers, her streets thronged with British soldiers.'[44]

There was nothing new in Lloyd George exploiting Jerusalem for political reasons; throughout its history controlling the city had been a way for foreign powers to show their military strength and religious authority. Almost twenty years before Allenby's victorious entry, Kaiser Wilhelm II of Germany had visited the Ottoman sultan and entered Jerusalem through the same Jaffa Gate, expanded to accommodate his imperial entourage. The alterations didn't go down well even among his fellow Germans, but in the kaiser's defence, the enlarged entry had not been his idea but that of his Ottoman hosts.[45] The same could not be said of the kaiser parading to celebrate the opening of the Holy Redeemer Church dressed in the white of the Teutonic Knights to the strains of Handel's 'See the Conquering Hero Comes'.[46]

British rule marked the beginning of a more modern style of pilgrimage to Jerusalem, and a more organised one. Transport links took another leap forward as the British wanted more efficient communications to better control Palestine. The improvements were a boon for pilgrims, and during the first Easter Week after the end of the war thousands of pilgrims of all faiths came by bus from neighbouring countries, and continued to do so well until into the 1960s. Better train routes, modern roads, more organised ports and shipping and eventually new airports all helped to bring larger numbers of pilgrims to the city. Bigger and more luxurious European-style hotels were built, and telegraph and telephone networks constructed.

However, things did not always go smoothly for Jerusalem's pilgrims, and there were arguments over who had the right to guide them around the city: Jews or Arabs. Each would present a very different view of Jerusalem, and tensions could run high.

The Western Wall (or Wailing Wall) is all that remains of the Second Temple, destroyed in 70 CE. It remains the primary place of pilgrimage in Jerusalem for Jews, who come to mourn the loss of their temple.

This was especially so when it came to the Western Wall. Under the Ottomans, the right of Jews to pray there had been recognised, and Suleiman the Magnificent had even ordered the construction of a plaza in front of it to facilitate access, though the rights of Jewish pilgrims weren't always respected. Things improved for the pilgrims in the nineteenth century, which led to an increase in numbers. However, this provoked the anger of Muslims living in the adjoining area of the city, and some of them took to walking their animals through the plaza and allowing them to defecate where the Jewish pilgrims were trying to pray. The British maintained the same position as the Ottomans when it came to access to the holy sites, passing a law known as the Status Quo of the Holy Places, but control of the Western Wall remained fraught, rioting over access breaking out in the 1920s.[47]

Meanwhile, the British were laying the foundations for a homeland for the Jews in Palestine, encouraging both pilgrimage and settlement in the rapidly expanding New City. Ethnically and religiously diverse, the Jewish settlers were nonetheless privileged by British policies, sparking further clashes and a Palestinian revolt against the British in the late 1930s. The issues were not resolved, and the situation rapidly declined from late 1947, leading to civil war and British withdrawal in May of the following year.

Jerusalem under Israel/Palestine

The end of British rule and the creation of the State of Israel in 1948 rewrote the pilgrimage map of Jerusalem. By the time the subsequent Arab–Israeli War was over, the kingdom of Jordan controlled the West Bank, and the city of Jerusalem itself was split between the Israeli west and the Jordanian-administered east. The Jewish half included Mount Zion and many important Muslim sites, while the Jordanians claimed the whole of the Old City and with it sites like the Church of the Holy Sepulchre and the Temple Mount. Critically for the Jews, the Jordanians now controlled the Western Wall and ignored the agreement that should have given Jewish pilgrims access.

This was a severe disappointment for the new State of Israel and for Jews more widely. The holy sites of Jerusalem had been harnessed by Zionists since the nineteenth century to promote the idea of Jewish nationhood, but despite establishing the longed-for homeland, Jews still could not access all their sacred pilgrimage sites.[48] Determined to create an alternative sacred landscape for his people, Dr Shmuel Zanwil Kahane, director of religious affairs, adopted existing shrines, invented origin stories and created altogether new places of pilgrimage. King

David's Tomb on Mount Zion, for example, had previously been of limited interest to Jewish pilgrims but now became the most important Jewish shrine in Israel. The Lion's Cave was promoted by Kahane using legends. It attracted pilgrims, though not everyone was convinced, and concerns were expressed that people would ascribe to it a sanctity the place never really possessed.[49]

Though Jewish Israel and Islamic Jordan had divided Jerusalem between them, Christians still wanted to come on pilgrimage, although their most important site, the Church of the Holy Sepulchre, could only be reached by a select few, predominantly church and monastic personnel. The difficulties of access almost caused a crisis when Pope Pius XII suggested to Catholics that they should go on pilgrimage to Jerusalem *and* Rome in the 1950 holy year. The Israelis calculated that 100,000 Christian pilgrims would converge on the Holy City and were seriously concerned. The places they would want to visit were in a parlous state after the recent war, and Israel simply wasn't in a position to cater for that many people in addition to its resident population, already swelled by post-war Jewish refugees from Europe. Food rationing was still in place. More worrying still was that a huge influx of pilgrims would lead to clashes between Jews and Christians. In the end, the Israelis, unable to stop the pilgrimage, accepted that it would go ahead, and coped very well with the underwhelming fourteen hundred who eventually arrived.[50]

The split between the two halves of Jerusalem, and the impact it had not just on pilgrimage but on politics, endured until the Six Day War of 1967, in which Israeli forces were victorious over a coalition of Arab states, taking control of the eastern half of Jerusalem. The Western Wall finally came under Jewish rule for the first time in nineteen hundred years.[51] The Israelis wasted no time in creating a vast open space around this most sacred of Jewish sites, sending the bulldozers in four days later and demolishing the homes of over six hundred people. With Jerusalem once again the capital of Israel, the Western Wall became intimately connected with the Israel Defense Forces. Since then they have used the site for activities like swearing-in and memorial ceremonies.[52]

Jerusalem, the centre of the world, has always been a contented political and religious place. Much of its history has been marked by violence against buildings, shrines and people, as different armies and religions have taken control and changed the city to suit their needs. In the process, the holy places of Jews, Christians and Muslims have been damaged or destroyed, but despite the difficulties this has created for pilgrims of all faiths, they have continued to come. Economically, Jerusalem built itself up on the proceeds of pilgrimage, especially in the nineteenth century when tourism and easier transport boosted numbers, and wealthy pilgrims wanted a more comfortable experience. Politically, global powers have argued over Jerusalem, leading to wars far away but also leaving marks on the place itself in attempts to show their power in the holiest city in the world.

5

MECCA

Saudi Arabia

In 1045, Nasir Khusraw embarked on a pilgrimage to Mecca because he was having a crisis of faith. We know this because Nasir tells us this at the very start of his *Book of Travels,* an account of his hajj from his home in Khurasan to the holiest city in Islam. Nasir was forty-two at the time. Following years of rather uninspiring administrative work in the revenue service, he had gone on a month-long orgy of drinking, which is of course at odds with Islam. Steeped in wine, Nasir then had a dream that told him to go to Mecca, so, shocked into sobriety by what seemed like a divine message, he packed up and set out.

According to sharia law – Islamic canonical law based on the teachings of the Koran and the traditions of the Prophet Muhammad – the hajj is the fifth pillar of Islam. It states that all Muslims who are financially and physically capable should undertake the pilgrimage to Mecca once in their lifetime, and it has been drawing pilgrims there for almost fifteen hundred years. Nasir's reason for embarking on the hajj is just one of the myriad motivating forces which have prompted individuals to step away from their ordinary lives and start on the road to Mecca. He had had some sort of epiphany about the way he had been living, and a religiously inspired dream had made him see the error of his ways.[1]

Mecca is a landlocked city in western Arabia, squeezed into a narrow valley half a mile wide and two miles long, overlooked on either side by high and inhospitable rocky mountains. It started life as a small oasis frequented by the trade caravans that crossed Arabia, ruled over by various tribes and little different to many other settlements in the region. Pre-Islamic pilgrims came there to honour Hubal, a god of divination, one of many deities they worshipped with varying degrees of interest.[2] It became an Islamic holy site, according to tradition, after Abraham and Ishmael, the sons of Hagar, built the House of God known as the Kaaba, an irregular stone cube fifty feet high. It was into one corner of its eastern side that the Prophet Muhammad set the foot-wide Black Stone particularly revered by pilgrims. The Kaaba is draped in huge piece of black brocade, the *Kiswa*, which is replaced annually and was manufactured in Egypt for centuries until the task was switched to Medina in the mid-twentieth century. As Islam's holiest city, Mecca is so central to their faith that Muslims across the world pray in its direction – *qibla* – five times a day, ensuring that their prayer mats (often depicting the Kaaba) are orientated towards the city. All mosques have a *mihrab,* a niche indicating the direction of Mecca, although in Casablanca, home of the world's second-biggest mosque, laser beams show the direction of Mecca during night-time prayers.

In about 560 CE, the man who became the Prophet Muhammad, the founder of Islam, was born in Mecca. Fifty years later Muhammad started to receive revelations, delivered by the Angel Gabriel, about a new monotheistic faith. Given that Mecca at the time was polytheistic, his preaching did not find a receptive audience, and he and his followers fled north to Medina. In 628, they returned on pilgrimage to Mecca, and though its inhabitants prevented them entering that year, the subsequent Pact of al-Hudaybiya protected the right of pilgrimage. Two years

Before Saudi Arabia's oil wealth, Mecca was a small town dominated by its surrounding mountains. Many of these have now been flattened to make way for the expansion of the city, including the construction of the Clock Royal Tower complex.

after *that,* the Prophet marched on Mecca with 30,000 followers, took control of the city, and its citizens converted to Islam.

Over the following years, the area around the Kaaba evolved slowly under Muhammad's successors as leader of the Muslims. The second caliph built a wall around the Kaaba to create an enclosed area, a wall that was added to and ornamented by later patrons. The third caliph found it necessary to enlarge the city's Great Mosque to accommodate the number of pilgrims and expand the area enclosed by his predecessor's wall. Mecca would eventually be transformed by pilgrimage, but in the first centuries of Islam it was not at the centre of the Arabian-Islamic world. For one thing, the Umayyad and then the Abbasid caliphs chose other cities as their capitals such as Medina, the second holiest city in Islam and the burial place of the Prophet Muhammad, and Baghdad, which for much of the early Middle Ages was the biggest city in the world.

The hajj itself usually takes place over ten days during Dhul-Hijja, the twelfth month of the Muslim calendar, though pilgrims can attend at other times of the year on the lesser pilgrimage known as the *umra*. Before reaching the Kaaba, pilgrims are supposed to perform a series of devotional rites in preparation: visiting sites around Mecca associated with the life and death of Muhammad, washing, dressing in a seamless white outfit that signifies and reminds them of death and the final judgement, and praying. Then in Mecca itself, they circumambulate the Kaaba seven times before visiting yet more important religious sites in the city.

In recent years Mecca has expanded to a city of one and a half million, covering ten square miles, with several hills flattened to accommodate its expansion, but for most of its history it was neither particularly big nor particularly affluent. The city was for centuries ruled by the Hashemite sharifs of Mecca, descended from the Prophet, but the sharifs were always vassals of some greater power: the Umayyad caliphate at Damascus, the Ottoman empire, the Egyptians. Yet control of Mecca and the hajj has long had a political dimension that has given power to those who claim it. Whoever has the city has religious authority by virtue of the fact that they control access to the Kaaba, a divine sign of their position as pre-eminent among Muslims. Even powers that were neither Muslim nor ever likely to control Mecca took an interest in the city and its pilgrims because of its importance to so many of the people they ruled elsewhere in the world. Britain's Queen Victoria and Winston Churchill (who referred to Britain as 'the greatest Mohammedan power in the world' because the British empire ruled over India's Muslim millions) were both aware of when the hajj took place.[3] Possession of Mecca has long conferred authority, and today it gives the Saudi royal family global influence, diplomatic leverage and international standing that it would not otherwise enjoy.

Medieval Mecca

During the Middle Ages, Mecca and the routes leading to it could be lawless and fraught with danger for pilgrims. Two annual pilgrimage caravans, from Damascus and Cairo, brought people in some safety from at least the last decades of the eighth century, and these grew in size and logistical complexity in the middle of the thirteenth century. However, political turmoil following the death of the seventh Abbasid caliph, al-Ma'mūn, in 833 meant danger for pilgrims and for Mecca, while attacks by the militant Islamic Qarmatians of eastern Arabia in the following century culminated in the seizure and removal of the Black Stone in 930. It would be twenty years before it was returned. By the last quarter of the same century, the Meccans were sufficiently confident in their position to make a push for independence, the Hashemite sharifs refusing to do homage to the Fatimid caliph in north Africa, but the city did not hold out for long. As the Fatimids expanded into Egypt they were able to cut off Mecca's trade and thus food, which brought the sharifs to heel, though this didn't stop Mecca's future leaders from trying to do the same.

Half a century of strong sharif rule under Abū Numayy I (ruled 1254–1301) was followed by almost a century of infighting, as the emir's thirty sons vied for control after his death. Calm and prosperity didn't fully return until the second half of the fifteenth century, when the Egyptian sultan undertook a major building programme in Mecca, but no matter the political situation in the city, the need for Muslims to complete the hajj meant that, sooner or later, some of the most important leaders of the Islamic world found their way to Mecca. This had consequences.

The famous 1324 pilgrimage of Mansa Musa, king of Mali, depicted in the 1375 Catalan Atlas as the wealthiest man of his day,[4] apparently required a caravan tens of thousands strong to accomplish his journey across Africa. It was the perfect opportunity to show off Mali's wealth and Musa's own power. As he travelled, Musa distributed some of that wealth to the cities he passed through, as well as to the poor. In the three months he spent in Cairo on his outward journey, he and his entourage allegedly spent so much gold that they effectively crashed its value in Egypt for years to come.[5] That might be an overstatement, but Musa's visit certainly had a significant impact on the country's commerce. Not all high-status pilgrimages were so economically disruptive. King Ali of Sudan's 1494 pilgrimage to Mecca allowed him to meet a prominent scholar and secure a selection of books on history, law and grammar, and he took the chance to get a statement of support for his rule to boost his regime at home.[6]

The arrival of pilgrims happy to spend some time in the city was increasingly central to Mecca's economic survival. One local saying went, 'We sow not wheat or sorghum; the pilgrims are our crops.'[7] The comparison is not surprising, given how inhospitable the land in and around Mecca was for pretty much any form of agriculture. For the early Islamic poet al-Hayqatan, Mecca was a place where 'winter and summer are equally intolerable. No waters flow ... not a blade of grass on which to rest the eye; no, nor hunting. Only merchants, the most despicable of professions.'[8] The sale of goods and the provision of services to the pilgrims were Mecca's twin lifelines, and guilds emerged to

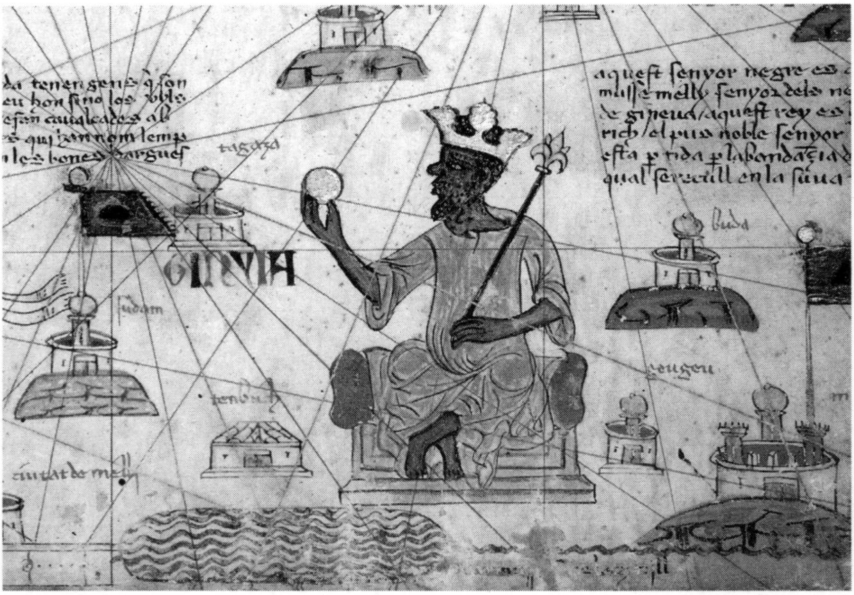

The obligation on all able Muslims to complete the hajj meant that the most important Islamic leaders in the world found their way to Mecca. Mansa Musa, a Malian king, travelled with such a large retinue that its spending had a severe impact on the Egyptian economy.

regulate the various interests – guides, those who provided water, camel brokers – though there was competition within the trades for the most lucrative work. The guides who worked with the richest pilgrims, for example, could demand higher fees and as a result achieved greater respect and social status than their peers.[9]

Mecca had been a trading centre long before the hajj. Muhammad was from a trading family, and in the Koran the materialism of the city's merchants – more concerned with money than helping others – was criticised. But after the Prophet's death, its merchants moved to Medina, and commerce in Mecca only revived because of the growth in pilgrim numbers. One thing that caught the attention of Ibn Jubayr, when he came to Mecca from al-Andalus (southern Spain) in 1183, was that many pilgrims brought things with them to trade, often whole caravans of goods that they sold to the inhabitants and their fellow pilgrims.

> Although there is no commerce save in the pilgrim period, nevertheless, since people gather in it from east and west, there will be sold in one day ... precious objects such as pearls, sapphires, and other stones, various kinds of perfume such as musk, camphor, amber and aloes, Indian drugs and other articles brought from India and Ethiopia, the products of the industries of Iraq and the Yemen, as well as the merchandise of Khurasan, the goods of the Maghrib, and other wares such as it is impossible to enumerate or correctly assess.[10]

Some groups, like the Saru tribe of the Yemen, arrived ten days before starting their hajj rituals with goods to barter, providing food that kept the Meccans supplied for the following year.[11]

By the end of the medieval period, Mecca had developed into a medium-sized town. A fire-damaged hospice was rebuilt, and old houses pulled down to make space for a new theological school. When Ludovico di Varthema went to Mecca as a mercenary in 1503, he found a place that was 'most beautiful, and is very well inhabited and contains about 6,000 families'.[12] The greatest compliment he could pay was that the houses he saw were as good as those back home in Bologna, though the place was too hot and water very scarce.

Mecca Under the Ottomans

In 1517, Mecca came under Ottoman rule when the Hashemite emir of the city, Bakarat, sent his son to voluntarily surrender the keys of both Mecca and Medina to Sultan Selim (known as Selim the Grim, a man of 'ferocious cunning' in the opinion of the Venetian doge) and recognise him as caliph; Mecca would remain under Ottoman control, barring a short blip, until 1917.

Suleiman the Magnificent (ruled 1520–66), Selim's successor and son, spent generously on repairing and extending the Great Mosque over the following decades, and on protecting the road between Damascus and Mecca with a series of fortresses extending right down into the Hejaz (the western part of the Arabian peninsula which includes Mecca and Medina). Given that he was also splashing out on improvements to Jerusalem at the same time, his spending on the pilgrimage centres within his territories must have been huge. Mecca's water supply system was renovated in the first years of his reign, and the Great Mosque itself a few years later by architects he dispatched especially for the job.[13]

Under his suzerainty the sharifs of Mecca brought stability to the city, and Suleiman's control of Mecca, Istanbul and Jerusalem created a connected network across the Ottoman empire across which pilgrims could travel, at least theoretically, in greater ease and security. But the relationship between Suleiman and his representatives was not easy, not least because of a lack of understanding. When the Ottoman sultan expelled Shi'ite Persians from Mecca (the Turks were Sunni Muslims) and forbade their pilgrimages, the potential impact of this on Mecca – reduced income, the likelihood of civic unrest – meant that the emir ignored the order.

Despite the money and energy Suleiman poured into Mecca, his improvements were focused on the pilgrimage sites and their immediate service infrastructure rather than the wider town. As a settlement, Mecca had not really developed since Ibn Jubayr was there in the 1180s. Joseph Pitts, in 1684 the first Englishman to perform the hajj to Mecca, and whose adventurous biography included being repeatedly sold into slavery, found it 'a ragged little town' and marvelled at how the influx of pilgrims could even be accommodated (in fact residents rented out their spare rooms to pilgrims and made a handsome profit).[14] The region he considered 'a barren place' where there was nothing to do, while everything still had to be brought into the city as it produced nothing itself, surviving only because of the annual pilgrimage.[15] It was also incredibly hot.

By the nineteenth century, although the Ottomans remained in charge, the Russians were looking at Mecca and saw an opportunity. The leaders of the Orthodox Church used the desire of Muslims living within Russian-controlled territory to go on pilgrimage to expand their influence and took de facto control of hajji travel within the empire, helped by the Russian government, which offered pilgrims protection via new laws and ensured cheap transport by building the infrastructure to take them from across Russia and Siberia down into Arabia.[16] This was motivated by Russian self-interest, as the imperial lands contained a large and multi-ethnic population, and moreover keeping them happy would help Russia's diplomatic relationship with its Muslim neighbours. Meanwhile in British-controlled central India, Sikandar Begum, nawab of Bhopal (ruled 1860–68), was concerned to safeguard those of her subjects who undertook the hajj. The first Indian leader to undertake the pilgrimage journey to Mecca, she had experienced the dangers of the hajj, being robbed and cheated repeatedly and her mother briefly kidnapped, so was fully aware of the need for protection and what the pilgrimage meant to her Muslim subjects.[17]

Protection for pilgrims had always been a concern. In the Middle Ages, the massive pilgrim caravans travelling across the desert covered hundreds of miles along routes with limited defences but peppered with facilities – markets, wells, way markers, accommodation – provided at intervals along the way. Even then there were still dangers, as Ibn Jubayr tells us that the people of the Hejaz 'treat the pilgrims in a manner in which they do not treat the Christians and Jews under tribute, seizing most of the provisions they have collected, robbing them and finding cause to divest them of all they have. The pilgrim in their lands does not cease to pay dues and provide foods until God helps him to return to his native land.'[18]

The pilgrim caravans took a knock at the end of the nineteenth century with the arrival of the railways. In the 1860s, a line was mooted to create a continuous route from the Ottoman capital of Istanbul to the holy cities of the Hejaz. The railway was about more than pilgrim travel (military considerations were also important), but rail access to Medina and Mecca would prove transformative. Financed by the Ottomans and opened in 1908, the line was supposed to cut the forty-day journey from Damascus to just four, but the line only went as far as Medina. It was never completed: the First World War interrupted any further construction. The railway still helped millions of pilgrims reach Mecca but was not without its dangers. When the English officer Arthur Wavell travelled to Mecca disguised as a Muslim pilgrim, his friend Abdullah warned him, 'If you are attacked in the train, or with the caravan, by overwhelming numbers, do not try to fight.'[19] Despite being relatively new, as the railway passed into the Hejaz it deteriorated too, the embankments littered with engines which had come off the poorly laid track.[20]

Even before construction began, the sharif of Mecca had complained that any rail route threatened the camel caravans, while others expressed alarm that a railway would bring non-Muslims and Europeans to the Hejaz, threatening its exclusively Islamic character.[21] International travel by train and ship (the Suez Canal had opened in 1869, meaning many shipborne pilgrims used that route to the Red Sea) meant a greater degree of mixing between Muslims and non-Muslims, if not on board, then at ports and stations. Mohammad Farahani, writing at the behest of the shah of Persia to explain the various new routes and methods of travel for potential pilgrims, was horrified by the debauchery and irreligion of many of the people that he encountered on his pilgrimage of 1885–6. He warned his readers that on the train the sexes and religions sat together. 'There is no way to avoid it,' he lamented.[22]

It is no surprise that the crowds of people who gathered annually in the small city of Mecca spread disease, as pilgrims had historically in other places. As long ago as the late 1340s, pilgrims had spread the Black Death, but it was the masses of the nineteenth century that really made this a problem. In the century after 1830, almost thirty cholera epidemics ravaged Mecca. This became such a problem that political leaders in Europe and elsewhere started to consider the public health implications of pilgrim travel. The measures they put in place were essentially forerunners of what would later become the World Health Organisation (WHO).[23] In the shorter term, after an outbreak in the 1860s, the British took responsibility – albeit reluctantly – for the health of pilgrims from India. Thomas Cook & Son was engaged as the Indian hajj agent from 1888 to 1893 to cater for and protect pilgrims following protests at the state of pilgrim transport.[24] The British state effectively underwrote the pilgrimages, making up the difference between the company's expenses and what it recouped from the pilgrims. This was a large undertaking and cost the exchequer a considerable amount, given that in 1880 the number of pilgrims from British-controlled India was 55,000, more than from any other area including the Ottoman empire. However, while the British authorities and Thomas Cook stepped up when it came to transport and had promised not to interfere in religious matters, they refused to accept that cholera was spread from person to person, and the Indian pilgrims they managed gained a reputation as spreaders of disease.[25] It was something of a PR disaster.

Similar problems with health dogged Mecca and its pilgrims well into the twentieth century. To counter this, hajjis were supposed to pass through quarantine stations, but many went to considerable lengths to avoid them. Thousands of west Africans crossed the Red Sea without stopping at the official ports from the 1920s to the 1950s. They travelled in such large numbers that such pilgrims were given their own nickname – dhow pilgrims – after the sailing vessels they used to cross the Red Sea.[26]

The Making of Saudi Arabia

The end of the First World War in 1918 marked the first major change in Mecca's status for four centuries. The Ottoman empire collapsed, and with it their rule in the Hejaz and its holy cities. What would this mean for Mecca, and the pilgrims who wanted to reach it? The Hejaz was now contested, as Egypt (effectively under British control) claimed a long-standing role in protecting the region, which lay just across the Red Sea from its own territory. Meanwhile the Hashemites, who had ruled the city of Mecca itself since the middle of the tenth century, were still in control there under Emir Hussein bin Ali. Hussein had ruled Mecca and the Hejaz on behalf of the Ottomans since 1908, but in 1916 tried to take advantage of Turkey's involvement in the First World War by making a bid for independence and declaring himself king and then caliph. This resulted in bomb damage to the Kaaba and the burning of the *Kiswa*, but he was victorious, and the revolt led to the (albeit short-lived) Hashemite

Kingdom of the Hejaz. Unfortunately for Hussein, he lacked external support, and under pressure from the forces of the charismatic Abdulaziz bin Abdul Rahman al-Saud, he was forced to flee to Cyprus.[27]

Ibn Saud completed his conquest of the Hejaz in 1925. The youngest son of the emir of Nejd, Ibn Saud had been exiled with his family from their Riyadh home in 1890, but twelve years later he returned to reclaim it. Since then he had expanded the areas under his control across Arabia. The Saudis had long wished to wrest the Hejaz from Ottoman rule, but previous attempts had all ended in failure. In Ibn Saud, they had a leader who could claim success. His capture of Mecca respected the sanctity of the city, with his envoys sent in wearing traditional pilgrim dress to read a proclamation offering peace. It wasn't perfect, not least because parts of the city – including the birthplace of the Prophet Muhammad – were destroyed, but the takeover was largely peaceful. Ibn Saud was acknowledged as king in a ceremony, he walked to the Kaaba to conduct his devotions, and Mecca became the capital of his new kingdom.

Mecca made Saudi Arabia. Control of Mecca legitimised Ibn Saud and justified his conquests. During the hajj of 1925, dressed simply but well and wearing sunglasses, Ibn Saud welcomed pilgrims in person, impressing those who met him.[28] At his opening address to the Islamic World Conference the following year, he explained it had been his duty to conquer the Hejaz because the Najidis of central Arabia had been prevented from going on pilgrimage to Mecca.[29] His reason for calling the conference, a forerunner of the World Muslim Congress, during the hajj season was to secure its approval of his control of the holy cities of the Hejaz.

Ibn Saud's support of the 1925 hajj and work on cleaning the Great Mosque gained him considerable credit.[30] Eldon Rutter's description of the pilgrimage of that year (the Englishman had converted during his time in Malaya) remarked on how smoothly it had gone, helping to promote the wonders of the new regime. He also recognised that Ibn Saud was a shrewd politician whose control of Mecca was useful for his ambitions. 'Abdul Aziz himself is not a religious fanatic,' he wrote after meeting him, 'but he is an ambitious statesman; and in the latter capacity he does not scruple to make use of religious fanaticism for the purpose of obtaining the objects of his ambition.'[31]

The next year's pilgrimage drew nearly 200,000 pilgrims, a sign of how accessible Saudi rule had made Mecca. Further cleaning, building and repairs were undertaken in 1927–8 at the king's expense, with large canvas awnings erected to protect pilgrims from the sun. The Great Mosque was electrified, and improvements to the electricity supply and building works carried out over the following decade. Ibn Saud's policies paid off. Saudi rule was seen as protecting the city's sanctity and the access needed by all Muslims. Control of Mecca brought him the support and recognition of the Islamic world as defender of the hajj and Mecca. With British backing, by 1932 Ibn Saud ruled most of the Arabian peninsula, and his kingdom was renamed Saudi Arabia in his honour.

Not everything went Ibn Saud's way. The years of his rise to power coincided with war and global depression, and by the mid-1920s pilgrimage income was so low that the government had to institute a new tax system based on the income generated by agriculture. While as many as 200,000 pilgrims visited Mecca in 1930, in 1933 the number had tumbled to just 20,000. This was particularly damaging as many absentees were long-distance pilgrims from places like Malaya or Indonesia, who tended to reside in Mecca for several months. Income from the head tax imposed on pilgrims, which had been the main source of income for the government, was now not enough to support Ibn Saud's regime,[32] but Saudi Arabia was saved by the discovery of oil in 1938. By the end of the Second World War, oil revenue had eclipsed what the pilgrimages used to generate. The taxes imposed in the mid-1920s were reduced and then abolished in the 1970s.[33]

The Saudis poured their new wealth into supporting pilgrims to Mecca. The city grew and modernised, and with the increasing numbers of pilgrims, the hoteliers, traders and merchants of Mecca prospered. In the 1920s, visitors noticed how few buildings reached three, four, or even five storeys.[34] In the following decade, the first modern hotels began to appear. By the turn of the twenty-first century, the pilgrims transported in from Medina on a fleet of 15,000 buses were staying in lavish hotels or housed in air-conditioned tents in the Mina Valley, while on the Plains of Arafat pilgrims were misted with water to keep them cool. By the first decades of the twenty-first century, much of what used to stand in Mecca, not to mention the actual mountains that confined it to its comparatively narrow valley, had been swept away to make space for the construction of the Fairmont Clock Royal Tower hotel and other buildings designed to serve the growing number of pilgrims, which today number about two million a year. The hotel itself, part of the largest building complex in the world, is supposed to accommodate 10,000 pilgrims.

The lavish hotels and shops have horrified many Muslims, but for some the erection of the Tower complex on the site of the Ottoman fortress has removed a sign of oppression. To others, though more people can now reach Mecca on hajj each year, the ease with which they can do so and the briefer time they spend in the city has had a detrimental impact on Mecca's capacity, in the words of Adam Silverstein, 'for spreading ideas, commodities, news, and the sense of a unified *umma* [Muslim community]'.[35]

The fact that only Muslims were (and are still) permitted access to Mecca has given the impression of an isolated city. The Frenchman Léon Roches disguised himself to gain access to Mecca and the Kaaba in 1841, and the Englishman Sir Richard Burton only succeeded in getting to Mecca in 1853 because he dressed and acted like a Muslim. But Mecca has long been a melting pot of people from around the world, precisely because Muslims, no matter where they are born or where they live, are supposed to go to Mecca. And pilgrims often stay, intermarrying with locals and further diversifying the ethnic mix. When the American human rights activist Malcolm X came on hajj in the spring of 1964, he saw this diversity as a sign that the racial divisions he had been fighting to overcome in America could in some ways be eradicated by faith.

> I have been blessed to visit the holy city of Mecca ... There were tens of thousands of pilgrims, from all over the world. They were of all colors, from blue-eyed blondes to black-skinned Africans. But we were all participating in the same ritual, displaying a spirit of unity and brotherhood that my experiences in America had led me to believe never could exist between the white and non-white... . We were *truly* all the same (brothers) – because their belief in one God had removed the 'white' from their *minds,* the 'white' from their *behavior,* and the 'white' from their *attitude*.[36]

He was overstating his case – prejudice and social division is found in Islam just as it is in all religions and societies – but Mecca is the one city that brings Muslims together for a common purpose.

In early twenty-first-century China, Muslim Uyghurs are only allowed to undertake the hajj once in their lifetimes, and they are only permitted to travel if they organise their pilgrimage through the China Islamic Association. The large deposits required make it too expensive for many Uyghurs, assuming they can even secure one of the limited number of places, with the stringent financial demands used to deter anyone hoping to use a pilgrimage to Mecca to flee China. In 2020 a law was passed that restricted pilgrims to those 'patriotic and of good conduct'. In earlier periods, the stories and presents brought back by returning pilgrims tied Uyghur communities to the outside world. Limiting and stopping Chinese Muslims from going on pilgrimage disrupts the links between them and their co-religionists.

Things aren't necessarily perfect in Mecca either, with the pace of development and the rising numbers bringing their own problems. Fourteen hundred pilgrims died in 1990 when a tunnel built to relieve overcrowding collapsed, and upwards of two thousand were crushed in the 2015 Mina stampede, prompting criticism of the Saudi regime's ability to manage the hajj.[37] In response – to show that they can be trusted with Mecca and the management of the hajj and like many administrators of places where pilgrimage traffic is significant – the Saudis have introduced a quota system to limit the numbers coming to Mecca. Each country has been allocated a number of places, one per thousand Muslim members of their population for each hajj. This system has its critics. 'What would Allah say to this?' asked one aspiring pilgrim, dismayed at the rising costs and the difficulty of getting a place.

Both the reality and perceptions of the Saudi regime's management of the hajj matter. The loss of Mecca would pose an existential threat to the regime, as without it the Saudis would lose their commanding position within Islam. In the early twenty-first century, the regime derives its wealth and authority from Mecca and its pilgrims, and from its production of oil. The latter will not last for ever, and if control of the former fades too, perhaps neither will Saudi Arabia.

6

ROME

Italy

In 1433 Pope Eugenius IV commissioned a new set of doors for Old St Peter's in Rome. He planned to restore the Porta Argentea, the famous ceremonial entrance that had once been beautifully decorated with silver. Eugenius was a pope who loved splendid things, so he wanted the best. His Florentine sculptor Antonio di Pietro Averlino, known as Filarete, designed and executed six panels of bronze (all surrounded by smaller scenes), each one depicting events from Eugenius' pontificate, as well as scenes from Ovid's *Metamorpheses* and Aesop's *Fables*. The doors were a bit of a political show, and were seen as so important that when the old basilica was replaced in the sixteenth and seventeenth centuries by the magnificent edifice that stands today, they were one of the few things from Old St Peter's to find a home in the new building.

Of the four small panels in the door's centre depicting scenes from Eugenius' pontificate, three are devoted to the Council of Florence (1438–42), held while Filarete was still working on his thirteen-year project. One panel, placed underneath a depiction of St Peter giving his keys to a kneeling pope, shows a procession of Ethiopian pilgrims, who had recently attended the council, entering Rome.[1] Eugenius, who had once been driven from the city and had had to fight for his authority following the Western Schism, was making a point: Look! Rome, my city, is drawing pilgrims from across the world.[2]

Rome occupied a very particular place in the medieval world, both spiritually and psychologically, but it was not always the thriving city of popular imagination. The ancient glories of Rome and the modern glamour of this city of faith give the impression that its history has been one of eternal greatness, but for long periods Rome was a place of political danger and ancient ruins, in desperate need of stability and investment. By the fifteenth century Rome was only a fraction of the size of the old imperial city, in long-term decline. When the Anglo-Welsh chronicler and lawyer Adam of Usk went to Rome in 1402 to seek 'clerical preferment' (a job), he didn't find what he'd expected. 'O God, how pitiful Rome is!' he lamented. 'Once it was teeming with princes and their palaces; now it is abandoned and full of slums, thieves, wolves and vermin, reduced to misery by the notorious internecine feuding of the Romans themselves.'[3] It was neither the biggest nor the most prosperous city in what is now Italy (those honours went to Naples and Milan).

What restored Rome to glory was pilgrimage.

Medieval Rome

The convert emperor Constantine the Great (died 337) and his Christian family are credited with building the Church of St Peter in the Vatican. He was fascinated by the cults of the early martyrs, so much so that his biographer, Eusebius, claimed that Constantine 'never ceased honouring the memorials of the holy martyrs of God'.[4] After Rome was sacked by barbarians in 410, the pope began moving the bones of the martyrs from the catacombs beyond its walls into the city for safety, while the pontificates of Damasus and Symmachus, straddling the year 500, promoted the martyrs of Rome, and pilgrimages in their honour, as central to the city's status. Pope Damasus 'searched for and discovered the bodies of many saints, and also proclaimed their [acts] in verses', claimed the *Liber Pontificalis*. Using the bones to boost the image of Rome, he transformed even those saints with a tenuous link to the city into distinctly *Roman* martyrs.[5]

The quantity of relics coming into Rome from the catacombs and from elsewhere was staggering. Processions of wagons wended their way into the city – twenty-eight to the Pantheon alone on one occasion in 609 – and some churches acquired over two thousand items.[6] The Lateran Baptistry and Palace, attached to St John Lateran, the seat of the pope as bishop of Rome, became a treasure house of relics including the heads of Saints Peter and Paul. By the seventh century, Rome had plenty of attractions for the keen pilgrim.

This success story was harnessed by successive popes, who took the credit for amassing this sacred collection wherever possible, erecting buildings to house relics of all kinds, to mark places of martyrdom and to shelter tombs.[7] The cult site of St Lawrence on the opening stretch of the Via Tiburtina, the road running north-east from Rome to Tivoli, featured an epigram reminding those who read it that the pope was responsible for improvements benefiting the people.[8] Over time, the cult of St Peter became the pre-eminent one in Rome, a process encouraged by Damasus' successor, Symmachus (ruled 498–514). Forced to spend most of his time in the Vatican, a rival having seized the Lateran, Symmachus elevated the importance of St Peter and his church.[9] This was the start of a gradual transfer of pilgrimage activity from the Lateran to the Vatican, which was only completed during the pontificate of Nicholas III (1277–80).

The loss of Jerusalem in the seventh century to Muslim conquest boosted the status and attraction of Rome to pilgrims. A pilgrimage to the city was often seen as of equal value to going to Jerusalem. Medieval guidebooks which covered both cities reminded their users that the spiritual rewards on offer in Rome were the same as those in Jerusalem.[10] The peace and relative stability of Italy at the same time also made it a more achievable journey.

Some of those pilgrims were from England. Bede, one of the greatest teachers and writers of the early Middle Ages, noted that pilgrimage to Rome was very popular and that the city was the best place to secure relics in order to create cult centres at home.[11] This indeed happened, the portability of relics allowing the Catholic Church effectively to franchise the pilgrimage business to regional locations. This became even more possible after the 1204 sack of Constantinople during the Fourth Crusade, when further quantities of relics were sent to Rome, making it the biggest repository of Christian relics in the world.

Among the huge range of objects, some were particularly revered. Such was the case with the Veronica (a corruption of *vera iconica* – true likeness), the cloth believed to have been used by St Veronica to wipe Jesus' face as he carried his cross on the Via Dolorosa to Calvary. It became more famous in 1216 after the image of Christ's face supposedly miraculously turned upside down while being carried in a papal procession, prompting the pope, Innocent III, to offer indulgences – spirit rewards in the form of time off from Purgatory – to those who saw the Veronica, said the Lord's prayer and recited the Hail Mary five times. This miraculous imprint of Christ's face was *the* relic that many pilgrims longed to see when they came to Rome, though it could strike fear into some. The German pilgrim Nichol Muffel claimed in 1453 that 'one's heart is struck with terror the moment one catches sight of it'.[12]

The Veronica was a cloth believed to show the face of Christ, imprinted when St Veronica used it to wipe his face. It was one of the most revered relics in medieval Rome and was adopted as the city's pilgrimage emblem.

Roman Jubilees

The importance of Rome to pilgrims increased dramatically with the institution of the first jubilee, or holy year, in 1300. The accidental brainchild of Pope Boniface VIII, who was largely pressured into the idea by crowds coming to Rome expecting him to announce something special, jubilees offered pilgrims particular indulgences if they visited the basilicas of Saints Peter and Paul in a given year. As the pope was the only person who could distribute these benefits from the Treasury of Merit, the virtual store of forgiveness created when Jesus died for humanity's sins, it gave him unique power over someone concerned for the good of their soul, and thus the capacity to create a highly attractive pilgrimage offer. It was all rather well promoted and marketed, and for the first jubilee an image of the already-popular Veronica was used on the 'branding'.[13]

The jubilees were wildly successful. The first one attracted so many pilgrims that Guglielmo Ventura (died *c.*1322), a merchant from Asti, 'frequently saw both sexes trodden underfoot' and was often in danger himself as he moved through the throngs who packed the city's streets.[14] Initially intended to be held every century, their popularity meant that the gap between holy years was repeatedly shortened until the 1450 jubilee, when Pope Nicholas V (ruled 1447–55) declared that they would take place every twenty-five years. The number of pilgrims flocking to Rome for each jubilee rose over time; that of 1400 was so popular that the pope extended the spiritual rewards it offered to pilgrims who came the following year. Imperfect records suggest that by 1600 the jubilee was attracting as many as half a million pilgrims.[15]

There were also occasional holy years to mark special occasions, such as the 1866–7 jubilee proclaimed to honour the recently canonised martyrs of Japan, or the 1933–4 holy year to mark the 1,900th anniversary of the death and resurrection of Christ. Another, fifty years later, was specifically identified as marking the 1,950th anniversary of human redemption.[16] In all, since the 1300 jubilee there have been around ninety of these events.

The success of jubilees brought challenges. The 1400 holy year coincided with an outbreak of the plague so severe that up to eight hundred people were dying a day. Most of them were pilgrims, as the disease spread easily among people accommodated in crowded inns or hostels.[17] Despite such risks, the Romans who provided for the pilgrims – innkeepers and hostel owners, apothecaries, provisioners, money changers, prostitutes, souvenir makers and sellers, those renting out spare rooms – benefited hugely from the busiest periods of pilgrimage. These caused strain though, with the food and space needed to feed tens of thousands of additional mouths prompting price rises and food shortages.[18] Pilgrims who couldn't secure somewhere to stay were left to hire straw mattresses and bed down on the street, which could prove fatal in winter.[19] Rome was, after all, often in a parlous state, not least during the Avignon papacy, when the popes abandoned the city for southern France. Francesco Petrarch (1304–74), Italian humanist and poet, appealed to Pope Urban V to return: 'How can you sleep, under your gilded beams, on the bank of the Rhone, while the Lateran, the Mother of all churches, ruined and roofless, is open to the wind and rain, and the most holy shrines of Peter and of Paul are quaking, and what was once the Church of the Apostles is but a ruin and a shapeless heap of stone.'[20]

Plenty of critics saw the jubilees as cynical money-making events. There was something to this, and not just because pilgrimages were Rome's main source of revenue during the Middle Ages. In 1390, Pope Boniface IX declared a jubilee and sold indulgences on a near-industrial scale because he needed cash to replenish the papacy's coffers.[21] The 100,000 gold florins the pope earned from the 1450 jubilee were used for building projects, including Pope Nicholas' glorious Vatican Library. Many of these buildings at least benefited the city, its inhabitants and pilgrims in the long term, but the revenue from the 1500 jubilee was allegedly given to the pope's illegitimate son, Cesare Borgia, to fight his wars in central Italy.[22] In the twentieth century, some more cynical pilgrims saw the jubilees as less about faith and more about papal power, though perhaps they always had been. When the American Eleanor Clark was in Rome in the holy year of 1950, she noted the celebrations praising the Virgin Mary (it was the Virgin's year) but wrote that it was 'even more visibly the year of Pius XII; there was perhaps never a holy year so stamped with the character of a pope'.[23]

Rebuilding Rome

Pilgrimage literally built the city of Rome. Walk its streets today, and in many cases you will be following routes set out to enable pilgrims to move around more easily, pass buildings designed to accommodate and feed them, or visit churches built to house the relics they came to visit. Shaping the city began almost as soon as pilgrimages to Rome took off. Pope Symmachus provided fountains and 'conveniences', and ordered remedial works in the catacombs and elsewhere after a damaging earthquake in 508.[24] As early as 556–61, Pope Pelagius I redesigned the Basilica of San Lorenzo so that the martyr's grave was easier for pilgrims to see.[25] Also in the sixth century, a semicircular ambulatory was added to St Peter's so that the crowds of pilgrims could process smoothly past the relics in the church.[26]

A second intensive period of construction took place in the

fifteenth century after the papacy returned from Avignon, and the schism which had sent them there ended, with Rome turned from a dilapidated medieval town to the capital of Christendom. In the lead-up to the holy year of 1450, a new road was built – the Via del Pellegrino – to facilitate access to the Ponte Sant'Angelo and on to St Peter's from the part of the city which contained the national pilgrim hostels. Like other major pilgrimage sites, Rome was peppered with churches and hospices that catered to people from particular places. Some of these facilities pre-dated this period, but the urban rebuilding project driven by the papacy in the fifteenth century prompted investment, and their number then grew significantly in response to the huge rise in pilgrim numbers.

The Church of Santo Stefano, constructed at this time, catered to Ethiopian pilgrims, who already had their own hospice, founded in the twelfth century; the English Hospice of 1362 (which became the English College after the Reformation, when a seminary was needed for English exiles) accommodated English and Welsh pilgrims. The two thousand men, women and children who set out from Danzig (Gdansk) for the jubilee pilgrimage of 1450 would almost certainly have been housed, at least in part, at the hospice at Santa Maria dell Anima, a fourteenth-century institution that welcomed German-speaking pilgrims. Most of these institutions kept records of the pilgrims who stayed there, and sometimes the items they left behind – their travel journals, itineraries and other ephemera.[27] From the late sixteenth century, pilgrims from all over Europe could also have their spiritual needs met by confessors at St Peter's, a group of Jesuits known as the *penitenzieri* drawn from a range of nationalities.

Unfortunately, the city's infrastructure still left something to be desired. The numbers thronging Rome a week before

Christmas 1450 were so great that when a mule crossing the Ponte Sant'Angelo started bucking, the ensuing panic tipped two hundred pilgrims to their deaths in the river below and crushed another hundred.[28] In response, the pope decided to make more space for pilgrims by clearing the bridge of shops.

Just as Rome was reaching new heights of popularity among pilgrims and the city was being transformed, the practice of pilgrimage itself came under attack. Martin Luther, a Catholic monk from Erfurt, first arrived in Rome in 1511, full of optimism about what it had to offer, but found churchmen and 'unlearned men' more concerned with earthly than spiritual matters. Despite this he was not initially critical of pilgrimage, concerned instead about the Treasury of Merit, which allowed the pope to dole out indulgences from a repository of forgiveness in return for certain acts like pilgrimage. He attacked indulgences in his famous disputation, the *Ninety-Five Theses* of 1517, posted on the church door at Wittenberg in Germany, though the following year he felt compelled to qualify his criticisms, stating that pilgrimage was worthwhile if done for the right reasons, and to the right places. Then in his 1520 *Address to the Christian Nobility* Luther asked German rulers to restrict or even ban pilgrimages to Rome altogether. 'There is no good in them,' he complained. 'Rather do these pilgrimages give countless occasions to commit sin and to despise God's commandments.'[29]

Luther's visit to Rome may not have borne fruit until after the mid-1520s,[30] but he was not the only one accusing the papacy and Catholic Church of all manner of religious and moral failings, in particular the corrupt practice of selling salvation in the form of indulgences. In one response to such attacks, the popes set out to show just how the Catholic Church was leading the way in spiritual matters by using the physical fabric of Rome. Building works in the city, which had been proceeding in bursts since before 1500 with the construction of the Via Sistina (*c.*1475), Via Alexandria (*c.*1500) and Via Giulia (*c.*1505), and the beautification of religious buildings by artists like Michaelangelo, became almost continuous as the papacy sought to improve streets, paving, accommodation and churches for pilgrims.[31] Rome had to match up to the spiritual ideals and authority that the papacy now needed to promote.

In the wake of the Council of Trent, a series of gatherings held from the 1540s to 1563 in response to the Reformation and to Protestant criticisms of Catholicism, Gregory XIII (ruled 1572–85) encouraged building and decorative schemes, and oversaw extensive urban regeneration.[32] But it was his successor, Sixtus V (ruled 1585–90), who set out to refashion Rome as 'a single holy shrine'.[33] More than any pope before him, Sixtus was determined to transform the experience of pilgrimage in Rome. In the year after he became pope, he issued an order that brought the routes pilgrims travelled through Rome under papal control.[34] He had ancient Roman and Egyptian obelisks erected outside four of the seven major pilgrimage churches, in part to show Christianity's triumph over paganism but primarily to create visual signposts for pilgrims. This was the Counter-Reformation in action, the papacy promoting itself as the sole authority over Christians in the face of the Protestant challenge. He also rebuilt the Lateran Palace, Christianised the ancient Roman columns of Marcus Aurelius and Trajan, and redesigned several streets, straightening and paving them to improve access to the pilgrimage sites.[35]

Just over sixty years later, Pope Alexander VII decided to commission a new scheme for the square in front of St Peter's. Old St Peter's had been demolished in 1505 and the new basilica constructed over the course of a century, largely funded by selling indulgences; it was finally consecrated in 1626. Over the space of twelve years from 1656, Gianlorenzo Bernini designed and built the vast elliptical space. In Bernini's conception, the columned sides of the square were the broad arms of God, welcoming the faithful into his most important church.

Preparing for pilgrims wasn't just about making physical space for them, so Urban VIII (ruled 1623–44) ordered a survey of the city to check that its population was suitably devout. He wanted to know if they had been receiving the sacraments, attending properly conducted divine worship and providing for the poor and sick.[36] This too was about showing that Rome had the right to call itself the supreme authority in religious matters, and that it was still right for pilgrims to quite literally put their faith in it. With the Reformation now firmly entrenched across large parts of Europe, some Catholics from Protestant countries focused on pilgrimage to Rome as a way to maintain and demonstrate (albeit not necessarily to the authorities at home) their faith, though most were fearful of the risks, and pilgrimage from England reached such a low point that there were debates over the future of the English Hospice.

This era saw a notable innovation – the printed pilgrimage map. Guides of various kinds had existed for centuries, the English priest Gregory Martin publishing his *Roma Sacra* in 1581, which showcased how many attractions the city could now boast.[37] But the revival and rebuilding of the city together with the rise of the printing press inspired and enabled the production of new maps aimed specifically at demonstrating the sacred identity of Rome to pilgrims. Antonio Lafreri's map *The Seven Churches of Rome*, produced for the holy year of 1575, showed pilgrims the seven sites they had to visit to gain their jubilee indulgence (they only had to visit four in 1450). As a practical schematic of the city, it was no use because it did not map Rome's streets (the historian Jessica Maier has called it 'a kind of CliffsNotes version of pilgrimage'), but then that wasn't the

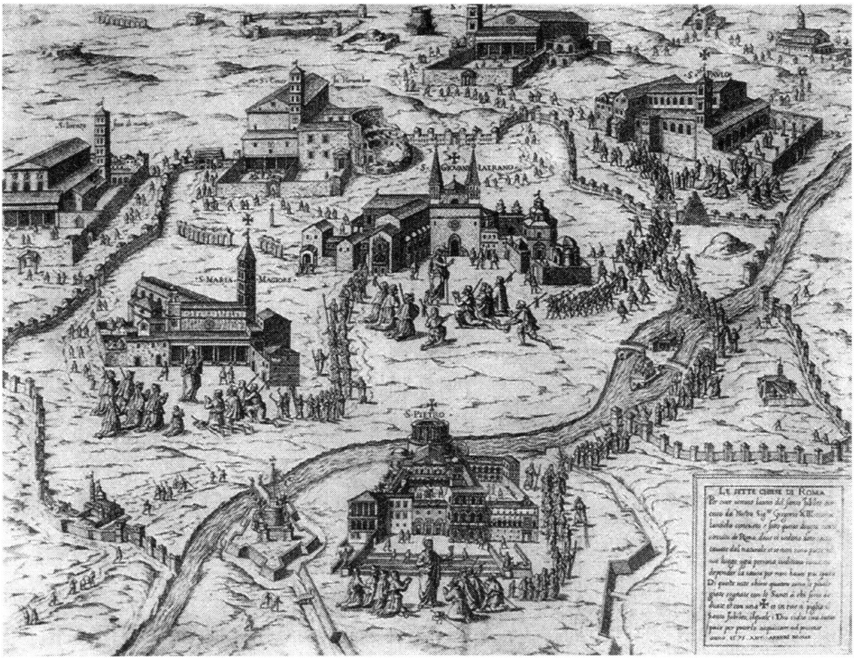

The growth of pilgrimage, especially during jubilee years, brought thousands of additional pilgrims and a lot of money into Rome. Some of the money was used to rebuild the city. To help the pilgrims find their way around, maps like this one by Lafreri were produced.

point.[38] It reinforced the idea that Rome was a sacred pilgrimage city and provided those who bought it with a handy souvenir that they could take home and show to friends and family.[39] The priest who became St Philip Neri set out a one- or two-day route that pilgrims could follow in 1552 to the same seven churches, which proved very popular. Another map was produced for the 1600 jubilee by Giovanni Maggi, showing the obelisks set up by Sixtus V. This map, and versions of it, remained popular for the next century and a half even though the map itself wasn't overly useful when it came to navigating the city, and only three of the seven churches appeared on it.[40]

Just as Rome was basking in the Counter-Reformation glories of the Renaissance and the huge rise in pilgrim numbers, the peak passed, and the city's pilgrimage business faltered once more. The eighteenth and nineteenth centuries were lacklustre for Rome and its religious attractions. As a temporal power, the papacy declined and was increasingly ignored, which left the pope still in charge of spiritual matters but with less overall authority. Rome was out of step with the European Enlightenment, seemingly stuck in its Renaissance heyday. Certainly, there were hardly any of the grand religious building projects of previous centuries. Increasingly visitors to the city came as part of the Grand Tour, interested in visiting Rome's churches and shrines for their artistic rather than spiritual merits, viewing its classical sights or, in the case of visitors from Britain, undertaking a literary pilgrimage to the home and grave of the Romantic poet John Keats, who died in the city in 1821 at the age of twenty-five.

In the early years of the nineteenth century the authority of the popes was at its lowest point since the 1500s. In 1799 Pope Pius VI had died in France, imprisoned by Napoleon for his refusal to relinquish his temporal power over the Papal States. His successor Pius VII was also imprisoned in France from 1809 to 1814 before returning to Rome.

The Politics of Pilgrimage

Throughout its history pilgrimage to Rome has always had a political aspect because for many centuries the pope, as head of the Catholic Church, has had immense influence. King Cnut, of Viking stock, went on pilgrimage in 1027–8 to secure papal approval for his rule over England, Norway and Denmark, but also to show that he was a Christian.[41] Spiritual redemption for his possible part in the killing of his brother-in-law earlier that year would have been a motive, but secular matters were undeniably also important to the pilgrim-king.[42]

Over nine hundred years later, the most influential pope of the nineteenth century, Pius IX (ruled 1846–78), was head of the Catholic Church in the decades when Italy became a unified kingdom. How the papacy and its territory would fit into this new system was a matter of some debate, known as the Roman Question, and one which the papacy initially seemed to lose. In 1860 Pius' army was defeated by the forces of the kingdom of Italy, and all the papal territories bar Rome and the area immediately surrounding the city, ruled by the pope since the middle of the eighth century, were seized. The city itself was taken ten years later, Pius XI becoming the so-called 'prisoner in the Vatican'. Pius refused to recognise the kingdom of Italy but actually controlled no territory. The solution to this problem was not reached until 1929 when the Lateran Treaty created the Vatican City, a papal state within the city of Rome, controlled by the pope.

One response of the Catholic faithful to what they saw as an attack on the papacy was to stage pilgrimages of support. Events held in Rome inspired significant numbers of locals and pilgrims. Large-scale national pilgrimages were also arranged, beginning before the final loss of Rome but if anything increasing afterwards. The first French national pilgrimage was in 1873, while the Spanish came three years later. Belgium (1877) and Ireland (1893) followed suit, as did many other countries.[43] Even when the papacy was on a surer footing, the national pilgrimages continued because they were so good at unifying Catholics at home. The 1909 Irish national pilgrimage in honour of Pius X's jubilee was seen by its participants as being 'creditable to Ireland', such was the national pride in those events. The Irish were shown the sites of the city and of the Vatican, including a more recent 'relic' – the door through which Pope Pius IX had fled when the papal palace was attacked by republicans.[44] For the three national pilgrimages from Mexico the deteriorating situation for Catholics at home was a spur. Years of secularisation had prompted a renewal of faith in the country and the foundation of religious orders. These were inspired by the European orders that organised national pilgrimages.[45]

The French Catholics had perhaps the greatest debt to pay to the papacy with their pilgrimages in the late nineteenth century, as it was the withdrawal of French forces from Rome in 1870 which had led to the capture of the city and the maltreatment – as they saw it – of the pope. Some believed they had consequently been punished by God. The war with Prussia had gone badly; territory had been lost. Things were considered so bad that France's Catholics had built the mighty Sacré Cœur on the hill of Montmartre in Paris and taken a 'national vow' to atone for 'allowing' Italian forces to capture Rome. In the 1870s, the French held pilgrimages to show their support for the pope and the restoration of the monarchy in France.

That support could turn physical, such as during the 1891 French workers' pilgrimage, when pilgrims clashed with Italian nationalists who they believed were undermining papal power. For some, pilgrimage to Rome was a rejection of the secular Third Republic, the system of government adopted in France in 1870 which lasted until the Second World War. For certain workers' pilgrimages from France, demonstrating Catholic unity and loyalty to the pope was a way of combating socialism.[46] To counter these demonstrations of papal support, republicans and secularists organised pilgrimages of their own.

The sixth anniversary of King Victor Emmanuel's death (1878) was marked by an Italian national pilgrimage to the Pantheon (consecrated as a church) to view his exhumed coffin.[47]

As the first ruler of an independent and unified Italy, he was lauded as the country's champion. The idea of a pilgrimage to the Pantheon had been mooted two years before in *La Riforma*, a socialist newspaper. It was already the burial place of some of Italy's great artists and would go on to be the resting place of King Umberto I and his queen. While the suggestion wasn't widely embraced, in 1900 secular pilgrimages were staged to sites in Rome that were distinctly anti-clerical.[48]

Just a few decades later, the fascist leader Benito Mussolini (ruled 1922–43) took the idea of pilgrimage for political ends to new heights. This had nothing whatsoever to do with religion, and everything to do with Mussolini – Il Duce – and his regime. He was, after all, an avowed atheist who regularly attacked the Catholic Church, though over time he softened his hostility to the papacy as it was politically expedient to do so. Under his dictatorship, Mussolini was promoted as a god-like figure and fascism as something resembling a religion. The rise of the new faith was rapid and widespread, as the *Weekly Dispatch* of London reported that British fascists were making 'a pilgrimage to Rome' in 1923, just one year after Mussolini came to power.[49]

After a decade in power, revering Il Duce was so baked into the fascist mindset that when four million people came to see the 1932 Exhibition of the Fascist Revolution, the regime referred to them as 'pilgrims'. This kind of activity was, in the words of Australian historian R. J. B. Bosworth, 'an obligation of all true fascists', one that gave the regime validity.[50] The exhibition played heavily on religious imagery. The last of the exhibition rooms was devoted to the 'Shrine of the Martyrs of the Fascist Revolution', a title which made it a pilgrimage destination almost by default, and there was a seven-metre-tall 'Cross of the Martyrs', lit up for dramatic effect.[51] The whole thing was intended to create a spiritual story about fascism and the country, and to achieve the maximum emotional impact on those who saw it. Little surprise that it was co-created by the set designer of a travelling theatre company.

These events had international appeal, with the regime encouraging ideological and political pilgrimages to Rome to spread its propaganda message beyond Italy and promote the cult of Mussolini. Youth members of the Organisations of Fascists Abroad enjoyed a pilgrimage to see Rome and Mussolini in the autumn of 1932, and the regime was sufficiently reconciled with the papacy for the pope to celebrate a special mass for them.[52] Romanians came on large-scale pilgrimages in 1929 and 1938, but it was their pilgrimage of 1933 that was particularly important to Mussolini. He so dominated that year's holy year celebrations, marking the 1,900th anniversary of Christ's death and resurrection, that the papacy, determined not to be outshone, displayed the Shroud of Turin in the northern Italian city, creating a rival pilgrimage destination. That same year Adolf Hitler had become chancellor of Germany, an event which prompted Mussolini, the most prominent fascist leader of the 1920s, to look for a way to show that *his* brand of fascism was better than the German variety. International recognition was the way to do it.[53] Romania had a fascist movement of its own, the Iron Guard, so they were a logical choice to invite to Rome on pilgrimage.[54] Other fascist leaders were also invited for similar political pilgrimages – from Switzerland, Bulgaria and France – with the express purpose of introducing them to Mussolini.[55]

Mussolini and his regime may have used pilgrimage to broadcast their ideology, but there was nothing new in this. For centuries the power of Catholic Rome had been spread by pilgrims returning home. The distribution of relics had begun in the early Middle

Ages, given to the devout as a way of expanding Rome's authority. In the eleventh century King Cnut returned to England with pieces of the True Cross and the manger in which the baby Jesus had lain. The 'rediscovery' of the overgrown Roman catacombs in 1578 resulted in a mass of supposedly holy items coming on to the market; many of them ended up in Germany to replace relics lost in the Reformation. There they were covered in gold and gemstones to create elaborate and colourful objects of devotion.[56] These were expensive items, usually only seen by the devout from afar, but in the fourteenth century the papacy hit upon a way in which more commonplace pilgrims could take something of Rome home for themselves. During the jubilees of 1300 and 1350, paper images of the Veronica were sold with the express purpose of pilgrims using them as a focus of their prayers in their own homes.[57]

Not all of these items were legitimately obtained, and Rome was at the centre of a large illicit trade in stolen relics. Which brings us back to Filarete, the sculptor whose ornate doors opened this chapter. In the end, he fled Rome in 1448 after an accusation that he had stolen the relics of John the Baptist.

7

ISTANBUL

Turkey

John Chrysostom (ruled 397–407) had been archbishop of Constantinople (today's Istanbul) for just over a year when he witnessed Empress Aelia Eudoxia (died 404) oversee the procession of some unnamed martyrs' relics to the church at Drypia, then a small settlement nine miles from the centre of the city. The procession set off from Hagia Sofia, Constantinople's most important religious building, and wended its way in the darkness west to the small suburb where the relics were to be translated to the church of St Thomas the Apostle. When everyone was assembled, the archbishop delivered a homily that captured the impact that such an event had on people at the time: 'What can I say? What shall I speak? I'm jumping with excitement and aflame with a frenzy that is better than common sense. I'm flying and dancing and floating on air and, for the rest, drunk under the influence of this spiritual pleasure.'[1]

The next day, the empress's husband Arcadius (ruled 383–408) came on a pilgrimage to see his wife's work accompanied by members of his imperial court, and the archbishop delivered a second homily. Relic translation in Constantinople – moving holy objects from one place to another (usually) more fitting one – was such a popular activity that John Chrysostom was kept busy delivering homilies on the merits of various martyrs throughout his time in charge of the spiritual life of the city. About forty years later, in 438, the bodily relics of the archbishop himself were brought back to Constantinople from Cappadocia, where he had been exiled, to place in a new shrine in his honour in the Church of the Holy Apostles, the most important church in the city at the time after Hagia Sofia. Though he had been exiled in 404 for attacks on the decadence of the imperial court, he was much loved by the people of the city, and bringing him back was a politically astute move by the regime.

A New Holy City?

Constantinople's pilgrimage story really began a century before St John Chrysostom's relics returned to the city, when Emperor Constantine the Great (ruled 306–*c.*337) refounded the ancient Greek settlement of Byzantion as the capital of the Roman empire. He called it Nova Roma – New Rome. Following the collapse of the western Roman empire, it became the capital of the eastern Roman, or Byzantine, empire. Constantine chose the site for strategic reasons – it lies on the Bosphorus, the straits connecting the Aegean and Black Seas. There was certainly nothing there to commend it on religious grounds, and this was a problem.

Constantinople (the name the city took on in the first half of the fifth century) had little in the way of sacred sites or holy objects to offer potential Christian pilgrims. The city did have two martyrs who could be promoted to attract pilgrims, St Mokios (beheaded in 295 after surviving a flaming oven and attempted death-by-lions) and St Acacius (scourged and beheaded in 305), but they had only local appeal. They were simply not big enough names for the capital of the Roman empire. Constantine and his successors had to provide suitably holy objects and places to reflect the city's sacred status. There were political reasons for addressing this issue, but the desire to acquire holy objects was also a reflection of the style of pilgrimage in the Byzantine empire.

In Western Christendom, holy sites were intimately connected to the landscape; pilgrimages were partly about the journey, and pilgrims trekked hundreds if not thousands of miles to places of martyrdom or burial and to sites connected with saints' lives. For Eastern Christians, the Orthodox faithful, pilgrimage was all about *proskynesis*, the act of veneration. Being in the presence of a relic or icon was what mattered, not where it was.[2]

Constantine wanted high-status relics to put his city on the sacred map, so sought out the bodies of the twelve Apostles to turn his city into a place equal to Rome, home of the most important relics of the Apostles Peter and Paul. Unsuccessful in this quest, he had to settle for the relics of some of Christ's lesser disciples instead. All was not lost, however. His mother Helena, from whom he seems to have gained his zeal for Christianity, went to Jerusalem on pilgrimage and sent him back nails from the Crucifixion, which were incorporated into Constantine's crown and his horse's bridle, and a piece of the True Cross. These were the first in a long line of major relics associated with Christ's life and death that made their way to the city.

Constantine the Great's successors took on relic collection with considerable gusto, just as they copied him in so many things, and in so doing they transformed the sacred landscape of Constantinople. New churches were built and dedicated to house them. His son, Constantine II, apparently inspired by Romulus, one of the founders of Rome, secured the relics of three saints to defend New Rome: Timothy, a disciple of Paul,

Hagia Sofia dominates the skyline of Istanbul. Originally a church visited by Orthodox Christians, who revered the building itself, it became a mosque in the fifteenth century and then a museum before reverting to a mosque in recent years.

in 357, the Apostle Andrew and Luke the Evangelist the year after.[3] He was also the builder of the first Church of Hagia Sofia (Holy Wisdom), though it did not get this name until about 430. This burned down in 404, and had to be rebuilt, as it would again in 532 under Justinian I.

It was really during the reign of the emperor Theodosius I (379–95) that interest in relics and pilgrimage took a leap forward when he outlawed paganism and declared Christianity the official religion of the empire. He was determined to make his city into one of the holiest in Christendom, declaring at a church council he hosted in 381 that it was now second only to Rome in the ecclesiastical hierarchy. Theodosius' claim didn't go down well with other important religious centres in the eastern empire like Antioch and Alexandria (or indeed in Rome),[4] but he needed to develop the city as a cult centre of international renown, one which would draw pilgrims and augment his political power. He was also very keen to acquire the right type of relic. Aware of the importance of relics and cults for his reputation, he took a prominent role in the process, personally carrying the head of John the Baptist into Constantinople (or at least *one* of his heads, as there was another in Damascus) and building the small Church of St John Prodromos to house it.[5]

Theodosius I's son Arcadius (ruled 383–408) and grandson Theodosius II (ruled 408–50) continued his policy of acquisition, as did Theodosius II's wife Eudocia and his sister Empress Pulcheria, wife of Marcian (ruled 450–57). The body of St Phocas arrived in the city in the last years of the fourth century, and that of Samuel appeared sometime the following decade. Arcadius processed them into the city accompanied by his guard and the whole senate. The year 415 was particularly busy for spiritual additions: the bodies of John the Baptist's father, Zachariah, and Joseph son of Jacob both arrived in the city. After several failed attempts, the pious Pulcheria also succeeded in acquiring the arm of St Stephen the Protomartyr, a relic so precious it was kept in a specially constructed chapel in the imperial palace. Pulcheria's sister-in-law Eudocia later acquired the rest of St Stephen, and he was placed in the Church of St Lawrence.[6]

In the century or so after Constantine the Great's death, the city became a treasure house of Christian relics, and under Theodosius II New Rome had developed such a reputation that it was referred to as another Jerusalem. The first person to use this epithet was St Symeon Stylites, the Syrian saint who famously lived atop a pillar. According to the *Life of St Daniel*, St Symeon met St Daniel (died 493) on the road to Jerusalem and advised him not to go there, 'but go to Byzantium and you will see a second Jerusalem, namely Constantinople; there you can enjoy martyrs' shrines and the great houses of prayer'. A relic of St Symeon was brought to Constantinople for the emperor after the saint's death, and St Daniel, who also became a stylite, living on the edge of Constantinople atop a pillar, was afterwards buried in a grave beneath the relics of martyrs, both men ultimately residing in the sacred city they had sought out some years before.[7] By the end of the century Constantinople could also boast the illuminated Gospel of St Matthew, which had been hidden in the grave of St Barnabas but was prised out of his skeletal hands and presented to the emperor.

It did not take long for Constantinople to establish its reputation as a holy city. The efficacy of its saints and shrines was promoted through written miracle collections, the first of which that of the healing twin saints Cosmas and Damian, whose shrine was outside the city walls on the inlet of the Bosphorus known as the Golden Horn, in the suburb of Blachernai. Justinian the Great (ruled 527–65) brought their reputed relics to the city and, after they miraculously cured him, he built a church in their honour. The thirty-eight miracles they would be credited with may or may not have occurred at their shrine – they are remarkably like miracles associated with other places – but that did not matter. Another collection, this time of St Artemios, whose relics worked miracles at the Church of St John the Baptist, showed how the sick could be healed in Constantinople.[8]

The focus of this activity was the mighty Hagia Sofia, when it was rebuilt, the largest building on earth. Justinian the Great had wanted 'an instant wonder of the world'.[9] Procoplus of Caesarea, our best source for Justinian's rule, claimed that visitors entering the church understood 'that it is not by any human power or skill, but by the influence of God, that this work has been so finely turned'.[10] Another important centre for relics and pilgrimage was the Chapel of the Virgin of the Pharos (Lighthouse) in the heart of the imperial complex, first mentioned in the late eighth century but redesigned by the child-emperor Michael III (ruled 840–67) over half a century later. The chapel possessed forty-eight relics associated with the Passion of Christ. There were multiple pieces of the True Cross, the most famous that obtained by Constantine the Great's mother, Helena, in the fourth century.

Constantinople as the New Jerusalem was a potent and lasting idea, so much so that when a Georgian archbishop saw the city in the 1750s, he cried at the sight of 'Constantinople ... the first city to adopt Christianity'.[11] But possessing all these relics wasn't just about creating more pilgrimage attractions; it made the rulers of Constantinople guardians of Christendom's holiest artefacts. The emperors' control of these sacred items underscored their 'god-guarded status' and right to rule.[12] The imperial complex was home to many churches and chapels containing relics accumulated over the course of the early Middle Ages: the right arm of John the Baptist, the Crown of Thorns, Christ's burial sheets and sandals, and the Mandylion of Christ, acquired in the mid-tenth century, a cloth miraculously imprinted with his image and one of the most famous relics of all. This was Constantinople's analogue of the Veronica in Rome. Almost as attractive to pilgrims (if not more so for some) were relics associated with the Virgin Mary, whom Constantinople adopted as its patron in the sixth century.[13] To boost its status and draw pilgrims, the empress Pulcheria (died 453) had already claimed Mary's camel-hair girdle for the city, as well as her veil or robe and an icon of Mary and Christ painted by

St Luke the Evangelist, brought to Constantinople by Eudocia, wife of Theodosius II, while the Church of Panagia Blachernai housed a well dedicated to the Virgin.[14]

High-status attractions like these were often off-limits to the regular pilgrim, locked in imperial chapels or only produced at certain times of the year. Alternatives were needed, and these were particularly popular if they had a curative specialism. St Artemios' relics could be visited in the Church of St John in Oxeia by anyone suffering from hernias or diseases of the genitals.[15] At the Monastery of Philanthropos, built into the city's sea wall, water from a holy well was channelled into a cistern for pilgrims. Where it spilt over onto the sand along the shore, pilgrims scooped it up and took it away to use for healing. Most famous was the Zoödochos Pege, the Church of St Mary of the Spring, where a natural miracle-working well prompted the emperor Justinian to commission a building using materials left over from the recent construction of Hagia Sofia.[16] Empress Irene was cured of a haemorrhage by the waters, after which the church was lavished with gifts in gratitude.[17]

The city's importance as a Christian centre and an alternative destination to Jerusalem grew following the loss of the Holy Land to Muslim forces in the 630s. The threat posed to Byzantium by Arab expansion led to the removal of several of Christendom's most holy relics, those associated with the Crucifixion, from Jerusalem to Constantinople. These were probably the ones seen by the Castilian ambassador Ruy Gonzalez when he visited in the first years of the 1400s and listed in some detail: the Church of St John the Baptist had a piece of bread from the Last Supper, some of Christ's blood, hairs from his beard, a piece of stone which his body had lain on, the head of the lance 'as fine as a thorn' that had pierced his side and the sponge on which he was given gall and vinegar during the Crucifixion, and a piece of his clothing made of red dimity. It also had yet another piece of the True Cross.[18]

Despite imperial investment in the city and its enormous growth, Constantinople suffered from one disaster after another in the seventh and eighth centuries. Attacks by Muslim armies, blockades and the loss of its main water supply, the ejection of inhabitants who could not provision themselves during sieges, and recurring earthquakes and enduring plague all diminished the population and impoverished the city. Many of the buildings built in Constantinople's early centuries were damaged or destroyed. In the ninth century some churches were at least reconstructed by Basil I (ruled 867–86), and Constantinople's trade, manufacturing and commerce recovered.

This recovery coincided with the emergence of a large group of potential pilgrims attracted to the city, the newly converted Slavs of Kievan Rus (Kyivan Rus in Ukrainian). A state roughly covering parts of modern Ukraine, Belarus and Russia from the ninth to the thirteenth centuries, Kievan Rus converted to Christianity in 988 after a century or so of rising interest. Contact between Rus and Constantinople pre-dated this, and the Slavs were aware of the spiritual riches Constantinople held. When, in 911, what was effectively a trade delegation came to Constantinople to sign an agreement, the pagan Rus were shown some of the emperor's precious relics. According to the *Primary Chronicle*, which records Slavic history *c.*850–1150, the emperor showed them the Crown of Thorns, the nails from the Crucifixion and several other relics with one aim in mind: to inform them about Christianity.[19] Four decades later, Princess Olga, widow of Igor of Kiev, travelled to Constantinople to be baptised as a Christian.[20] She returned to Rus and tried without success to convert her son; instead, Rus converted during the reign of her grandson, Vladimir the Great, who turned to Christianity so that he could marry the sister of the Byzantine emperor.

Whatever Kiev's motives, its adoption of the Orthodox Christianity of the Byzantine empire meant that Constantinople acquired the spiritual authority over Slavic Christians that Western Europeans gave to Rome. As more eastern Europeans joined the Orthodox fold, the city's pool of potential pilgrims expanded, pilgrimage activity grew and Constantinople's influence increased.[21]

The Ages of the Crusades

At the end of the eleventh century, Constantinople became a stopping place for crusading armies en route to, or returning from, the Holy Land. Pilgrims heading for Jerusalem had visited the city from at least the fourth century, when the pilgrim Egeria visited 'all the churches – that of the apostles and all the martyr-memorials, of which there were very many' on her way through.[22] A few years before the First Crusade was preached in 1095, Joseph, a monk from Canterbury, had already completed his Jerusalem pilgrimage when he decided to detour to Constantinople with some friends to see its 'incomparable treasury of relics'. He wanted to 'commend himself in person to their blessings'.[23] The advent of the Crusades meant large groups of armed pilgrims were heading east, and travellers who might not otherwise have visited the city wanted to view its treasures. Fulcher of Chartres, a French priest travelling with the armies of the First Crusade (1096–9) was dazzled by the riches he saw.

> Oh, what an excellent and beautiful city! How many monasteries, and how many palaces there are in it, of wonderful work skilfully fashioned! How many marvellous works are to be seen in the streets and districts of the town! It is a

> great nuisance to recite what an opulence of all kinds of goods are found there; of gold, or silver, or many kinds of mantles, and of holy relics.[24]

When the pious Louis VII of France (ruled 1137–80) passed through in 1147 on the Second Crusade, he was shown some of the most sacred relics in Constantinople. 'Along with the emperor,' the Byzantine writer John Kinnamos tells us, 'he went to the palace [Blachernai] south of the city, to investigate the things there worthy of awe and to behold the holy things in the church there: I mean those things which, having been close to the body of Christ, are signs of divine protection for Christians.'[25]

The easier, and theoretically safer, access to Jerusalem achieved by the successes of the early Crusades inspired an increase in the number of pilgrims from Europe to the Holy Land, and many of them passed through Constantinople. But this militarised pilgrimage traffic ultimately proved massively damaging to Constantinople: the armies of the Fourth Crusade of 1204 diverted to the city on their way to Egypt, and sacked it with considerable vigour.

Just a few years before, a pilgrim from Kievan Rus, Anthony of Novgorod, had written an account recording what he saw on his pilgrimage, providing a snapshot of Constantinople's sacred possessions just before so many of them were lost. Anthony managed to take in seventy-six shrines in the city itself, and another twenty-one in the surrounding suburbs. Chief among them was Hagia Sofia, which Orthodox pilgrims seem to have venerated as much as the relics within it. He prayed over bodies and bones, Passion relics and items owned by the Virgin Mary, not to mention various sacred crosses, icons, a sheepskin, a table and the trumpets of Joshua.[26]

When the crusaders arrived at Constantinople in 1204, they found a city overflowing with spiritual riches which they promptly seized and sent back to Europe for themselves and as gifts, both personal and diplomatic. One of the crusaders was Robert of Clari, a knight from Picardy in France. His wonderfully detailed account of the attack describes how 'one found there two pieces of the True Cross as large as the leg of a man ... and one found there the blessed crown with which He was crowned, which was made of reeds with thorns as sharp as the points of daggers'.[27] He witnessed them being carried off, but he wasn't just an observer. Robert brought back his own selection of relics to grace the town of Corbie in northern France: half of the Virgin's girdle, St Mark's arm and one of St Helena's fingers. Robert of Clari wrote a whole list of the items he picked up in Constantinople, fifty-four in all.

The supernatural bounty taken from the shrines and pilgrimage sites of Constantinople had a transformative impact on many places in Europe. Acquiring relics enabled churches and monasteries to attract their own pilgrims, and gave them status and prestige. St Luke's body was spirited away to Venice, prompting a dispute with the Benedictines in the nearby city of Padua who claimed they already had him. The Venetians also got St Paul the New Martyr, and the relics of St Lucia, who became Venice's most important female saint.[28] A relic of St Andrew was taken to Amalfi, John the Baptist's head to Amiens, the head of St Anne to Chartres, and a sliver of the True Cross ended up in the small priory of Bromholm on the Norfolk coast of England. The Cistercian monastery of Pairis, in Alsace, was graced with a choice array of saintly bones, feet and arms, as well as part of the rock from in front of Jesus' tomb and a piece of the table used during the Last Supper. They were brought back by the monastery's abbot, Martin, who had grabbed handfuls of relics and bundled them into his habit before whisking them away from the Monastery of the Pantocrater (Ruler of the Universe).[29]

The shock the sack of the city and the looting of their treasures caused the Byzantines was profound. One of them, historian Nicetas Choniates, mourned the violence of the crusaders' attack: 'O, the shameful dashing to earth of the venerable icons and the flinging of the relics of the saints ... into defiled places!'[30]

The plunder of most of Constantinople's relics was initially well organised, the crusaders appointing the bishop of Troyes to oversee collection and redistribution to Europe. Unfortunately, his death on the return journey to Europe and the lax application of the rules by his successor, the papal legate, meant some relics did not go to their originally intended recipients. Nor did the losses end with the Fourth Crusade. Baldwin II, the last Latin emperor of Constantinople (ruled 1228–73, in exile from 1261), used most of the rest of the city's Passion relics as surety for a Venetian loan in 1235. He defaulted, and the Venetians seized the relics, which included the Crown of Thorns. They sold the Crown to Louis IX of France, who placed it, together with the other Passion relics he had collected, in his new, purpose-built, jewel-like Sainte Chapelle on the Île de la Cité in Paris.

The Latin empire of Constantinople lasted just over half a century, though Baldwin II and his successors continued to use the title of emperor even after they were displaced by the returning Byzantines in 1261. Despite the crusaders' attempts to strip the city of everything of spiritual worth, a lot was left behind and more acquired when the Byzantines reclaimed the city. Pilgrimages by the Orthodox to venerate icons and relics quickly resumed. During his visit to Constantinople in the late 1280s, Rabban Şauma, a traveller from China and an honoured guest of the emperor, found there were still plenty left, as his account of the city shows. Some were very important relics like a stone purportedly removed from Christ's tomb and the hand of John the Baptist, which begs the question of whether the Latin rulers of the city had even known they were there, or if they did, had retained some relics in the city to preserve its spiritual prestige.[31]

Icons, central to the Orthodox faith but not of any particular interest to Latin Christian pilgrims, had also largely survived the sack of the city. For instance, St Luke's revered icon of the Virgin Hodegetria (She Who Shows the Way) was kept at the Pantocrator complex where it escaped the attentions of the crusaders. By the fourteenth century, it had emerged as the pre-eminent pilgrimage icon in the city. Many of the healing shrines overlooked by the city's Latin inhabitants were also revived and became popular with pilgrims once more. This resurgence in religious fervour within Constantinople coincided with the emergence of new Orthodox saints, chief among whom was Athanasio I (died by 1323), patriarch of Constantinople, whose shrine became a place of healing three years after his death.[32]

Over the following centuries, a renewal of the connections between Constantinople and Russia coincided with the decline of the vast Mongol empire, making travel easier for potential pilgrims. Stephen of Novgorod (in present-day Russia) and his eight companions embarked on a pilgrimage in 1348–9, hoping to 'venerate the holy places and kiss the bodies of the saints'.[33] Their week-long sojourn in Constantinople included visits to Hagia Sofia and other major sites, where Stephen meticulously documented their encounters with numerous relics and icons. They must have been wealthy (indeed, Stephen may have been bringing money for the repair of Hagia Sophia's dome)[34] as they engaged the services of a guide to take them around the city, and of some importance, as they had the privilege of meeting the patriarch of Constantinople, something ordinary pilgrims rarely did. Forty years later, Ignatius of Smolensk, a lordship on the western fringes of modern-day Russia, embarked on a pilgrimage, accompanying the metropolitan of all Russia on his third pilgrimage to the city. Ignatius chronicled not only their experiences within the city, but the journey starting with their departure from Moscow on 13 April 1389.[35]

Pilgrimage from Novgorod to Constantinople, where Anthony had come from just a few years before the sack of 1204, was again popular. Novgorod, one of the most important European cities of the age, managed to escape destruction by the Mongols in the mid-thirteenth century by surrendering before it was attacked. Regarded as the cradle of Russia, it was a city of ethnic diversity and cultural vibrancy, so much so that the Russian philosopher Prince Eugene Trubetskoy (1863–1920) called it 'our own Russian Florence'.[36] A flourishing mercantile republic with a strong democratic tradition, Novgorod maintained strong ties with Constantinople, and trade had made many of its inhabitants wealthy. Travel between Novgorod and Constantinople encompassed not only pilgrimage traffic, but also the migration of artisans from Constantinople to decorate Novgorod's churches, and clergy to provide spiritual guidance for its citizens.

Just over a dozen years after Ignatius of Smolensk's pilgrimage to Constantinople, the Spanish nobleman Ruy González de Clavijo embarked on a remarkable journey. Appointed ambassador of the Castilian King Henry III (ruled 1390–1406) to the court of Timur the Lame, brutal ruler of the central Asian Timurid empire, he found himself detained in Constantinople during the harsh winter of 1403–1404 by inclement weather. Accidental pilgrims, de Clavijo and his companions sent a message to the emperor that they were 'desirous of seeing the city, and the churches and the relics which it contained'.[37]

Their subsequent wanderings around Constantinople included viewing the left arm of John the Baptist, 'withered so the skin and bone alone remained', and in another church his right arm, 'fresh and healthy'.[38] He saw a relic of the True Cross, the bread Christ gave to Judas at the Last Supper 'about three fingers in breadth', some of Christ's blood, the stone his body had lain on and the lance that pierced his side at the Crucifixion, as well as dozens of other arms, bones, thumbs, heads and other relics, and also some icons.

De Clavijo marvelled at the abundance of pilgrimage sites, estimating that there were around 3,000 churches, and the innumerable relics in the city. 'Even though the visitor should day by day return, seeing all he could, yet always on the morrow there would be new sights to see.'[39] However, despite admiring its spiritual riches, the Spaniard concluded the account of his pilgrimage by lamenting, 'This city of Constantinople contains many great churches and monasteries, but most of them are in ruins; though it seems clear that, in former times, when the city was in its youth, it was the most renowned city in the world.' The city had been in decline for centuries. Around a hundred and fifty years before de Clavijo's visit, the last Latin emperor of Constantinople, Baldwin, had stripped the lead from the city's roofs in a desperate attempt to raise cash for its defence.

The Islamic City

Christian pilgrimage to Constantinople came to an abrupt halt when the Ottoman sultan Mehmed II (ruled 1451–81) led his forces into the city on a late spring day in 1453 and made it the new capital of his empire. Mehmed had made his ambition to seize Constantinople clear two years earlier when he became sultan, driven by his desire to fulfil the Prophet Muhammad's prophecy that his followers would take Constantinople.[40] The Ottoman Turks then set out to reconfigure one of the great pilgrimage centres of Christianity as a Muslim city where the faithful could live according to the rules of Islam. Following the old imperial playbook, they transformed the sacred landscape of their new possession to suit their own religious needs and bolster their position as the leading Islamic power. Churches were converted into mosques. Notably, Hagia Sofia, the embodiment of Orthodox Christianity and the epitome of Byzantine architecture, had four minarets added under the direction of the empire's chief architect Mimar Sinan (*c.*1489–1588). Among the many conversions, the Monastery of Saint John the Baptist at Stoudios, renowned for the powers of its relics in the decades preceding the city's fall, was transformed into the Imrahor Camii Mosque.[41]

Divine approval of the city's conquest was signalled when Mehmed's spiritual adviser found the tomb of Ayyub al-Ansari, the standard bearer of the Prophet Muhammad. Killed during the failed assault on Byzantine Constantinople in 674–8, Ayyub's tomb was built into the wall of the Eyüp Sultan Mosque on the Golden Horn, where it became a revered shrine and an instant pilgrimage destination for Muslims.[42] The shrine attracted pilgrims with a variety of needs. If they had business troubles, for example, they could collect some sacred water from one of the four taps in the mosque's courtyard. The shrine's importance was cemented by the decision to hold the ceremony where new Ottoman sultans received the Sword of Osman there. The sword, once owned by Osman I (died 1323), the progenitor of the Ottoman dynasty, conferred legitimacy and a sense of connection on the empire's ruler.[43] Investing new sultans at Ayyub's tomb forged a symbolic link between the current Muslim leadership and the Prophet Muhammad, mediated through Ayyu al-Ansari, and turned his shrine into a pilgrimage destination clearly associated with the authority of the Ottomans. The shrine also transformed Constantinople into a Muslim pilgrimage city, the most important in all Turkey.

When the Moroccan ambassador saw the shrine in 1591, he reported that 'the grandees of the empire compete for the burial places available near him [Ayyub]. They acquire plots there at the highest price. All good men even of modest condition also do all they can to obtain their place beside this tomb.'[44] Most of the dead lay in the extensive cemetery next to the mosque, but Mehmed II was buried in a domed mausoleum in the mosque itself. This too became a place of pilgrimage. New sultans who aspired to embody Mehmed's qualities came to pray at it, as did pilgrims from all ranks of society looking for aid.

In addition to these prominent shrines, Constantinople also boasted several lesser-known sites that became pilgrim destinations during Ottoman rule. For instance, the water in the holy well of Merkez Efendi (died 1552), a Sufi scholar and healer, supposedly had therapeutic qualities and was used for bathing. The city also contained a multitude of tombs – up to five hundred associated with revered individuals which formed the focus of *ziyarat*, the Islamic term for the act of visitation or pilgrimage to a tomb. Some of these shrines were only known in their local area.

Just as Constantinople's greatest Christian relics had been those linked to Christ, the new Islamic capital's foremost sacred relics were connected to the Prophet Muhammad. Following the Ottoman empire's acquisition of Arabia in 1517, its sultans started to bring Islamic relics from there to Constantinople. They were housed in the Topkapi Palace, residence of the sultan, in a room known as the Chamber of the Holy Relics. The collection included a hair of the Prophet's beard, his sandals, one of

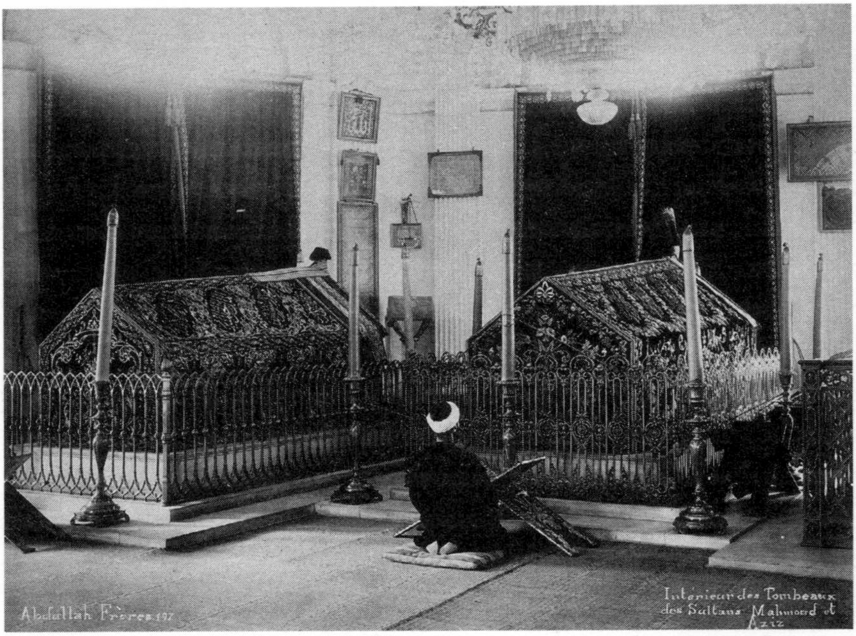

Tombs of Islamic leaders, like these of Ottoman Sultans Mahmud II (ruled 1808–39) and Andulaziz (ruled 1861–76) in Divan Yolu Street, Istanbul, became the focus of visitations or pilgrimages to tombs.

his teeth, his sword, the dust from his tomb and imprints of his feet preserved in stone. Prominent among these relics was the Khirqat al-Sa'ada, a mantle that once belonged to the Prophet, which was the focus of regular celebrations. A second mantle of the Prophet was later housed in a new building commissioned by Abdülmecid I (ruled 1839–61) which, though called a mosque, was supposedly intended to provide pilgrims with access to the mantle. The presence of pilgrims in the palace, particularly during Ramadan, underscored the piety of the sultans and enhanced their religious authority.[45] In reality, housing the relics within the imperial palace meant few but the elite would ever see them.

With this in mind, the footprint of the Prophet (of which

there were many) was accommodated in the tomb of the pacifist Sultan Abdülhamid I (ruled 1774–89). Before his death he secured an agreement from religious leaders that access for pilgrims would be possible, and the footprint was displayed on the tomb's northern wall. His concerns around pilgrims stemmed from a calculated decision as he knew how important pilgrimage could be for demonstrating imperial power. At the time, the sultan was dealing with concerns regarding his ability to lead and safeguard the Islamic world, particularly following the recent loss of Crimea and its large Muslim population to Russian control. The spectacle of pilgrimage was a way to demonstrate his religious authority and shore up his faltering legitimacy.[46] This wasn't the only time that Constantinople's sultans used relics and holy sites to boost their declining power; this happened repeatedly throughout the nineteenth century.

The deposition of the sultans and the replacement of the Ottoman empire by the secular Republic of Turkey between 1922 and 1923 was transformative. In 1930 Constantinople was formally redesignated Istanbul, a name that had been used in various forms since at least the tenth century. Emblematic of the new state's commitment to secularism was the conversion of the mosque housed in the former Church of Hagia Sofia into a museum; it became a mosque again in 2020. Secularism was strictly adhered to until the end of the Second World War, when political changes ushered in a gradual reassertion of Islamic values: mosques were rebuilt, religious brotherhoods were revitalised, and Turks were able to go to Mecca once more.

The revival of pilgrimage to sites treated for decades as of purely historical interest created a strange situation. Unlike in Mecca, where non-Muslims were, and remain, forbidden, secular tour groups visited sites alongside the most devout of pilgrims. In shrines that had functioned as museums for years, tourists freely wandered through displays while pilgrims sought the tombs which were the original focus of the buildings. However, this has come to be seen as an opportunity rather than a problem. Whether facilitating the hajj to Mecca or pilgrims visiting Istanbul, supporting Muslim pilgrimage while welcoming outsiders became an important part of the Turkish state's desire to promote itself as a bridge between East and West, a 'broker' between Western and Islamic countries.[47]

As Constantinople and as Istanbul, both the city and its pilgrimage attractions have enjoyed a long history of bolstering political regimes, as well as catering to the religious and medical needs of ordinary pilgrims. And the importance of relics to the city's status and its relationship with the rest of the world shows little sign of abating. In November 2004, some of the relics of St John Chrysostom, the archbishop instrumental in the early development of Constantinople as a sacred city, were translated to the Cathedral of St George, the principal Orthodox cathedral in Constantinople. Stolen from Constantinople in 1204, they had been kept in Rome for the previous eight centuries, although the papacy had strenuously denied this. Giving up the pretence, the papacy now returned them housed in a crystal and alabaster casket, where they lay on yellow velvet cushions. The decision to return them was, according to the elderly Pope John Paul II, to 'purify our wounded memories' through a gesture of reconciliation with the Orthodox Church.[48]

Just like the emperors of Constantinople and the Ottoman sultans who came after them, the pope had employed 'relic diplomacy', but John Paul knew how important control of relics was and still is in the power struggle between the two political and religious capitals; he kept some of St John's bones in Rome.

8

IONA

Scotland

In the autumn of 1773, the lexicographer Samuel Johnson and his friend and biographer John Boswell spent seven weeks touring the Inner Hebrides off the west coast of Scotland. Writing about their journey, Johnson described arriving late off the coast of the island of Iona and being carried onto 'that illustrious Island' (they couldn't dock) to visit the cradle of Celtic Christianity. For the devout Anglican Johnson, it was clearly a moving experience, and the idea that anyone could be indifferent to the island repelled him. 'That man is little to be envied,' he claimed, 'whose patriotism would not gain force upon the plain of *Marathon*, or whose piety would not grow warmer among the ruins of Iona!'[1]

Iona is widely considered the birthplace of Scottish Christianity, and the saint who established it as a Christian centre, St Columba (Colum Cille in Irish, 521–97), is commonly credited with introducing Christianity to Scotland, though there were Irish Christians there before he arrived. In many respects, historical reality, or at least the reality of Iona as it has come to us via hagiographies and legends, matters less than what people believe the island to be. The poet Archie Lamont called it the 'shrine of a nation yet to be'.[2] IONA IS THE SOUL OF SCOTLAND, proclaimed a headline in the *Aberdeen Press and Journal* in the summer of 1949. The author of the article which followed, Rowntree Harvey, wrote with concern that many people in his country had not heard of the island, or did not appreciate its significance in the history of Scotland. 'Columba made Iona what it is,' he informed his readers, 'a place in which you feel you are all the time surrounded by a cloud of witnesses who have made the island what it really is – the shrine of the soul of Scotland.'[3]

St Columba's Island

In 563, in a small currach (wicker-framed boat covered with leather), Columba crossed from Ulster to the western shores of Scotland, accompanied by a dozen companions, including his uncle Ernán and two cousins. At around forty years old, this Irish princeling was making one of the most significant voyages of his time. Columba, a member of one of Ireland's royal families, likely saw the wisdom in leaving his homeland after the Battle of Cúl Dreinne three years before. This battle was possibly connected to a dispute over a psalter copied by Columba. Though some suggest he was banished for his role in the strife, his hagiographer Adomnán offers a different perspective. He claims Columba's true motivation was religious: a desire 'to be a pilgrim for Christ' and to find a new home where he could live an ascetic monastic life. Whatever his motivation, Columba's voyage was a pivotal moment in the spread of Christianity. [4]

If that was his plan, Iona was the perfect choice. This small island, just three miles long and one and a half miles wide, lies off the west coast of Mull, the second-largest island of the Inner Hebrides, separated from it by a narrow strait. Encircled by pale sandy beaches and crystal-clear waters, in Columba's time Iona was likely uninhabited, offering a pristine, untouched landscape. Whether he intentionally chose Iona, stumbled upon it by chance or was granted it by the King of Dál Riata in exchange for converting the Picts, the island presented a blank canvas.[5] Here, he could realise his vision and build a centre for his faith.

Columba's practice of that faith was founded on principles of austerity and withdrawal from society, yet it wasn't long before Iona's success meant that people were seeking him out, coming to ask for spiritual advice as pilgrims, or appealing to him on theological matters. The bishop of Lindisfarne asked for his advice on the complicated matter of how Easter should be calculated.[6] Some pilgrims got more than they had bargained for. When two brothers arrived on the island, they told the saint that they had come 'to be pilgrims in your monastery for this year'. Columba would only accept them if they took monastic vows and became permanent members of the island's community. The two agreed, such was Columba's reputation.[7]

Under his guidance, Iona blossomed into a revered spiritual haven. When Adomnán (*c.*624–704), Iona's ninth abbot and another future saint, authored a life of St Columba in the last years of the seventh century, he infused the text with comparisons to Jerusalem. This is perhaps no surprise given that Adomnán's other book, *On the Holy Places,* was a description of Jerusalem and other sites of the Holy Land and Egypt, which could almost be used as a guide to Iona itself.

Pilgrims arriving on Iona would take the path from the landing area on the island's eastern shore up to St Columba's shrine. This was known as the Street of the Dead and was laid out to echo the pilgrimage route to Christ's tomb in Jerusalem along the Via Dolorosa.[8] Iona's spiritual atmosphere was also enhanced by legends that placed this isolated spot at the heart of the Christian story. One claimed that the Virgin Mary had visited Iona, while another foretold that Christ himself would appear on the island on the Day of Judgement.

At the time Adomnán was writing, the cult of St Columba had yet to develop. Columba had been buried in the monastery cemetery in 597, but there is no indication that pilgrims came to visit his grave. The few who arrived would probably have venerated the books he had written or the tunic Columba was wearing when he died; Adomnán put them on the altar of the monastery church when he prayed for good weather for the delivery of building supplies, so we know they were on the island during his time as abbot. But no real effort was put into developing Columba's grave or the wider island as a pilgrimage centre for the simple reason that Adomnán probably didn't want to do so, and may have actively discouraged pilgrims and other visitors from coming.[9] However, within half a century of Adomnán's death, things had started to change. There may have been a shrine containing Columba's relics by the 750s, as several legal proclamations at the time suggest that relics were available as part of legal ceremonies, where swearing on sacred items was important. That is what happened in Ireland anyway, and the religious practices and traditions of Iona and Ireland were intimately connected.

Iona's fame and wealth attracted Viking raids. Martyrs' Bay just south of the island's modern landing stage is named for sixty-eight monks who were massacred by raiders in 806. Around 825, the Vikings came looking for the reliquary housing St Columba's relics, likely adorned with gemstones. Walafrid Strabo, a Swiss monk writing fifty to sixty years later, recounted the tale of how the acting abbot, Blathmac, was martyred for refusing to disclose the location of the reliquary. Warned of the impending raid, Blathmac and his fellow monks had buried the casket of 'precious metal' in a trench, concealing it with turf.[10] Before its concealment, the reliquary may have been kept in a small chapel near the current abbey's west door, which was known as St Columba's shrine by the thirteenth century.[11]

Blathmac was buried on Iona, revered as a saint, and miracles began to take place in his name.[12]

By the twelfth century, pilgrims could also see the burial place of St Oran (or Odrán), a companion of St Columba. Although he had died centuries before, it was only in the twelfth century that his cult gained traction when people came to believe that Columba had told Oran, 'No one will be granted his request at my own grave unless he first seek it of you.'[13] A chapel dedicated to him was built to the south of the abbey, and pilgrims would pass it as they walked from the island's landing place to the shrine of St Columba, allowing them to respect the saint's warning by stopping at St Oran's Chapel first.

As Iona was remote, it was difficult and expensive to add to the monastery or build more shrines, so particular spots on the island were developed for pilgrims to visit, some marked with crosses, others simply named to associate them with St Columba. This was done to such an extent that a circular path developed around the island, similar to some pilgrimage routes in Ireland. Pilgrims who followed the path could visit such sites as the bay where Columba and his companions landed when they first came to Iona, or the Hill of Angels, where he had conversed with the messengers of God and where there may once have been some sort of chapel.[14] There was also a large eighth-century cross dedicated to St John the Evangelist placed immediately in front of the abbey's west door to mark a place of prayer, and several wells adopted as holy places over the course of the island's history.

At the northern extreme of Iona, the Well of the North Wind allegedly secured favourable winds for sailors who sought it out. Near the now-ruined St Mary's Chapel, a well dedicated to the Irish monk St Ceathan (or Kian) may have had something to do with easing the passage to heaven as people asked for its

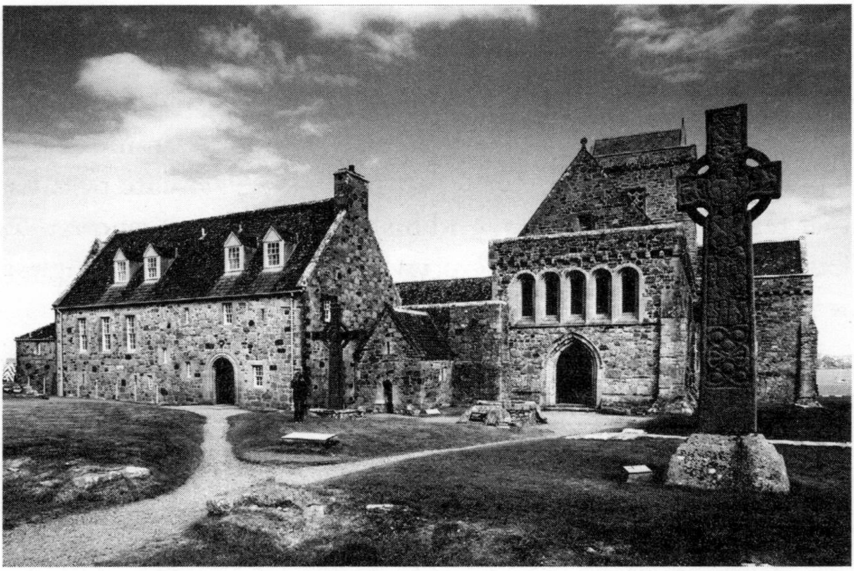

Iona Abbey, rebuilt in the twentieth century, is now a place of ecumenical pilgrimage. Pilgrims come to honour St Columba, who may have been buried in the small cell to the left of the abbey's west door, and to experience the sacred landscape of the island.

water on their deathbeds.[15] On the top of the Dun, the island's highest point, was another natural water source, this one credited with the ability to confer eternal youth or grant wishes; it had been allegedly blessed by the Irish abbess St Brigid.[16] This made it one of the oldest holy wells not just on Iona, but perhaps in all of Scotland.

In the last decades of the eleventh century, Iona started to attract both high-status pilgrims and wealthy patrons. The famously pious St Margaret (died 1093), wife of the Scottish king, paid to rebuild the decaying abbey church. Magnus Barelegs, king of Norway (ruled 1093–1103), must have seen the renovated building when he came on pilgrimage in the 1090s, not long after he gained control of Iona. His decision to visit the island shows he revered the saint, but he was also careful to respect Columba's church. In the *Heimskringla*, one Norse saga recounts his exploits and tell us how Magnus 'wanted to open up Columba's little cell, but did not enter into it, and immediately closed the door again, saying that no one should dare to enter that church'. Given that he and his men were happy enough to harry and burn just about everywhere else they went, Magnus was clearly in awe of St Columba's sanctity.[17]

Around 1200, the introduction of a community of Benedictine monks to the abbey by the sons of Somerled, king of the Isles (died 1164), prompted more building work and the further development of Iona as a pilgrimage destination. They had buried Somerled on Iona and turned it into a royal mausoleum of sorts. This meant a new chapel, St Michael's, was erected to the north of the abbey, and a community of Augustinian canonesses was established near the landing place for those crossing from Mull. The island also benefited from a rebuilt parish church, St Ronan's, and a pilgrims' chapel in the cathedral dedicated to St Mary.[18] Donald, lord of the Isles (died 1421) gifted a gold and silver reliquary to hold the hand of St Columba.[19]

Unfortunately, despite this largesse, Iona, much like other pilgrimage centres in Scotland, struggled to attract pilgrims, and those who did come were usually Scots; late medieval Iona was not an international pilgrimage destination by any stretch of the imagination. By 1428, the abbey was again in need of repair; the timberwork in the choir had collapsed.[20] Abbot Dominic offered pilgrims indulgences, but it was too little too late. With the Reformation monasticism on Iona was swept away, and the island became the seat of the new Protestant bishop of the Isles. This, however, was a short-lived creation, abolished at the end of the seventeenth century, after which Iona's religious life went into sharp decline.[21]

Revival

In common with so many post-Reformation holy sites across Europe, Iona, once the destination of reverent pilgrims, later became the focus of sightseeing and literary pilgrimages. A treasure trove of antiquities and history, it was just the sort of place which attracted travellers in the years after road building improved access across Scotland. Gentleman travellers and antiquarians toured the Highlands and islands, and many wrote accounts or drew landscapes of Iona.[22] Samuel Johnson, John Keats, Walter Scott and Robert Louis Stevenson all made the trek to the island, drawn by its remoteness and romanticised history, and the notion that they would perhaps find something lost. 'I know not whether you have heard much about this island,' the poet John Keats wrote to his brother Tom in July 1818. 'I never did before I came nigh to it.'[23] Iona's ruins gripped the imagination of Scottish artists, who painted them repeatedly in this period. One of them, John MacCulloch, explained his fascination:

> The ruins of Iona are the soul and centre of the Painter's Landscape. Without them, the landscape is nothing; with them, it is every thing; because, in it, they are, themselves, every thing. But, still more, are they the centre of the landscape of the Poet; because History has surrounded them with a magic and an interest beyond the reach and power of the pencil ... They speak not to the eye, but to the mind ... This is Iona.[24]

Iona inspired William Wordsworth when he visited in 1833, lamenting the state of this 'Glory of the West' that was once home to monks and nuns.[25] The island was a picturesque ruin, its religious life all but done. Visiting in 1828, the Reverend

Norman MacLeod opined that Iona was 'left without church or settled preacher or public worship. It was a sad change which came over Iona and shameful to relate,' but concluded prophetically, 'but a better time is coming.'[26]

Iona underwent a massive revival in pilgrimages in the second half of the nineteenth century. This was happening all over Britain. The 1829 Catholic Emancipation Act and the restoration of the Catholic hierarchy in England and Wales by the pope in 1850 had given new freedom and confidence to Britain's Catholic population, which grew rapidly through immigration and to a lesser extent conversion. And there was growing interest in St Columba and Iona from antiquarians, who identified a large stone which once stood next to the saint's grave as St Columba's Pillow,[27] and from tourists. Both developments helped to promote the island as a destination. The Columba Hotel opened in the former Free Church manse between the landing stage and the abbey at the end of the 1860s, reflecting the need for visitor accommodation, which had been seriously lacking.

There was also considerable interest in faith and the history of the island. One of the most influential authors of this time was Fiona MacLeod (the pseudonym of William Sharp 1855–1905), who was a regular pilgrim to Iona from the early 1880s onwards. He used his pilgrimages to the island to develop the persona of his alter ego, in an attempt to make her the accepted expert on the Scottish Celtic Renaissance. Sharp wrote extensively on how the faith of Iona was rooted in older Druidic beliefs, and believed that to tell the story of Iona was 'to go back to God'.[28] His books did not stand the test of time, but the idea of Celtic Iona remains strong, and some modern pilgrims believe the island brings them closer to a simpler, pre-medieval faith.

The rising interest in Iona's religious past coincided with the island's ownership by George, eighth duke of Argyll, who inherited it from his father in 1847, the year after its inhabitants were hit by the potato famine. His predecessors had tried to protect the abbey ruins by walling them off and instructing their tenants to look after the derelict nunnery, but these efforts had met with limited success. Under the duke there was some restoration, and he took an active interest in improvements. He also wrote and published *Iona* (1871), a study explaining the importance of the island. He was not sympathetic to the idea of pilgrimage or the reverence for St Columba, which he considered superstition, but that did not stop the island from becoming a pilgrimage destination once more.[29]

The first large national Catholic post-Reformation pilgrimage to Iona was held in the summer of 1888.[30] Pilgrims came from across Scotland and flocked to the port of Oban on the west coast of Scotland, where they took the steamer to Iona. This was probably the most important pilgrimage in the island's history, for both religious and political reasons. Scottish Catholics, the historian Katherine Grenier has argued, had organised the pilgrimage to Iona in order to assert their pre-eminence on an island considered the birthplace of Christianity in Scotland and important to the country's national history.[31] The timing was significant: 1888 was the three-hundredth anniversary of the English Protestant victory over the Spanish Armada and two hundred years after the Catholic King James II of England (VII of Scotland) was deposed. St Columba was an Irish-Scottish saint, but the Catholic diocese of Argyll and the Isles had chosen him as its patron. Unsurprisingly, the pilgrimage was not popular among Protestants. One reporter for the Glasgow *Daily Mail* claimed that 'it would be safe to say that a plebiscite of the resident population would not have supported the permission given' to hold the Catholic pilgrimage. To some Protestants the pilgrimage seemed a statement of intent: 'the Romans want a footing in Iona' claimed an alarmed J. F. Campbell.[32]

In 1897, the thirteen-hundredth anniversary of St Columba's death, two large pilgrimages were held to Iona, one Catholic, one Protestant. The Protestant Presbyterians got in first, staging their commemorations the week before the Catholic pilgrimage arrived. The Presbyterian pilgrims were welcomed into the ruins of the abbey church, where a temporary pulpit and high altar had been set up. The following week, five hundred Catholic pilgrims came to the same place and celebrated mass.[33] In a show of unity and to embrace as many of the pilgrims as possible, the Catholics were treated to a 'most impressive' sermon in English, courtesy of the archbishop of St Andrews and Edinburgh, and another in Gaelic by a Jesuit father who took copious quantities of snuff throughout.[34] Things were not always organised so smoothly and sometimes events clashed. In 1936 the Catholic mass and the Protestant service coincided, and the congregations could hear the other event.[35]

The renewed importance of Iona to faith and pilgrims led the duke of Argyll to gift the consolidated ruins of the cathedral and nunnery to the Iona Cathedral Trust in 1899. His motive was to safeguard 'buildings of such great historic interest to the whole Christian world'.[36] Work began on restoring the church, a process that was finished in July 1913.

The most recent major event in Iona's history was the founding of the Iona Community in 1938 by George MacLeod, a Church of Scotland pastor from Glasgow. Having turned to religion after the trauma of fighting in the First World War, five years earlier he had been on pilgrimage to Jerusalem with his father, a journey that made a lasting impression on him.[37] He was clearly a man looking for something more from his faith and came to believe that he should found an ecumenical Christian community where divisions could be healed. Coming from Scotland's industrial belt and thus only too familiar with hardship and unemployment, MacLeod also hoped that the renovation of Iona's ancient structures would give purpose to people who had lost their jobs.

The idea of establishing some sort of community on Iona had been mooted in the previous decade by David Russell, a wealthy paper-mill owner, but come to nothing, although the Iona Fellowship, set up in 1929, facilitated spiritual retreats to the island. Another proposal, to establish a 'Gaelic University', had come from New York's American Iona Society in 1935, and yet another from the Catholic marquis of Bute in 1938, who wanted to buy the island to build a Catholic seminary there. Clare Vyner, owner of the majestic ruins of Fountains Abbey in Yorkshire since 1923, also expressed an interest.[38] The Iona Cathedral Trust chose the scheme proposed by George MacLeod.

Over the following decades, MacLeod and the community raised the funds and provided the labour to rebuild the rest of the abbey's buildings. He was also responsible for starting the weekly pilgrimage tours around the island. These increasingly took on the form of pilgrimages to the places associated with the sacred history of the island, but initially seem to have been an attempt by MacLeod to take a break from the noise and activity of the almost permanent building site that the abbey became.[39] The pilgrimages mixed a good walk with spiritual refreshment, a combination often echoed in the responses of modern pilgrims to Iona, who find its remoteness and quiet a refreshing contrast to their usual life. These pilgrimage walks still take place each week, starting at St Martin's Cross outside the west front of the abbey church and visiting places like the marble quarry on the island's southern shore (provider of the abbey's Benedictine altar stone), the bay where Columba landed and a reputed hermit's cell, before heading back to St Oran's Chapel.

The whole point of the Iona Community was, and is, to bring together different faiths. Initially, this was to restore the abbey and its surrounding buildings, but the community has developed into an organisation with members throughout the world, who come on week-long visits from places as far afield as America and Australia, and often more than once. As one man put it in 1977, 'I have been unable to keep away. I am drawn back continually to this place which speaks to me in so many ways of God'.[40] Other groups have arranged their own pilgrimages – Orthodox Christians, Episcopalians – and in 2014 there was an interfaith pilgrimage of Jews, Sikhs, Hindus, Muslims and Buddhists.

Though the message of the community is very much one of faith and harmony, not all the pilgrims who came to Iona in the second half of the twentieth century did so in the spirit of ecumenism. During the 1963 St Columba's Day pilgrimage, the Anglicans opted to conduct their worship service separately.[41] Still, the hope that Iona could be a place where faiths come together was no better illustrated than in 1982, when Pope John Paul II, on his UK visit, called on Christians in Scotland to go there on pilgrimage 'hand in hand', no matter their denomination. The leaders of the Iona Community responded to this call by offering Iona as a place for joint worship, and two years later the Scottish Church Leaders' Gathering met on the island in a historic gathering. But as with the experience of some twenty years before, things were not as harmonious as they could have been. Some Protestant extremists, led by the activist anti-Catholic pastor Jack Glass ('Scotland's answer to Iain Paisley', according to *The Times*, though Glass thought Paisley too liberal), 'took over St Columba's Cell and barracked the guests as they arrived'.[42]

Permanent Pilgrimages

Throughout its changing fortunes, Iona has been a destination for what may be called permanent pilgrims – like St Columba, who did not intend to return to his home, but knew he would live out his life in search of God. A life of the saint written in Old Irish likened his actions to those of the biblical Abraham, who undertook a journey in search of the 'Land of Promise' – a 'perfect pilgrimage' as instructed by God.[43] Others went on a sort of long-term pilgrimage. An Irishman of royal descent, Aid Black, was brought to Iona by a priest named Findchan (who also seems to have been his lover) with the aim of being 'for some years a pilgrim' with St Columba. Aid seems to have been racked by guilt about the deaths he had caused, particularly that of Diormot son of Cerball, ruler of all Ireland. He afterwards became a priest.[44]

King Artgal of Connacht was a true permanent pilgrim. Abdicating in 782, he set out the following year 'with pilgrim's staff' for Iona. His was a one-way ticket; he lived on the island for the best part of a decade until his death.[45] Amlaíb Cuarán, the king of the Norse in Dublin, also spent the rest of his life on Iona. His pilgrimage was one of repentance, so the medieval Irish *Annals of Tigernach* tells us, prompted by his recent defeat at the hands of the Irish, who forced him to hand over treasure and jewels.[46] Having lost his city in 980 to Máel Sechnill, high king of Ireland, the elderly Amlaíb fled Ireland for Iona, where he died the same year.[47]

Perhaps unsurprisingly, death has become a prominent feature of many pilgrim landscapes. Pilgrimage sites frequently have associated cemeteries and burial places nearby, the devout wanting to remain in death as close as possible to those they venerated in life. At Iona there is no escaping the cemetery, as all pilgrims travelling from the harbour to the abbey have to pass along the Street of the Dead. There may have been as many as nine cemeteries across the island at various times. In Shakespeare's *Macbeth*, written for performance at London's Globe Theatre in about 1606, the Scottish nobleman Ross seeks the whereabouts of his king. 'Where is Duncan's body?' he asks. MacDuff tells him that Duncan has been

> Carried to Colmekill,
> The sacred storehouse of his predecessors,
> And guardian of their bones.[48]

Colmekill is Iona, and it seems that by the time Shakespeare was writing, Iona's reputation as a pilgrimage destination had been largely eclipsed by its identity as a burial place, though his audience would also have known of the island's connection with St Columba.

In the last years of the twentieth century, after the burial of the Labour Party leader John Smith on Iona in 1994, visits to the grave of a political leader on the island were again popular, though not with the islanders themselves. Previously some had objected to permission being granted for the burial, given that John Smith was not from Iona. Now the island's residents were lamenting the damage caused by the sheer numbers of people visiting his burial site, so many that they were damaging the surrounding graves. The *Independent* reported that some locals hoped 'that one year after his death the number of political pilgrims would drop sharply'.[49]

9

KARBALA

Iraq

On the 10th of Muharram (10 October) 680, Husayn Ibn Ali, the grandson of the Prophet Muhammad, was killed battling the Umayyad caliph, Yazid I. Their forces had met on the banks of the Euphrates in present-day southern Iraq to settle the question of who should rule over the Muslims.

Yazid was far from the ideal candidate for caliph: anti-Islamic and irreligious, he was a drinker with lax morals. Unsurprisingly, there was some opposition to his accession. Although the Sunni Muslims supported him, the Shia believed Husayn to be the true caliph, on the basis that the right to lead the faithful, the imamate, descended through the male descendants of the Prophet Muhammad's daughter, Husayn's mother Fatima. The people of the Iraqi garrison town of Kufa accordingly called on Husayn, then in his mid-fifties and in Medina, to take power.[1] On his journey north to the town (or on his way back – accounts don't agree), accompanied by friends and family members, he was intercepted by Yazid and an army. Husayn camped on the plain outside Karbala, where negotiations between the two sides took place. When they broke down and Husayn refused to take the pledge of allegiance to Yazid, a battle took place.

Husayn wasn't best placed for a fight, given that his force

consisted of at most a couple of hundred men accompanied by his harem and family members, some of whom were women and children. In stark contrast, the caliph had a fighting force of about 4,000 men. The result was brutal. Husayn, his brother and two of his sons were killed, as were all the men in his party, their severed heads taken as grim trophies of Yazid's victory. Husayn's remains were desecrated and his body stripped of its silken robe, cloak, sword and sandals until it 'lay bare on the sands of Karbala'.[2] He was buried on the battlefield, about sixty miles south-west of Baghdad.

Husayn's willingness to stand up to the caliph and his martyrdom (for that is how his death was framed) became central to Shia Islam. The mosque and shrine built in his honour, later topped by a gilded dome, evolved into focal points of devotion and pilgrimage, and Karbala became one of the four Shia shrine cities in what is now Iraq known as the sacred thresholds.[3] The shrine also housed the tombs of his friend Habib, the man who had written to Husayn from Kufa asking him to take power, Husayn's slaughtered sons and his companions. Just to the west of Husayn's mosque, a separate shrine was built to honour his half-brother and standard bearer at the Battle of Karbala, Abu Fadhl al-Abbas. Despite efforts to limit their growth, the two shrines expanded in the century after the Battle of Karbala, eventually drawing thousands, and then millions, of pilgrims each year.

As the third imam of the Shias, Husayn's death was a historical marker in the development of Islam. Until then, Shia and Sunni Muslims had not been theologically distinct. Husayn's martyrdom changed all that: as the historian Philip Hitti put it, 'Shi'ism was born on the tenth of Muharram.'[4] Until then, the divisions between the supporters of one side or the other had been largely political, but with Husayn's martyrdom they became

The burial of Imam Husayn at Karbala following his martyrdom created Shia Islam's most important pilgrimage destination. The pilgrims, who come in their thousands to mourn Husayn, drive the local economy and impact the relationship between Iraq, Iran and India.

firmly theological. Husayn's sons, grandsons and descendants down to 874 completed the line known as the Twelve Imams. Adherence to them became known as Twelver Shi'ism and was centred on Karbala. The number of imams stopped at twelve because of the belief that Muhammad Ibn Hasan al-Mahdi, the twelfth, did not die. Rather, he is said to be hidden and will return at the end of time as the Mahdi to restore justice and peace to earth.

Imams from the time of Husayn's son and successor onwards imbued Karbala with an increasing number of sacred connections, but it was Husayn's martyrdom and burial at Karbala that have made the city such an important and influential place for Shia pilgrims. While Mecca is a place of pilgrimage for all

Muslims, an obligation set out in the Koran, pilgrimage to the shrines of Husayn and his half-brother is a *ziyarat*, a voluntary visit to a holy tomb. Pilgrimage to Karbala is also a matter of Shia identity, unity and power.

Pilgrimages of Mourning

The first pilgrims appeared in Karbala a few years after the fateful battle to weep over Husayn's grave, though one tradition states that the Prophet Muhammad's friend Jaber heard a voice in faraway Medina, announcing Husayn's death, and immediately hastened to Karbala to mourn him. Two years after Husayn's death, the surviving female members of his family were freed from imprisonment at Yazid's court in Damascus and came on a pilgrimage of mourning to Karbala. Perhaps three years after that, a thousand men from Kufa came as penitential pilgrims to atone for their failure to save Husayn from the battle into which they had unwittingly led him, weeping, screaming and praying around the martyr's tomb.[5] Given such a start to Karbala's pilgrimage history, it is little surprise that pilgrimages of mourning became central to Shia practice, and reciting prayers and poems in Husayn's honour was recommended on the way to, and at, his tomb. Doing so came with its own rewards. 'Whoever recited couplets of poetry for al-Husayn and weeps, and makes then people weep,' advised the poet al-Sayyid al-Himyarī, writing in the century after Husayn's death, 'he and they shall go to paradise.'[6]

The first poet to compose an elegy in Husayn's memory was Iqbah ibn Amr al-Sahmi, a poet-pilgrim who undertook a *ziyarat* to Karbala in the decades after Husayn's death.

> I passed the grave of Husayn in Karbala, and on it my tears flowed copiously.

> I continued to weep and grieve for his suffering, and my eye was well assisted by tears and sobs. And with him I mourned a group of men whose graves surround his own.
>
> May the light of an eye, seeking consolation in life when you [Husayn and his followers] were frightened in this world, be darkened.
>
> Peace be upon the dwellers of these graves in Karbala … May peace be upon them with the setting of the sun and its rising: peace carried from me by the winds as they blow to and fro.
>
> Men in troops continue to flock in pilgrimage to his grave, where on them flows its musk and sweet fragrance.[7]

Accounts of the sadness of pilgrimage to Karbala often feel at odds with the joy expressed by pilgrims to other places, but sorrow is central to the experience of honouring the memory of Husayn. 'Everyone knows how one feels on such a day,' Sakineh, former wife of the Qajar shah of Iran, wrote in her diary in 1889. Nine years earlier, Mehrmah Khanom (daughter of a Qajar prince) had stopped at Karbala as she travelled on the hajj to Mecca and went to Husayn's shrine, where she 'wept a bit about the unreliability of this world and the vicissitudes of life and asked God for forgiveness'. Begum Sarbuland Jang, wife of the chief justice of Hyderabad in India, had a similarly moving experience in about 1910. 'The moment we arrived, my heart was overwhelmed by a strange sensation that I am incapable of describing,' she wrote. She told her husband, who replied, 'Just look at the effect that this place has on the heart,' to which she answered, weeping, 'It was my heartfelt desire never to part from there.'[8] Many others recorded similar experiences.

Some Shia pilgrims go beyond weeping, engaging in rituals of flagellation and self-mortification that are supposed to echo the suffering of Husayn and his family (*tatbir*). In extreme cases men may strike the front of their heads with swords, drawing blood. This is said to commemorate Zaynab, Husayn's sister, smashing her head against a pole upon seeing the severed head of her brother. Though the practice has been banned in Iran and Lebanon, it is still carried out by thousands of devout pilgrims.[9]

The suffering and death of Husayn is the inspiration for the largest Shia pilgrimage in the world, the annual Arba'in, a walking pilgrimage that coincides with the end of the forty days of mourning following Ashura, the day of the Battle of Karbala. In some traditions, the pilgrimage reflects the journey taken by Husayn's severed head from Damascus (where it had been taken by Yazid), back to Karbala for burial forty days after Husayn's death. Over three weeks, millions of pilgrims from across the Middle East, from India and Turkey, walk to Karbala. They don't necessarily cover the entire route on foot; it has become more usual to converge on the cities of Basra and Najaf, and walk from there. That is still a distance of between about fifty and seventy miles, so a trek of several days, which allows the pilgrims to reflect on the suffering of Husayn. A lot do it barefoot, or in socks, and as the pilgrims are in mourning, many wear black, just as Umm Salama, the Prophet Muhammad's sixth wife, did after Husayn's martyrdom.[10] Pilgrims also engage in abstinence and weep copiously, the latter sometimes stimulated by the consumption of grilled lentils, which are believed to soften the heart.[11]

Supporting Arba'in pilgrims is a pious act in itself for which Shia hope they will be rewarded. Money to provide food and accommodation pours in from the wealthy but also from those who can barely afford it. Some people along the pilgrimage routes let people stay for free. Others give out food and drink at the roadside or offer a free massage. The hospitality of the road is a huge part of the Arba'in pilgrimage.[12]

As a place of sacred tombs and holy mourning, Karbala is a sought-after burial place, and some pilgrims come hoping to die in the city. This is partly about proximity to the martyrs, but what also draws them is the belief that the very soil of Karbala is holy. Various stories about its sanctity have been included in pilgrimage manuals and devotional works, such as one in which the Angel Gabriel took the Prophet Muhammad to Karbala and gave him soil that smelled of must, making him weep as he learned that it was where his grandson Husayn would die.[13]

Pilgrims have sought death and burial at many of the sites in this book – Constantinople, Amritsar, Shikoku – attracted by the possibility of spending eternity in the place they believe to be the holiest on earth. At Karbala, burial, ideally in the Wadi al-Imam cemetery, is prized because of the belief that it will open a gateway to heaven, and earn the dead Husayn's intercession on the Day of Judgement. 'Never is one who rests at Karbala debased,' wrote Shahid-e-Salid (1549–1610).

> No matter his state, though he be reduced to dust
> For he shall be taken up and fashioned into a rosary
> A rosary, worn about pious hands.[14]

So popular was burial at Karbala that the transport of the dead became known as 'corpse-traffic'. Unfortunately, this was a conduit for disease, and despite the belief that the earth of Karbala itself could also cure, the city was often the site of epidemic outbreaks.[15] According to the Shia theologian al-Mufid (died 1022), 'The soil from the tomb of Husayn ... is a cure for every malady. Upon eating it, say, "In the name of God and by God. Oh Lord make it abundant sustenance, beneficial knowledge and a cure for every malady. You are powerful over everything."'[16] Writing a guidebook for pilgrims in the sixteenth century, Muhammad Bakir al-Majlisi claimed the clay at Karbala was healing, but only if it was taken from the area near Husayn's tomb. This power made it a sought-after souvenir. Consequently, Karbala clay has been fashioned into tablets and exported to India, and made into prayer beads, like rosaries (*tasbihs*), which are sold to pilgrims. In Karbala itself the devout sometimes prostrate themselves on the tablets to pray, and there have been requests from India for Karbala clay to be sent for incorporation into the construction of new mosques.[17]

Power

The popularity of Karbala has frequently made Sunni Muslims uneasy. As a result, over the course of its 1,300-year pilgrimage history the city and its tombs have been attacked, destroyed and rebuilt, only for the cycle to repeat itself. Harun-al Rashid, the fifth Abbasid caliph, whose capital was Baghdad, only about sixty miles from Karbala, stopped pilgrimage to the city during his reign (786–809), and Husayn's grave was obliterated to remove any marker to guide future pilgrims. Apparently this didn't work, because in the middle of the ninth century another caliph ordered the destruction of the grave and the ploughing up of the land; the pit that was left was filled with water.[18]

The shrines were rebuilt but destroyed again, this time in 971 by Hanbalis, a military Sunni sect from Baghdad who burned them down.[19] In response, Adud ad-Dawla, a powerful nominal vassal of the Abbasid caliph (ruled 949–83), reconstructed the shrines in the last decades of the tenth century and, aware of the financial benefits of pilgrims coming to Karbala, developed the surrounding area.[20] The new buildings remained intact only until 1016, but at least this time damage was accidental, as a fire sparked by two large candles destroyed the dome of Husayn's shrine. It was once again rebuilt. Thereafter the shrines survived, being improved and expanded over time. Mahmud Khan, a descendant of the Mongol emperor Genghis Khan, visited in 1303 and left expensive gifts.[21] When the Moroccan traveller Ibn Battuta visited in the 1320s, he found

> a small town, surrounded by palm groves and watered from the Euphrates. The sanctified tomb [of Husayn] is inside the town, and beside it is a large college and a noble hospice, in which food is supplied to all wayfarers. At the gate of the mausoleum stand chamberlains and guardians, without whose leave no person may enter ... Over the sanctified tomb there are lamps of gold and silver, and upon its doors there are silken curtains.[22]

Husayn's shrine at Karbala has always been central to religious and political power in Iraq and the wider Shia world, and as such its leaders have seen pilgrimage to Karbala as a way to consolidate their rule. During the Iraq campaign of the (Sunni) Ottoman sultan Suleiman the Magnificent in the 1530s, he visited Husayn's grave at Karbala as a sign of his authority over it, and to mark his defeat of the (Shia) Safavid rulers of Persia. Suleiman was acutely aware of the importance of controlling the major pilgrimage sites in his territories, as can be seen by his patronage of the holy sites in Jerusalem and Mecca in the years after they came under his rule. The Safavid Shah Safi, grandson and successor of Abbas the Great (died 1629), came on pilgrimage to Karbala in the early years of his reign.[23] The young monarch was a ruthless and politically astute man who used the pilgrimage as a method of legitimising his rule.

Suleiman ordered the construction of a canal to bring water to the city, but it was apparently poorly designed or maintained, as the city was reportedly devoid of pilgrims by the end of the sixteenth century due to a lack of water. The problem was not addressed until the first decades of the eighteenth century, when the canal was improved on the orders of the Ottoman governor Hasan Paşa (ruled 1704–24), creating a steady and reliable water supply for Karbala. This was critical in helping the site become the most important of the four shrine cities of Iraq.[24] With greater pilgrimage numbers came a stronger economy, and surplus wealth that could be used to build Karbala into a centre of Shia learning. The city continued to grow, and the two shrines benefited from generous gifts, acquiring lavish ornamentation.

In the spring of 1801, approximately 12,000 Wahhabi fighters, puritanical Sunnis from central Arabia, pillaged Karbala and its shrines, killing thousands of Shias. The Wahhabis were determined to return Islam to what they saw as its pure form, which meant getting rid of tombs and shrines like those in Karbala and stamping out what they saw as idolatrous Shia practices. The Mamluk governor of the city fled, leaving its surviving inhabitants to rely on the help of Fath Ali Shah, the ruler of Persia, a Shia and a member of the Qajar dynasty.[25] However, the Wahhabi attack on Karbala and the other important shrine city of Najaf only made the Shia more determined to rebuild their city and convert the Sunni tribes of Iraq. The Shia in Karbala had an established tradition of sending out missionaries, and they were able to spread their faith with little or no opposition. As a result, the Shia population in southern Iraq went from strength to strength.

Unfortunately, although the Shia faith was spreading, Karbala itself was descending into lawlessness. From the 1820s onwards crime, corruption and opportunism, coupled with a violent gang culture, threatened the city's stability. As Ottoman control weakened, a power vacuum emerged in the city into which those who controlled the shrines stepped. The custodian of Husayn's shrine became the city's unofficial governor, and under his patronage over a dozen gangs extorted protection money from residents and visiting pilgrims. Karbala's de facto rulers were able to exercise an effective veto over the city's Ottoman governors, forcing out those they opposed or murdering them.[26]

Gaining control of Karbala would be a significant win for anyone wanting to assert their authority over the Shia, but few were as adept at using pilgrimage to the city to advance their cause as Suleiman the Great or Shah Safi had been. Ali Reza Pasha, Ottoman governor of the Iraqi capital of Baghdad, tried to make use of a pilgrimage to demonstrate his political strength in 1841 but failed.[27] The city's authorities, aware of what Ali Pasha was trying to achieve, decided to welcome him but with certain conditions, insisting that he bring only a party of fifteen with him. Ali Pasha chose to cancel his pilgrimage to avoid being publicly humiliated by being forced to arrive with such a small entourage.[28] However, the Ottomans got their revenge, besieging and taking Karbala in January 1843, massacring over 5,000 Shia and installing a new governor, Najib Pasha. Many of the faithful left Karbala for Najaf, a spiritual brain drain which shifted the centre of Shia faith and learning to the more southern city.[29]

After something of a high in 1844–5, perhaps because of the appearance of a man claiming to be the physical manifestation of the hidden twelfth imam, the importance of Karbala declined rapidly. Towards the end of the First World War, large parts of the Ottoman empire came under British control, and in 1921 the kingdom of Iraq was created, ruled by the Sunni Hashemites under British suzerainty. Even so pilgrims to the city remained vital to its economy. When she wrote to her stepmother about her visit to Karbala in January 1918, the Englishwoman Gertrude Bell claimed it was Husayn's shrine that 'makes the fortune of Karbala'.[30]

A pilgrimage to Karbala undertaken with the aim of consolidating and validating authority did not guarantee political survival, as demonstrated by the fate of the final shah of neighbouring Iran, Muhammad Reza Shah (ruled 1941–79), whose reign ended in revolution.[31] Given that approximately 80 per cent of his subjects adhered to Shia Islam, he embarked on pilgrimages to Mecca, Karbala, Qom and Mashhad (the final two of these in Iran and specifically Shia pilgrimage destinations) and used religious symbolism to boost his credibility in the complex socio-political landscape of Iran. However, his policies and events during his reign suggested his attachment to Shia Islam was at best superficial. He also apparently believed that God had been guiding his actions since childhood.[32]

Consequently, though the genesis of the revolution that removed him from power was political and economic, it acquired distinctly religious undertones when symbols associated with Karbala and the martyrdom of Husayn were used by the rebels. The narrative of Husayn's defiance of authority and subsequent martyrdom chimed with the shah's opponents, who refused to recognise his claim to rule in Iran just as Husayn had refused to recognise Yazid's accession to the caliphate. Ayatollahs delivered sermons drawing parallels between the shah and Yazid, portraying both as tyrants, and crowds chanted, 'Everywhere is Karbala, and every day is Ashura.' The Shia Muslim form of pilgrimage and mourning, which takes place forty days after a funeral, was even repurposed as political demonstrations.[33]

In the 1980s, those who had died during the revolution were commemorated through murals in Tehran in which they were depicted like the martyrs of Karbala.[34] Iranian pilgrimages to Karbala were suffused with nationalist revolutionary fervour, with some pilgrims carrying photographs of the popular General Soleimani, commander of the Iranian Revolutionary Guards, to show how powerful Iran had been in 'securing the region' and safeguarding the interests of Shia Muslims.

Back over the border in Iraq, where Sunni Muslims are outnumbered approximately two to one by Shias, when Saddam Hussein (a Sunni, died 2006) first came to power in 1979, he had tried to cultivate an alliance with the influential ayatollahs of Karbala.[35] When these attempts proved futile, Saddam punished the Shia by banning the Arba'in pilgrimage altogether, and imposed restrictions on a range of Shia religious activities. He also enacted policies designed to deny foreign pilgrims access to visas in a bid to control religious practices and cripple the economies of Karbala and the other shrine cities. Like so many rulers before him, he also feared that pilgrimages served as a pretext for his opponents to come together and conspire against him.[36]

In the aftermath of Iraq's defeat in the First Gulf War (1991), a Shia uprising led to significant damage to Husayn's shrine, which was shelled by Saddam's forces. Despite reconstruction, Shia communities, their religious leaders and shrine officials endured oppression and persecution. Throughout the 1990s and early 2000s, the shrines remained a focal point for conflict, with pilgrim access increasingly difficult. Following the fall of Saddam Hussein, Shia pilgrims regained the freedom to go on pilgrimage to Karbala, with tens of millions making the pilgrimage each year in the early decades of the twenty-first century. But freedom did not mean safety, and during and in the aftermath of the Iraq War (2003–2011) the pilgrimage was perhaps more fraught with danger than ever, as the emerging fundamentalist Sunni Islamic State took over parts of Iraq.[37] Between 2004 and 2010 alone, ten bomb attacks specifically targeting pilgrims and the Karbala shrines claimed the lives of over five hundred people and injured many times that number.

Global Connections

Throughout all these trials, Karbala has retained its profound significance as a cornerstone of Shia identity, with pilgrimage serving as a mechanism for fostering community cohesion, sectarian allegiance and a shared sense of self. In Saddam's Iraq, Karbala played a pivotal role in enabling Shia Muslims to assert their own distinct identity against the oppression of a Sunni-majority government. Karbala's influence also extends beyond the borders of Iraq, serving as a unifying symbol connecting Shia populations in other countries like Bahrain, ruled by the Sunni al-Khalifa family since the eighteenth century, and Lucknow in India, which has emerged as a prominent centre of Shiism.[38]

For centuries, the pilgrimage to Karbala has linked India and Iraq. The burgeoning trade relationship between the two regions from the sixteenth century onwards facilitated the influx of a considerable number of pilgrims and their wealth into the city. Gifts also flowed in from the inhabitants and rulers of the north Indian state of Awadh (Oudh) in the eighteenth and nineteenth centuries, like the canopy of velvet and silver for Husayn's shrine, as well as money.[39] This income – known as the Indian money (*pul-e Hindi*) – was considerable and made Karbala financially reliant on India.[40] The Indian money was augmented by the Oudh Bequest in 1849, a payment established by the king of

Awadh to benefit the shrine cities of Karbala and Najaf, with the total of over six million rupees sent over a fifty-three-year period intended to support the shrine custodians in Karbala, students and the poor. Further gifts were used to bring a canal to Karbala, improve conditions for pilgrims and build a wall around the city in the wake of attacks by fundamentalist Sunni Wahhabis. Indian generosity has been a lifeline for the city in hard times.

In India the numbers of pilgrims prompted cities to set up facilities for them. In Karachi, for instance, the Bohra community established a 'reception hall' for pilgrims at their mosque shortly after 1880, providing comfortable accommodation. Mosques and travel agencies did the same in other Indian cities. Merchants also took an interest in supporting pilgrims. Guides like Musajī's 1923 *Rāhe Karbalā* show just how intertwined the relationships between mercantile interests and pilgrimage from India were. It included advertisements for various essentials, including incense and ghee, ensuring pilgrims procured their supplies locally before embarking on the journey abroad.[41]

Not everyone in Karbala was happy about the influx of Indians. One critic in 1932 complained that the numbers of pilgrims didn't help with building the local Shia community, but hindered it, exacerbating divisions and stirring up arguments. This was certainly true of the Twelver Khoja and Bohra pilgrims. The caste distinctions which divided these two groups in India were not overcome by their shared reverence for Karbala. Some Karbala clerics also saw the presence of these organised groups as a threat to their interpretation of Shia Islam and their influence over pilgrims to the city.[42]

Equally significant were the historical ties between Iraq and neighbouring Persia, which, in a reduced form, was renamed Iran in 1935. Under the Safavid dynasty (1501–1763), Sunni practices had been suppressed, forced conversion to Shia Islam took place, and pilgrimage to Karbala and Najaf took precedence over the hajj to Mecca.[43] Karbala had benefited immensely from its proximity to Shia-dominated Persia. The influx of Persian pilgrims brought so much wealth to Karbala that when the Ottoman sultan Murad IV (ruled 1623–40) wanted to take revenge on the Shia for an attack on Iraqi Sunnis in 1623, he refrained from targeting pilgrims because of the damage it would cause to the city's prosperity.[44] Pilgrims were given tax exemptions in the mid-eighteenth century, leaving them more to spend in Karbala. The connection with Persia also gave the Shia of Karbala considerable leverage with Iraq's rulers, not least because any threat to them could lead to a cessation in the pilgrimage trade, which would have damaging financial repercussions not just for Karbala and the other shrine cities, but for Baghdad itself.[45]

Across the centuries, Karbala has served as a unifying force for Shia Muslims, fostering a sense of community, identity and devotion. Pilgrimage to the city sustained Shia Muslims in the immediate wake of Husayn's martyrdom, and continues to do so, while facilitating international cultural exchange and trade, and driving the city's economy. To Shia Muslims across the world, Karbala is also a metaphor for suffering and resistance, a shorthand for oppression and martyrdom.

10

CHICHÉN ITZÁ

Mexico

Opposite the title page of Theodore Willard's *The City of the Sacred Well* (1926), his New York publishers included a frontispiece painting of a reputed historical event. It showed a Mayan man in priestly garb, his large feather headdress touching the top of the doorway in which he stood, one hand outstretched towards the large sinkhole to his left. Hundreds of people were arranged around its edge to witness two men, long-haired and clad only in the most minimal of coverings, carrying an unconscious young woman to its rim. The caption below read, 'A last forward swing and the bride of Yum Chac hurtles far out over the well.'[1] This misleading and colonialist view of Mayan practices very much set the tone for the rest of Willard's book, and for many popular (and scholarly) ideas about what pilgrims got up to at the giant sinkhole at the Mayan settlement of Chichén Itzá: the Cenote Sagrado, or Well of Sacrifice.

Willard's rather florid account was based on the excavations, research and theories of the archaeologist and Maya enthusiast Edward Herbert Thompson. In 1885, the twenty-eight-year-old Thompson moved to the Yucatán peninsula in Mexico to take up the position of American consul. The job had been secured for him by the American Antiquarian Society, and part of his brief was to conduct research into the Mayan ruins that dotted the landscape. His previous work on the lost city of Atlantis had attracted some attention, and members of the AAS, which is still based in Thompson's hometown of Worcester, Massachusetts, thought that he was just the man for the job. Over the following forty years, he lived and studied in the Yucatán, uncovering much of the history and archaeology of the Maya. He became particularly obsessed with the history of Chichén Itzá, including the Cenote Sagrado, a place of Mayan pilgrimage, which in 1894 led to his purchase of the hacienda built in the shadow of the ruins. The task of exploring and excavating the site would occupy him for several decades.[2] He referred to his exploration of the Cenote Sagrado as 'the crowning event of my life's work'.[3]

In 1923, Thompson sat down for an interview with the journalist Alma Reed, offering her 'an exclusive story on "the greatest archaeological adventure of the New World"'.[4] He told Reed about his discoveries in the cenote, and specifically about the recovery of human remains that he believed were the result of human sacrifice. Reed reported in the pages of *El Palacio* that 'prisoners of war and virgins of flawless loveliness were sacrificed at the cenote. From early childhood, the maidens had been cared for with physical perfection as a goal. Their spiritual training had martyrdom for the public good as its ideal.'[5] Thompson had his own theories as to why and how these girls had been sacrificed, telling Reed that they were 'drowned in a mystical wedding ceremony that united them to the deity they wished to appease'.[6] The image of young virgins thrown into the well by a pre-Columbian society was a very potent one, and it was regularly repeated. Fourteen years earlier, Channing Arnold and Frederick J. Tabor Frost, having been shown bones from the well by Thompson and told of their age and sex, had been convinced by their fellow American's arguments. 'From these facts alone only one deduction is possible,' they wrote, 'namely that sacrifices in the cenote did occur, and that such sacrifices were of young girls who were hurled by the priests into the chasm, possibly after defilement by the high priests in the small building at the pool's edge.'[7]

Such theories say far more about the men (it was always men) who conceived them than historical reality. For one thing, how did they know that these were the skeletal remains of virgins, let alone ones of 'flawless loveliness'?

About 120 miles west of the modern Mexican city of Cancun, Chichén Itzá was once the capital of the Maya in the Yucatán. Today all that remains are the ruins of vast temples, courtyards and other buildings, probably built over the period 550 to 1250. The settlement – there is some dispute about whether it can be called a city – had several sacred centres and two giant sinkholes filled with water and called cenotes, one of which was a place of pilgrimage. This was the Cenote Sagrado, a place so important that it gave the neighbouring settlement its whole identity: Chichén Itzá translates as 'mouth of the well of the Itzá' or 'at the edge of the well of the Itzá'.[8] The cenote itself is sixty metres wide, and looking down from its edge the surface of the water in the well is twenty metres below. The water itself is over thirteen metres deep.

While for the Maya the pilgrimage island of Cozumel was the place to go for assistance with pregnancy and divination, and the Maya went to Izamal for cures, Chichén Itzá was the pilgrimage destination of choice if pilgrims wanted to appease the gods of weather. According to Bishop Diego de Landa, Spanish inquisitor of the Yucatán in the 1550s and 1560s, Cozumel and the cenote at Chichén Itzá were held 'in the same veneration as we have for the pilgrimages of Jerusalem and Rome'.[9] For Sylvanus Morley, a Carnegie Institution archaeologist, it was 'an

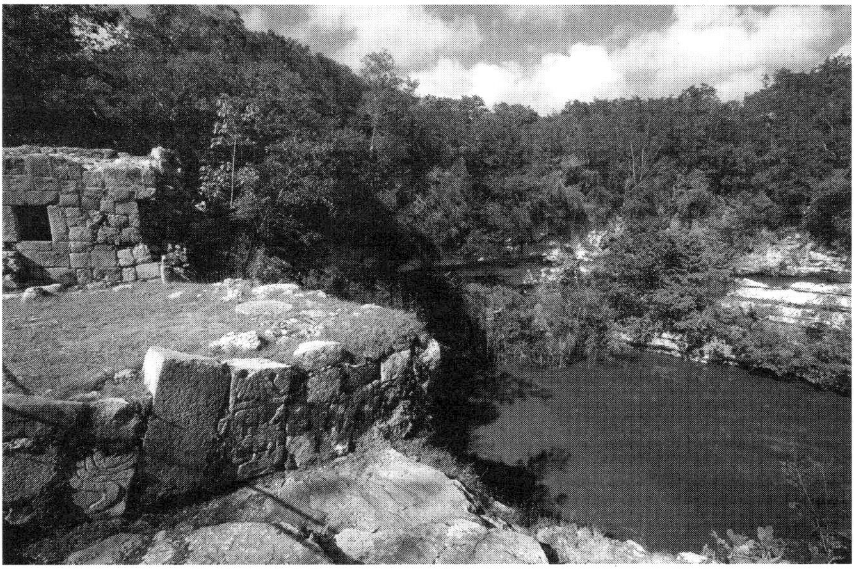

The limestone of Mexico's Yucatán peninsula creates sinkholes across the terrain. The one at Chichén Itzá became a pilgrimage site, perhaps used to appeal for rain in a landscape without rivers.

ancient American Mecca' which in the thirteenth and fourteenth centuries was the 'holiest city in the New Empire, and what is more, the Mecca of the Maya World'.[10]

The Maya and the Cenote Sagrado

The Maya of pre-conquest Mexico lived in the Yucatán from the mid-third century CE until 1697, when their last independent city, Nojpetan, built on an island in the middle of a lake, was seized by the Spanish. Chichén Itzá itself had been conquered far earlier, in the mid-sixteenth century, when the conquistador Francisco de Montejo seized it as a capital for his conquered lands in the Yucatán peninsula. Between the eighth and the turn of the thirteenth centuries, Chichén Itzá was one of the biggest

Maya settlements in the area, though its fortunes fluctuated dramatically. At first, it was a bustling trading hub and the home of priests, boasting several shrines which they served. Then for some reason it suddenly fell on hard times, and declined to the point where the settlement was all but abandoned. It may well have been almost empty in the thirteenth century when pilgrims passed through on their way to the cenote. New life was breathed into it by the arrival of the Itzá people, who reinvigorated the northern parts of the settlement,[11] but in the 1400s, it declined once more and never recovered, not least because of the arrival of the Spanish in the sixteenth century.

The one constant was Chichén Itzá's religious importance as the location of the cenote. The Maya had moved their main settlement to Mayapan, south of Merida, but despite this, the pilgrims kept coming. Venerating a sinkhole shows how rooted the faith of the Maya was in the landscapes of Yucatán. The peninsula juts north into the Gulf of Mexico and is devoid of major water sources. However, rainwater passing down through fissures in its water-soluble limestone has created sinkholes and underground streams. Given that pilgrimage to water sources of all kinds features in many world religions, it is no surprise that a particularly massive sinkhole took on a sacred identity and drew pilgrims from across what is now Mexico. Water itself was central to Mayan cosmology, a link to the underworld and a reflection of the past, present and future.[12] In cenotes it was also symbolic of the water left over from the time of creation, when land emerged from the original water that covered the world, and the sky was created.[13]

Chichén Itzá reached the peak of its influence in about 950, in the period between *c.*800 and *c.*1000 when the largest droughts in world history took place. At this time some of the city's largest buildings were constructed, and its rulers extended their control over the northern Maya lowlands.[14] This coincided with a time when the southern Maya powers were on the wane, so Chichén Itzá's rulers could capitalise both on their decline and the fact that they controlled a large source of sacred water.

Theories about cenote worship abound. One is based on the belief that a crocodile came out of the water to receive sacrifices, suggesting the site was a place for the worship of Itzamná, a Mayan creation god.[15] Another is that people went on pilgrimage to ask for a good harvest, or to seek health and longevity. The discovery of the remains of a rattle in the bottom of the Cenote Sagrado suggested to Thompson (and a Professor Saville) an offering to the god Xipe Totec, lord of the coastland and patron of goldsmiths, who is sometimes depicted wearing a flayed human skin and carrying a staff mounted with a rattle.[16] Chichén Itzá may also have been recognised as an international centre for the worship of the Aztec god Quetzalcoatl (Kukulkan, in Maya), the feathered serpent deity. The range of offerings found in the well suggests that several deities were revered there, but there was a substantial amount of jade (associated with Quetzalcoatl) in the form of plaques and beads.[17] Worship of Quetzalcoatl spread across the region with pilgrims and other kinds of travellers, and Chichén Itzá was an important centre for the expansion of the cult from the third to the tenth centuries. In artistic representations on the site's ruins, he often appears as a plumed rattlesnake, a creature associated with wind and rain.[18]

It seems highly likely that some pilgrimages to the cenote were part of political rituals. For the Maya, Chichén Itzá itself was just one *tollan* of several in the world, places where the landscape was linked to ancestry and political power. These were where leaders were invested with power and authority, which made the sites politically as well as religiously important, with those who had authority over them able to portray themselves as having dominion over life and death. This is just one interpretation for the construction of a large causeway several hundred metres long running north from the Great Temple of Kukulkan (now known as El Castillo), Chichén Itzá's patron deity, to the edge of the cenote, as it suggests some sort of ceremonial purpose, though as we'll see it may have had a considerably darker function.

Despite some dramatic stories – such as the assassination of Napot Xiu, a rain-seeking priest, and over thirty members of his family in 1536, en route to the cenote on a pilgrimage they hoped would bring an end to a lengthy drought – it seems that pilgrims travelled some distance to Chichén Itzá and the Cenote Sagrado via a well-organised network that provided for their needs. Just as on the way to other pilgrimage sites around the world, pilgrims needed to be housed and fed as they travelled. William Ringle and others have suggested that this hospitality worked as a 'dispersal mechanism' for the cult of Quetzalcoatl/Kukulkan, who had a temple dedicated to him at Chichén Itzá. This was the original centre of his cult, but the fact that it spread to places like Belize and Guatemala suggests that people would have wanted to visit his first temple.[19] That could have prompted the growth of places like Xuenkal, a settlement around thirty miles north of Chichén Itzá.[20] We also know that pilgrims travelled the Maya's *sacbe* or white roads, elevated highways that lifted them above the surrounding terrain of swamp or forest, taking them from one important settlement to the next. These were sacred roads, protected by divine power and thus theoretically safe for pilgrims.[21]

Pilgrimages of Sacrifice

Human sacrifice was one of the main reasons to come on pilgrimage to the cenote at Chichén Itzá, no matter which deity a pilgrim was appealing to or what remedy they sought. Edward Thompson was right about that.

Diego de Landa, a Spanish Franciscan friar, arrived in the New World in 1549 and began a campaign against the religion of the Maya, attacking their beliefs and smashing their icons. Stories of missionaries and conquerors are replete with tales of brutality, but de Landa was a cut above in terms of cruelty. He conducted an auto-da-fé, a public punishment of heretics, in 1562, as a result of which he was able to collect almost 150 testimonies of human sacrifice in Yucatán, many of which had allegedly taken place inside Christian churches. He was summoned back to Spain and tried for overstepping his authority, but unfortunately the charges did not stick. In 1573, de Lana sailed back to Mexico as the new bishop of Yucatán, his behaviour having earned him promotion rather than punishment.

Because de Landa burned the texts he found that described Maya society and religion, our main source for what was happening at Cenote Sagrado comes from the pen of the man himself. Drawing on the 'evidence' he had extracted under torture he wrote *An Account of Things of the Yucatán* (*Relación de las cosas de Yucatán*) in about 1566, in which he claimed one child had been sacrificed and thrown into the well, while another was supposedly put into the water alive on the orders of Nachi Cocum of Sotuta in the expectation that he would return with a message from the oracle. He presumably drowned, as the man left to await his message was forced to return to his chief empty-handed.[22] In one version of this sacrificial ritual recounted by de Landa,

Lords and dignitaries of all the provinces of Valladolid [in

> Yucatán] practised the custom (after fasting for sixty days without laying eyes on their women, not even to those who brought them food); and they did this so that arriving to the mouth of that zenote [*sic*], they would at dawn throw in several Indians owned by each of the Lords who were told to plead for all the good things they might desire, as they were thrown in the waters. These Indians were not tied but were thrown in from the heights, making a big splash. Around noon they would begin to shout and a rope was lowered to bring them out half dead. Large fires were built around them and they were purified with copal [a sort of incense]. Coming back into their wits they said that inside the cave there were many of their nation, both men and women, who gathered it, and no sooner they lifted their heads to see these people, they received knocks about the ears so they were obliged to keep their heads down in the water, which was filled with many chambers and pits; and they would answer their questions about whether there would be a good year or bad, in accordance with the question asked by the Indian, and whether the devil was angry at any of the Lords who had thrown them in, knowing that if the Indian did not plead to be pulled out by noon, this would mean the devil was displeased with the Lord, and this Indian would never come out … then, seeing that he did not emerge, all of them including that Lord and his men would throw great stones into the water and run away shouting in fear.[23]

Of course, de Landa's account was hardly impartial, and the evidence collected in the trials he instigated was probably heavily embellished, or else the Mayans he questioned were just telling him what they thought he wanted to hear. He did though record what he saw at Chichén Itzá, including a now-lost structure on the lip of the cenote where he found 'idols made in honor of all the principal edifices of the country, almost like the Pantheon at Rome'.[24] This building may well be the one depicted in the frontispiece of Willard's book.

However, archaeological evidence recovered since the time of Edward Thompson onwards is testament to the large number of people who actually did end up in the Cenote Sagrado. Overall, of the remains found, roughly 60 per cent were male, while about 70 per cent were from children aged between seven and fifteen.[25] Aside from showing us the age and gender of the victims, analysis has also shown that, just like the objects left as offerings, these people came from all over Mexico and further afield.[26] Assuming it is evidence of human sacrifice, this is horrific, but for the Maya, their children may have been the most precious offerings they could make, and they may have believed that their youth meant the children were closer to the gods and their own Mayan ancestors. Whether these unfortunates were sacrificed elsewhere (such as in the temples of Chichén Itzá, where images of dismemberment and heart removal decorate the walls) and then brought to the cenote, or dispatched at the edge of the well (a knife, recovered in three parts from the bed of the cenote, might suggest this) will probably never be known.[27]

Pilgrimage Offerings

Human sacrificial victims unsurprisingly dominate the stories of pilgrimage and offerings at the Cenote Sagrado, but most pilgrims probably offered less gruesome things, from the ornate and valuable to the everyday and mundane. Thompson's excavations, as well as those conducted later by Mexico's National Institute of Anthropology and History, recovered all kinds of

Items like these ceramic faces were thrown into the well as offerings by pilgrims. The origins of such objects suggest that pilgrims travelled some distance from other parts of Central America.

objects from the bottom of the sinkhole: offerings made of silver and gold, copper, carved jade and obsidian, as well as ceramic items and incense from the *pom* tree. Animal remains, pieces of fabric and wooden objects had all been preserved in the thick silt at the bottom of the sinkhole.[28] Subsequent recovery efforts have found rings and bells, rubber and rock crystal, mother of pearl and onyx, five jaguars carved from stone and several wooden buckets.[29] The latter were presumably lost by people trying to collect water from the cenote.

Some of the most famous high-status offerings are gold discs, hammered thin and decorated with symbolic scenes. These discs were broken into pieces, crumpled up or burned before being thrown into the water. One shows a victim of heart sacrifice, while another more detailed survival portrays a naval battle presided over by a winged deity.[30] Such a wide variety of objects suggests offerings were made over many hundred years, during different historical periods, but they are hard to date. Jade and gold may have been offered early on, when Chichén Itzá was still populated by the Mayan elite, copper bells and wooden objects later, after they left.[31]

Of the hammered gold discs may have been put into the water by a pilgrim seeking favour during conflict with an enemy, or it could have been a thank-offering for surviving a battle.[32] Another disc is decorated with a scene of victory – images of the heart of a vanquished warrior, as well as breast shields and a votive *atlati*, designed to launch a spear twice its usual distance, all suggesting some sort of link between warfare and going on pilgrimage to the cenote, either to ask for protection or to thank a god for victory.[33]

The offerings also show that pilgrims came from a reasonably wide geographical area: Chiapas, Guatemala and Tabasco. Metal objects found in the well have been traced back to Guerrero and Oaxaca on the Pacific coast of Mexico, Honduras, Coclé and Veraguas (both in Panama) and Colombia.[34] A plaque found in the well depicts a ruler holding a cacao tree and standing by a column covered in circular hieroglyphs, showing it came from Pacific Guatemala, the only place where these were used. The Guatemalans also used cacao as a tribute offering across ancient Meso-America. Many small bells made from gold were also recovered, possibly from Panama or Costa Rica, though gold bells made in Veraguas were in particularly high demand and a lot of the gold in the well came from this area. Other items made of Pachuca obsidian and plumbate suggest trade across the Gulf of Mexico.[35] Jade was a precious and valued stone, unknown in Europe until the conquest of the New World, and it is not surprising that it was used for carved offerings. There was a rich source in southern Mexico. It had symbolic meaning too, and that could explain some of the pilgrim offerings.

Conquered Chichén Itzá

The last recorded pilgrimage to the Cenote Sagrado was that of the doomed rain-seeker in 1536, although some maintain that pilgrimages to the cenote continued until the time of the Caste War, a Maya revolt against the dominant Hispanic population that encompassed the whole of the second half of the nineteenth century and the first fifteen years of the twentieth.[36] If they did, there is no evidence of this at Chichén Itzá. The visit of American explorer John Lloyd Stephens in 1842 found a place that appeared long disused. 'A mysterious influence seemed to pervade it,' he wrote, 'in unison with the historical account that the well of Chichén was a place of pilgrimage, and that human victims were thrown into it in sacrifice.'[37] Stephens' journey marked the rediscovery of Mayan civilisation, which just over forty years later led to the arrival of Edward Thompson in Yucatán.

More recently, Chichén Itzá has become a pilgrimage site once more. Pilgrims come not to visit the cenote but to witness the play of the sun on the ruined city's central pyramid, El Castillo, during the spring and autumn equinoxes. As the equinox sun sets, the light and shadow create the impression of a snake undulating down the steps of the pyramid, a snake that supposedly marks the descent of the deity Kukulcan to earth. First noticed in the 1920s as the building was undergoing restoration, it isn't known if the phenomenon was intended by its original builders or is a happy accident. Either way, the pattern of moving light is now interpreted by some as a sign of the sacred.

It's considered so special that the vernal equinox, which marks the beginning of spring, was declared a state holiday in Yucatán in 1976.[38]

Pilgrimage to Chichén Itzá gained yet another dimension in 2012, when people converged on the site from South America, Europe and Asia believing that year would see the end of the world.[39] Others came convinced that aliens would land, that they would witness the dawn of a new age, or that Chichén Itzá had been built at the intersection of ley lines and that a 'vortex' would emerge. None of the pilgrims seemed particularly alarmed at the prospect of these things occurring, least of all the possibility that their own destruction was imminent. One Indian pilgrim laughingly told a curious reporter, 'At least we can die saying we've seen the end of the world.'[40]

11

MUXIMA

Angola

In the south-western African country of Angola, local legend tells the story of a group of Portuguese sailors, led by the navigator and explorer Diogo Cão, who at some point in 1491 discovered a statue of the Virgin Mary on the banks of the River Kwanza in what was then the kingdom of Kongo. Convinced that this was a divine sign, the sailors took the statue to the nearby village of Muxima, where a chapel was built to house it. As the statue was believed to have miraculous origins, it wasn't long before pilgrims started to visit the shrine of Our Lady of Muxima. These included both Portuguese Catholic colonists and indigenous Africans converted to Christianity by their new rulers.

Diogo Cão did explore the kingdom of Kongo, and the part of it that became Angola, but as he may have been dead by 1486, him finding a miraculous statue five years later would have been, well, miraculous. The date may have been chosen because it was the year that King Nizinga (ruled 1470–1509), ruler of Kongo, converted to Christianity. He was said to have 'immersed the country in Catholicism'.[1] Where the statue of Our Lady venerated in Muxima came from is not recorded. Still, it is certainly the case that just over a century later a church was built in Muxima by the Portuguese in honour of Our Lady of the Immaculate

Conception, who locally became known affectionately as Mama Muxima. At that point a statue or image of her was installed inside the shrine. Since then, the comparatively small, plain white church overlooking a bend in the Kwanza has become Angola's most visited pilgrimage site. Muxima is celebrated in poems and novels, and one of the country's most famous songs, popularised by N'Gola Ritmos, tells of lighting candles in Muxima in the hope of bringing peace and prosperity'.[2]

Colonialism and Pilgrimage

The Portuguese settlement at Muxima was established in 1595 when a fort and prison were built on the river. Twenty years before, the Portuguese had started to expand into the area from their base in the coastal settlement of Luanda. The Jesuits, an order of Catholic priests noted for their teaching and missionary work, were part of that expansion, evangelising the local population. At that time, the area around Muxima was ruled by a Quissama chief, Muxima Quitangombe, who welcomed the Portuguese because they and the Quissama had a common enemy in the N'Gola kingdom. A church was built in Muxima to provide for the spiritual needs of the garrison of the fort, and as a centre for the Jesuits' missionary activities.[3]

In seventeenth-century Angola, and indeed in the eighteenth and nineteenth centuries, the Catholic Church was used by the Portuguese as an important means of colonisation and control. As the Portuguese empire grew, many churches dedicated to the Virgin Mary were built in the conquered areas. Some of them, like the Jesuit church of Nossa Senhora da Assunção (Our Lady of the Assumption) in Ambaca became places of pilgrimage, but on nowhere near the same scale as Muxima. Being open to worshippers, the church was quite a departure from the

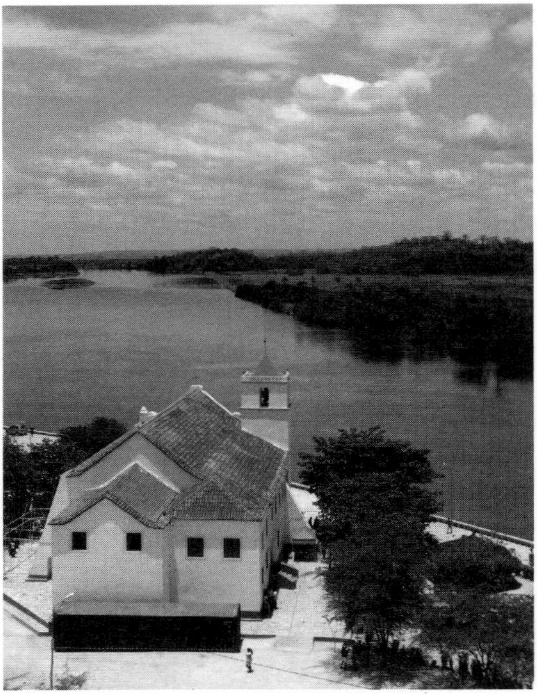

Overlooking a bend on the River Kwanza, the simple white church at Muxima is the most important pilgrimage destination in Angola. Despite its origins as a Portuguese foundation where enslaved people were forcibly converted, it is revered by Catholic Angolans.

traditional architecture of the area, where settlements, meeting places and houses were typically protected by high walls.[4] And the message of Catholicism and Our Lady of Muxima was taken beyond the town. When the area was suffering from a drought in the summer of 1641, the image was dispatched to the Casa de Misericórdia, a Portuguese charitable foundation in Luanda, to provide spiritual succour and hopefully generate some rain. By the end of the century, miracles of Our Lady of Muxima were already being reported.

In those early decades, Portuguese expansion into Angola

did not go unchallenged. In 1640 the Dutch took control of Luanda, and allied with Queen Ndongo and the kingdom of Kongo. Seeking aid wherever they could, the Portuguese looked to their faith. In early 1643, Governor Pedro César de Meneses set out on a campaign against the Dutch accompanied by the statue of Our Lady of Muxima. Unfortunately the Virgin failed to prevent the Calvinist Dutch attacking the Portuguese encampment, and their Congolese allies carrying the image away to Mbanza Congo.[5]

The statue was soon either recaptured, returned or replaced, as three years later, in 1643, the Virgin was apparently once more the protectress of Muxima, although further trials soon followed. Following the destruction of most of the town by Dutch forces in 1646, the Portuguese besieged in the fort at Muxima constructed a rough wooden chapel in the centre of the fortress and placed the statue, rescued from the church, on its altar.[6] It was '8 palms in height, with a very right crown on her head, dressed in cloth of gold'. During the siege, the roof of this rudimentary building caught fire and its walls were hit by 'four salvos of artillery' and riddled with holes. Yet the statue was untouched. 'When the besieged people saw the miracle,' wrote the Capuchin missionary Giovanni Cavazzi, 'they raised their voices giving infinite thanks to her who had liberated them, and [made] vows to her.' And when the enemy tried to use the church at the bottom of the hill as cover for their assaults, the Virgin drove them out. Cavazzi concluded, 'the mother of mercy did not allow her House to become a shelter for the enemies of our Holy Religion to the offence of her devoted followers'.[7]

Centuries later, the story of the country's conquest by Christians and the importance of Muxima were promoted in the colony's capital. Inside the fort in Luanda a number of panels of blue and white tiles were installed at the end of the nineteenth century, with one panel depicting a map of southern Angola flanked by historical scenes. To the left, the tiles showed the funeral of Queen Njinga (died 1663), the famed ruler of the Matamba kingdom in northern Angola, who fought against the Portuguese but converted to Christianity in 1623. Her funeral procession, led by Capuchin friars and members of the Brotherhood of the Rosary, 'bore greater resemblance to that of a Christian monarch than of an Mbundu/Imbangala leader'.[8] On the other side of the map were tiles depicting the church at Muxima, shown as it would have looked to someone travelling on the river. The panel combined images of one of the country's most famous indigenous leaders and a picture of its premier Christian shrine, testimony that faith and place were an intrinsic part of the history of Angola.

The Slave Trade

Muxima was one of a string of Portuguese forts, *presídios*, built along the Kwanza River as it flowed west, reaching the Atlantic Ocean just south of the Angolan capital of Luanda; the others were at Massangano (*c.*1580) and Cambabe (1609) further upriver. These were built to collect tributes from the Africans in the form of commodities and enslaved people which the Portuguese could then trade overseas.[9] As the supply of people in the area immediately around Luanda began to dry up, the slavers moved further into the heart of the country. In the early seventeenth century the colonialists worked with Imbangala, African warriors who captured people on their behalf, a tactic that resulted in a dramatic increase in the numbers captured in the Kwanza basin and traded through Luanda primarily to Brazil, where they were put to work on sugar plantations.[10]

Sourcing people to enslave from the interior meant more time spent searching and more captives dying before they even reached the ships heading across the Atlantic. Even so, by the middle of the seventeenth century, Luanda had outstripped the ports of the Congo in the numbers of enslaved people being exported to the Americas.[11] As much as 40 per cent of the New World's ten million enslaved people originated in the Congo and Angola, so the traffic of people along the river to the coast was substantial and lucrative.[12] In the late eighteenth century, the captain of the ports along the Kwanza was Álvaro de Carvalho Mattoso (died 1798), a notorious slave trader who seems to have inherited the business from his father, who headed the forts before him. Mattoso's former home in Luanda is now fittingly Angola's National Museum of Slavery.

Priests played a large role in Angola's slavery business, including owning and selling enslaved people. At Muxima, Francisco Travassos Valdez witnessed 'a neat little church of freestone ... to which [was] attached a number of slaves, for the immediate service of the church'.[13] Priests also engaged in the forced conversion of the enslaved, infamously one of the primary roles of the church at Muxima.[14] Other churches along the trafficking routes were put to the same use. Some priests did not believe that there was any point in trying to convert the Africans, but the Portuguese authorities thought it useful so persuasion was backed up by military force. A decade before Muxima was established, Father Garcia Simões dispatched a letter on this topic to the Jesuit provincial: 'Almost all have verified that the conversion of these barbarians will not be achieved through love, unless they have first been made subjects and vassals of the King Our Lord through arms.'[15] Travelling in western Africa at the turn of the twentieth century, Mary Kingsley declared that African professions of faith were about convenience, claiming they would 'superficially adopt the religious ideas of alien people with whom they have commercial intercourse'.[16]

Conversion to Catholicism was often less than total; it wasn't unknown for reverence for Mama Muxima to combine with traditional African beliefs. In a scene from the comedic novel *The World of 'Mestre' Tamoda* by the Angolan nationalist Uanhenga Xitu (1924–2014) one character declares, 'I'm going to bury a red cockerel alive and you'll die! If you escape that, I'll go to Saint Anna's Church, or Our Lady of Muxima, because you've no right to ruin other people's lives.'[17] Before the Portuguese arrived, the area around Muxima was largely monotheistic, and it was not a huge leap for the local people to identify their abstract deity, Nzambi, with the Christian god. And Nzambi was a broad enough concept to include other spirits in the form of saints and holy figures.[18] Likewise, the Bakongo, one of the country's largest linguistic groups, practised a traditional religion based around the spirits of their ancestors and were able to integrate the variety of figures found in Catholicism quite easily into their beliefs.

Mixing beliefs could, however, lead to trouble. In 1715 Vincente de Morais, a mixed-race soldier at Muxima in the service of the Portuguese, was investigated by the Inquisition when he was found in possession of a 'Mandingo charm'. He was accused of making a talisman that combined a piece of stone stolen from the church's altar and a prayer card with non-Christian charms, and of misusing Christian prayers. He told his questioners that the charm bundle protected him during encounters with his enemies, by which he largely meant people within the fort itself. Condemned for unorthodox practices, he was sent to Portugal and sentenced to hard labour. De Morais' story was not an extraordinary one. Many soldiers serving in the fort at Muxima, as well as across Angola and in Portugal itself, mixed charms with Christian practices; indeed de Morais claimed he had been given the charm bundle by someone he served with at Muxima called António Dias, and that all the men in the fort wore similar bundles.[19]

In 1836, slavery was prohibited across the Portuguese empire by Queen Maria II. The Catholic Church, however, remained central to Portuguese colonial control, and Muxima was one of the most important of all their possessions. Reporting on a visit to the Angolan interior in the summer months of 1846, Manoel Alves de Castro Francina, a member of the Creole *angolense* elite and government official, warned that the church at Muxima needed to be maintained. '[W]e cannot by any means afford to lose it, not only because it is a Christian temple of worship, but also because the pagans have a great faith in the miracles of Our Lady of the Conception of Muxima ... It is one of the main factors, perhaps the only one, keeping them at bay, and these hinders will disappear if the church is allowed to fall into ruin.'[20]

Just a few years later, the Catholic Church became the established church of Angola and the Portuguese state now expected its priests to make a 'missionary contribution to the colonial task'.[21] There were two main reasons for this: the first the arrival of Protestant missionaries in Africa, which threatened Catholic Portugal's influence;[22] the second that Portuguese rule was not that secure, with the interior of the country largely beyond their control. Using religious networks and the reputation of places like Muxima was a logical way to consolidate and expand their power.

Nineteenth Century

Despite the close association of the Church of Our Lady of Muxima with slavery, and of faith with colonialism, both settlers and indigenous Angolans alike went on pilgrimages to ask Mama Muxima for help in the 1870s, with the church prospering from the offerings they made. Two decades earlier, the British mining engineer Joachim John Monteiro arrived in the village and described the church as 'held in the greatest veneration by the natives far and wide ... and even the natives from Luanda seek there the intercession of the Virgin Mary as represented by an image in that church; and I was shown a chest full of plate, chains, rings, and other offerings of the pious pilgrims to its shrine'.[23] But Monteiro found the village itself a 'dead-alive place'; the settlement had at most five hundred houses, and by the end of the century Muxima was 'almost in ruins' due to a decline in trade,[24] with pilgrimage the only thing that kept the town going.

Pilgrims were coming in increasing numbers. This was the case across most of the Catholic world, as large-scale pilgrimages were on the rise after 1850, especially to destinations associated with the Virgin Mary. At Muxima mass pilgrimages were held on 31 August and 1 September each year, and the shrine was becoming famous throughout Angola, so much so that descriptions of pilgrims flocking to Muxima in the late nineteenth century found their way into António de Assis Júnior's 1934 novel *O Segredo da Morta* (*The Secret of the Dead Woman*).[25]

In 1889 the widely travelled editor and writer Mabel Loomis Todd was able to report that the church at Muxima 'preserved still some jewels and furniture presented by devout Europeans as well as natives'.[26] By then the building was lavishly decorated and possessed a silver incense boat, crafted in Brazil in the first half of the eighteenth century, and a statue of St Anthony holding a sword, again from Brazil.[27] That enslaved people had been sent out to Brazil and gifts returned from there to the church might well suggest that the pilgrimage shrine had benefited from the proceeds of slavery. In 1907 the incense boat was taken to Portugal as a souvenir by a Portuguese prince, and at some point many of the riches were removed, their lack obvious when a 'Registration of Cultural Goods' was drawn up in 1913, but apart from the boat, it wasn't clear where the 'rich objects of worship' from Muxima's church had gone.[28] St Anthony was an interesting choice for a church in northern Angola. At the end of the seventeenth century a Bakongo prophetess called Dona Beatriz Kimpa Vita claimed that the saint possessed her and spearheaded a movement to end the civil war in the kingdom of Kongo and reclaim the territories of the kingdom lost to the Europeans including northern Angola.[29] She was burned for heresy.

In the first years of the twentieth century an epidemic of trypanosomiasis (sleeping sickness) struck the area around Muxima. It first appeared among plantation workers in the mid-1890s, and by the beginning of the following century entire families were being wiped out. European traders abandoned Muxima as there were too few people to sustain their businesses.[30] The replacement of the Portuguese monarchy by a republic in 1910 was a setback for the Catholic Church and probably had a knock-on effect on pilgrimage to Muxima, but the republic's replacement by the authoritarian, conservative and pro-Catholic regime of António de Oliveira Salazar in the 1930s resulted in increased conversions to Catholicism in Angola, and in the following decade an agreement with the Holy See gave the Catholic Church responsibility for school education.[31] This ensured that future generations were educated in the benefits of pilgrimage to Muxima.

Over the course of the twentieth century, facilitated by rising literacy levels in Angola, more and more of the faithful would write to Mama Muxima to ask for her help. Hundreds of thousands of letters arrived at the sanctuary. These appeals were, in the words of the local priest, Father Honório, 'written in unrefined Portuguese' and reflect the fears of their writers about their health, love lives and work.[32] Sending a letter was a safer way of appealing to the Virgin than risking the journey in person, especially during the dangerous years of the war of independence from Portugal (1961–74) and the civil war of 1975–2002. Things have since improved, and numbers of pilgrims have grown year on year, helped by the construction of a paved road and a bridge, which have cut the journey from Luanda from one day to one hour.

Not everyone in Angola reveres Mama Muxima. In the middle of mass one Sunday in October 2013, five men and one woman from the Prophetic Church of Judaic Bethlehem's Ark burst into the church at Muxima. Armed with stones and sticks, they attacked the statue of Mama Muxima. The congregation rushed to defend it, wrestling the attackers to the floor. The motive of the attackers was their belief that the statue was a symbol of 'witchcraft-fuelled idolatry'.[33] The statue sustained only limited damage, but other items were wrecked. The local archbishop deplored the 'moral damage' to the hearts of the faithful caused by the attack.[34]

For a site so intimately linked to colonial rule, it is interesting to see how Muxima has become central to modern Angolan politics. When President José Eduardo dos Santos was celebrating his fifty-sixth birthday in 1998, the week of festivities included a pilgrimage to view some restoration work taking place at the shrine of Our Lady of Muxima. This was the 'climax' of this corrupt ruler's 'presidential personality cult'.[35] Then, in the run-up to elections in 2006, in response to a mass Pentecostal event at a stadium, Catholics staged a pilgrimage to Muxima.

They were concerned that they were losing ground to the evangelical churches, which had been growing since at least the early 1990s. The response was massive, as wealthy politicians flew in by helicopter, and others took to the road in luxury cars or came by bus.[36]

Religious divisions in Angola have long reflected political loyalties. Both before and after independence, the Catholic Church was seen as an agent of the Portuguese colonisers, while the Protestant churches tended to attract their opponents. Attempts have been made, however, to unify people across the country and smooth tensions using Muxima as a rallying point. During the national pilgrimage of 2008, the seventh held since the end of the civil war, organisers took as their theme '*Boa governação dentro e fora da igreja*' (Good government inside and outside the church). Pilgrims travelled for days along Angola's mud tracks to pray for the government and people of the country to work for the common good. In 2017, the date of the pilgrimage to Muxima was even brought forward by a few weeks so that people could complete it before going off to vote in the general election.[37] From being symbols of colonial rule and the slave trade, Muxima and its pilgrimages to honour the Virgin Mary have become integral to broader Angolan society.

12

BEAR BUTTE

South Dakota, USA

At some point in the decades on either side of 1900, the Oglala Lakota historian and artist Amos Bad Heart Bull (died 1913) sat down to sketch a map of the Black Hills in South Dakota. Just off-centre on the page, he drew the lumps and bumps of the hills, shaded them in and put a yellow oval outline around the whole thing. This was labelled 'Ki Inyanka Ocanku' (The Racetrack), site of the celestial race which had formed the Black Hills. The rest of the page was free of notable features – there were some lines denoting watercourses and a few words here and there identifying rivers or settlements – except one spot just to the north-east of the hills where Amos Bad Heart Bull drew the head of a bear staring out from the page.[1] A second map, drawn on a piece of packing paper in the 1940s by a Lakota artist named Dragonfly also showed the Black Hills surrounded by a racetrack (this time with creatures described in its associated legend) and a hill in the form of a brown sleeping bear.[2] This was Mato Paha, Bear Butte, one of the four pillars around the Black Hills that hold the earth and sky together, and one of the most important pilgrimage destinations for the Cheyenne and Lakota of North America.[3]

For thousands of years, pilgrim access to Bear Butte for prayer and religious rituals was unimpeded, but the arrival of white colonisers in the nineteenth century marked the beginning of more than a century of struggle over the site, as the hill itself, and access to it, became subject to legal and physical barriers. The story of Bear Butte mirrors that of Native American religion in the United States, where the First Amendment was supposed to guarantee religious freedom but paid only lip service to the right of people to worship in their own way, while pilgrimage to the site reflects the changing fortunes of the Native Americans who revere the hill.

A Sacred Landscape

Bear Butte, a large isolated hill lying just north-east of Dakota's Black Hills, is a bulge in the terrain formed by molten rock forcing its way up through the earth's crust. The Lakota claim that their historical association with the area stretches back eleven thousand years, though their regional hegemony is a relatively recent phenomenon,[4] and in the oral history of the Oglala Lakota the Butte is known as the Groaning Bear, perhaps dating from when it was still a laccolith, a mass of molten rock emitting noises.[5] The shape of the hill, when viewed from the right direction, also resembles a sleeping bear, which accounts for its name.

Bear Butte is sacred to many Native American nations from what is now the United States and from Canada, including the Arapaho, Kiowa, Mandan and Arikara, though it is most significant to the Lakota and Cheyenne.[6] Several tribes received their most sacred objects on the mountain: the Arapaho their seven sacred bundles or Medicine Bags, and the Kiowa the Bear Kidney, a religious object associated with the Sun Dance.[7] For the Mandan, it is akin to Mount Ararat, where Noah's Ark came to rest after the biblical Flood; Bear Butte was where the Great

Said to resemble a sleeping bear, the hill of Bear Butte dominates the area east of South Dakota's Black Hills. Since the nineteenth century access for Native American pilgrims has been threatened by legal restrictions, white settlement and tourism.

Canoe of the Mandan people beached after their Great Flood.[8] The Mandan were supposed to come on pilgrimage every year in honour of this event and to stave off the danger of another inundation.[9]

The Lakota have many stories and sacred items intimately linked to Bear Butte, making it central to their religion. They revere Bear Butte as the place where the Creator spoke to his prophet, and liken it to Mount Sinai, where Moses received the Ten Commandments, to convey its significance to Christians and Jews.[10] It is also uniquely where their seven sacred elements can be found, including rocks essential to the performance of the Lakota's purifying sweat lodge rituals.[11] Also important are several plants growing on the slopes of the hill, which are used for spiritual and medicinal activities. Bear Butte was also the place where the Lakota were gifted the Sacred Calf Pipe by the Creator. This is their holiest object and plays a central role in their spiritual and cultural life. The Lakota were taught to pray with this pipe by White Buffalo Woman, and its possession and use is important to their well-being.[12] The Lakota also believe that the spirits of their dead congregate at Bear Butte, and so pilgrimage there can relate to mourning or loss.[13]

For the modern Lakota, a displaced people, pilgrimage to Bear Butte is like going home. Pilgrimage is an opportunity to meet up with relatives, decide laws that govern their nation and hold or arrange marriages. 'If I am to be Lakota,' claimed the activist Charlotte Black Elk, 'it involves a number of things. One of these is the preservation of religious sites ... Bear Butte contributes to my being Lakota.'[14] Whatever an individual's specific reason for pilgrimage, the Lakota believe that the mountain pulls people towards it with its spiritual strength, making pilgrimage more an obligation or compulsion than a free choice. Richard Two Dogs, a Lakota healer, explains: 'The religion is rooted to the land. And you can't have the religion without the land ... We can't practise without the sacred places because that is where we draw our religion from.'[15]

For the Cheyenne or Tsitsistas, the dominant people in the Black Hills until about 1850, Bear Butte is Nowah'wus, the Good or Holy Mountain. Somewhere between four and one thousand years ago, so tradition says, an exiled teenage Cheyenne called Sweet Medicine stayed in a cave on the hill for four years, and the four arrows (two which gave power over men, two which gave power over buffalo) he received were accompanied by spiritual teachings and information on laws and the right way to rule. A Cheyenne elder, Walter R. Hamilton, explains: 'The four sacred arrows ... came from within Bear Butte as a covenant with the Almighty ... [the mountain is, therefore] the holiest place to the ... people, who use the mountain regularly for pilgrimages, and who think about it every day, and who mention it in their prayers.'[16]

The arrows also represented four things forbidden to the Cheyenne: incest, adultery, theft and murder. On his descent from Bear Butte, Sweet Medicine imparted his new knowledge to his people, enabling them to draw up the rules of their society, rules they still adhere to. The arrows remain sacred to the Cheyenne, their custodian the holiest man of the tribe. In 1945, they were carried from Oklahoma back to Bear Butte on a pilgrimage to spiritually recharge them, and again in 1948.[17]

The hill itself remains a place where Cheyenne leaders go on an annual pilgrimage to seek advice on how to govern their two nations, now located in Oklahoma and Montana, and to maintain the link between the Cheyenne and Bear Butte every man in the tribe wears a small bag with red paint made from a mineral pigment found at the hill around his neck.[18] It is such an important place for their culture that the Cheyenne orientate the opening of their camp circle in the direction of Bear Butte when they gather for the holy *massaum* ceremony, a five-day re-enactment of the creation of the world which was first performed at Bear Butte by Sweet Medicine.[19] The tribal buildings at Lame Deer Reservation in Montana, two hundred miles north-west of Bear Butte, have all been built to face towards it.[20] Some Cheyenne do the same when constructing a home.[21]

For the Lakota, Bear Butte is a place for vision quests. These rituals, where the future is revealed, need to be completed before participation in the Sun Dance, which takes place in the valley below Bear Butte.[22] Vision quests can take place elsewhere, but if Bear Butte is chosen, whether by a holy man or through someone feeling a call, that is where the Lakota have to go.[23] One belief is that the great bear who sleeps beneath the hill preserves the dreams of the Sioux nation, of whom the Lakota are part, and that this is why Bear Butte is the preferred location for the quests.[24] Following preparations spanning several years, vision seekers seek the quiet and solitude of the Butte to communicate with the Creator. Over several days and nights, the seekers fast and pray in solitude on the hill. Bear Butte is also important to a range of other rituals that are central to Lakota beliefs, rituals that need to be completed or disaster follows.[25] George Bushotter, the first ethnographer of the Lakota, wrote that they used to camp on the flat top of a mountain, and he may have been referring to the vision seekers.[26] The Cheyenne conduct similar ceremonies, seeking aid through visions at times of uncertainty.

For all Native Americans, whether seeking answers or honouring their ancestors, Bear Butte is integral to their beliefs, which are strongly linked to particular places.[27] The land is part of Native American culture. The Creator chose Bear Butte as a sacred place, and alternatives – somewhere relics can be moved to, for example – just aren't an option. For the Lakota, Bear Butte is a sacred presence and where holy ceremonies can be performed to the greatest effect.[28]

Bear Butte and the White Man

Native American pilgrimage to Bear Butte and the performance of spiritual rites went on largely undisturbed for thousands of years until the arrival of white settlers in South Dakota. In the first decades of the nineteenth century, the state (then part of the Territory of Louisiana) was bought from the French by the United States, explored and partially settled by fur traders. By the 1850s, the US Army had a base at Fort Randall, and European settlement was increasing.

Old Crazy Horse (*c.*1818–1881), an Oglala leader, went on pilgrimage to undertake a vision quest on Bear Butte in the summer of 1839. Reaching the top of the hill, he spread his buffalo robe on the ground on top of some sage leaves and began his vigil. Three days later he received a vision in which he saw that warfare between the Indians and the white people was coming, and that his people would endure hardships and poverty. Old Crazy Horse also foresaw cars and planes, and the two world wars, after which his people would eventually find peace and spiritual awakening.[29]

When his son Curly Hair was considered to have come of age and into his warrior strength, he was given his father's name and told of his visions. Old Crazy Horse claimed that the bear 'gave to me powers to conquer all earthly beings, including the white men who are coming into our land'.[30] This transition took place at the tribal council held at Bear Butte in August 1857, which had been called in response to growing concerns about encroachments onto Indian lands in the aftermath of the treaty signed with Colonel William Harney the year before, which promised to limit their movement through Indian lands but unsurprisingly had failed to do so. The location for the council had no doubt been chosen with the aim of inspiring some sort of collective vision.

The threat to their land was very real. Commenting on the possibility of the discovery of gold in the Black Hills, a report by an army officer that same year claimed it made war with the Native tribes almost inevitable. It was probably only the outbreak of the American Civil War in April 1861 that averted a conflict.[31] The tribal council, however, was an important moment for Bear Butte. Thousands of Indians and their horses descended on the area. Sitting Bull and Red Cloud, both Lakota leaders, advocated a forceful response to drive the white man back. The Black Hills and Bear Butte had to remain free of the incomers. If not, the Lakota would retaliate.

However, it wasn't long before the settlers moved in.[32] Under the terms of the Homestead Act (1862), the US government seized swathes of land in South Dakota and redistributed them to incomers. Sporadic conflicts throughout the 1860s resulted in the Treaty of Fort Laramie, signed following the Native American victory in Red Cloud's War (1866–8). The treaty was supposed to secure Native access to Bear Butte, but the crucial oral agreement protecting the Black Hills was not recorded in the written treaty.[33] Access to Bear Butte for Native pilgrims was threatened, and settlers continued to arrive. Perhaps inspired by the vision his father had received on Bear Butte, the young Crazy Horse and the Lakota leader Sitting Bull forged an alliance with other Plains Indians to take on the threat. Engaging around seven hundred men of the US 7th Cavalry under Colonel George A. Custer at the Battle of Little Bighorn (1876) in southern Montana, the Native tribes killed over a third of the US force including Custer. One legend tells how Custer had offended the spirits of Bear Butte by climbing the hill before the battle, and that led to his defeat.[34]

Pilgrimage and Oppression

Custer's Last Stand may have been a victory for the Native Americans but it failed to ensure access to Bear Butte for those Indians who sought to visit it. Gold had been discovered in the Black Hills two years before Custer's defeat, and in 1877 the US government confiscated the land close to Bear Butte. Miners and their equipment quickly began moving in and the settler population grew.[35] Deadwood, twenty miles to the west of the Butte, and founded illegally on Lakota land, grew to sustain seventy-two licensed saloons.[36]

As part of efforts to undermine Native associations with the Black Hills and Bear Butte in particular, writers like Edwin Denig and Richard I. Dodge had already claimed that the tribes had no interest in the area. Dodge was a colonel in the US Army and escorted the Black Hills geological expedition of 1875, while Denig was a fur trader and ethnographer whose writings (which were very judgemental of Native morals, or what he considered their lack) were inspired and heavily influenced by the Jesuit Father Pierre-Jean de Smet. His disapproval did not stop Denig from enjoying 'country marriages' with at least three Native women, but when the tribes threatened his economic interests, he was quick to take the moral high ground.

Things went from bad to worse from the end of the 1870s. The US government's Peace Policy (originally instituted in 1868) aimed to make the Indians more 'European' by moving them off their traditional lands into reservations and sending their children to boarding schools, where they could be removed from the influence of their parents and turned into 'civilised' Americans.[37] The government also supported Christian missionary efforts and denigrated Native religious practices as supposedly backward, and sought to stamp out a variety of rituals through the Code of Indian Offences (1883).[38] Pilgrimage to Bear Butte was now fraught with danger. Pilgrims could be arrested and imprisoned for thirty days.[39] Rituals like the Ghost Dance and the Sun Dance – the first to unite the people with their dead and halt the expansion of the white man, the second for healing – which had been used by Native American resistance movements as a form of protest against settler dispossession, became more difficult to conduct.[40]

Attempts to integrate Native Americans into white society were cemented by the 1887 Dawes Act, which aimed to end the sovereignty of the tribes and gave them parcels of land – allotments – to live on. In the same decade, several laws were passed to suppress Native religious practices, and both the Sun Dance and the Ghost Dance were stopped by the military. In

1890, Senator Jones of Arkansas declared 'that this educating the Indian without religion is an utter impossibility. I do not believe that you can ever make any civilization that is not based primarily upon the Christian religion.'[41] The following year, the last great pilgrimage made by all the Cheyenne took place.

One of the biggest obstacles to a pilgrimage to Bear Butte was the prohibition placed on Native Americans travelling beyond the borders of their new reservations. For the Cheyenne, this was especially serious, as the ability to seek spiritual advice at Bear Butte underpinned their tribal governance.[42] The Cheyenne were forced to conduct their pilgrimages in secret or by using some other pretext for travelling. Spotted Tail's grandson, a Lakota, went on a pilgrimage and fast in 1913.[43] Whistling Elk went as a pilgrim in 1920 and received a message from the Creator that presaged the atomic bomb, 'something that isn't big, but it is very powerful'.[44] Four Cheyenne heading out to fight in Europe during the First World War went on pilgrimage to fast on the mountain. Being in the army freed them from the constraints of the reservation, and enabled them to complete a pilgrimage without the authorities knowing.[45] A group of around eighty Lakota, drawn from across the tribe's seven bands, undertook a pilgrimage to alleviate the drought of 1935; successful, they returned the following year on a pilgrimage of thanks.[46] These Lakota were the lucky ones, as the many hardships which befell Native Americans during these decades were often attributed by them to not being able to conduct their traditional religious ceremonies or seek advice on the way forward. However, Fools Crow of the Oglala Lakota managed to go on pilgrimage to Bear Butte to pray for change: for better harvests, an end to drunkenness among his people, and for the young to come back to the ways of the Cheyenne.[47]

In 1934 President Roosevelt appointed John Collier as commissioner of Indian affairs, and things began to look up.

Instructions were issued that no 'interference with Indian religious life or ceremonial expression will hereafter be tolerated. The cultural liberty of Indians is in all respects to be considered equal to that of any non-Indian group.' Collier ordered that Native religious life and cultural expression should not be interfered with, and the Indian Reorganization Act passed the same year protected Native American lands, and gave Collier the authority to redefine, add to and protect the reservations.[48] However, in practice, Congress worked towards ending the degree of self-government which the Native American nations had enjoyed. During the so-called Termination Era (*c.*1945–*c.*1968), the US government sought to terminate its treaty obligations to tribal communities under the guise of assimilating Indians into wider American society.[49]

The Threat of Tourism

It took several more decades before Native beliefs would gain greater protection, but in the meantime there was an increase in pilgrimage to Bear Butte. The first substantial Cheyenne pilgrimage took place in late September 1939, and was led by four 'old warriors' who lived at the Tongue River Agency in Montana: Nelson Medicine Bird, John Black Wolf, Charles Spotted Elk, and ninety-two-year-old Robert Yellow Nose, who had taken part in the fight against Custer over sixty years before.[50] According to one of the participants, Eugene Fisher, president of the Northern Cheyenne Tribal Council, the pilgrimage was intended to help locals – those living close to Bear Butte, irrespective of ethnicity – explore Bear Butte's history. They hoped to gain recognition for Bear Butte as a national monument, and thus protect it from further external threats and commercial development.[51]

The pilgrims and the tribal council members obviously wanted protection for Bear Butte to preserve its religious character, but others were thinking about its potential as a tourist destination. A teacher and historian, Thomas E. Odell wrote several articles published in local newspapers suggesting that the mountain should become a national monument. One year after the four elders went on pilgrimage, the Bear Butte Company was founded by two local families, the Bovees and the Hollis Devers, to promote the hill to tourists.[52] Bovee family members offered donkey rides up Bear Butte.[53] Ezra Bovee had started buying land on the eastern slope of the Butte at the end of the nineteenth century, and then secured more, including the Butte itself, over the following years.

During the Second World War, in the summer of 1944, a young Cheyenne called David Deafy dreamed of four naked men painted yellow and, unable to interpret his vision, went to the priest Whistling Elk for advice. He was told that his dream meant four men should go on a pilgrimage to Bear Butte 'to find a way to end the war'.[54] Deafy prepared to set out only to be scuppered by fuel rationing, but in June 1945 he and twenty others managed the pilgrimage. On Bear Butte, Deafy received a vision which was interpreted as that the war would end with American victory over Japan. After the war, pilgrimages giving thanks for peace took place.[55]

In 1962, the State of South Dakota bought the hill and the surrounding area, designating it Bear Butte State Park. Development changed both the physical form of the site and its atmosphere: routes and walkways were moved or built, and parking lots and a visitor centre were constructed. Tourist numbers climbed steadily. This was anathema to Native American pilgrims, who visited Bear Butte only for religious reasons: they did not hunt or live there and built no permanent structures.

From the late 1970s onwards, tourists watched ceremonies from viewing platforms, photographing them despite requests not to do so. 'Imagine if we flip things around,' complained Chris Spotted Eagle in 1984, 'and we had Indian people dominating Christian churches. There would be signs on the church aisles saying DON'T PHOTOGRAPH THE CHRISTIANS. We Indians would stroll in there with our popcorn and watch you practice your religion.'[56] He had a point. As long ago as 1927, the Sioux had been approached about performing the Sun Dance 'inoffensively' for visiting tourists, offering 'a sideshow without its most sacred aspects'. Fools Crow went on a pilgrimage to Bear Butte to ask when things had started to 'go wrong' for his people and how they had reached the point where they were asked to do such things. The answer he received was that it was the First World War (not the arrival of Europeans), and the pensions given to Indian veterans, who then had no incentive to work but money to drink.[57]

Freedom?

After a century of prohibition, stagnation, persecution and, more recently, tourism, the situation of Native Americans and the practice of their religion finally improved. Democrat Morris Udall stood on the floor of the House of Representatives in Washington in July 1972 and explained the importance of sacred places in the landscape like Bear Butte for his listeners:

> For many tribes, the land is filled with physical sites of religious and sacred significance to them. Can we not understand that? Our religions have their Jerusalems, Mount Calvarys, Vaticans and Meccas. We hold sacred Bethlehem, Nazareth, the Mount of Olives and the Wailing

> [Western] Wall. Bloody wars have been fought because of these religious sites.[58]

The passage of the American Indian Religious Freedom Act (AIRFA) the following month meant that it was again legal to practise indigenous religions, though the new law was not always applied fairly and was not without its problems. In Hawaii, for example, native Hawaiians were 'prevented from taking pilgrimages to sacred sites because they are on restricted lands – lands owned by the military, the state or by private companies and individuals'.[59] But there was a sea change at Bear Butte. When the Cheyenne were offered first refusal on some privately owned land at Bear Butte the same year, this was tacit recognition that they had some sort of claim to it. The Cheyenne could not afford the purchase price, but in 1973 the secretary of the interior bought it on behalf of all Native Americans.[60] Then in 1980 the US Supreme Court ruled that the Black Hills and Bear Butte had been seized illegally in the nineteenth century in one of the most 'dishonourable' acts in the country's history.[61] The justices concluded that the 1868 Treaty of Fort Laramie gave the Lakota title to about 60 million acres of land, which included Bear Butte. However, this did not mean that the Indians got their land back. Instead, the court awarded them $102 million in damages.[62]

Two years later, the Lakota and Cheyenne took on the State of South Dakota in the courts in the famous *Fools Crow v. Gullet* case.[63] Frank Fools Crow, aged about ninety at the time the case was brought, was an Oglala Lakota leader and a fierce defender of Native rights in the Black Hills. He and his supporters argued that all future developments at Bear Butte should be prohibited and uninterrupted use of the site for religious purposes guaranteed. Access to the site for pilgrims had been difficult for many years, but more recently the imposition of time-limited visitor permits, which meant that Indian pilgrims could stay for five or sometimes ten days only, had interrupted their ceremonies. They were also required to pay for a camping pitch, meaning they were treated as tourists, and many could not afford the fee anyway. The plaintiffs also wanted all the physical changes made to the site – the roads, viewing platforms, parking lots, bridges – removed, and one million dollars in damages. They lost.

Even a limited degree of religious freedom comes at a price. In recent years, Bear Butte has become a pilgrimage destination of a different kind, and one that means the Native pilgrims must share Bear Butte with other worshippers. Now people from around the world travel there for the Harmonic Convergence, a belief that the universe aligns in such a way that strong forces are brought to earth. This happens at only a few places, and one of them, at 6 a.m. on Sunday, 15 August 1987, was Bear Butte. To the Native worshippers these pilgrims are simply another form of tourist.[64]

13

AMRITSAR

Punjab, India

In April 2004, the *Times of India* ran a news story about a specially chartered flight leaving the airport at Amritsar, a city of about one million people in the north-western Indian province of Punjab. Those on board were heading for Toronto's Pearson International Airport and travelling in some style, all 150 of them carried across the tarmac to the plane on luxurious cushions, draped in shawls and delivered to their reserved seats by specially selected attendants. They had already been carried on the heads of the same men past crowds of joyous people as they left the city, and were seen off by high officials and members of the Sikh faith. People showered the procession with petals and handed out gifts of biscuits, fruit and religious photographs. Displays of swordsmanship entertained the crowds, and groups of smiling schoolchildren dutifully lined up to wish the passengers well. When they arrived in Toronto many hours later, the plane was met by the Canadian prime minister, Paul Martin, and Canada's Sikh leaders. From there they were taken to a gurdwara, a Sikh place of worship, before travelling to other gurdwaras across the country.[1]

Each one of the 'passengers' was a copy of the Guru Granth Sahib, the holy book of the Sikh faith. This is revered as a living eternal guru, the source of all spiritual wisdom and advice on how to live. The copies needed by the Canadian Sikhs had to come from Amritsar as nowhere else in the world is allowed to make them, and had to be transported with due reverence. In the city itself, the original Granth Sahib, a collection of texts by the first ten gurus of Sikhism, is kept in the Harmandir or Golden Temple, the holiest place in the Sikh world. Given Amritsar's importance as the home of the Granth Sahib, the Harmandir and the tank of sacred water which surrounds it, it is not surprising that it is the Sikhs' most important pilgrimage destination too.

Amritsar was never intended as a pilgrimage centre by the faith's founder, Guru Nanak (1469–1539). Born in what is now Pakistan, Nanak was a married clerk and father of two, an otherwise unremarkable man when he disappeared while bathing with a friend in the river. When he emerged unscathed several days later, he declared, 'There is neither Hindu nor Muslim,' and established his own religion. Nanak left his job and embarked on a long tour around India, preaching and singing of his new beliefs. When he eventually returned home, Nanak took his family and founded a new settlement at Kartarpur. People flocked to hear him preach, and he left behind him a community who had settled around him. From there he set off for the place that later became Amritsar, just over thirty miles south of his home: his destination may have been a lake where he simply hoped to meditate. The place was virtually uninhabited, surrounded by forest.

It was only after Guru Nanak died that Amritsar became a place of pilgrimage in his honour, even though Nanak had not been a great advocate of pilgrimage. He thought it 'barely worth a sesame seed' unless people undertook some form of internal spiritual pilgrimage beforehand.[2] 'Why should I bathe at sacred shrines of pilgrimage?' he asked rhetorically. 'My pilgrimage is spiritual wisdom within, and contemplation on the Shabad.'[3] Even so, he did single out one pool as a special place, which was so effective it was called the 'pool of the nectar of immortality' by Guru Nanak in his poetry. He told his followers, 'sins are washed away by bathing in Amritsar'.[4] Whether he meant the pool at Amritsar in a literal (the water) or metaphorical (bathing the mind in spiritual teaching) sense is debatable.[5] Clearly many have taken his statement literally, and this has made the site important enough to become the home of the Sikh gurus and the location of its eternal guru, the Granth Sahib. Despite this, the influential Shiromani Gurdwara Parbandhak Committee refuses to acknowledge pilgrimage as part of Sikhism, perhaps because it seems uncomfortably close to Hindu practice.[6] Perhaps someone should tell that to the thousands who flock to Amritsar every year?

As a place of Sikh pilgrimage in a country where they are a minority, Amritsar has been seen as a place of community solidarity, a centre for fomenting rebellion, as well as an important possession for those who want to control the Sikhs. It is little wonder that it has been subjected to repeated attacks – destroyed, defiled, and rebuilt over and over again. Despite this, Amritsar and its pilgrimage have only grown, and over six million pilgrims now visit each year.

The Foundation of Amritsar

The plan to establish a new settlement for the Sikhs was initially the idea of Guru Amar Das (died 1574), the third of the ten Sikh gurus or spiritual leaders of the faith. There are at least two legendary stories about how the necessary land was acquired. In one version his successor Guru Ram Das (died 1581) bought land from the villagers of Tung for 700 rupees, money raised from donations. In another (probably unlikely) account, he was gifted the land by the Mughal emperor Akbar in gratitude for the latter's success in capturing the fort of Chittor in 1567–8.

However the site was acquired, Guru Amar Das ordered a survey of the land and the excavation of a large tank to enclose the only pool, while the work was carried out by his successor, Ram Das. The new settlement was initially called Ramdaspur, the town of Guru Ram Das. Visitors were asked to contribute to the cost of creating the pool (amrit Sarovar), which is about the size of nineteen Olympic swimming pools. Ramdaspur was renamed of Amritsar after the pool. The water that flowed in cleansed the devout by removing dirt from their bodies and by washing away their sins.

Enough money came in to fund the construction of the rest of the complex in Amritsar and another sacred tank about ten miles south called Tarn Taran (Pool of Salvation), which became famous for healing leprosy.[7] To service the growing visitor traffic, Ram Das also invited Sikh traders and artisans to come and settle the area. Pilgrims arriving at Amritsar were fed from a large communal kitchen, the Guru Ka Langar, where volunteers working in shifts prepared hundreds of free meals for those who came, irrespective of their means. This was a good thing for the surrounding area as farmers had steady demand for their produce. Four and a half centuries later, the kitchen caters to 100,000 people a day on the same terms.

In the last years of the 1580s, Guru Ram Das's third son and successor and the fifth guru, Arjan Dev (died 1606), began construction of the Harmandir Sahib (Temple of the Absolute) on a platform that projects into the pool. The Harmandir was built with all four sides open to pilgrims to reflect the fact that it welcomes all Sikhs irrespective of class, race or caste. Constructing

The Temple at Amritsar was gilded by Maharaja Ranjit Singh, one of the last great Indian rulers. He was a devout Sikh, but his generosity to the shrine was an expression of power.

this temple gave Sikhs a physical focus for their faith, one which naturally functioned as a pilgrimage destination, something that the gurus may have intended all along.[8] Around the complex, various other sacred attractions were added or recognised over time, such as the Dukh Bhanjani Beri (Tree that Ends Sorrow), underneath which people bathe in memory of Bibi Ranji's pilgrimage with her leprous husband who, failing to find healing at a range of Hindu sites, was cured by the water of Amritsar. There was also a shrine to the martyr Baba Deep Singh (died 1757), killed in a battle to defend the temple at Amritsar, and the Lach Ber, the tree under which Arjan Dev sat when he was supervising the building of the Harmandir.

The foundation of the pilgrimage centre at Amritsar was

critical in providing a political and spiritual capital from which the Sikh faith could expand. It helped that Amritsar lies in a fertile area, which made it a commercial hub; a steady flow of people and goods, and with them substantial offerings and voluntary labour, could be relied on. It also helped that Amritsar was located on the Grand Trunk Road, a major trade route that has stretched across Asia for at least two and a half thousand years. Running from Kabul in Afghanistan via the Khyber Pass and the Indus and Gangetic plains down to Bangladesh, this road benefited from periodic improvements. When the Englishman Rudyard Kipling wrote his novel *Kim* (1901), he had an old man tell his protagonist, 'And now we come to the Big Road ... Look! Brahmins and chumars, bankers and tinkers, barbers and bunnias, pilgrims and potters – all the world going and coming'.[9]

In the first few years of the seventeenth century, the Harmandir was finally finished and a copy of the Adi Granth, the first iteration of the Granth Sahib, was placed inside by Guru Arjan Dev. Around half of it consisted of his own writings, as he was a prolific author and poet. Arjan Dev instructed Baba Buddha, a man who had known the first guru and was ninety-eight years old at the time (he allegedly lived to 124), to take on the role of the first *granthi*, ceremonial reader of the book. It was his job to read from the text every day so that the advice of former gurus could be heard by anyone coming to the shrine. The already-sacred site now housed a work that became so revered that its printers have to abstain from alcohol and tobacco, and any by-product of the production process – misprints, waste paper – is ceremonially cremated.[10]

Guru Arjan Dev was probably tortured and certainly killed in 1606 by the Mughal emperor Jahangir, making him the first Sikh martyr. Previously peace-loving, the Sikhs were now encouraged by their seventh guru, Arjan Dev's only son

Hargobind, to become militant. Non-violence only encouraged evil, and it was only by fighting that the community could be protected. At his investiture, Guru Hargobind conspicuously adorned himself with two swords, which he told his followers symbolised his spiritual and temporal authority.[11] He also organised the construction of the Sri Akal Takht Sahib (Throne of the Timeless One), placed opposite the Harmandir, a move that angered the Mughal emperor, who within his realm had the exclusive right to sit on a throne.

The Akal Takht gave Hargobind an earthly seat of power at his faith's most important holy site. His militant guruship was marked by clashes with the Mughals, including his victory at Amritsar in 1634, which was held to demonstrate divine approval of his militarisation of the Sikhs. Guru Hargobind was imprisoned for a time by the Mughal emperor (though he was released, and they became friends), but Guru Har Rai (died 1661), his teenage grandson and successor, continued in the same militant vein. Rai's own son, Guru Har Krishan (died 1664), hardly had an impact on Amritsar, being guru from the age of five until his death aged only eight, while his successor, Guru Tegh Bahadur (died 1675), fell out with the emperor, who had him caged, tortured and beheaded.

The last living Sikh guru, Gobind Singh (died 1708), succeeded to the guruship while still a child in 1675. He had been trained in martial arts and was a keen horseman, so it is little surprise that he continued the work of turning the Sikhs into a militant faith and founded the Khalsa warrior community in 1699. As the son of a martyred father, his relationship with the Moghuls was understandably tense, and his guruship was marked by a series of battles. As all of his sons were killed during his lifetime, just before he was killed by Afghan Pathan assassins in 1708, Guru Gobind Singh declared that his successor would not be a man but an object. Thus the last of the gurus was, and remains, the Granth Sahib, the living eternal holy book of the Sikhs kept at Amritsar. [12]

The Eternal Guru

The absence of a living Sikh leader created a power vacuum in the Punjab, which threatened both the town of Amritsar and its holy shrine, and pilgrimage to it. Gobind Singh's potential successors refused to accept that the guru was now a holy book, and for some years Sikh history was dominated by assassinations, battles between different factions and conflict with the Mughals as rival groups fought for control of the Harmandir. It became dangerous to visit Amritsar, and many of those who served the shrine and the pilgrims decided it was wiser to leave. With no agreement on who should take charge, the Sikhs of Amritsar appealed to Mata Sundari, widow of Guru Gobind Singh, who had become something of a focus of Sikh power at her home in Delhi. In 1721 she dispatched her husband's childhood friend and oldest disciple, the scholar Bhai Mani Singh, who had been active in Amritsar some years before, asking him to take control as the site's ceremonial leader. He thus became the next *granthi*, reader of the Granth Sahib.[13]

Opposed by those Sikhs who believed that there should be a new human guru rather than a book, Bhai Mani Singh succeeded in calming the situation in Amritsar, although pilgrimage to the shrine remained a dangerous proposition. The Sikhs' Mughal overlords forbade pilgrimage to Amritsar and bathing in the holy water, and sent soldiers to the outskirts of the town to arrest any pilgrims who tried to enter. Pilgrimage may have been off the table, but other religious gatherings were possible, so in about 1733 Bhai Mani Singh asked for permission to hold festivities for Diwali. It was granted on the proviso that he paid a punitive tax. It is entirely possible that the Mughal authorities were hoping to gather a large number of Sikhs in Amritsar in order to kill them. Whether or not that was their intention, Bhai Mani Singh was spooked (apparently tipped off by the Sikhs of Lahore) and he advised potential visitors not to come. Of course, no pilgrims coming to Amritsar meant that he couldn't collect their offerings to pay the required tax,[14] so Bhai Mani Singh was dragged off to Lahore and dismembered. His removal gave the Mughals an excuse to seize the holy site, the occupiers watching dancers in the Harmandir and throwing dead animals into the sacred tank. Seven years later, some Sikhs sneaked into the temple in disguise and beheaded the Mughals' local commander, Massa Ranghar, but the shrine remained under the control of the emperors.[15]

For the remainder of the century, Sikh power was mainly vested in the armies of the twelve Sikh confederacies known as the Army of Khalsa. These forces were involved in conflict with the Mughals, though they eventually turned on each other. Amritsar and its holy shrine were subject to repeated attacks, re-won and lost again, and defiled. Those who reached Amritsar were doomed to disappointment as rubbish had been thrown into the tank around the Harmandir, polluting the water.[16] Most did not even make it. One Muslim writer of the time told how 'Sikh horsemen were seen riding at full gallop towards their favourite shrine of devotion. They are often slain in the attempt, and sometimes taken prisoner; but they used on such occasions to seek instead of avoiding, the crown of martyrdom.'[17]

Under Mughal Muslim occupation, Sikhs were barred from entering Amritsar, with the penalty for doing so death.[18] Yet even when the Sikhs regained control, things were still dangerous: the temple was attacked and thousands of Sikhs massacred when Ahmad Durrani, the founder of modern Afghanistan, led a jihad into India – in part to subdue the Sikhs, but probably to plunder too.[19] In this attack the Harmandir was destroyed, though reconstructed two years later, with the Sikhs forcing their Muslim captives to clean out the pool they had desecrated,[20] only to be blown up in the spring of 1762 by Ahmad Durrani on his sixth campaign in India. The guesthouses around the tank were demolished and the rubble pushed into the water. Again, the Sikhs retook their city, which was rebuilt over the next three decades.[21]

The repeated attacks on Amritsar were intended to destroy Sikh unity and the focus of their faith, and the Mughals weren't the only power in India to recognise the city's strategic importance. As British control of the subcontinent expanded and consolidated in the eighteenth and nineteenth centuries, they became aware of Amritsar's significance. Captain Bingley of the 7th Bengal infantry explained to his fellow Britons in a handbook on the Sikhs that by building Amritsar, the guru had 'provided his followers with a common rallying point'.[22] Protecting the Harmandir and its surrounding tank was a matter of honour for Sikhs. And the place itself inspired them: bathing in the sacred pool instilled valour in devout Sikhs. 'Whenever an important expedition was undertaken by the Sikhs,' wrote historian G. S. Chhabra, 'they started with a dip in the tank. Once this was done, lambs were converted into lions.'[23]

Life improved significantly for the Sikhs of the Punjab during the reign (1801–39) of their co-religionist Maharaja Ranjit Singh. The Lion of the Punjab, as he was known, was an astute leader, militarily successful and tolerant of all religions, and he ruled his newly conquered lands with a considerable degree of skill. Ranjit Singh was twice victorious at battles at Amritsar before he became maharaja, in 1797 and 1798, successes that made him a hero in Sikh eyes. In 1802, he decided to capture the spiritually symbolic site of Amritsar as a way to rubber-stamp his control over his fellow Sikhs, though he had moved the political centre of his empire from Amritsar to Lahore. The prestige it would give him was an additional attraction. Essentially invited in by city merchants sick of being extorted by tax collectors, he was welcomed into the city with no resistance at all. The resulting stability allowed the city to focus on developing its trade and industry, and reviving pilgrimage.[24]

Ranjit Singh's patronage of Amritsar resulted in the Harmandir's fabulous gold covering. The gilding for this lavish gift was long thought to have come from pillaged Mughal monuments.[25] Whatever its origin, the gold was applied ten to twelve layers deep and gave the temple an opulent glow. Soon it was no longer referred to as the Harmandir, but the Golden Temple. He made further gifts to the Harmandir complex throughout the rest of his life, as did members of his family: marble for walls, more gold to plate four pairs of doors, and a gold umbrella set with gems and a sapphire- and pearl-encrusted peacock.

Ranjit Singh was a devout Sikh, but his generosity may have been prompted by more than piety; the maharaja may have intended his gifts as acts of expiation. One account of his life says that in his earlier years he had been overly fond of alcohol and opium, and offended the Sikhs he ruled by taking a Muslim wife, a dancing girl called Moran. A visit to Amritsar, where some pilgrims gathered there accepted his apology, led him to correct his ways.[26] He undertook further pilgrimages: in 1826, when he thought he was dying; after military successes, of which there were many, like the conquest of Kashmir; and on holy days and holidays.[27]

Amritsar under the Raj, 1849–1947

During the first half of the nineteenth century, the tradition of pilgrimage to Amritsar and the vitality of the Sikh faith appeared robust. However, the onset of British colonial rule in the Punjab in 1849 posed challenges to both. In an administrative report written shortly after the British annexation, Sir Richard Temple claimed that at one time 'men joined [the Sikh faith] in thousands, and they now depart in equal numbers. They rejoin the ranks of Hinduism whence they originally came, and they bring up their children as Hindus. The sacred tank at Amritsar is less thronged than formerly, and the attendance at the annual festival is diminishing yearly.'[28] A few years later, he did concede that Sikhism seemed to be bouncing back despite the focused efforts of the Protestant mission at Amritsar to convert the locals. However, the Sikh faith and its holy book were attacked in the press, and British officials suggested letting the Golden Temple fall into disrepair, allowing the faith to wither through neglect.[29]

These suggestions were not adopted as policy; rather, a more interventionist approach was taken in an attempt to control the Sikh population and influence them to support the colonial government.[30] Though legislation was passed to divest the colonial authorities of control over Indian religious institutions in 1863, the Golden Temple was an exception, and the British continued to take a role in the shrine, appointing site managers responsible to the deputy commissioner of Amritsar until 1925. This was not popular as the managers were accused of corruption, and it took years of protest and negotiation to get the guilty removed. In many respects, the British continued the policy of the maharajas, who had also appointed managers, but their motives were very different. Whereas Ranjit Singh had been a devout Sikh, the British were Christians who believed that mismanagement or a dispute at the shrine might inspire the volatile Sikhs to rebel.[31]

Neither the temple nor Sikhism collapsed and the British attempts at control weren't wholly successful either. Baba Ram Singh, a former soldier in Ranjit Singh's army and founder of the Namdhari sect, which attracted thousands of Sikh peasants and members of the untouchable caste, was probably the first major thorn in the British side at Amritsar. The growth in his popularity and his message to boycott all things British – from schools to the postal service – led to government scrutiny. He was allowed, albeit reluctantly, to go to Amritsar with his followers for the Baisakhi celebrations, but there were suspicions that he was fomenting a rebellion. The fair had long been a time for Sikhs to meet others heading to the Harmandir, and a morning of bathing and spiritual activity was sometimes followed by an afternoon of political rallies.[32] Consequently, from 1863 to 1866 he was confined to his village of Bhaini. The year after his release, he led a pilgrimage to Amritsar of some three and a half thousand, accompanied by a military escort, and while he was there he held court like a maharaja, converting pilgrims to his sect. In many ways, Baba Ram Singh and his followers were exactly what the rulers of India had for centuries been afraid of: potential rebels gathering at Amritsar under the pretence of pilgrimage. Ram Singh was exiled to Burma and died there in 1885.

The British continued to be suspicious of pilgrimages to Amritsar, assuming the gathering together of so many Sikhs necessarily meant trouble. Rioting in India in 1893, chiefly in Bombay, was believed to have been religiously inspired, and similar problems were expected in the Punjab. 'Amritsar in the pilgrimage season is another notorious place for riots,' warned *The Age*, 'and the garrisons within the city and at the fort ... are strengthened during that period to meet all contingencies.'[33]

Despite their best efforts, under the British, Amritsar became one centre of the events which led eventually to India's national struggle to throw off colonial rule and achieve independence. One notable and tragic event in this process occurred at Amritsar on 13 April 1919, when a peaceful crowd of up to 20,000 men, women and children which had gathered in the Jallianwala Bagh (a large walled public space) near the Golden Temple complex despite a ban on meetings, was fired on by Sikh and Gurkha soldiers of the British Indian Army. The crowd had come out to demonstrate against the arrest of Dr Saifuddin Kitchlew and Dr Satyapal, who had addressed meetings protesting against the Rowlatt Acts of the month before – legislation which extended wartime powers allowing indefinite detention without trial. The troops, under the command of Colonel Reginald Dyer, had entered the city to deal with what they considered to be rebels. During the previous day's protests several Britons had been assaulted, and a female British missionary had been beaten and left for dead. Trapped in a space with few exits, the crowd was decimated. Dyer's men fired into the crowd of protesters, only stopping when they ran out of ammunition. In Dyer's own words, delivered to the inquiry that investigated events, he did not want to make 'a fool of myself' by asking the crowd to disperse, as he thought they might mock him by returning to the garden later.[34] The 379 dead included pilgrims who had come to the city for Baisakhi, the Sikh new year.

If Dyer's intention had been to assert British control over Amritsar in particular and India in general, his actions were a spectacular failure. The world, including much of Britain, was horrified – although for some of the British Dyer was a hero – and the Indian independence movement was galvanised. In Amritsar, Dyer added another layer to the pilgrimage landscape, this time in the cause of resistance to colonial power. Among the publications that emerged in the wake of the massacre, one collection of poems, *Jallianwala Bagh ka Mahatma*, called the garden in Amritsar a place where 'the martyrs of the motherland and the gems of the country were robbed' and suggested that it should be thought of as a place of pilgrimage.[35] This in fact happened immediately after the massacre, and the following year plans were drawn up to erect a monument in memory of the dead, though it wasn't built until India gained its independence in 1947. Decades later, a writer in the *Contemporary* claimed, '*Jallianwala Bagh* is a place of pilgrimage for those who hold the cause of independence dear to their hearts.'[36]

The Partition of India had a considerable impact on Amritsar. Much of its Muslim population moved out to the new state of Pakistan, though not before some attacked the city's wealthier Sikh and Hindu populations, forcing 50,000 of them to take refuge in the Golden Temple complex. In the months before the British left and Lahore and Amritsar were separated by the new border, a series of attacks by members of the Muslim League destroyed half of Amritsar's walled city. Sikhs from the surrounding area flooded in, bringing stories of massacres across the Punjab, news which only served to strengthen the resolve of Sikhs to hold Amritsar come what may. It was now a frontier city as the border between Indian and Pakistan lay only seventeen miles away, and as early as 1948 it was being written off as a place in steep decline.[37]

What the Sikhs had demanded but failed to secure during Partition was the creation of their own state, Khalistan, and campaigning continued in the decades after 1947. By the 1980s Sikh militants were a significant force, and events climaxed in 1984 when the Golden Temple itself was the scene of a massacre. Indira Ghandi, Indian prime minister, sent troops in to capture the leader of a Sikhist independence movement who had taken up residence inside.[38] The attack, known as Operation Blue Star, damaged the Harmandir and the Akal Takht, with further harm caused during the occupation of the site for three months by the Indian army. The assault was successful, but among the dead were pilgrims caught up in the siege. Somewhere between fifteen hundred and five thousand men, women and children were killed; the authorities never confirmed the number or the names of the dead.[39]

The shock caused by the attack on the Golden Temple was deep and enduring, leading to years of unrest and retaliatory massacres. Khushwant Singh, an Indian MP and one of the country's best-known writers, visited the site a few days after the operation and witnessed the destruction and the emotions of the devastated Sikhs. 'In my articles and speeches I pleaded with Mrs Gandhi to go to the Golden Temple as a pilgrim,' he wrote, 'and ask for forgiveness. I assured her that Sikhs were an emotional people and the gesture would assuage their feelings of hurt.'[40] Amritsar was so important to the Sikhs and the struggle for India's independence that recognising its spiritual significance through pilgrimage would have done much to heal the wounds. Mrs Gandhi didn't heed his advice. Later the same year she was assassinated by two of her bodyguards. They were Sikhs.

14

LOURDES

France

When Marie-Bernarde Soubirous, known to everyone as Bernadette, reported seeing visions of the Virgin Mary at Lourdes in 1858, it was not as unusual a phenomenon as you might think. Young people, usually peasant children, had been reporting visions of the Virgin for centuries, and mid-nineteenth-century France was no stranger to such events. The mother of God had appeared to a young nun in Paris in 1830 and two shepherd children at La Salette in south-eastern France in 1846, so when Bernadette claimed she had seen the Virgin in a riverside cave known as the Massabielle Grotto, there were plenty of people willing to believe her.

A sickly and uneducated girl of fourteen, Bernadette was the daughter of an unemployed man who had once run one of Lourdes' mills but was now reduced to living with his wife and children in a dank cellar room of the town's dilapidated old jail. On 11 February 1858, Bernadette was out collecting firewood on the outskirts of the town with her sister and a friend when she saw her first vision at the cave. She said this was of a woman wearing white, surrounded by a soft light. The woman was carrying a rosary and made the sign of the cross. Although clear to Bernadette, no one else could see her. On subsequent visits to

The grotto where Bernadette saw visions of the Virgin Mary in 1858 rapidly became a major pilgrimage destination. The small town of Lourdes was transformed by building work, and a souvenir trade sprang up to cater to the pilgrims, many of them sick, who flocked there.

the cave Bernadette saw the woman again. In the local dialect she told Bernadette that a chapel should be built at the grotto. On the woman's ninth appearance, Bernadette dug into the earth and uncovered an underground spring, and during her sixteenth vision the woman told Bernadette that she was the Immaculate Conception, a reference to the Catholic doctrine that the Virgin Mary was free from original sin – the state of sin into which all humans are born – from the moment of her conception.

By this point Bernadette was already attracting followers.[1] She was nevertheless attacked in the French press, threatened with arrest by the local police and slapped by a woman as she walked home from school. To her detractors she was an illiterate and hysterical girl who was seeking attention or mentally ill. The police removed the religious paraphernalia that had begun to collect at the site, and the cave was barricaded; even Bernadette could not get in, seeing her final vision on 16 July from across the river. Soon after, she withdrew to a local hospice to escape unwanted attention, and from there joined the nunnery of the Sisters of Charity at Nevers. She died there in 1879 at the age of just thirty-five.[2] The grotto's closure and Bernadette's disappearance into a nunnery might well have resulted in Lourdes retreating into its previous obscurity, yet the town went on to become one of the most popular pilgrim destinations in the world, famed for its cures and miracles, and as a place of peace and reconciliation in a world riven by war.

In the first decades of the twenty-first century, Lourdes is the most-visited tourist destination in France after Paris, and the most-visited pilgrimage destination for Catholics after Rome. House prices once rivalled those of the French capital. The flood of pilgrims to Lourdes has led to its development from a small town, relatively isolated from the outside world by virtue of its location in a remote valley high in the northern foothills of the Pyrenees, into a global destination. Today this municipality of 13,000 people has over 350 hotels and 40,000 beds, and draws in as many as 6 million pilgrims a year.

It helped that miraculous cures started happening soon after Bernadette saw her first vision. The first 'approved' miracle probably took place on 1 March, when a local mother who had injured her hand falling from a tree prayed and bathed her hand at the grotto, and was instantly cured. Several days later, a fifty-five-year-old quarryman from the town called Louis Bouriette had the sight restored in his right eye. Three further cures, all later approved by the Catholic Church as miraculous, happened before the visions stopped. These were widely reported in the press and inspired more people to come. Within three years, at least one hundred cures had been claimed, of which fifteen were deemed miraculous after investigation in 1861.[3]

Initially non-commital, in 1862 the Catholic Church declared Bernadette's visions genuine. Now there were no limits to the growth of Lourdes. The diocese had already begun to develop the town as a pilgrimage destination: the land around the grotto was purchased, and missionaries of the Notre-Dame de Garaison – who became known as the Grotto Fathers – were invited to take control.[4] Buildings were demolished and new roads laid out to facilitate the movement of pilgrims. Over the next decade, a new shrine was built, a church began, a statue of the Virgin was placed in the grotto, and railings erected to channel the growing crowds.

With the arrival of the railway in 1866, Lourdes became a destination for mass pilgrimage. The new train line was originally supposed to go from Tarbes to Pau without including Lourdes, but as luck would have it the minister of finance, Achille Fould, had recently bought land nearby and persuaded the railway company to bring the line past Lourdes and his own estate.[5] Railway access was critical. Marian shrines without rail connections, like La Salette in France and Knock in Ireland, developed to nothing like the same degree as Lourdes.

In the 1870s a second church was opened, and later consecrated in front of a crowd of 100,000, but the numbers continued to grow, so a third church was started in 1883, a vast Romano-Byzantine edifice named the Rosary Basilica capable of holding 1,500 worshippers. New rituals were developed and became regular events at the sanctuary, including torchlit Marian processions, and in the years before the First World War a Via Crucis (Stations of the Cross) was constructed on the hill above the grotto.[6]

Most of the pilgrims flocking to Lourdes in its early years were women, and they came for the most part from rural France. The feminine bias appears to have endured. In 1894, pilgrims from the Diocese of Cambrai came en masse to Lourdes: of the 5,600 who took part, only 400 were men. Critics claimed this was because women were more irrational, hysterical and susceptible to suggestion.[7] A better explanation is perhaps that the feminine bias was a reflection of the girl Bernadette, and early responses to Lourdes as a place of the marginalised, away from the mainstream church and state controlled by men. But Lourdes also attracted some of the elite. The emperor Napoleon III's son's governess went there to obtain water to treat her charge's sunstroke; Napoleon himself ordered the reopening of the shrine in the autumn of 1858 to boost his popularity after its closure by the police.

Lourdes rapidly became an international pilgrimage destination with organised groups coming from Belgium and Canada (1873), and from the United States the following year. During the rest of the decade, these visitors were joined by German,

Italian, Polish, Spanish, Irish and Swiss pilgrims as the popularity of Lourdes spread across Europe, before the Catholics of South America began to arrive from Brazil, Argentina, Bolivia and Venezuela.[8] Pilgrims initially came by ship or train, but after the Second World War were able to take advantage of the expanding airport at Tarbes. Shrines and images of Our Lady of Lourdes were established all over the world as proxies for those who could not visit in person. Many modern migrant women from Africa choose Lourdes as their first pilgrimage when they reach Europe because European missionaries brought the cult of Our Lady of Lourdes to Africa in the late nineteenth century.[9] She also attracts Non-Catholic pilgrims. Muslims, Buddhists and Hindus visit Lourdes and pray there alongside Catholics. There are churches (and pilgrims) from other Christian traditions, such as the Ukrainian Orthodox church, built in 1982.[10] Lourdes is truly a global pilgrimage place, welcoming people of all faiths or none, and from almost everywhere on earth. Masses are offered for congregations made up of international pilgrims, while at the Chapel of the Reconciliation priests hear confession around the clock in almost every European language.

The Lourdes of Healing

Pilgrimage sites around the world have been places of healing for thousands of years, but at Lourdes the relationship between faith and medicine has been perhaps more important, and more hotly debated, than anywhere else. Yet healing was never mentioned in the messages that the Virgin gave Bernadette, so why has Lourdes become not just a place of healing, but the pilgrimage above all others that is associated with health and cures? Indeed, its fame is so great that other pilgrimage sites around the world, many far older than Lourdes, have cast themselves in its image. Istanbul has the Church of the Vivifying Source, a Byzantine Lourdes famed for miracles and cures; Kibeho is the Lourdes of Africa, Chimayó the Lourdes of America, Las Lajas the Lourdes of South America; while in the British Isles, Knock claims the title of the Irish Lourdes, Carfin is the Scottish Lourdes, and St Winefride's Well in Wales (not dedicated to the Virgin but a place of healing since the eighth century with a cure record to rival Lourdes) was marketed as the Welsh Lourdes from the 1890s onwards.

Though miracle cures occurred from the start, it was not until the mid-1870s that the sick became a significant proportion of the pilgrims arriving at Lourdes. Over the second half of the decade, several hundred reliably came each year, sometimes brought by special trains, often in wheelchairs or carried on stretchers. The journey was especially difficult in hot weather, or when the trains were full. Sick pilgrims were cared for by friends and family, if accompanied; if not, the well helped out as an act of faith. In 1877 as many as a third of those who came by rail were sick or dying, a situation that necessitated the rapid development of medical facilities. Baths were built, followed by pools in the 1890s. As the number of pilgrims grew, so did the pressure on facilities, and in 1955 larger bathing pools were opened. The severely disabled were helped by *brancardiers*, 'stretcher-bearers to the poor'. At first, these men were from a hospital in Toulouse, and they were sometimes accused of bullying the pilgrims, but over time volunteers took over this role.[11] There were also two hospitals – the domain of women nurses and carers – set up to care for the most seriously ill.

The growing numbers of sick and corresponding claims of cures and miracles led to greater scrutiny. In 1883, concerns over the way cures were being assessed and recorded by the Grotto Fathers led to the foundation of the Bureau de Contestations

Medicales. It eventually settled under one of the ramps leading up to the Rosary Basilica, the perfect spot to interview pilgrims claiming to have been cured. Only if they met strict criteria could cures be approved as miraculous.[12]

To date, only seventy of the cures investigated by the bureau have been declared miracles. The most recent occurred in 2008, when an elderly nun called Sister Bernadette Moriau was cured of the spinal complaint that had kept her in a wheelchair since 1980. The cure was declared miraculous in 2018.[13] As medicine has advanced, the number of cures recognised as miraculous has diminished, although the number of people who believe they have been cured has, if anything, grown. The sanctuary formally recognises the attendance of around 50,000 sick pilgrims each year, though the real numbers are no doubt much higher.

The Business of Pilgrimage

Across the river from the sanctuary, Lourdes became a boom town as the locals set up businesses to cater to the pilgrimage trade, while entrepreneurs made full use of the gamut of promotional tools available to them, as a result of which the story of Bernadette was spread far and wide. Images of Lourdes appeared in the early works of the French pioneers of the moving image, the brothers Auguste and Louis Lumière. The popularity of Lourdes meant that guides to the town and sanctuary were among the bestsellers of their day, the French journalist Henry Lasserre's 1869 book running into 142 editions in just seven years.[14] By the end of the century, it had been translated into eighty languages. As pilgrims poured in, people turned their homes into boarding houses, hotels were thrown up, and souvenir shops opened on the town's narrow streets, selling everything from Virgin-shaped bottles for holy water, prayer books, Bibles, photos of Bernadette, prayer cards and rosaries, to tea towels, pill boxes (useful for the many sick pilgrims), mints made using water from the holy spring, and glow-in-the-dark rosaries and statues of the mother of God. The town also developed sights to draw in pilgrims and tourists, including a waxwork museum depicting scenes from Bernadette's life, which opened in 1974. Not for nothing has Lourdes been called the Disneyland of God.[15]

The commercialisation of Lourdes at the end of the nineteenth century led the historian Suzanne Kaufman to argue that it was an important place for the emergence of modern consumer culture – the first modern capitalist shrine[16] – and many have criticised the development of the town and the proliferation of souvenir shops. But pilgrimage places have always catered for those who want a memento of their visit. One person's tourist tat is another's holy keepsake, the tourist and the pilgrim investing the same object with entirely different meanings. One guidebook advised pilgrims to 'scour the city for material souvenirs, images, rosaries with all the benedictions and indulgences, medals and pretty trinkets and jewelery' to take back for friends and family, as these objects would come under the protection of Mary, and thus convey her grace back to the pilgrims' homes.[17] Lourdes is a fascinating example of the pull between the secular and the sacred at holy places, where the two overlap and are often embodied in the same thing.

Keen to avoid charges of greed and exploitation, the religious authorities distanced themselves from the rampant commercialism, banning hawkers and sellers from the sanctuary itself, but they were quick to exploit the mass media to spread the message of Lourdes. Their newsletter, *Le Pelerin*, was launched in 1873 to promote Lourdes and its cures. Stories of sanctuary events regularly found their way into the national and foreign press too, either because journalists came to Lourdes, or because the church authorities actively circulated the information. The Grotto Fathers established a candle factory to supply their own needs, while water from the holy spring was (and is still) bottled and shipped all around the world.[18] The fathers have argued that this is the continuation of a long tradition of generating income to support a sacred site while simultaneously spreading its benefits to those unable to visit, but critics complain it's simply a money-making scheme on the part of the rapacious Catholic Church.

Critics of Lourdes' commercialisation and the rapid development of the sanctuary have been highly vocal in the press and in fictional works. In Émile Zola's *Lourdes* his protagonist Pierre saw the town in a dream: 'He beheld Lourdes, contaminated by Mammon, turned into a pot of abomination and perdition, transformed into a huge bazaar, where everything was sold, masses and souls alike!'[19] There were complaints about the number of street sellers pushing their wares on to pilgrims, and about the beggars who harassed them. Another writer, Joris-Karl Huysmans, visited Lourdes in 1905 and complained about the 'plethora of vulgarity' and 'haemorrhage of bad taste' that were the sanctuary and its buildings.[20] The increasing numbers of hotels and tourist facilities during the twentieth century did nothing to improve matters. 'Lourdes was an intoxicating place,' Arthur Matthews has his protagonist complain in his novel *Well-Remembered Days*, about his visit in 1964, '[but] I remember thinking that it was probably what Las Vegas would have been like if casinos and nightclubs had been replaced by Catholicism.'[21]

Others disapproved of how pilgrims reached the town. Railway travel was a practical and speedy way to get there, and companies laid on special services to transport thousands of them. These 'trains of hope' brought people from all over Europe, and without them many of the sickest pilgrims would never have been able to reach Lourdes, but they attracted criticism from non-Catholics, who saw rail travel as cheating. Pre-modern pilgrimage had often involved tough and even dangerous travel, and the fact that some pilgrims went first class in considerable comfort didn't help matters. The Catholic authorities took a different view, embracing the rail journey as part of the religious experience. Manuals and handbooks for prayer on board were handed out, services were conducted by priests, and every effort was made to ensure that the devout were catered for. It might not have been the trek across hundreds of miles on foot that sceptics demanded, but it was a religious experience, nonetheless.

However, it was a modern experience. Lourdes was not to everyone's taste and was at odds with what many thought a pilgrimage should be, which was in essence medieval – or at least what they *thought* was medieval. A Belgian pilgrim called Joseph Demarteau complained in 1906 that new religious buildings had been thrown up like modern five-storey houses, that the souvenirs were mass-produced in Paris, and that this 'brutality' clashed with any attempt to create the impression of an ancient and venerable place.[22] The previously isolated town offered round-the-clock electricity, comfortable modern hotels and a selection of fine places to eat, but what had any of that to do with pilgrimage? Maria Warner, writing about Lourdes in her brilliant *Alone of All Her Sex: the Myth & the Cult of the Virgin Mary*, asked 'why Lourdes should leave so many visitors hollow and dry'? In answer she pointed to its lack of 'artistic greatness' as seen in places like Rome or Florence, the mosaics of 'singular weakness and vulgarity' decorating the basilica, and the poured-concrete underground basilica used for pilgrim worship, built in the 1950s to house 25,000 worshippers, which 'resembles an underground carpark'.[23]

These might sound like criticisms born of some sort of misunderstanding regarding the power of faith in stirring pilgrims, but Warner rightly noted that the Catholic Church has always used beauty and the stimulation of the senses – whether sight, touch, smell or hearing – to convey sanctity. For her the lack of sensory stimulation at Lourdes made the place feel empty, though for the thousands who flock there each year this seems not to be a problem.

The Politics of Lourdes

Though the story of Lourdes is overwhelmingly one of faith and pilgrimage for healing, it is also a political symbol, a sacred national site that developed in response to war and disease in France. It was quickly adopted as a place where political statements could be made under the guise of faith. 'Everything about Lourdes,' claimed Miri Rubin, 'was a challenge to the [secular] state.'[24] This was part of a wider trend. France was a hotbed of Marian devotion in the nineteenth century, with apparitions of Mary, basilicas built in her name, and new religious orders dedicated to the Virgin. In 1871, in an atmosphere of anti-Catholicism that had already seen the archbishop of Bayonne murdered, pilgrims at Nantes were attacked as they travelled home from Lourdes.[25] There had been a distinctly political bent to the pilgrimage that year, in support of the restoration of the Bourbon monarchy following the collapse of Napoleon III's empire.

The following year a rally was held at Lourdes, organised by a priest called Victor Chocarne and one of his parishioners, Marguerite de Blic, who led a procession through the town of banner-carrying pilgrims, who laid them down in the basilica as a sign of their faith in the strength of France. Dubbed the Rally of the Faith and Hope of France to Our Lady of Lourdes, and also known as the Pilgrimage of the Banners, it was the first large-scale national pilgrimage to the shrine. The *Daily News* in England reported that the pilgrimage was 'evidently political'.[26]

In 1873 a national pilgrimage to Lourdes was established by the Parisian Augustinian Fathers of the Assumption (the Assumptionists), and the Grotto Fathers promoted it as a way the French could atone for the sins that had in part brought about their defeat in the Franco-Prussian War two years before. Around the same time there was also a push to remind visitors to Lourdes about France's medieval Christian past, and many of the pilgrims of 1873 wore a small red cross made of wool, recalling the crusaders of the Middle Ages and signifying that they were taking part in a pilgrimage to save France.[27]

At the beginning of the twentieth century, Lourdes hit a rough patch when a scandal led to the removal of the Assumptionists and Grotto Fathers and the seizure of the grotto itself by the state. The local bishop was soon able to rent the sanctuary land back, but the affair showed how the site had become a focus of conflict between secular French republicans and Catholic monarchists. It was not restored to church ownership until after the defeat of France by Nazi Germany in 1940. The following year Marshal Pétain, head of the puppet Vichy regime, was invited to visit. This brought with it its own problems and further controversy due to Pétain's collaboration with Nazi Germany.

The separation of church and state which has defined French politics since 1905 was tested in 2008 when Pope Benedict XVI came to France on a three-day visit, the first since he became pontiff. The trip included a pilgrimage to Lourdes to celebrate its 150th anniversary, something which need not have been controversial but for the behaviour of the French president, Nicolas Sarkozy. A thrice-married 'cultural Catholic', he had recently taken to referring repeatedly to God in his speeches in a way that was more akin to the behaviour of American politicians. Consequently, there was concern that the papal visit to France, and particularly Lourdes, was a sign of a shift back to closer ties between the Catholic Church and the French state.[28]

The Lourdes of War

Of all the Christian pilgrim destinations, Lourdes is the one most associated with military pilgrimage. Early in the shrine's history, army officers from prominent French families were involved in organising the French national pilgrimages, reinforcing the connections between the Virgin, Lourdes and the church militant. In the wake of the two World Wars, however, Lourdes became a place of reconciliation, forgiveness and peace for those who had served on all sides of the conflicts. Lourdes was in many ways a natural choice. Though Mary is usually seen as the embodiment of peace and nurturing, she has also been portrayed as the protector of those who appeal to her and as a patron of armies. In this dual role, she has appealed particularly to Catholic members of the military, both offering them comfort when they are injured in body or mind and supporting them in battle.

French devotion to Our Lady of Lourdes was notable in the trenches of the First World War, where she was the focus of prayers for protection and of pilgrimage vows made by desperate soldiers. In 1915 one fighter wrote a letter of prayer to her, which he left in the sanctuary at Noulette in the Pas-de-Calais, northern France. 'Our Lady of Lourdes I turn to you so you can give me the grace of coming home some day to my little home with my whole little family how far away I am. Preserve me against the disasters I see every day, and I beg you, stop at last this terrible carnage that makes so many corpses.'[29]

The following year, France's bishops prayed to Our Lady of Lourdes for victory in the war, promising that they would organise a national pilgrimage in her honour when it was over. True to their word, when the war did end, military pilgrimages of thanks were held and hundreds of ex-servicemen marched south. In March 1919 the Knights of St Columba, a religious fraternity founded as a mutual benefit society to support immigrants to the United States, took three thousand American 'boys in uniform' who had been stationed across Europe on pilgrimage to Lourdes.[30] There was also an Allied forces pilgrimage, led jointly by the archbishops of Reims and Westminster. Whereas those pilgrimages before the First World War that had had a political or military aspect had been at least in part inspired by resistance to the French state and secularisation, those afterwards were more often about healing and international reconciliation.

In the decades between the two World Wars, military pilgrimages to Lourdes continued to develop and grow, drawing ex-servicemen and sometimes their family members from around the world. The National League of Ex-Combatant Priests organised French veteran pilgrimages, while other pilgrimages were supported by Pax Romana. They grew in popularity across Europe, America, Australia and New Zealand, with new organising groups and annual pilgrimages established each year.

The reputation of Lourdes as *the* pilgrimage destination for soldiers and veterans received a boost, especially in Britain, when a disabled veteran called Jack Traynor was cured while on pilgrimage in 1923. Mr Traynor, a Catholic from Liverpool, served in the First World War, where after only a month of active service he was injured in the head by shrapnel from an exploding shell. Following a five-week coma and a spell in a military hospital in England, he was sent out to Egypt. It wasn't long before he was shot in the knee. What caused the real damage though was the hail of machine-gun bullets he ran into at Gallipoli in May 1915, one of which entered his right arm and, travelling up, came to rest under his collarbone. As he had lost the use of his arm, he was discharged from the army and sent home. Epileptic fits increased in severity over time, and despite specialist treatment and an operation on his skull he eventually could not walk or stand. Confined to a wheelchair by July 1923, the military authorities offered him a place at the Mossley Hill Hospital for Incurables.

The same month, news reached him that a pilgrimage from Lancashire to Lourdes was being planned. Though his wife and doctors objected, Mr Traynor was determined to go. The story caused quite a stir and featured in the local press. Interest grew to such a point that Mr Traynor got his brother to wheel him through Liverpool's back streets to the pilgrimage train to avoid the crowds. He endured a punishing journey to Lourdes that many thought he would not survive. At Lourdes itself, he bathed in the holy water and improved a little each time. After the ninth bath and a blessing, he could suddenly move his arm. Early the next morning, after a restless night, he leaped out of bed and ran down to the sanctuary, even though he had been unable to walk for four years. Moved by his experience and determined to give thanks to the Virgin for her help, he abandoned the only vice he had left, and stopped smoking.

The English press seized on Jack Traynor's story, and by the time he returned to Liverpool, he was quite the sensation. When his wife arrived at Lime Street station to meet him, she had to force her way through the crowds to the platform, where several dozen other women, all claiming to be *the* Mrs Traynor, were already waiting. The reaction of the British army to the change in his circumstances is illuminating. Apparently unable to recognise the possibility that a miraculous cure may have occurred at Lourdes, they continued to pay him his disability pension even though he was hale and hearty, went on to set up and work for his own company, and never needed a wheelchair again.[31]

Jack Traynor's pilgrimage was important in demonstrating the possible benefits of Lourdes to disabled veterans, but organised military pilgrimages remained relatively rare until the following decade. Then in 1934 a papally approved pilgrimage involved up to 80,000 First World War veterans from at least nineteen countries.[32] The pilgrimage was a source of pride for many of the pilgrims; the names of some of the British men chosen to take part were printed in their local newspapers, often accompanied by details of their service. Press coverage was also substantial because the pilgrims included ten holders of the Victoria Cross. The growing reputation of Lourdes as a place of peace and reconciliation led the Catholic archbishop of Birmingham, Dr Thomas Williams, to call on Hitler to let German troops join the pilgrimage to 'invoke the peace of the world'. He also delivered a sermon suggesting that Hitler himself should come as a pilgrim as a reflection of the 'profound love of peace' he had gained fighting in the trenches of the World War One. 'What a fine impulse towards real peace in Europe it would be if Herr Hitler were to attend,' he told his congregation. 'It would encourage the Catholics of Germany who fought so splendidly for their country in the War to come and join their former foes in praying for peace.' With hindsight the archbishop's hopes seem woefully naive, but they remain a testimony to the belief held by people of faith that pilgrimage has the power to bring people together and effect real change through the power of prayer.[33]

Two years later, another even bigger peace pilgrimage to Lourdes, led by bishops who were themselves war veterans, drew 120,000 ex-servicemen.[34] The 1934 pilgrimage had managed to steer clear of politics, but rising tensions in Europe meant that this event was more political in flavour as pilgrims worried about another war and prayed for peace. Although the Virgin failed to answer their prayers, throughout 1939–45 pilgrims still came in their tens of thousands despite the difficulties imposed by wartime conditions.

The period after the Second World War saw massive growth in the Lourdes pilgrimage. Whereas in an average pre-war year about 250,000 pilgrims had visited, the annual figures rapidly rose into the millions after 1945. In part this was down to the energies of Monseigneur Théas, the post-war bishop of Tarbes, the diocese which includes Lourdes, who was appointed in February 1947, and quickly set about reviving the fortunes of the shrine. As president of Pax Christi, he was also committed to promoting reconciliation between France and Germany.[35]

He was building on firm foundations, as peace and reconciliation pilgrimages were already under way when he was appointed bishop. One of the earliest of these pilgrimages took place the year after the end of the war. When the pilgrims approached Lourdes in September 1946, they were met with an impressive sight. The field across the river from the grotto had been converted into a map of Germany, with all the prisoner-of-war and concentration camps marked with fifteen-foot-high statues, painted in different colours to identify the type of camp and category of prisoner. One hundred thousand pilgrims from Buchenwald, Dachau and other camps thronged the field, some meeting fellow prisoners they had not seen since their liberation.[36] This Lourdes pilgrimage offered the chance for people from all over France and further afield who had spent time together under terrible circumstances to find each other again. It was also a pilgrimage born of thousands of vows, as in the camps many prisoners had sworn to go to Lourdes if they survived. The following year, Bishop Théas assisted in the visit of 700 pilgrims from the Saarland just over the German border in the hope that their faith would reconcile them with their former enemies.

In 1958, the hundredth-anniversary pilgrimage to Lourdes was held, with great celebrations to mark the milestone. A few months later the first of the international military pilgrimages to Lourdes took place when the French armed forces invited their German counterparts to accompany them to Lourdes as an act and sign of reconciliation.[37] Since then, pilgrimages to Lourdes have become the cornerstone of the annual activities of many of the world's military bishoprics, and not just for veterans of the Second World War. America's Warriors to Lourdes programme sends thousands of pilgrims each year, including veterans of the conflicts in Iraq and Afghanistan and serving soldiers, many seeking cures for injuries and disabilities.[38] Lourdes has also been a powerful tool for reconciliation in internal wars. In 1992, as Yugoslavia was riven by civil war, the Croatian military and police pilgrimage to Lourdes was set up, and over time military representatives from other countries have joined the Croatian pilgrims.[39]

15

SAINTES-MARIES-DE-LA-MER

France

On a Friday evening in the summer of 1941, the station platform at Arles-Trinquetaille in southern France was crowded with pilgrims. Unable to travel by road due to the wartime shortage of petrol and the scarcity and cost of horses, this large group of Gypsies (the term used by the community in the UK and by several Romany groups across Europe)[1] had decided to travel by train. The carriages were packed, and those who could not fit inside were obliged to climb onto the roofs. Everyone was dressed in their finery – men in suits, women and girls in their best dresses – and excited to cover the last twenty-five miles across the watery landscape of the Camargue, inhabited by wild white horses, bulls and flamingos, to the small coastal town of Saintes-Maries-de-la-Mer for the annual pilgrimage in honour of St Sara and the two Marys after whom the place is named.[2]

This pilgrimage has brought Europe's Gypsies together since at least the mid-nineteenth century, though Les Saintes, as the town is usually known, has been a destination for pilgrims for far longer than that. It is undoubtedly one of the most important Gypsy pilgrimages in Europe, but it has also become an event about heritage and exploitation. The event has been repackaged to create a cultural and touristic spectacle that the Catholic

Church simultaneously dislikes and insists on controlling, and the Gypsy community and those drawn to its sense of freedom are continually trying to take back.

The Two Marys

The town of Les Saintes is probably named in honour of Mary Jacobe, mother of St James the Great, whose own relics are at Santiago de Compostela in Spain, and Mary Salome, two of the three Marys (the other was Mary Magdalene, who some mistakenly believe came with them) who carried myrrh to Jesus' tomb and found that he was no longer there.[3] According to legend, the two women then sailed across the Mediterranean and were washed up on the delta of the River Rhône at a small village. They lived there for some years and, on their deaths, were buried in the village church, which was later rebuilt and dedicated to Mary, mother of Christ. In 1521 Vincent Philippon recorded this story in *The Legend of the Saintes-Maries*, the manuscript of which is now in the library at Arles, and mentioned a serving woman in the little seaborne party, Sara, though, as we shall see, this is just one of the stories told about her origins. Gypsies, who had arrived in the nearby town of Arles in the late 1430s, venerate this woman as St Sara.[4]

During the Middle Ages, evidence for pilgrimage to Les Saintes is almost non-existent, though Bishop Pierre Benoit of Saint-Pol-de-Léon in Brittany credited the Marys with healing his gout and followed up his cure with a pilgrimage of thanks in 1357, so evidently pilgrims were going to the church.[5] Situated by the sea, the town was vulnerable to pirates, which may have discouraged regular pilgrimage, and it was defended by ramparts. The church itself was heavily fortified and served as a refuge in the event of attack.

Pilgrimages probably took off in the fifteenth century after the relics of the saints were rediscovered in 1448 by René, duke of Anjou, then ruler of Provence and father of Margaret of Anjou, queen of England. The excavations he oversaw turned up their bones, as well as lead coffins and pottery and the possible remains of St Hippolytus of Rome, martyred in 235. The site was presumably identified by some sort of marker soon after that, as Hans von Waltheym, a young pilgrim from Saxony, saw the graves of the two Marys in 1474. He took back some soil as a sacred souvenir.[6] Also found were a marble table thought to be the altar the two women set up in their home, and a smooth piece of marble, now embedded into the wall of the crypt, identified as the pillow of the saints. The relics of the two Marys were housed in a reliquary which was burned during the French Revolution, which also interrupted pilgrimages. The reliquary was replaced in 1798, and the name of the town was changed to the plural by the commune in 1838 to encompass both Marys – from Sainte-Marie-de-la-Mer to Saintes-Maries-de-la-Mer.[7]

The renaming of the town was part of its inhabitants' project to revive the fortunes of Les Saintes. Given that the surrounding terrain was malarial swamp, and the town itself had little to offer, the most logical thing was to develop Les Saintes as a pilgrimage destination, using what they already had: relics and a good story. A stream of pilgrims had been coming for centuries, so they were not starting from scratch; reporting on religious activities in the town in 1820, the mayor described celebrations and the presence of pilgrims. Five years later, the count of Villeneuve explained that so many pilgrims flocked there to venerate the Marys that they had to shelter in tents, as the town was too small to accommodate them all. They came for healing – apparently rabies was a real issue at the time – and to receive indulgences.[8] The procession of the two Marys to the sea was

The two Marys who give the town its name are the focus of the Catholic pilgrimage procession which takes place on 25 May. St Sara, venerated by Gypsy pilgrims, had her own procession the day before.

re-established in 1862 as a focal point for the pilgrimage, and later in the century, to ensure as many came as possible, the start time of the celebrations was shifted to fit in with the arrival of the morning train.[9] Les Saintes, small and already too crowded during the pilgrimage, could now attract religious day-trippers.

The celebrations for devotees of the two Marys have come to comprise two key events. The first takes place on 24 May, and is the lowering of the reliquary chest holding the saints' remains on thick ropes from a room at the top of the church using a winch. The right to operate the winch is the preserve of the men of Beaucaire, a town on the banks of the Rhône north of Arles.[10] The chest, painted with scenes of the Marys' arrival, is an object of veneration, and pilgrims vie with one another to get as close to it as possible in order to reach up and extinguish their candles on its base, and then, when it reaches the altar, touch the chest itself.[11] It remains on the altar until the completion of the second key event the following day, the procession down to the sea. The procession attracts large crowds and important pilgrims. Monsignor Roncalli, who became Pope John XXIII a decade later, presided over a special procession held in 1948 to commemorate the discovery of the relics five centuries before.

The Gypsy Pilgrimage

The pilgrimage to Les Saintes is two pilgrimages in one: the Catholic pilgrimage in honour of the two Marys, venerated in the church, and the Romani pilgrimage to St Sara, whose statue is hidden away in the crypt underneath the church. They take place in the same week and overlap. St Sara's statue can only just be seen beneath the layers of clothing she is dressed in on the evening of 23 May, each item a gift from a devout pilgrim. Returning pilgrims traditionally retrieve their previous year's offering and take it home, cutting it up and giving the parts as gifts to family and friends.[12] The dark colour of the statue comes from the thousands of candles which have been burned in the crypt. It is possible that there was also a reliquary containing her bones, as John Manson reported seeing it in 1901, the glass scratched by the touches of countless pilgrims, but there is no trace of it now.[13] How early Gypsies started to come, we don't know, but it is possible they were visiting Les Saintes in the fifteenth century, as Arles is close enough for news of the rediscovery of the relics to have reached there.

Some Gypsies believe that Sara is one of their own, a Gypsy who lived in southern France and welcomed the two Marys when they arrived, wading out into the sea to help the women reach the beach.[14] Others that she was a Gypsy from Egypt, where many believed Gypsies originated, who came in the boat with Mary Jacobe and Mary Salome, perhaps as their servant.[15] That is how she is described in a poem of 1357 by Jean de Venette, who wrote that the two Marys, having been brought from Italy by a French knight (rather than arriving by sea), were buried at Les Saintes. Venette's verse was popularised in the early sixteenth century by its translation into prose by Jean Drouyn, which ran through several editions between 1506 and 1511.[16] Yet another work claims Sara was the wife of Pontius Pilate.[17] A proportion of the legends surrounding Sara might have bled in from other faiths, and some of those who support the theory that the Gypsies originate in India believe that her name in Romani, Sara La Kali or Kali Sara, suggests an association with the Hindu goddess Kali.[18] In the Hindu faith, a statue of the goddess Sati Sara is carried into the Ganges. However, statues of religious figures being carried into the sea is not uncommon in the Catholic tradition.

Gypsies were only allowed into the church to take part in the lowering of the two Marys' reliquary after the archbishop of Aix gave his permission in 1921. After the lowering of the chest and mass in the church on 24 May, Sara's statue is carried in procession along the town's narrow streets and into the sea accompanied by four men on white horses and the shouts of pilgrims, many of whom collect water from the sea. The two Marys get their own procession the following day. The procession then forms up for the return journey to the crypt of the church.

The involvement of Romani in the pilgrimage, like so much of their history, is not well documented. They were certainly taking part by the 1850s, as their attendance was reported in *L'Illustration* in 1852.[19] The poet Frédéric Mistral, writing about his own pilgrimage of 1855, provided the best early account of the pilgrim Gypsies. When he and his companion reached the church, they found it 'full as an egg of people from Languedoc, women from around Arles, invalids, and Gypsies, all in fact on top of one another. It was the Gypsies who burned the biggest tapers, but only at the altar of St Sara.'[20] The scene of chaos included some women from Nîmes fighting over a sleeping spot in the church itself, who had brought cushions but needed to secure chairs, and people singing a number of different hymns all at once. The smell of the mass of people and animals made Mistral 'gasp for breath'. The seething crowd in the church contrasted with the more romanticised and picturesque image of pilgrims portrayed in paint. When Vincent van Gogh painted some Gypsies who had probably stayed on in the town after the pilgrimage in about 1888, he was captivated by their apparent representation of 'a myth of primitive survival'.[21]

The Gypsies come to ask Sara for help with all kinds of problems, leaving prayers and requests on slips of paper before her statue, or more tangible things like wedding bouquets.[22] Many of the pilgrims are looking for some sort of cure. Mistral arrived on a cart with a friend and a Gypsy woman with her daughter. Abandoned by the man she had eloped with and 'not right in the head since', the girl's mother hoped Sara would 'distract her or cure her'.[23] In the church itself he witnessed sick pilgrims drinking 'glasses of brackish water from the well of the Saints' in the nave, while others scratched away at the stone pillow, collecting the dust to use in some sort of cure.[24]

The Gypsy pilgrimage has always been important in bringing together a people who are usually scattered across Europe. American art historian Marilyn Brown has called it 'an annual convention for the Gypsies of continental Europe'.[25] For most, pilgrimages are a chance to get away from ordinary life, to leave behind the everyday and engage in quiet contemplation, but the Romani who come to Les Saintes do the complete opposite.

The pilgrimage is an opportunity for a people continually on the move to come together to conduct the business of life: weddings and christenings, parties, family gatherings and deals.[26] It is at the heart of Gypsy culture. The annual get-togethers at Les Saintes spawned the band the Gipsy Kings (at first called Los Reyes) when two families met on the 1970 pilgrimage and began to play together. When Django Reinhardt, arguably the most famous of Gypsy musicians, wrote a mass during the days of the Nazi occupation he did so in homage to Saintes-Maries-de-la-Mer. He never recorded it but told a reporter he hoped 'that my mass will be adopted by my people throughout the world and that it will be consecrated at our annual gathering at Saintes-Maries-de-la-Mer'.[27] The Gypsies' connection with the area could unfortunately be used against them. Following the lead of their Nazi masters, the Vichy regime built an internment camp for Gypsies at nearby Saliers on the basis that the area was, in the words of the camp's architect, the 'cradle of their race'.[28]

Whereas they had previously dismissed it or been outright hostile, after the Second World War, the Catholic Church began to promote the Gypsy pilgrimage to Les Saintes. The pioneers of the Catholic Gypsy chaplaincy, Father Jean Fleury and Father André Barthélémy, arrived in the town in 1950 and 1953 respectively to begin the process of inserting themselves into a pilgrimage that had already been going on for decades if not longer.[29] Their motives were less about supporting the Romani than concern that they were switching to Pentecostalism in large numbers, particularly after the Pentecostalists set up their Mission Évangélique Tzigane in 1958.[30] The Catholic Church was perhaps right to be worried, as in 1949 one visitor noted that, with the exception of the war years, there were fewer Gypsies than ever before on the pilgrimage.[31] The church also wanted to bring the cult of Sara more into line with orthodox

Catholic practice, which they attempted to do by introducing the statue of Our Lady of the Gypsies into the processions from 1958 onwards.[32] This did not go down well, and the angered Gypsies crowned St Sara to show her primacy in their pilgrimage.[33] The local clergy were also unhappy about the arrival of the new priests, and were only calmed when Fleury and Barthélémy were officially designated 'priests of the Gypsies' with no authority over parochial matters.[34] Pierre Causse, who took a close interest in the history and practice of the pilgrimage, was appointed to liaise between the two groups to smooth relations.[35]

Pilgrimage to Les Saintes grew exponentially as easier and cheaper travel in the post-war years transformed an essentially local pilgrimage into one that attracted Romani from across Spain, France, Italy and Germany. This was even though Gypsies traditionally eschewed passports and travel documentation, which limited their ability to cross borders.[36] That said, this is a reasonably recent shift. In a survey taken at the church door in Les Saintes in 1974, eleven years before the European Community opened its internal borders, although 28 per cent of pilgrims came from outside France, of the Gypsies questioned only 3 per cent did. Most (53 per cent) came from the local region, while 44 per cent were from further afield in France.[37] The rise in numbers put increasing pressure on the town, as more space was needed to accommodate the sudden influx of tens of thousands of people into a town of just a few thousand. The place de Gitans, once large enough to accommodate the caravans of all the Gypsies who came for the pilgrimage, was no longer able to do so in the years after the Second World War.[38]

Gypsies have not always been welcome in Les Saintes. A ban was placed on Gypsy pilgrims in 1895 by prefectural degree, though it was lifted after three years, and in 1907 the deputy of

Savoy, Fernand David, suggested banning them from the May pilgrimage.[39] At one time, Gypsy pilgrims were only allowed to visit the crypt via a back door of the church.[40] Monsignor Coste, archbishop of Aix in 1934, banned them from carrying the statue of Sara on the 25 May procession, though the prohibition was lifted the following year after an appeal from a local aristocrat, the marquis de Baroncelli, who was largely responsible for the official recognition of St Sara. The local priests were unenthusiastic about the cult of Sara, at best tolerating it.[41]

Efforts to stop St Sara being carried into the sea in 1953 were met with fierce opposition, and presumably in an effort to bring the practice more firmly under church control, priests were involved for the first time. Even as late as 1966, the local chaplaincy tried to replace the procession with Stations of the Cross, a move that resulted in 'violent incidents'.[42] Support for the procession the following year, from no less a figure than the archbishop of Aix, put a stop to attempts to suppress it. At a press conference in May, according to *La Provencal* newspaper, he declared, 'The cult of Saint Sara is an immemorial cult. That is why I maintain it in its traditional form. Like many other saints, it is not possible to give any truly historical details about the character of Saint Sara. But it is for historians, not the bishop, to delve deeper into this problem.'[43] Even so, prejudice if not outright opposition continued. When a French radio station broadcast a three-hour programme in the summer of 1972 about Saintes-Maries-de-la-Mer and its pilgrimage, they managed to do so without once mentioning the Gypsies, which was quite a feat.[44]

Acceptance of the Romani within the Catholic Church has long been a bone of contention, while suspicions about their beliefs have been directed at Gypsies all over Europe and from all faiths.[45] Much of this is thinly veiled (or not-veiled-at-all) racism. Jean Aicard's 1890 novel *King of Camargue* complained about 'so many mischievous gipsies [*sic*]' at Les Saintes, and suggested they were 'impelled by a curious sort of piety, mingled with a desire to pilfer from the pilgrims'. The Gypsy pilgrimage was the 'rendezvous of the last savages of the faith'.[46]

At Les Saintes, a good deal of criticism has focused on how Gypsies conduct their pilgrimage, which conflicts with how Catholic pilgrims behave. This is true of Gypsy pilgrim destinations all over Europe like Knock in Ireland, or St Winefride's Well in Wales, but the sheer numbers who descend on Les Saintes make it more of an issue. Walter Starkie, who was invited into the crypt for the overnight vigil in 1951, was 'scandalised by the behaviour' of Romani youths, who talked for much of the night and threw wax at each other.[47] The fact that Gypsies conduct an overnight vigil in the crypt has done plenty to fuel the imagination of those suspicious of their motives: they must be celebrating a black mass or electing a new Gypsy queen; sacrifices were offered, secret rituals of all kinds conducted.[48] The imaginations of mainstream (or intolerant) Catholics ran riot. 'Despite their excessive zeal,' observed a local priest around 1900, 'their enthusiastic demonstration, their diligent abandonment, one cannot help but ask themselves if they are truly Christians, and if it is indeed the love of the Holy Marys that inspires their conduct.'[49]

However, Gypsy pilgrims follow their own strict code, one that specifies particular forms of veneration and requires sexual abstinence. Romani men will kiss and touch the statues of the two Marys, but not the statue of Sara because she is a Gypsy, and the same rules must be adhered to for her as for all Gypsy women.[50] This begs the question: who decides on what is the appropriate way to conduct a pilgrimage?

A Pilgrimage of Performance

Despite the ancient origins of the stories of both the two Marys and St Sara, and the antiquity of the church at Les Saintes, the modern pilgrimage was the brainchild of Marquis Falco de Baroncelli-Javon (1869–1943), a town councillor, cattle farmer and zealous defender of the Camargue's unique culture. Having moved to the area in 1895, he spent the following years promoting Provençal traditions, staging processions on horseback and greeting pilgrims to Les Saintes in person. He was passionate about authenticity, whatever that might mean, and like many others of his class he was fascinated with the exoticism of Gypsy culture, which seemed so separate from 'normal' society. Joining the Gypsy pilgrimage involved crossing some sort of boundary. When writer Ernest Hemingway visited Les Saintes on pilgrimage during his 1927 honeymoon with his second wife Pauline, they 'stained their faces with berries and got lost among the Gypsies', as if a disguise was necessary.[51]

In 1935, in his capacity as a town councillor Baroncelli managed to reintroduce the procession of Sara's statue down to the sea . Baroncelli had church approval for his support of the Gypsy pilgrimage, but his real motive wasn't so much spiritual as driven by his desire to create and promote a cultural identity for the town.[52] The logic behind his focus on the Gypsy pilgrims sat on shaky foundations. The origins of the two Marys and St Sara are obscure, but Baroncelli added an even more fanciful element, to the effect that they were descendants of one of the four tribes of the lost city of Atlantis.[53] Nevertheless, his role in reviving the Les Saintes pilgrimage is such that a ceremony is still held at his tomb in the town on the day after the processions end.

The pilgrimage as re-created by Baroncelli has become a mix of faith, tourism and heritage, with people dressed in nineteenth-century costume encouraged by the local tourist office.[54]

The Gypsy pilgrimage has been commercialised to such an extent that costumed performers are preferred by many locals to genuine Gypsy pilgrims.

Visitors seem to love it, posing for photographs with the 'traditional' Gypsy pilgrims, but it reinforces the impression that the pilgrimage is a performance rather than an act of devotion. Every year major newspapers around Europe run photo essays and reports on the 'unusual gathering' in the Camargue, hardly mentioning its religious significance. PARTYING WITH THE GYPSIES IN THE CAMARGUE read one headline in the *Guardian*.[55] Advertising materials and tourist office publicity utilise Gypsy imagery to promote the pilgrimage and the town itself. To promote the 1962 pilgrimage, its organisers commissioned local artist Henry Couve to produce a poster. He was known for creating vibrant images of horse shows and bullfighting, activities full of movement and energy. His poster was in the same vein, its right-hand side given over to practicalities like the days and times of events, but the rest covered in bright pictures that created a very particular impression of the pilgrimage. At the bottom left were a man and woman dressed in Gypsy finery on a horse, the woman's rich blue skirts striking against the white coat of their mount. Above them, two women lounged outside a traditional Gypsy caravan, dressed in bright clothes. At the top of the poster was a depiction of the banner of the two Marys, and on the top right the tower of the village's fortress-like church loomed large. There was no sign of St Sara.

Despite the use of Gypsy imagery to promote the pilgrimage, Romani arriving on pilgrimage have long been treated with considerable suspicion in Les Saintes. Policing levels are increased, and other visitors are warned of a potential rise in crime during the period of the pilgrimage. Many of the townspeople seem to resent the Gypsies. Whereas most pilgrimage places around the world welcome the arrival of visitors as a significant source of income and trade, at Les Saintes many business owners shut up shop and go on holiday to avoid what they consider an invasion.[56] For those who remain and continue to trade, while they welcome the income from tourists they want the *right kind* of pilgrims. In recent years, the election of a right-wing mayor in the town, who, together with his deputy seems to have gone out of his way to cause offence to Sara's devotees, has coincided with increasing complaints against Gypsy pilgrims and suggestions that the town no longer wants or needs them.[57]

Just as the pilgrimage to Saintes-Maries-de-la-Mer has changed before in the interests of reviving the town, perhaps it will simply evolve once more. Some recent pilgrims to the town believe that St Sara was the love child of Mary Magdalene and Jesus, a notion advanced in the internationally bestselling pseudohistorical *The Holy Blood and the Holy Grail* (1982) and made even more popular thanks to the 2003 international blockbuster *The Da Vinci Code.* In Brown's version of events, the pregnant

Mary Magdalene flees the Holy Land after Jesus' death and gives birth to their daughter, Sara, when she reaches France.[58] Both books have been widely derided, but believers in the legends of the two Marys and St Sara hardly seem no more concerned with hard evidence, so why should the new pilgrims?

The Gypsy pilgrims who still come to Les Saintes are drawn by the sense of community it brings them. Once the prayers and processions are over, and the tourists and other pilgrims have gone home, the Romani stay for a while to conduct the business of their lives on one of the few occasions they meet as a large group. 'While the tourists and the faithful storm the little tram, the Gypsies gather at the fair, in the cafes, around the caravans and hold their family council,' reported the pilgrim on the journey of 1941 which opened this chapter. 'We deal with common affairs, we form marriage plans, we discuss, we argue, we help each other. On this day of pilgrimage, peace is established between families.'[59] Like Bear Butte, Les Saintes brings together a scattered people.

16

RĀTANA PĀ

New Zealand

On 8 November 1918, a Māori man called Tahupōtiki Wiremu Rātana, a mild-mannered forty-five-year-old farmer, had a vision. A strange cloud appeared, and a manifestation of the Holy Spirit told him he was to show the Māori people of New Zealand how to turn away from their traditional beliefs and cultural practices in favour of a version of Christianity. This news was not met with joy by his family, who initially thought he had lost his mind, not least because Rātana started to speak with what he claimed were the voices of the archangels Michael and Gabriel. But over time they started to believe in his visions. He had also previously had a vision in which two beached whales featured, apparently signifying that Rātana would be a fisher of men, or alternatively that his mission would have two facets, spiritual and material.[1]

Exactly what happened next is a bit uncertain, but accounts generally agree on the following. At this time one of his twin sons, Omeka, was in hospital. A needle was lodged in the flesh at the back of his knee, which was presumably causing septicaemia, but the doctors were either unaware of it or unable to remove it. Rātana took Omeka home, where he prayed and fasted for a week. He then declared, 'Son, I bestow health on you in the name of God and his faithful angels.'[2] The needle in his son's leg then came out of its own accord, and he was cured. Rātana had demonstrated that he was a messenger from God. Shortly afterwards, Te Kahupūkoro, a Māori chief, took his bedridden daughter to Rātana, who told her to rise and walk. She promptly did.

Rātana's reputation as a healer grew, prompting people to seek him out at the family farm.[3] The pilgrimage to Rātana Pā was an established event as soon as 1920.[4] The following year there was talk of needing special trains to bring the thousands of pilgrims expected to come for healing at a special Christmas meeting.[5] By this point, the settlement around the farm was being called the Mecca of the Māori and the Lourdes of New Zealand, and people were living there in tents and worshipping at a small wooden chapel.[6] But the miracle cures would eventually cease, and the nature of the pilgrimage changed (either by accident or design) to become a wholly political event.

Healing Pilgrimages

Given that Rātana first became known as a healer, it is no surprise that many people sought his help. At the time, the global pandemic sometimes called Spanish flu was sweeping across New Zealand and ravaging Māori communities. A Māori doctor, Te Rangihiroa, called it 'the severest setback the race has received' since the early years of Western settlement in New Zealand. It killed more Māori than the First World War,[7] and eight times as many of them as white settlers. Rātana himself appears to have caught it, causing him to lose his hearing. After reading the New Testament and the verses on Christ's healing of the centurion's servant, Rātana fasted and prayed for six days until he was cured. Early reports of Rātana's cures focus on the flu, such as the one of a woman made blind by the illness who recovered her sight when she went to see him.[8]

The pandemic seems to have been the catalyst that spurred an already discontented people – angered by losing their land to settlers, something which particularly infuriated war veterans – to look for a solution to their problems, and what they found was Rātana. Devotees arrived in such numbers at his homestead on the North Island that it developed into a *pā*, a village, and the centre of a new movement. Followers sold their homes and built houses in Rātana Pā, or if they had no money, relied on Rātana and lived in tents on the farm. The farm grew from only four houses in 1921, to over a hundred by the middle of the following decade. One of the buildings was a long shed which functioned as a sort of hospital where stretcher-bound pilgrims were housed while they waited to be cured. It seems it only took a day or so before this happened, and they were then able to move into the village houses for a few days before leaving.[9] This meant a lot of accommodation was needed, particularly when Rātana's followers gathered for Christmas, when he apparently cured one hundred people at his first annual gathering in 1920.[10] Little surprise then that so many Māori pilgrims came bringing sick family members that the small railway halt, established at the request of Rātana's family some years before, struggled to cope.

At the start of 1921, Mr Tuki Shortland claimed to be the first person from the city of Auckland to be healed, in his case from asthma. 'By corry he's the feller to make a fine cure,' he told a reporter, showing off how easily he was now able to breathe. When he reached Rātana Pā, he saw 'crowds, hundreds, all around. Ha, plenty there with sticks waving them around' because they no longer needed them.[11] Rātana claimed to have healed a girl, bedridden for a decade;[12] Tupu, brother of King Tawhia, was cured of an unspecified problem with his legs and

The simple church built at Rātana Pā is the focus of the community to which pilgrims come in honour of its founder. Originally pilgrimages of healing, Rātana's shift towards pushing for Māori rights has made his settlement into a political pilgrimage destination.

invited Rātana to come to the Waikato district to preach;[13] and the minister of native affairs regained his sight.

A record of all the people Rātana managed to cure was kept, patients being asked to sign it to testify that they had recovered through the intercession of the Holy Spirit. By the spring of 1921, there were allegedly 4,722 signatures, collected over one eighteen-month period, which would have averaged sixty a week.[14] Mr H. M. Stowell of the Native Department visited during that period and claimed he witnessed 327 people cured in just one day.[15]

The early pilgrimages in search of health and healing were ad hoc events, with people coming as and when they could by car or on boats from the South Island. Only Māoris were allowed into Rātana Pā; a sign on the gate informed visitors that the only non-Māoris permitted were reporters with 'proper credentials'. Given that Rātana did not court publicity and shunned recognition of any kind, this was an odd exemption.[16] And when people weren't cured, that fault was not Rātana's. 'But what else could you expect,' asked one man, relating the story of a married couple, the husband cured, the wife not, 'when she did not fully explain the disease to him? When you go to the doctor you should tell him everything, and it is the same with Rātana'.[17]

As Europeans were not generally allowed in the *pā*, they were healed remotely, with pilgrimages of thanks occasionally taking place after the fact.[18] They were strongly encouraged to write to Rātana instead of trying to visit, and over 80,000 letters arrived in one twelve-month period alone.[19] Replying to them was largely the task of Rātana's secretary, and it took up most of his time. Letters came in from all across the world – Iceland and Sierra Leone, Russia and Romania, China and Canada – and Rātana claimed 100,000 cures. Some people sent newspaper clippings that reported on their newfound health. One of Rātana's most famous successes was of a woman called Miss Fanny Lammas (or Lomas in some reports) from Nelson on the South Island, who was cured of some crippling disease and afterwards came on a pilgrimage of thanks to meet the man himself.[20] According to an interview she gave, Rātana had restored her health through 'a single interchange of letters'. Miss Lammas claimed she knew other European New Zealanders who had been cured by Rātana.[21] This led to a debate about who Rātana should help, and in the end he decided to confine his help to his fellow Māoris, so that his powers would not be 'dissipated too wide' and lose their potency.[22]

Conversion to Rātana's beliefs

Rātana spread his message via a tour of the North and South Islands, and far beyond New Zealand. His fame resulted in a trip to Japan, where he met with a warm reception, but when news of his complaints about the Treaty of Waitangi reached New Zealand the country's political leaders became suspicious of Rātana and his followers.[23] The Treaty of Waitangi (1840), signed by a representative of the British crown and Māori chiefs, was supposed to recognise Māori ownership of their lands, but due to some inexact translation (perhaps deliberately on the part of its translator, Henry Williams) led to years of disputes. In 1924 Rātana travelled with a delegation to London to present a petition asking for redress for breaches of the treaty to King George V and the Prince of Wales, but the New Zealand government intervened to make sure the meeting never happened. A visit to the United States of America followed in 1925. For a brief period, Rātana's reputation was harnessed to try and improve the situation of Māoris, but with the exception of the support he gained in Japan, he met with little success.

Where he was successful was as a healer, and it was this ability that cemented his reputation as a holy man and brought pilgrims flocking to Rātana Pā. Physical evidence of his abilities started to accumulate very early in his career. The meeting house at Rātana was festooned with crutches and goggles, glasses and rejected medicine bottles, as well as a discarded invalid chair.[24] The museum or Curio House at Rātana Pā showed off unwanted wheelchairs and surgical supports.[25] Discarded walking sticks, glasses, bandages and ear trumpets suggest the range and number of ailments he alleviated.

Rātana's healing powers disappeared over the course of the 1920s, and by 1927 reports of cures had completely dried up, though at the now-lost village of Atene, around fifty kilometres north of Rātana Pā, the devout reported they had been cured by Rātana's enduring influence long after his death in 1939, and still went on pilgrimages of thanks.[26] Explanations for the loss of his powers included Rātana's growing worldliness, his increasing involvement in national politics and reneging on his own teaching to abjure drink. In 1927 he was arrested for driving without a licence and while drunk.[27]

Sceptics said he never had any powers in the first place and dismissed his claims to be able to cure the sick. Many visitors to Rātana Pā noted that they never saw any healing take place. And the stories that appeared in the press all appear to have reached journalists via Rātana's secretary Pita Mōko, 'the mouthpiece of Rātana to the English-speaking world'.[28] One unidentified Auckland vicar thought those who believed in his cures were 'too gullible'.[29] Despite the attacks, the settlement and church at Rātana Pā continued to attract pilgrims. For the devout, pilgrimage to Rātana Pā still had spiritual value even without the cures. The anniversary of his birthday is a particularly spiritual occasion for his followers, many of whom read from the Rātana service book as they travel and go to the church on arrival to give thanks for their journey.[30] For Māoris of the 1980s, 'the pilgrimage to the pā [was a] time for reminiscing and seeing whether "Dad's" teachings are still being followed'.[31]

A New Faith

Though Rātana's healing powers waned – something he predicted would happen – the new faith he established and his reputation as a prophet still made Rātana Pā a place that drew in pilgrims. Rātana had a Methodist mother and an Anglican grandfather, and came from a long line of Māori prophets. His aunt, Mere Rikiriki, was a healer and prophetess, and while Rātana denied he was a prophet his followers nevertheless revered his words. Six years before he had his vision, Mere Rikiriki is said to have claimed he was destined to become a messenger of God who would unify the Māori. Rātana's faith was a sort of melding together of elements of Christian belief and Polynesian/Māori traditions, though he also made a point of challenging what he saw as the more superstitious aspects of Māori beliefs.[32]

Rātana aimed to use his faith, which relied heavily on angels, to bring together the fractured Māori. The movement he created grew to number around 40,000, and there were more Rātana priests at one point than Anglican clerics in New Zealand.[33] Although it was one in a long line of Māori religious movements, many of which focused on the idea that their members were descendants of the lost tribes of Israel, Rātana's was the only one which had any lasting impact.[34]

The new faith was formally established in May 1925, and a church built and dedicated on Rātana's birthday (25 January) in 1928. One of its articles described Rātana as the 'mouthpiece of Jehovah'.[35] The Anglican Church, previously quite supportive, thought this a step too far and declared Rātana schismatic. Otherwise seemingly modest, he had a carving of himself added to a series depicting Christ's Twelve Apostles.[36] The Christian trinity was venerated and there was a hierarchy of 'True or Faithful Angels'. On the altar of the church at Rātana Pā, a Bible sat alongside the Blue Book written by Rātana himself.

By the 1930s, the faith was increasingly about Rātana himself (references to Jesus in prayers were dropped), and when his sons Arepa and Omeka died in the early years of the decade, he had his followers treat them as saints. During Rātana's lifetime almost 20 per cent of New Zealand's Māori became adherents of his movement,[37] and the annual pilgrimage on his birthday drew as many as 12,000 people. Rātana's death in the autumn of 1939 did not appear to dent the enthusiasm.[38] Long after his death, the date he received his visions, 8 November, is the most important day in the Rātana calendar, when pilgrims flock to his home. Also prominent is the anniversary of his birthday, celebrated as a religious festival at Ratāna Pā. Remembering her childhood visits, Waerete Norman (1942–1999) recalled:

> The journey to the pā was a pilgrimage, always begun two or three days earlier, leaving around 21 January. In that time we caught the train, the special train, which was called the Rātana Express. The train was originally arranged by one of the four Māori MPs ... Something I still do even today is go to the Rātana 25th celebrations ... Sadly, the days of the Rātana Express are no more.[39]

In 1929, Rātana handed over control of his church to a committee, announcing that his spiritual role had come to an end and that he would now concentrate on political matters aimed at improving the lot of New Zealand's Māori population, chiefly through the repeal of the Treaty of Waitangi. His political leadership was certainly inspiring. Part of his appeal was the sense of agency he gave to his fellow Māoris. According to one report, he convinced some that the European settlers would be 'driven into the ocean'.[40] He made serious efforts to reclaim Māori lands, raising considerable amounts of money to support legal actions.[41]

He had long been politically active despite protests to the contrary on the part of his secretary, who insisted in 1924 that Rātana did not 'interfere in politics'. As early as 1920, Rātana had been approached by Tupu tai-Ngakawa and Rewiti Te Whena, two leaders of the king movement at Waikato, which aimed to unite the Māori under a single sovereign. They came to seek help 'not [for] the ills of the body but the ills of the land',[42] wanting Rātana to use his growing influence to help the Māori in practical ways. And in a speech delivered at Christmas 1923 he committed to a partial political programme. Two years later he began to secretly support the New Zealand Labour Party, selecting candidates for the 1928 election whom he swore to loyalty.

This strategy was not a success, but in 1932 the first Rātana MP was successful in a by-election. Though the fortunes of the movement had wobbled in the preceding years, the suffering caused by the Great Depression gave it new impetus, much as the First World War and flu pandemic had done over a decade before.[43] The focus of campaigning was on honouring the Treaty of Waitangi. Three years later, Rātana's son Tokouru won the movement's second seat, and the third and fourth were won in 1938 and 1943. For twenty years afterwards, Rātana members held all four of the Māori seats. The support of the Rātana MPs gave Peter Fraser's Labour government a majority in the late 1940s, although critics complained the administration was being kept in power by adherents of what they saw as little more than a cult.[44]

Pilgrimage and Politics

In the closing days of January 2012, New Zealand's *Herald on Sunday* ran an article under the headline THE POLITICAL PILGRIMAGE OUR LEADERS FEAR TO MISS.[45] The story referred to the visit of many of the country's members of parliament to Rātana Pā to court the Māori vote during the pilgrimage in honour of Rātana's birthday. The *Otago Daily Times* reported:

> It can only be assumed that the continued fuss attendant upon the pilgrimage to Rātana is down to tradition and

> political theatre, an opportunity to strike a pose and try out a few lines – a dress rehearsal for the resumption of Parliament and Waitangi Day to come. This week, Prime Minister John Key used the occasion to trumpet his party's record of success with Māori initiatives, contrasting it with Labour's, and to stress the importance ... of education, health and welfare reform.[46]

This was the legacy of Rātana's decision to switch his attention from the spiritual to the political domain in the late 1920s. In the mid-twentieth century the Labour Party, allied with the Rātana MPs and benefiting from their support, had been reasonably successful, with periods in government in 1935–49, 1957–60 and 1972–5, but after that political fragmentation made it increasingly necessary to court the Māori vote. In 1996, Labour lost the Māori seats they had historically dominated to New Zealand First. The formation of the Māori Party eight years after that shock, and the presence of Māori candidates in other parties like the Greens split the Māori vote even further.

The date of the first political pilgrimage to Rātana Pā is obscure, but in 1996 representatives of all New Zealand's political parties visited. Since then, the pilgrimage has become the unofficial start of the political year. The press don't seem to have referred to it as a pilgrimage until 2009, the year a third of the country's MPs made the trip to the North Island. Just over half of them were members of the National Party, led by Prime Minister John Key, though Labour came in a close second. Since then, the event has repeatedly been called a 'political pilgrimage' or a 'pilgrimage of the politicians'. Jacinda Ardern, prime minister 2017–23, has had a close association with Rātana Pā. Raised a Mormon, she rejected that faith and became agnostic. As a sign of support and her good intentions, Ardern gave her childhood

Bible to the Rātana church.[47] She also chose to deliver the last speech of her premiership on the Rātana pilgrimage.

The political pilgrimage to Rātana Pa has been attacked as little more than theatre and a chance for politicians to 'strike a pose and try out a few lines' that will probably end in the not-too-distant future.[48] And it is true that most if not all of them have little sympathy with the spiritual teachings of the Rātana movement. But for the time being many New Zealand politicians will continue to take part. Missing the event gives an opponent the chance to advance their cause unopposed and, more importantly, is an indication that the politician does not respect the Māori people and its beliefs or care about Māori concerns.

17

BUENOS AIRES

Argentina

In the Argentinian capital of Buenos Aires, plans for a vast monument in honour of the president's wife, Eva Perón, were unveiled in 1953, the year after her death. In *The Sphere*, a British illustrated newspaper, an artist's impression of the 445-feet-high structure depicted an Argentinian worker on a massive pedestal, the whole thing dwarfing other globally famous monuments like the Statue of Liberty (151 feet) and Christ the Redeemer in Rio de Janeiro (124 feet). The paper printed a handy graphic for comparison. The monument would stand opposite the presidential palace in Buenos Aires and tower over the whole city. Inside the base of this vast work, a silver sarcophagus would hold the remains of Eva, her sleeping figure moulded on top. The report claimed that Eva had had some input into the design, influenced by a visit she had made to Napoleon's tomb in Paris. It would be, *The Sphere* told its readers, a place of pilgrimage for the people of Argentina.[1]

The monument was never built. Instead, for years the question of what to do with the earthly remains of the former first lady of Argentina, and indeed whether to commemorate her at all, took up considerable official time and energy, not to mention column inches in both the Argentine and international press.

Attempts to control Eva Perón's remains and manipulate

Born into poverty, Eva Duarte's marriage to Juan Perón transformed her into the elegant First Lady of Argentina and darling of the country's poor. During her life and after her death, her image was carefully managed to portray her as the country's spiritual leader; some believed she deserved to be made a saint.

her memory played a significant role in Argentinian politics in the second half of the twentieth century. The potency of Evita's memory and her veneration by certain sections of Argentinian society meant the lack of an official focal point did not deter people from undertaking pilgrimages in her name. While other famous figures of the twentieth century – Elvis, Lenin – have tombs which are treated as shrines, Evita became the focus of a cult which was most like that of a saint, complete with religious imagery and talk of miracles. The story of Eva Perón, Buenos Aires and pilgrimages to the sites associated with her is one of control and rivalry. The people who loved her sought her out on pilgrimage from the moment of her death; those who feared her symbolic power tried to prevent them. What the veneration of Evita in Buenos Aires shows is how potent the site of a political pilgrimage can become, and how it can enter into the national conversation of a country.

Creating a Saint

Eva Perón was born Eva Duarte but became known to the world as Evita. She was the youngest of five illegitimate children, and she and her siblings were abandoned by their father when Eva was just one. Desperate to escape poverty and determined to become an actress, at the age of fifteen she moved from rural Argentina to Buenos Aires. Success as a radio performer followed. She met Colonel Juan Perón at a fundraising gala for earthquake victims in January 1944. They married in the autumn of 1945 when Eva was twenty-six, and the next year Perón was elected president of Argentina. She was pivotal to Perón's campaign, using her radio experience to deliver speeches on the air directed particularly at the poor, and touring the country by his side. Six years later she was dead from uterine cancer.

During his presidency, Eva ran the Ministry of Labour and the Ministry of Health, and founded the María Eva Duarte de Perón Foundation for those in need. Though her unofficial political role was much broader, she concentrated her efforts on helping the class she had come from, the *descamisados* (shirtless), Argentina's poor. For them she was the Lady of Hope, and to one admirer 'our little Madonna of the Ministry of Social Welfare'.[2] The poor and destitute, who called her Mother of the Humble and Needy,[3] wrote to her in their thousands, and she kept cash in her office to give to those who came in person so that no one went away empty-handed. She would also touch the sick and diseased, even if there was a risk of contagion, to show her sympathy and to give comfort. The fact that she never contracted any illness from these activities confirmed to those who adored her that she was a saint. She just happened to be one dressed head to toe in expensive designer clothing that probably cost more than a *descamisado* would earn in a lifetime.

The Peronist regime worked hard to create a saintly persona for Evita and to a lesser extent her husband, including on the international stage. Her whirlwind 1947 European tour was described as 'a miracle' to the people of Argentina.[4] In Franco's Spain, she was named Handmaiden of Honour to Our Lady of Hope Macarena. In Argentina indoctrination started young. Eva's book, *The Reason for My Life*, was required reading in Argentina's primary schools, and Argentinian schoolchildren were taught that Juan Perón was from 'that class of people who create new religions'.[5] On her sickbed, Eva reportedly told one visitor that people she had met looked at her with 'an expression of adoration, as though I were a supernatural being'. She also claimed that a child had approached her once and said, 'Mamma Eva, give me your benediction.' As she was dying, her husband described her as the 'woman given to me by providence, to guide my steps'.[6] No effort was spared to make her into an iconic figure at the heart of Argentine life. This culminated in the announcement that she had been given the title Spiritual Leader of the Nation by the Argentine Congress on what turned out to be her final birthday.[7]

Eva was not universally loved. Far from it. Nevertheless, her cult, both in her lifetime and afterwards, was powerful and widespread, boosted by mass-circulation magazines and newspapers in Argentina, as well as numerous books. What their adoring authors claimed about Eva was republished, repeated, quoted as authoritative – solidifying her blameless reputation on actually shaky foundations.[8] Eva was described as saintly (literally and metaphorically) because of her work with the poor, especially through the foundation she established, because of her willingness to touch and care for the sick, because of her illness and suffering in her final months, and because of her death at thirty-three, the same age Christ was when he was crucified. It helped, of course, that one of the papers most keen to promote this image of her, *Democracia,* was one she had owned since 1947.

Martyrdom

Perhaps if she had lived, Eva would have lost some of the aura that surrounded her, and like her husband would have ended up deposed and widely despised. But her death on a warm summer evening in July 1952 turned her into a martyr.

The outpouring of grief in Argentina was massive. Following the announcement, cinemas immediately stopped their films; plays were halted mid-performance; bars and restaurants ejected their patrons and closed their doors; newspapers were printed with black borders of mourning; shop windows fell dark. Some people took to the streets, screaming and crying. Instructions were given to open all the churches so that people could pray for her soul, and the numbers who flocked to do so were, according to one newspaper, unprecedented. The atmosphere of religious fervour during the mourning period was only heightened when a cross from Jerusalem carried by Franciscan missionaries, travelling on an unrelated tour of spiritual crusade and penance from the Holy Land, arrived in Argentina.[9]

The numbers who turned out to venerate it, combined with those seeking religious solace at a time of national mourning, created a sort of religious mania. Nowhere was this more apparent than when the Cross was carried in procession through the northern Argentinian city of Tucamán on a gun carriage, watched by massive crowds. A friar called Antonio Rivas delivered a speech to the crowd from a temporary pulpit in the city's main square and drew direct parallels between Christ and his suffering on the Cross and Eva's illness and death. She had borne herself, he claimed, with 'the memory of Calvary'. Images of Eva were used in domestic shrines, complete with flowers, candles and rosaries, and even placed inside churches. Pilgrimages were staged to several places so that people could pray for Eva. In the town of Trancas in northern Argentina, mourners carried a statue of St Francis Solano to their local holy well, praying for Eva's soul as they went.[10]

It is no surprise then that the language of pilgrimage was being used even before Eva was interred – which, as we'll see, was a protracted process – whether applied to the people flocking to the Unzué Palace in Buenos Aires, where Eva died, or to those who headed to the city to see her body. The *Illustrated London News* described the crowds as part of 'a country-wide pilgrimage to the Ministry of Labour and Welfare', where Eva's body lay in state from the day after her death for thirteen days.[11] Covering her funeral, the American magazine *Time* reported,

'Last week, in near-freezing rain, some 700,000 Argentines made pilgrimage to her bier in Buenos Aires.'[12] Yet more lined the route taking her to the trade union confederation headquarters from Congress

That the adulation of Eva reached such fevered heights is not surprising when you consider that Peronism had essentially replaced the Catholic Church in Argentina.[13] Both Perón and Eva had had the support of the Church, but they were both also adept at using it for their own purposes. Juan Perón rounded off his first presidential campaign with a visit to the shrine of the Virgin of Lujan because he knew a show of faith was vital, while after his victory both he and Eva borrowed heavily from religious imagery to cast themselves as the spiritual leaders of the nation. Eva did this particularly assiduously. And when she died, the official photographs of her body lying in state emphasised the link between Eva and the Catholic faith.[14]

Eva's premature death elevated her status to new heights, with the period of mourning and much of what came afterwards closely controlled by the Peronist regime. The decision to cast her as a saint was very deliberate.[15] All printed images of her had to have official approval; her widower and his supporters pushed the idea of Evita as the Virgin; and the city of La Plata, just down the coast from Buenos Aires, was renamed in her honour.[16] *Democracia* called her a saint, while the French daily *Le Monde* described her as the 'Madonna of the Argentinian poor'.[17] Efforts to remember Evita in the image of the Virgin intensified.[18] In a hymn she was the 'redeemer of peoples', and schoolchildren prayed to her: 'Evita, I promise to be as good to you as you wish me to be, respecting God, loving my country; taking care of General Perón,' and 'My mummy taught me to pray. In my prayers I never forget Eva Perón, our spiritual mother.'[19]

There were even calls in Argentina for her canonisation; one trade union petitioned the Vatican.[20] For her supporters, the fact she was never canonised was a woeful omission by the pope. When a Buenos Aires-born priest by the name of Jorge Mario Bergoglio became Pope Francis in 2013, Eva's supporters in the union again tried to have her canonised, thinking the Peronist-leaning Francis would be sympathetic.[21] These appeals have not been successful; instead, in the absence of official recognition, a cult has grown up around Eva Perón that has made Buenos Aires hallowed ground for those who revere her. This even extends to the outer suburb of San Vincente in the south of the city, where the home of her husband was visited by a group of pilgrims in 2021 carrying a statue of Our Lady of Lujan with the former president's initials engraved on the Virgin's cloak. The pilgrims apparently revered both Juan and Eva Perón, and one of them, Gabriel Duna leader of the neo-Peronist Evita Movement, claimed that Eva's actions and the policies of President Perón 'most resembles [*sic*] the Gospel'.[22]

On the first anniversary of Eva's death, commemorative events were held in Buenos Aires. The building where her body lay in state was adorned with flowers, and thousands of people packed the streets of the city carrying candles and praying for her. A speech praising her was delivered to a silent crowd in which she was called 'the miracle of love, the proverbial and sublime apostolate ... woman and symbol ... the chosen of the people ... mother of the humble'. Shop windows displayed memorials in her honour, and Congress paid tribute to her as the 'most faithful interpreter of Perón's true message'. The model for her future monument was put on display and crowds queued for hours to see it.[23]

Eva's Travels

Immediately after her death, Evita's body was prepared for embalming by Dr Pedro Ara. After a quick initial treatment to delay decomposition, she was taken to the Ministry of Labour building and put on public display. For thirteen days, thousands trooped past her in a procession that was only stopped when the body began to dehydrate. Removed from the ministry, the body was taken past thousands of mourners to the trade union confederation building. Over the following year, Dr Ara worked there to prepare her body for permanent embalming.

Eva was supposed to be interred in the fantastic national monument mentioned at the start of this chapter. Perón, it has been argued, wanted to use Eva's body as a focus for popular pilgrimage to boost his own position, but the monument took time to build.[24] No one quite knew what to do with Eva, so she stayed where she was, and, when her husband was forced out of Argentina in 1955 by a military coup, he left Eva's body behind. His circuitous journey via Paraguay, Panama and Venezuela into exile in Spain would have been made more problematic by a coffin, but he seems to have simply forgotten her. Work on the national monument was stopped: the new regime in Argentina wanted all signs of Peronism erased, so the last thing it was likely to do was sanction a memorial to Evita. Nonetheless, it had inherited the question of what to do with her.

Wanting to avoid the body becoming a focus for a Peronist cult, a few days before Christmas 1955 the junta 'kidnapped' Eva and moved her into the attic over the office of the head of army intelligence. He apparently planned to bury her, but whenever he tried to move Eva's body, a pop-up shrine would appear next to the truck designated to move her across the city.[25] So he kept the body in his office, propped upright, for two years, before forgetting to tell his successor about it, who stumbled over it a few days after taking up his position.

Eventually the junta decided to send Eva overseas for burial. To throw her devotees off the scent, the junta filled twenty-five identical coffins with ballast and dispatched them all over Argentina. There were also rumours that she had been sent across the Atlantic to the Argentinian embassies in Italy, Germany and France. The ruses and rumours worked; nobody was sure where Eva had gone. Some claimed she had been buried in Chile or Uruguay; some said she was on Martín García Island in the River Plate; others thought she had been cremated overseas.

Eva's body wasn't located until 1971. She had been interred in May 1957 in Milan's largest cemetery in the district of Musocco under the name of Maria Maggi Magistris. Secretly exhumed, Eva's embalmed but slightly the-worse-for-wear body was driven to Spain, where it ended up in the home of Juan Perón and his third wife, Isabel. Eva was kept in the dining room of their house, where dinner guests were able to see her.[26]

The Tomb Without Peace

Juan Perón returned to Argentina and power in 1973, and Peronism was fashionable once more. The cult of Evita received a fresh injection of state support, and posters depicting her appeared across Buenos Aires once more, but Eva herself was still in Spain, where Perón and his wife had left her. It was only when Montonero guerillas stole the body of former President Armaburu from the Recoleta Cemetery and demanded the repatriation of Eva's body that it was flown home.[27] There were then yet more plans for a grand tomb, but Isabel, who had become president after Juan's death in July 1974, chose to display Eva in the crypt of the presidential palace alongside her husband. When the

The Duarte family mausoleum in La Recoleta Cemetery, Buenos Aires, has become a place of pilgrimage for devotees of Eva Perón, who leave flowers and gifts at her tomb. Her body is buried deep underground to protect it from potential theft or desecration.

Argentinian military displaced Isabel in 1976, Eva's body was removed.

On 22 October 1976, her body was finally given to her family and laid to rest in Recoleta Cemetery in Buenos Aires. Despite all the plans for vast monuments and elaborate tombs, there is little official acknowledgement of her presence. The family tomb, a small Gothic edifice hidden among a sea of others, is relatively plain and bears the name of the Duarte family. Eva herself was given a small plaque, which would be easy to miss if it was not for the offerings left by pilgrims. To make sure her body would not be disturbed again, a company accustomed to building bank vaults was hired to construct a secure chamber beneath the main tomb, with another beneath that for Eva herself.

The tomb continues to attract pilgrims, whether curious tourists or devout followers, in large numbers. A photo essay on the seventieth anniversary of her death printed in a British newspaper was accompanied by an image of a close-up of a woman's hands, nails painted black, holding a white carnation and a portrait of Eva a bit smaller than a playing card, its condition suggesting she had owned the picture for some time. The portrait showed Eva in front of a white circle, giving her the halo of a saint. The caption read, 'A woman holds a photo of Perón as she waits her turn to visit the first lady's tomb'.[28] This was just one of tens of thousands to visit the cemetery that year. So busy is her grave, it is sometimes called *la tumba sin paz* (the tomb without peace).[29]

Over time, almost all sites in the city associated with Eva, and to a lesser extent with her husband, have become places of pilgrimage for people who believe her to be a saint or revere Peronism. To prevent devotees focusing on the Unzué Palace, where Eva died, in 1958 the regime that ousted Perón demolished it and the plot was turned into the site of the National Library of Argentina. Other places survive. A popular destination is the cafe where Juan and Eva Perón regularly ate, now so revered that it has a shrine dedicated to Eva inside. Places well outside Buenos Aires have been drawn into the Evita pilgrimage circuit, like her childhood home, which is so visited that it has become another shrine. If you're open to such ideas and looking for evidence of Eva's sanctity, the fact that the 1996 premiere of the movie *Evita*, starring Madonna, took place at the Shrine Auditorium in Los Angeles might seem significant.

The plethora of shrines and pilgrimage destinations associated with Eva Perón is perhaps not so strange. Catholic Argentina had, and still has, a tendency to create secular saints; just think of the country's love for Diego Maradona. Eva capitalised on this tendency during her time as Perón's wife, using symbols and events associated with the Virgin Mary to fashion her own public image. Her popularity also reflects changing economic times in Argentina. In the early years of the twenty-first century, when unemployment rose more than 20 per cent, and almost half of the country was living in poverty, there was a surge of interest in her.

Buenos Aires gained a new focus for pilgrimage in the late summer of 2004 when the shroud that covered Evita's body during the three years it lay in her husband's dining room was donated to the Argentinian Congress. A gift of the Aerolíneas Argentinas Foundation, the shroud had been bought by Antonio Mata in a Roman auction held by renowned auctioneers Christie's. Mindful of the political sensitivities surrounding Evita and Peronism, Argentina's politicians decided to keep it in a glazed casket in the Blue Room, a neutral space in the congressional building.[30] Fifty-two years after her death, her cult in the capital city was still potent and politically sensitive.

18

SHIKOKU

Japan

In 1918, at the age of twenty-four, a reporter called Takamure Itsue recorded her journey around Japan's fourth-largest island, Shikoku. Her pilgrimage was a 750-mile trek, taking in the island's temples and shrines, and took several months. It was serialised in over one hundred parts in the *Kyushu Daily Newspaper* that year, and turned out to be surprisingly popular. This wasn't the first time that an account of the pilgrimage had been written, but it was novel for being by a woman, and a single woman at that, and for being by a layperson, so different in tone to previous accounts.

One of its features was that her pilgrimage was relatable. 'Even I myself don't know why I resolved to make the pilgrimage,' she told her readers, though she seems to have had several motivations, as she was an energetic and fiercely intelligent woman who had an independent spirit. Writing to Miyazaki Daitarō, her editor, she elaborated: 'There is nothing in the world more painful than stagnating. I even think that venturing recklessly into an unknown world has perhaps more significance than that.'[1] She initially considered undertaking the Saigoku pilgrimage, a route comprising thirty-three temples in western Japan, but was inspired by hymns to choose the route around Shikoku.

The ideals she espoused were lofty, claiming that it was more important to engage in spiritual practice than to learn theory, but she had other, much more worldly reasons for her pilgrimage. She was having difficulties with her boyfriend Hashimoto (she had vowed eternal love, but his response was lukewarm, though they later married), and she was unemployed.[2] A pilgrimage to Shikoku, serialised in print, would bring in much-needed income, and give her some space.

Faith and Pilgrimage

Shikoku pilgrimages are undertaken in honour of the Buddhist monk Kukai (774–835), commonly known by the name bestowed on him by the Japanese emperor Daigo (died 930), Kōbō Daishi. He founded Shingon Buddhism in Japan, a school of thought that believed that all beings had once been enlightened and that people could regain this state through mudras, mantras and mandalas, gestures, words and visual representations on which Buddhist practices and teachings are based. Shikoku pilgrims (known as *henro*) believe that Kōbō Daishi walks with them as they travel – 'two people, one practice'.[3] The most committed wear a white shirt and broad bamboo hat, known as a *kasa,* on which a poem usually written on coffins has been inscribed. They also wear a sash bearing the words *dōgyō ninin* to show they are walking with Kōbō Daishi, and carry a bag and a box for the pieces of paper they collect at each temple they visit. They walk with a staff.

The current pilgrimage route takes pilgrims clockwise around eighty-eight numbered temples, each one dedicated to one of the main Buddhas of Shingon Buddhism, or to Kōbō Daishi himself. Of the temples, some pre-date the visit of Kōbō Daishi (for example numbers 77, 78, 80, 82, 85 and 86) and so

Pilgrims walk a circuit of Shikoku's eighty-eight temples in honour of Kōbō Daishi, whose image dots the landscape. Completing the circuit is time-consuming and arduous, so many pilgrims now do it in sections over several years, or use buses and cars.

were known to him; some were built or rebuilt by Kōbō Daishi (for example 75 and 78), while others were built after his death. Pilgrims can start from anywhere, and no temple or shrine is intrinsically more important than any other, though people have their favourites; the only requirement is that all eighty-eight are visited. Pilgrims can collect red wax stamps to prove where they have been on a document known as a *nokyo-cho* (stamp book). Since at least the eleventh century, some adherents of Shingon Buddhism have added an eighty-ninth stop at the end of their pilgrimage – Mount Kōya on the Japanese mainland, the place where Kōbō Daishi built a temple complex.[4]

How the pilgrimage came to encompass eighty-eight sites

has been the subject of some debate, and there is no consensus. A priest called Jakuhon (1631–1701), writing in about 1690, believed that the route was established by Kōbō Daishi's disciple Shinzei (800–860), who went on pilgrimage immediately after his master's death.[5] More convincing is the case for Prince Shinnyo Shinnō. The third son of Emperor Heizei, he went to Shikoku in 861 at the age of sixty-two and died about four years later. The tomb he now rests in was built at the Kiyotakij temple (35). While on Shikoku, he may have set out the numbered route that pilgrims still follow.

The medieval origins and history of the Shikoku pilgrimage in honour of Kōbō Daishi are widely assumed, but very poorly evidenced. Early stories and legends about Kōbō Daishi were spread by itinerant priests, but records of pilgrimage to Shikoku only started to appear in the twelfth century, when pilgrim priests travelling the coasts of Shikoku 'went along the road of Shikoku to Iyo, Sanuki, Awa, and Tosa'. However, there were other spiritual reasons to visit Shikoku, and there is no indication that they were specifically there to honour Kōbō Daishi.[6] Some probably were. The pilgrimage of the monk and poet Saigyō in 1168 followed Kōbō Daishi's traditional route, and involved a visit to the tomb of Emperor Sutoku (died 1164), who had been Saigyō's benefactor, to appease his ghost. He went when he was at what he thought of as an 'advancing age' with the expectation that he would stay on pilgrimage until he died, though he was only about fifty at the time, and didn't die for another twenty-two years.[7] In another case, exile to Shikoku facilitated a pilgrimage. The priest Dōhan was banished to the island in 1243 for his role in a dispute that ended in the burning of the Demböin temple in Tokyo.[8]

This all suggests pilgrimage to Shikoku was the preserve of monks, priests and religious ascetics. One twelfth-century poem described pilgrims cleansing themselves before completing the pilgrimage:

> How we looked, in our asceticism
> Stoles of endurance hanging on shoulders,
> And wicker baskets on our backs;
> Robes always soaked in brine.
> Endlessly we round the edge of Shikoku Island.[9]

And for almost the entirety of the Kamakura (1185–1333) and Muromachi (1333–1578) periods, the Shikoku pilgrimage seems to have been largely the preserve of those who had already opted for a religious life. It was in the late 1400s that lay pilgrims started to emerge, as evidence of a parish pilgrimage in this period survives in a faded inscription in Temple 88.[10] By the end of the sixteenth century it was more common, perhaps in part because crossing the Inland Sea to reach the island had become easier as piracy had been brought under control in the last decades of the century by Hideyoshi (died 1598), Emperor Go-Yōzei's (ruled 1586–1611) chief adviser.

Organising Pilgrimage

In the Edo period (*c.*1603–1868), Buddhism became the main religion in Japan, and Shikoku's importance as a place of pilgrimage grew in response. The regime took a particular interest in Shikoku and its pilgrimage, using it to 'build a sense of national consciousness and identity'.[11] This was a much more stable and prosperous time. People could afford a period away from work and home, and travel was easier. They were also protected, at least to some extent, by regulations set out by Shogun Tsunayoshi's government in 1688. Though the 'Circular concerning the treatment of travellers and oxen and horses' was written to aid travellers on the Tōkaidō road from Kyōto to Tokyo, it was adopted elsewhere in Japan, including on Shikoku.[12]

Other important factors were the growth of the print industry in Japan and improved education. The first known written account of the pilgrimage was composed in 1638 by Kenmyō, a pilgrim monk, and fifteen years later the first guidebook to the Shikoku pilgrimage, *Record of the Diary to the Pilgrimage Temples*, was for sale at a lodge on the pilgrim route. A copy was bought by Chōzen, a monk from Chishakuin in Kyōto, who wrote an account of his own experiences in 1653. His record is the first time that a pilgrimage to all eighty-eight temples was recorded, but if Chōzen was following an existing guide, it is reasonable to assume that this was already an established practice. The earliest surviving guide was not produced until 1687, when a priest and serial pilgrim called Yuben Shinnen from Osaka produced *The Guide to the Shikoku Pilgrimage*. Shinnen has been called the 'father of Shikoku *henro*' because of his influence. His guide numbered the temples, with his own base at Ryōnzenji as number 1.[13]

The following year Shinnen (died 1691) wrote down a collection of miracles that showcased the benefits of pilgrimage, which included the possibility of a cure for problems ranging from tumours to speech impediments. Shinnen undertook the Shikoku pilgrimage anywhere between ten and twenty times. He was responsible for setting up some of the wayside markers to guide pilgrims (complaints had been made about a lack earlier in the century),[14] funded through donations, as well as several wayside shrines that could be visited in addition to the temples.[15]

The guides and written accounts were soon harnessed to promote Shikoku and its pilgrimage more systematically.

Shinnen-bō was a publishing entrepreneur from Osaka in the Genroku period (1688–1704), a time of great commercial growth and urban revival. Osaka, a city north-east of Shikoku on the coast of Honshu, Japan's main island, was a publishing centre, and its merchants and entrepreneurs supported Genroku culture, which encouraged freer use of leisure time. Osaka was also increasingly connected to Shikoku at the time through trade, particularly in salt and indigo, which spread information about the pilgrimage and facilitated movement between the two islands. One of the Shingon temples on Shikoku even sent its most important sacred image to Osaka, where it was displayed in the Jimyoin temple to promote the Shikoku pilgrimage.[16]

One of the works that Shinnen-bō published was by the monk Jakuhon. Shinnen-bō was keen to secure an author from a respected monastery, while Jakuhon was keen to write a work in honour of Kōbō Daishi. Jakuhon's work, *An Account of the Journey Around the Spiritual Sites of Shikoku* (1689), was illustrated with woodcuts, and must have been popular as it was reprinted several times. It was also very large, running across seven volumes, and emphasised how the pilgrimage had deep historical links to Kōbō Daishi. The anthropologist Ian Reader believes Jakuhon's *Account* was about the 'Kōyasan Shingon authorities' exerting their authority over the pilgrimage by defining it in print, but it also advised pilgrims on where they could secure a pair of free sandals or other gifts from the devout.[17] What it did not do was number the eighty-eight temples in order, and instead listed a total of ninety-five locations, which might suggest that the sequence set out by Shinnen two years before was not a given, or alternatively that Jakuhon did not see it as a pilgrimage requirement.[18]

Artistic representations of both pilgrimage and pilgrims also started to appear in the seventeenth century, and by the middle of the eighteenth century the Shikoku sites had been mapped by Hosoda Shūei. According to Michael Pye, the earliest map was made in 1747, inspired by the pilgrimage that took place that year, but it seems the map, known as the Shikoku Henro Ezu, did not appear in print until 1763.[19] It showed the eighty-eight temples that are visited today with the figure of Kōbō Daishi in the middle, a format that has frequently been copied.

More visitors meant more facilities were needed on the island. Many pilgrims relied on charity from the islanders, who gave them alms as this was seen as akin to giving to Kōbō Daishi himself. More substantial support was provided by the devout. Bukkai, an ascetic from Iyo on Shikoku who undertook twenty-one pilgrimages in person,[20] set up pilgrim lodges in the mid-1750s. Despite the freedom to start and finish the pilgrimage where they chose, pilgrims were kept to a reasonably tight regime, which included needing to obtain a pilgrim passport. The island's four provinces had different rules about how long visitors could stay within their borders, and pilgrims had to produce their passports at checkpoints to prove that they hadn't overstayed. Delays due to sickness were tolerated, but pilgrims could be blocked from completing their pilgrimage if the rules were flouted. The regulations and checkpoints were clearly an attempt to keep the pilgrim traffic moving and prevent excessive or fraudulent begging. The sick and infirm, the solitary young or very old were prevented from even starting the pilgrimage.[21]

Despite these strictures, many people went to Shikoku on pilgrimage specifically because they were sick. Stomach cramps, immobility following childbirth and trauma brought on by stress all feature in accounts, as do pilgrimages to give thanks for healing.[22] Leprosy impelled some to effectively become permanent pilgrims, forced to stay on the Shikoku circuit to get the alms they needed to live.[23] Others went to Shikoku when they thought their lives were coming to an end so that they could be buried there. Some completed the pilgrimage for the spiritual benefit of a dead relative, a common motive at many pilgrimage sites around the world. At the other end of the spectrum, a Shikoku pilgrimage could be about coming of age, demonstrating a man or woman's transition to adulthood and readiness for marriage.[24] Henry Noël, writing about pilgrims in the 1930s, claimed that young women 'were especially anxious to visit the Eighty-eight Temples [because] ... there is a belief among them that they may have difficulties in finding suitors unless they fill this part of their education'.[25]

Yakudoshi, a belief that some ages (such as 25, 37, 49 or 61) were particularly unlucky, was another reason for a Shikoku pilgrimage, as were poverty and hardship. Pilgrims sought solace and support during the Tenmei famine of the 1780s and the Tenpō famine of 1833–7, when hundreds of thousands died after heavy rains, flooding, cold weather, disease and insect infestation decimated crops.[26] Writing a century after these events, Alfred Bohner listed pilgrims' motives, and ended:

> One more motive may be mentioned, among those that urge on many people along the highways of Shikoku. Sometimes there come moments in our lives when simply everything fails; when every undertaking, every plan, no matter how well thought out, miscarries ... In such cases, many Japanese reach for the poison, throw themselves onto the railroad track in front of a train locomotive, or cast themselves into the sea. Others however tie up their bundles, equip themselves as well or as poorly as their means allow, and set off on a pilgrimage ... Even if luck has not changed for them on their return, they are able to see life from another angle,

and this often makes possible a change of fate and sets them on the right road.[27]

Desperate pilgrims were a problem. In the 1780s they were deported from Shikoku because the locals barely had enough for themselves, and in the 1830s there was an outright ban on giving alms to pilgrims on Shikoku for the same reason.[28] Large numbers of pilgrims always have the potential to put a strain on resources, but at times of shortage can be a threat to the well-being of the resident population. Even during times of plenty, pilgrims seeking alms may be viewed with suspicion, and misbehaving children threatened with kidnap by them.[29]

The most distinctive aspect of the Shikoku pilgrimage is the repeat pilgrim. There are many examples of pilgrims repeating the circuit until they die, probably in imitation of the early ascetics who spent their lives walking the route. Ian Reader and John Schultz have argued that this is the 'dominant theme' of the pilgrimage. Takeda Tokuemon (died 1814) embarked on a pilgrimage after the death of a son and four daughters and completed the pilgrimage thrice annually over a period of about fourteen years. He was from the northern part of Shikoku, so at least he was comparatively local. Nakatsukasa Mōhei (born 1845), unlucky in love, started his first pilgrimage in his twenties, and carried on for fifty-six years. In total, he completed perhaps as many as 282 circuits of the island (or 254, according to a sign in Mukuno village), more than any other known pilgrim. Both men were responsible for setting up some of the way markers that guide pilgrims along the route. Tada Emon (died 1862) from the Hiroshima region managed 136 journeys before his death on pilgrimage.[30]

The route around Shikoku is littered with memorials to those who died along the way and whose families had the money to pay for one.[31] These deaths peaked in the seventeenth and eighteenth centuries.[32]

The Heritage of Pilgrimage

In the first half of the nineteenth century, the Shikoku pilgrimage went through what Nathalie Kouamé saw as something of a golden age.[33] Indeed, Shikoku's spiritual benefits were seen as so valuable that it was emulated elsewhere in Japan, inspiring routes to spring up across Japan 'as bamboos after the rain', for those who could not or did not want to go to the island itself, or who perhaps wanted to practise on a shorter circuit before attempting Shikoku. Three were pre-eminent: Sasaguri on Japan's southern island of Kyushu, Shōdoshima just off the northern coast of Shikoku, and Chita Hantō, founded in about 1809.[34] Sasaguri, a thirty-seven-mile route, is said to have been established by Jinin, a nun inspired by her own pilgrimage to Shikoku. On her return home in 1835 she found her town devastated by disease and, believing that Kōbō Daishi had trained near Sasaguri and that it was blessed as a result, prayed to him for help. The town recovered, and the pilgrimage was founded in thanks. Shōdoshima, on a small island just off the tip of Shikoku itself, was also associated with Kōbō Daishi as he visited there for contemplation.[35]

The heyday of the Shikoku pilgrimage was not to last. After the Meiji Restoration in 1868, when the emperors returned to power, the pilgrimage was derided for being outdated and superstitious. The new regime wanted to present Japan as modern and forward-looking.[36] Even those who persisted in going faced problems, as during the 1870s and 1880s pilgrims were prevented from accessing some of the sites on the traditional pilgrimage circuit. The Separation Edict of 1868 ordered Buddhist priests at Shinto shrines to become Shintos, so priests could not henceforth be both Buddhist and Shinto. Shintoism was promoted to bolster the divine status of the emperor and Buddhists were persecuted, with temples attacked, statues smashed and images defaced.[37] On Shikoku, this meant the closure of nine of the temples in Tosa on the island's southern side, some for over two decades. Other temples were destroyed outright.[38] Temple 30, Zenrakuji, was demolished in 1870, and not rebuilt until 1964. Two years later, Buddhist monks were banned from begging for alms, and unable to sustain themselves on the pilgrimage, some were forced to abandon it, while ordinary pilgrims were persecuted as representing the benighted peasantry of the past.[39]

However, over the course of the twentieth century, the Shikoku pilgrimage recovered to become synonymous with traditional Japanese culture.[40] The shift in attitudes began after the change of regime in 1912, which led to the pilgrimage receiving a more favourable press. By the 1920s, the characteristics of the Shikoku pilgrims that had previously been criticised – their outdated ways and poverty – were being lauded as examples of cultural continuity in the face of the relentless onslaught of modernity. Japanese intellectuals, who had previously shown very little interest in the pilgrimage, now treated it as a sort of heritage tourism experience. It helped that the Shikoku route was rural and remote compared to popular alternatives like the Saigoku pilgrimage, which went through large cities like Osaka and Nara.

The growing interest in pilgrimage-as-heritage was facilitated by the foundation of interest groups in places like the Japanese capital, Tokyo. One of these, Henro-Dogyokai, was established in 1928 or 1929 and published a journal about the pilgrimage that emphasised its traditions. It also organised parades and a training programme for potential pilgrims, as well as lectures. The group was strongly opposed to the 'decadence' of the 'modern *henro*' who travelled on coaches or used cars to complete their pilgrimage.[41] When the editor of the group's journal, Murakami Nagando, heard about the transport being used by some pilgrims in 1931, he wrote,

> I was surprised when I learned that a lot of people were using vehicles, breaking a prohibition on the use of transport. Ship and rail companies sell discount tickets, taxi companies persuade pilgrims to use their services by tugging at their sleeves. Devils are setting up nets of temptations everywhere. I am irritated to know that there are some salesmen lurking in the sites of sacred temples in particular ... I believe that undertaking the pilgrimage on foot is important, therefore I want to terminate the unpleasant trend of pilgrimage using transport.[42]

Nagando was fighting a losing battle, but his complaint was one heard all over the world. The same year Alfred Bohner acknowledged that a pilgrim seeking 'to receive the greatest good' should walk or 'hobble as well as they can on crutches', but for his own Shikoku pilgrimage he opted for 'travelling luxuriously by train and auto'.[43] The railway had come to Shikoku in 1887 and was then extended in stages until the mid-1930s. Those parts of the island not served by train were reachable by bus. This led to a shift in the type of pilgrim, as more middle-class and educated people made the journey, encouraged by government promotion of tourism and information printed in newspapers. The *Osaka Asahi News* explained to its readers how they could undertake the pilgrimage using rail and other forms of public transport, and how to find comfortable accommodation. From the later 1930s, the government encouraged foreign tourists, publishing magazines and guides in England and establishing overseas tourist offices. The 1970s saw an uptick in pilgrimage-as-heritage, with Japanese railway companies promoting travel to the more rural (and thus traditional) parts of the country.[44]

By the later twentieth century, most pilgrims were doing the circuit by car or bus.[45] This meant many were completing the circuit in one visit, or returning year after year to accomplish the pilgrimage in stages. Just as there was opposition to railway use in the first half of the century, this attracted disapproval. Oliver Statler, a researcher who completed the pilgrimage several times and led tours in the 1970s and 1980s, expressed the view that 'going around in a bus or a car may be meritorious, but it is not ascetic exercise and it is not performing the pilgrimage'.[46] Easy travel is not the only thing considered a threat to 'proper' pilgrimage, as the focus on Japanese heritage has prompted extreme reactions. After the first Korean guide put stickers along the route to assist her compatriots, signs appeared urging Japanese people to protect the pilgrimage 'from the hands of the Koreans'. The Association for Protecting Japanese Pilgrimage asked people to remove the Korean stickers, and there was widespread agreement that they were somehow a threat to Japanese culture.[47]

With easier transport and shorter journey times, Shikoku opened up to international pilgrimage. Frederick Starr, an American academic, may have been the first foreign pilgrim when he completed part of the route, from Matsuyama to Komatsushima, in 1917; he returned in 1921 to cover the rest. This was such an unusual occurrence that his journey was tracked in the Japanese press.[48] Starr was surprised by the physical demands of the pilgrimage, writing to his mother, 'If I had really realised its length and difficulties, I doubt I would have had the courage to undertake it.'[49] When the German Alfred Bohner came to Japan in 1922, he did so because his brother Hermann, who had been held at an internment camp on Shikoku during the First World War, invited him over to work. Five years later Bohner completed the pilgrimage and published a study and account of his experiences in 1931, the first by a Westerner.

Around the time of Bohner's pilgrimage a lot of emphasis was placed on the importance of walking, though this wasn't about pilgrimage so much as state attitudes to health. The Japanese government, inspired by Nazi Germany, was promoting physical fitness to prepare the population for war, and in the summer of 1940, a ban was put on alternative forms of pilgrimage travel. A few months later, Japan formally entered the Second World War, and the ban endured in an attempt to ensure a combat-ready people, although after the war a more pragmatic approach prevailed. During the conflict pilgrims continued to visit Shikoku and complete the circuit, many no doubt seeking support and praying for peace, and in its aftermath many veterans came on pilgrimage. One man returned from war to find his home and family annihilated, and embarked on a permanent pilgrimage for the next three decades.[50] One consequence of the war and Japan's defeat was a collapse in charitable donations to pilgrims.[51]

Shikoku doesn't compare to many of the world's most important pilgrimage destinations in terms of numbers. In the late 1960s, despite easier transport and economic prosperity, there were still only about 15,000 pilgrims a year.[52] At the start of the twenty-first century this had risen to around 80,000 each year, a substantial increase but still modest by comparison with many other places.[53] Yet the government recognises that the pilgrimage has the potential to bring people from around the world to Japan, and is going to increasing lengths to promote it. The circuit was improved by the Ministry of Construction in 1981 to facilitate long-distance hiking,[54] and in the summer of 2017 the Japanese authorities collaborated with the Museo das Peregrinacións in Santiago de Compostela, Spain, to host an exhibition, 'El camino de Shikoku'.[55]

Japan has tried repeatedly to gain UNESCO recognition for Shikoku, part of which involves convincing the organisation of its 'universal value', but has not yet succeeded. As a result, argues Sara Kang, 'in the process of its UNESCO nomination, Shikoku Henro has become "nationalized" in the sense that its "cultural" values have become preferred over its "religious" values as the symbolic embodiment of a collective, national past'.[56] There is some truth in this. In associating itself with Santiago de Compostela, a destination mainly known for the long-distance routes leading to it, those seeing recognition by UNESCO have chosen to emphasise Shikoku's heritage, rather than the spiritual motivations pilgrims have had to complete the circuit. Shikoku has long been promoted for myriad reasons, and those who walk it do so for many, many more.

19

SANTIAGO DE COMPOSTELA

Spain

Late at night on 29 January 1879, a small group of men was hard at work in the cathedral in Santiago de Compostela under the supervision of Antonio Lopez Ferrerio, canon of the cathedral. For months they had been searching for the crypt, a mission which had been kept concealed with the assistance of Ferrerio's superior and collaborator, Archbishop Miguel Paya. Inside they hoped to find the remains of St James the Great, brother of St John the Evangelist, member of Christ's inner circle and Apostle, martyred (according to Acts 12: 2), possibly around the year 44. These had apparently been hidden behind the altar when the English attacked nearby La Coruña in 1589, and had not been seen since.[1]

That night they found the crypt, and within it the treasure they had been looking for: hundreds of fragments of the bones of St James himself, together with those of two of his disciples.[2] A week later the archbishop publicly announced that what had been portrayed as cleaning works had actually been a search for the saint, and that the searchers had been successful. Five years later, a papal bull, *Deus Omnipotens*, formally recognised the fragmentary remains as those of St James, and those of two of his disciples, Athanasius and Theodore. The pope declared the

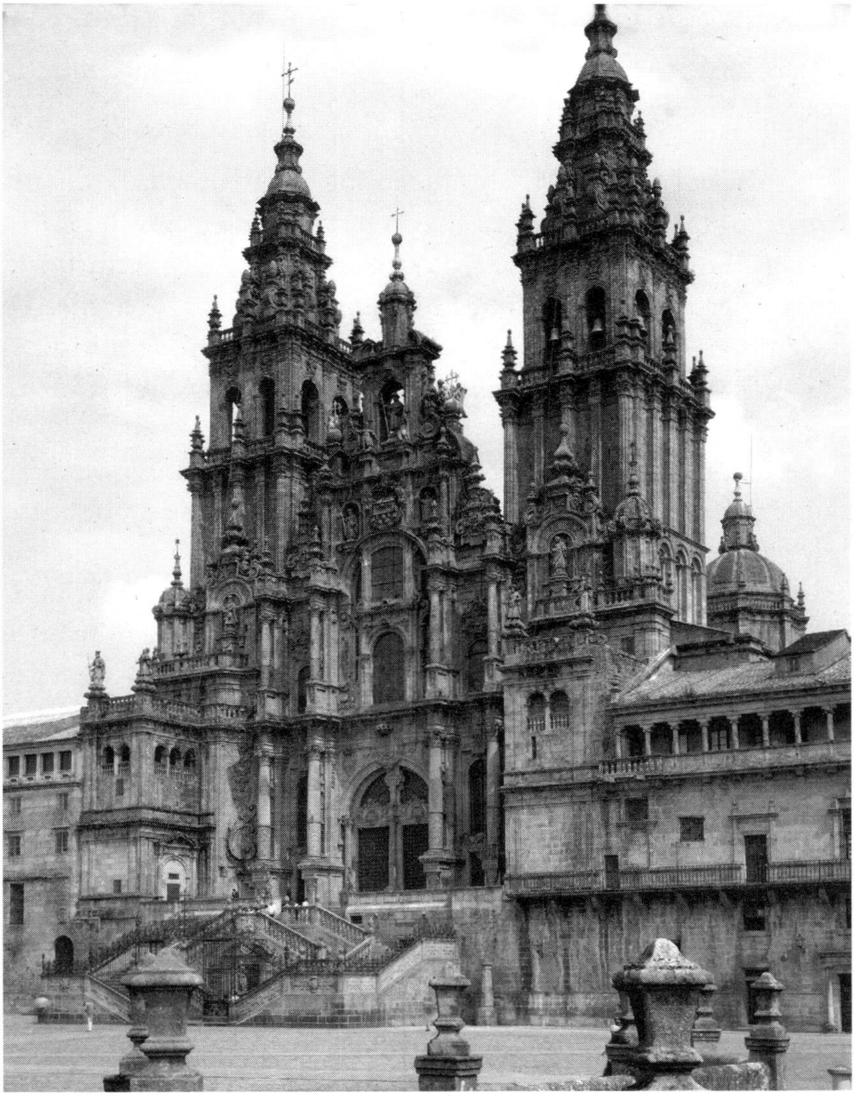

The cathedral in Santiago, home of the tomb of St James, is the final destination for pilgrims who walk to the city. The saint's cult developed from a local to a national then international phenomenon during the Middle Ages, and was used by medieval kings and the fascist leader Franco to bolster their power. Santiago has come to be considered the model on which all other pilgrimages should be based.

following year an extraordinary holy year, and thousands converged on the city in celebration.

This chapter is about Santiago de Compostela but also about the network of pilgrimage routes to it, as the city and the Camino de Santiago (Way of St James) cannot be separated. For many Santiago de Compostela has become the model pilgrimage to which all others are compared. It represents what pilgrimage is, what pilgrims must do and how pilgrimage can be harnessed for cultural, political and economic purposes. Modern historians and anthropologists have called this the 'Caminoisation' of pilgrimage.

The pilgrimage to Santiago de Compostela is today so famous that people assume it has always been massively popular, but in fact the rediscovery of the relics of St James was just the start of a process which took over a century to make it what it has become. Nevertheless, the city and its saint have long been central to not just Spanish history but that of Europe, and the pilgrimage and access to the relics of St James have always had international significance. When they were first found in the ninth century it was at a time when Muslim rule extended across almost the entire Iberian peninsula, and when the relics were hidden in the sixteenth century the very idea of pilgrimage itself was under attack by Reformation thinkers. And in 1879 the papacy was facing problems in Italy, with the Catholic Church and faith struggling against political as well as spiritual opposition. Santiago de Compostela might today be known chiefly as a destination for long-distance walkers, secular and Christian, but for centuries it had considerable political significance.

The Birth of the City

The cult of St James emerged during the seventh and eighth

centuries, while pilgrimage to Santiago de Compostela itself probably began in the middle of the ninth century after Theodemir, bishop of Iria, claimed he had discovered the remains of St James the Great in what was then the kingdom of Asturias around the year 820. The *Concordia* of 1077, the oldest source for the discovery of St James's grave, explains how, having seen lights and heard music over the woods of Mount Libredon, a local hermit called Paio found the relics and informed the bishop. In antiquity the area had been under Roman control, and there had perhaps been a temple with an altar dedicated to Jupiter. How the bones of St James, martyred in the Holy Land, had come to the north-west tip of Spain was a puzzle, but one explained away by a story which recounted how his bones were brought to Galicia by sea. Several of his disciples had come ashore, then walked inland to a predestined burial site.[3]

Whatever the origin or authenticity of the relics, the city named after the saint, Santiago, soon became a popular destination for pilgrims. Alfonso II, king of Asturias (ruled 791–842), came on pilgrimage in 834, possibly the first person to do so, and certainly the first person of note. He ordered the construction of a church to house the saint's tomb and granted land to sustain the religious community he founded. Alfonso III (ruled 866–910) came twice in the 870s, the second time with his wife Jimena, and gave goods seized from a rebellious count and an elaborately decorated cross, sadly lost in 1906. He also made substantial donations for the rebuilding of the church itself and built hospitals along some of the pilgrim routes.[4] The church would endure for the next two centuries. The royal devotion seems genuine, but it had a political motive too: the kings were essentially buying themselves regional loyalty. They also wanted a patron saint for the kingdom of Asturias, and James, one of the twelve Apostles, was perfect.

The new shrine also had a role in the wars against the Muslims on the Iberian peninsula, which continued on and off until the end of the fifteenth century. Christian kings saw St James as a *miles Christi,* a knight of Christ; they came to Santiago to pray for his assistance against the infidels, and if they were victorious made pilgrimages of thanks or gave gifts to the church. The association between St James and war with the Muslims began under Alfonso II, who adopted the saint as protector of the Christan army. On the eve of the Battle of Clavijo, King Ramiro I of Asturias (ruled 842–50) allegedly dreamed that the saint would help him to win. The story may or may not be true, but there is no doubt that St James and his shrine were important in *la Reconquista* – the Christian reconquest of Spain.

Santiago was so important to the Christians that in 997 al-Mansur (died 1002), the effective ruler of the Umayyad caliphate of Cordoba, the most powerful state in Iberia at the time, attacked the city, burned the church and made off with its bells. They were melted down and the metal reused in Cordoba's Great Mosque.[5] Fortunately, the fleeing bishop had already removed the saint's relics, so once the city was regained Christian pilgrims returned. These included Ferdinand the Great, king of Leon (ruled 1037–65), who conquered the city of Coimbra in what is now central Portugal in 1064 with the saint's help. According to the *Historia Silense*, a twelfth-century Latin work which promoted the figure of Santiago Matamoros – St James the Moor Slayer – he appeared to the king and showed him the keys to the city, and then fought with him on a white horse. Ferdinand went on a pilgrimage of thanks the following year with his wife Sancha and their children.

A Pilgrimage for Europe

In the twelfth century, Santiago de Compostela developed from a site of Spanish significance into one of the major pilgrimage destinations of Christian Europe. Santiago was already attracting international pilgrims from France in the 950s, and the promotion of the Camino Francés (the French route to Compostela) by Ferdinand the Great (died 1065) made it easier for them to come in significant numbers over the Pyrenees. The city they were heading for was also being developed to promote the cult and accommodate its growing number of pilgrims.

This began under Bishop Diego Peláez (1071–88), who started the reconstruction of the cathedral church in 1078, a process continued by his energetic successor Bishop (Archbishop from 1120) Diego Gelmírez (1100–40). The bishop's palace was destroyed in 1117 in an uprising, but this was a small blip in the city's otherwise relentless rise under Gelmírez, who completed major building programmes that benefited both the city's inhabitants and incoming pilgrims. These included coastal defences, freshwater fountains in the streets, rebuilding the bishop's palace after 1120 and hospitals to care for sick and infirm pilgrims. He also persuaded the Cluniac monastic order (to which he belonged) to provide accommodation for pilgrims at their monasteries along the route to Santiago, and developed settlements at key points along the pilgrimage routes to the city. In the cathedral itself, the old altar was replaced by one decorated with gilded silver. This was all paid for by the money brought in by pilgrims, and because the city was permitted to mint money, a privilege usually reserved for kings.[6]

This was the cathedral described in *Codex Calixtinus*, a work that was part pilgrim guide, part saint's life, part miracle collection, part collection of hymns and prayers.[7] Parts of the *Codex* are historically inaccurate, but it was effective in putting

Santiago on the European pilgrimage map despite its remote location in north-west Spain. Chief among its spurious claims was the assertion in Book IV that Alfonso III invited Charlemagne to help him fight off the Muslims who had attacked the Asturian capital of Oviedo, and that Charlemagne came to the defence of the tomb of St James himself. There is no truth in the tale – Charlemagne died in 814 before the saint's relics were even discovered – but it was a good story and a successful piece of promotion, taken at face value both then and now and used to show the importance of the saint and his city.

Book V of the *Codex*, a first-person pilgrimage-account-cum-guide, was probably written by the Poitevin cleric Aymeric Picaud in the last years of the 1130s. It set out four routes to Santiago across France that met at St-Jean-Pied-de-Port in the Pyrenees, and then continued as one across the north of Spain. There were other routes already in existence at this point, but this was the most famous and is still the most popular route followed by pilgrims today. Most modern walkers believe foot travel is the most 'authentic' form of pilgrimage as this was the method used by their medieval forebears, but the *Codex* shows that this was not the case. The second chapter of Book V broke the journey from the Cize Pass, which takes pilgrims across the Pyrenees to Roncesvalles, to Santiago into thirteen stages and recommended a mix of walking and riding depending on distance.

The efforts made to promote Santiago soon showed results. High-status international pilgrims like Henry of Blois, bishop of Winchester and brother of King Stephen, and the earl of Salisbury came on pilgrimage from England.[8] So did a repentant William X, duke of Aquitaine, dying in 1137 in rather dramatic style in front of the altar in the cathedral.[9] Archbishop Gelmírez's hope that his city would become recognised as one of the pre-eminent pilgrimage destinations in Europe was realised only a decade after his death. In 1150, the Muslim writer al-Idrisi, composing a book of travels for the court of Roger II of Sicily, wrote,

> This church is known as a destination and place of pilgrimage. The Christians come to it on pilgrimage from all places and no church is more impressive, with the exception of the one at Jerusalem. It resembles the Temple of the Resurrection (Holy Sepulchre) because of the beauty of its construction, the breadth of its space and the treasures that it guards, the fruit of very generous offerings and gifts of alms.[10]

In the following centuries, all manner of kings, queens, saints and common people flocked to Santiago despite the difficulties of the journey. From Sweden, St Bridget, her father, grandfather and great-grandfather all completed the pilgrimage.[11] The greatest of these royal pilgrimages was that of Isabel of Portugal, queen from 1282 to 1325 and known for her piety. In the summer of 1325, the recently widowed Isabel left the city of Coimbra with a train of lavish gifts for Santiago which included her own crown. As she approached the city, Isabel stripped to her shift and walked barefoot. Ten years later she allegedly repeated the pilgrimage in the guise of a poor pilgrim, minus the expensive gifts. When she died soon afterwards, the queen was buried with a crozier and scarf decorated with scallop shells that had been given to her by the bishop of Santiago on the occasion of her first pilgrimage.[12]

If Isabel's motives were purely spiritual, other monarchs came to Santiago because of the political benefits to be gained from a pilgrimage to the shrine of St James. Alfonso XI, king of Castile for two decades by 1332, staged a ceremony that year in which he was knighted in the cathedral by a mechanical arm of St James.[13] Like so many of his predecessors, Alfonso was fighting the Muslims in southern Spain and sought the saint's support. He later returned to give thanks for his victory at the Battle of Rio Salado, a decisive encounter that forced the North African Marinids to return to Morrocco and gave the Christians control of the Straits of Gibraltar.

For the next century and a half, the fortunes of the city fluctuated with political instability, making it a problematic destination for pilgrims and a harder place to reach. During the Hundred Years War (1337–1453) between England and France, the Camino Francés was fraught with danger, and William Wey, bursar of Eton College, travelled by sea from England to La Coruña in 1456, just as the war came to an end.[14] A voyage across the Bay of Biscay might seem the easier option for northern European pilgrims, but medieval travellers who took ship regularly described the horrors of sea travel and the danger of shipwreck – if they could find a boat at all.[15] Margery Kempe, mother of fourteen who abandoned her family to become a serial pilgrim, waited for six weeks in Bristol in 1417 for a ship because they had all been 'detained and requisitioned for the king'.[16] Some sea-going pilgrims barely made it out of the harbour before they were drowned, as happened to a group of pilgrims who set sail from Dunster in Somerset in 1332.[17]

Despite such dangers, whether coming by land or sea, Santiago still pulled in pilgrims from across Europe. Jean de Tournai, a wool merchant from Valenciennes, embarked on a pilgrimage encompassing Rome, Jerusalem and Santiago de Compostela in 1488–9. A few years later Mártir, bishop of Arzendjan (Erzincan in present-day Turkey), used the opportunity of a diplomatic mission to Europe to journey on to Santiago.[18] By the turn of the sixteenth century, the city was flourishing and bustling with pilgrimage activity. This was a period of substantial rebuilding for the city and cathedral. Hospitals and hostels, many of them catering to pilgrims, were built or rebuilt, and new streets and squares laid out. The cathedral itself got a new roof, additional towers, several new chapels and a cloister.

Reformation and Rivalry

Unsurprisingly, the Protestant Reformation was not good for Santiago de Compostela. Spain, it's true, remained Catholic, but pilgrim numbers declined as much of northern Europe including Germany, Scandinavia and England turned to the new religion. The pilgrimage routes crossing northern Spain fell into decline, and Santiago shifted from being a great international pilgrimage destination to a Spanish, even a local, attraction reviled as a place of superstition in countries from which pilgrims had flocked only a generation before. Erasmus, that great Reformation thinker, mocked the pilgrimage to Santiago even though he had once been himself, and Martin Luther delivered a sermon attacking the credibility of its relics, pointing out that pilgrims had no way of knowing if 'St James or a dead dog or his dead pet is buried there'.[19] It was still important to the Spanish – King Philip II of Spain met an English delegation there to sign his contract of marriage with Mary I, and they celebrated mass in the cathedral to mark the occasion – but its heyday as the destination of Europe's kings and prelates was over.[20]

By the end of the sixteenth century Santiago was suffering. An outbreak of plague killed many people in 1560, and in 1589 an English fleet led by Francis Drake landed an army which besieged the pilgrimage port of La Coruña, prompting the clerics at Compostela to hide the relics of St James.[21] The conquest of Granada, the last Muslim outpost in Iberia, in 1492 had also diminished the importance of St James as a unifying figure for Christian Spain, and the country's monarchs no longer felt the need to go on pilgrimage to Santiago. Meanwhile, St James himself was under threat from within the Catholic Church. In 1592 Cardinal Robert Bellarmine wrote a report for the pope with recommendations for what should and shouldn't be included in a revised version of the *Roman Breviary*, a book of liturgy for daily use by the clergy. On the basis that St James had never preached in Spain, Bellarmine suggested removing references to him, but in the end Spanish pressure persuaded the pope to leave St James in the book.[22] Less than two decades later, the nun and mystic Teresa of Ávila was canonised and made joint patron saint of Spain by Philip III (ruled 1598–1621).[23] Saints Michael (1643), Joseph (1678) and Gennaro (1701) were all proposed as replacement national patrons, though James held out and ultimately triumphed.[24]

In an attempt to boost pilgrim numbers to Santiago, religious foundations were encouraged to send representatives to the holy year pilgrimages. As the only place in Europe bar Rome where one of Christ's Apostles was buried, Santiago was entitled to celebrate a holy year whenever St James's birthday fell on a Sunday – so every few years. Holy year pilgrims received a plenary indulgence – remission of punishment for all sins. The religious authorities at Santiago also tried to get Spanish royalty to come on pilgrimage and almost succeeded in persuading Philip III and his influential wife Margaret of Austria to visit in 1610 and 1625. Philip (known as the Pious) failed to come but at least sent his chaplain, laden with gifts, to Santiago in his stead.[25] His son and successor Philip IV (ruled 1621–65) supported Santiago by pouring considerable sums into the construction of a sort of show-tomb for St James that, unlike his actual relics, was visible to pilgrims. Philip IV also introduced the *Ofrenda*, an annual donation from the Spanish crown to Santiago, reinforcing the national status of the saint.

Unfortunately for the fortunes of Santiago, despite royal support and the occasional noble visitor – Cosimo de Medici and his entourage stayed for a few days in 1669, the year before he became grand duke of Tuscany – most pilgrims at the time tended to be poor, so had less to spend en route and in the city itself.[26] And no matter how rich or poor, they had to be determined, as many potential pilgrims were prevented even from setting out. Conflicts in France and the Spanish Netherlands lessened the number of pilgrims heading south, and Portugal's prolonged struggle to re-establish its independence from the Spanish crown (1640–68) dealt another blow. So too did legislation enacted by the French, which prohibited pilgrimage altogether in 1617 and 1687.[27] The following century was no better. When the Italian pilgrim Nicola Albani illuminated his pilgrimage diary in the 1740s, he included a depiction of the robbery and attempted murder of a pilgrim on the road to Santiago.[28]

The reality was that by the eighteenth century, though Santiago still attracted pilgrims, and both the cathedral and city underwent almost continual rebuilding, the place no longer had European significance. During the Napoleonic Wars Santiago was captured by Marshal Soult and the cathedral trashed by his troops. The giant thurible, the incense burner that hung from the cathedral's cupola, was stolen.[29] Santiago lost its status as a regional capital to the port of La Coruña in 1833, and two years later the convents and monasteries that supported the city's religious life and accommodated its pilgrims were closed.[30] By the time the Hungarian priest János Zádori arrived in 1868, having conducted his pilgrimage by rail as far as Astorga, the city had lost its pilgrim bustle.[31]

This wasn't surprising, given the lack of support for pilgrimage at the time. The Spanish government had abolished the *Ofrenda*, and there was less money to support the network of pilgrim hospitality.[32] Pilgrim numbers for most of the nineteenth century were small, perhaps a few hundred at most in the holy years, and even fewer the rest of the time. However, the feast of St James (25 July) was still popular in Santiago and Galicia, where there were extended celebrations. In the late 1870s, the regional railway company started to promote these celebrations, inspired more by the prospect of pecuniary reward than devotion to St James. Attempts to promote the railway to pilgrims had been made since the middle of the century, with several Spanish-language histories and guides including train schedules, but pilgrims remained scarce.[33]

This all began to change with the rediscovery of the saint's relics in 1879, even if the effect on pilgrim numbers or the city's status was not immediate. Despite newspapers reporting a 'great influx' into Santiago for St James's feast day, official records do not indicate any notable increase in the number of pilgrims.[34] Cardinal Archbishop Miguel Payá y Rico (in office 1875–86) was determined to change that. He organised and funded the search for St James's relics in 1879, enjoyed royal support and succeeded in getting King Alfonso XII to visit the city twice, once on St James's feast day. Archbishop Rico felt confident enough in the status of his city to tell the pope in 1884, the year that he presented evidence that the relics discovered in Santiago were indeed those of their titular saint and Saints Theodore and Athanasius, 'in truth, the standard of St James is the symbol of unity and cohesion for this Spanish people, always and constantly Catholic'.[35] The pope accepted Rico's evidence, declared via a papal bull, *Deus Omnipotens,* that the relics were genuine and encouraged Catholics to make the pilgrimage to Santiago once more.[36]

An extraordinary jubilee year was celebrated in 1885, attracting pilgrims with the promise of additional spiritual rewards. Rico's work was continued by Cardinal Archbishop José Martin Herrera, who ensured that mass pilgrimage processions were organised, personally (and very visibly) took part in celebrations in honour of St James, and called on pilgrims to visit Santiago in support of the Spanish war effort in Cuba in 1896. Some of those who came benefited from discounted rail travel (the city mayor secured a 50 per cent reduction on tickets for pilgrims in 1897),[37] and the growth in tourism helped to swell the crowds. The holy year in 1909, for example, coincided with the staging of the Galicia Regional Exhibition in Santiago de Compostela, further increasing numbers.[38]

Rail travel gave the pilgrimage a rather different complexion. Katherine Lee Bates, an American author and poet, went by train. 'Degenerate pilgrims that we were,' she wrote in her 1900 book, 'we had taken a first-class carriage reserved for ladies.' She did see plenty of walking pilgrims, and ones in traditional dress, including a German man from Wittenberg who said he had 'footed his way to Jerusalem and other distant shrines' following his conversion from Lutheranism. Bates did not find the relics at Santiago particularly impressive. The cathedral of Oviedo around 180 miles to the west in Asturias claimed to possess far more remarkable items, like a piece of the True Cross and thorns from the crown worn by Christ at the Crucifixion.[39]

Santiago and Franco

Francisco Franco (ruled 1939–75) was a fan of St James. Born in Ferrol, Franco was a Galician, so St James was his regional saint. Recalling Spain's medieval monarchs, Franco claimed that his victory at Brunete (1937) near Madrid over the Republicans had been secured with the aid of St James, and undertook a pilgrimage in 1938 to give thanks for his successes in the civil war.[40] It provided an excellent photo opportunity for the fascists, and pictures of Franco at the shrine were used to demonstrate divine support for his cause. The political Catholicism General France espoused during his dictatorship adopted the saint as its spiritual figurehead, and St James's status as the country's official patron saint, which he had lost during the country's brief period (1931–6) as a secular state, was resurrected. The *Ofrenda* was also restored, and St James's Day became a national holiday. Under Franco, Catholicism became a tool of the state and integral to the regime. Portraits of Franco with St James appeared, and the saint was used to 'guarantee the ideological values of State policy'.[41] The Catholic Church reciprocated by portraying Franco's fight against Marxism as a holy crusade under James's protection, echoing his role in the *Reconquista* centuries before. To remind Spaniards of Santiago's importance to the country's past, the city was declared a 'historic-artistic monument' in 1940, sparking a new building programme.

Franco went to Santiago several times, as did his wife Carmen Polo. Large group pilgrimages were arranged by members of the Falange, Spain's fascist party, and three holy years (1937, 1943 and 1948) were celebrated in considerable style.[42] Economic assistance came in the form of government-backed improvements to local infrastructure, and promotion of the saint and his city throughout Spain.[43] In 1942, the Institute of Spain ran a writing competition on pilgrimage to Santiago, resulting in two substantial books which told the history of Compostela and St James, as did the prize-winning poetry written for the 1945 Floral Games held in Santiago, and presided over by Franco's daughter.[44] During the 1943 holy year, the fascist writer Ernesto Giménez Caballero, claimed, 'Compostela was and will continue to be the greatest European and Catholic symbol against the Orient … like a latter-day Almanzor, Stalin could send his armies to the gates of Compostela so that his beast could drink the blessed water of the Apostle.'[45]

In an attempt to broaden the appeal of pilgrimage to Santiago, the holy year of 1954 was promoted overseas, and rising interest in tourism and the rebranding of St James as an Apostle-pilgrim, coupled with popular books about pilgrimage and interest in long-distance walking combined to create a boom in visitors to the city, symbolised by the conversion of the Royal Hospital into a luxury hotel in 1954. The government also funded the restoration of historic buildings along the Camino as *paradores,* luxury hotels.[46] In 1962, the Camino de Santiago was placed under national patronage, and the famous scallop shell and cross of St James were adopted as symbols of the pilgrimage. Two years later, the government stated that it wished to turn the traditional pilgrimages into tourist activities,[47] something it then did with growing success.

Many of the key features of the modern Santiago de Compostela pilgrimage appeared under Franco, and not only have they come to define that pilgrimage, but they have been copied on other pilgrimage routes and destinations around the world. As a result of the clearer and better-supported route, walking became an increasingly important part of the pilgrimage to Santiago. Pilgrims in the past had walked, and as we have seen also went by rail, but over the twentieth century, hiking the Camino increasingly became seen as a requirement for pilgrims. The activist movement Catholic Action relaunched Santiago as a walking pilgrimage in the 1940s, and in 1963 three pilgrims in medieval dress accompanied by a mule and cart followed the route on foot.[48] People had been walking the Camino for centuries because they had no other option, but these pilgrims were making a point. Thereafter, walking the full route was increasingly seen as necessary to be considered a proper pilgrim.[49] Then in 1965, the first holy year for eleven years, the first certificates were awarded to pilgrims who had walked at least 300 kilometres of the Camino to reach Santiago. A pilgrimage certificate – called the Compostela– had been issued since at least 1321, when a pilgrim called André le Breton received his, but this was the first time a stipulation was made about walking a minimum distance.

Press coverage of the 1965 holy year was global, the number of pilgrims much higher than before, and descriptions of individual pilgrimages were published in significant numbers. First-person accounts of the pilgrimage have become something of a publishing phenomenon since the middle of the twentieth century, kick-started by the Irishman Walter Starkie's record of his penitential pilgrimage from Arles (where he witnessed the Gypsies going to Saintes-Maries-de-la-Mer) in 1954. Starkie would have approved of the new walking requirement, as he scoffed at the 'pilgrimages without tears' that modern people undertook, believing them to be 'the complete antithesis of the original idea of pilgrimage'. (It is worth pointing out that Starkie also used a bus.)[50]

Global Santiago

After the death of Franco in 1975, the now-well-established pilgrimage to Santiago continued, though the numbers who actually reached Santiago were now small. Even in 1971 and 1976, both jubilee years, the official records only counted 500 and 240 pilgrims respectively.[51] Fortunately for Santiago de Compostela, the 1970s was in many respects the calm before the post-1980 deluge of pilgrims.

A significant figure in the twentieth-century history of Santiago de Compostela and the Camino was Elias Valiña Sampedro, parish priest of the tiny and remote hilltop Galician village of O Cebreiro from 1957 to his death in 1989. Pilgrims passed through O Cebreiro because it was on the pilgrimage route and had been stopping there since at least the ninth century, but it also had its own religious attraction as the site of a fourteenth-century miracle. The story goes that a farmer who struggled to the church through vile winter weather found only a despondent priest simply going through the motions of saying mass. To shake the priest out of his indifference, God turned the wafer and wine into actual flesh and blood, the blood leaped from the chalice and a statue of the Virgin Mary in the church dipped its head. Relics of this miracle were placed in a reliquary in the church, and the farmer and priest were buried at a side altar to remind pilgrims of the tale.[52]

Sampedro oversaw the restoration of his village as well as the church and hostelry used by pilgrims and cleared overgrown parts of the route.[53] A historian and avid researcher, he also wrote two guidebooks, published in 1971 and 1985, intended for those driving rather than walking the route to Santiago.[54] He took part in the 1985 meeting that discussed the introduction of a pilgrim's card, but most significantly of all, during the 1980s Sampedro and a group of volunteers marked the whole route from Roncesvalles to Compostela with yellow arrows. The colour, the result of the fact that Sampedro was using leftover paint given to him by a company that painted road markings, has become key to the branding of the Camino. His efforts were supplemented by signs indicating distances and by the much-copied concrete way markers featuring a scallop shell, which were set up by the government of Galicia.

Sampedro's efforts coincided with renewed international

interest in Santiago and its primary pilgrimage route, including two visits in 1982 and 1989 by Pope John Paul II (ruled 1978–2005). In his 1982 homily delivered at Santiago, Pope John Paul related Santiago and its pilgrimage to Europe's Christian identity.

> The meaning, the pilgrim style, is something deeply rooted in the Christian vision of life and of the Church. The Camino de Santiago created a vigorous spiritual and cultural current of fruitful exchange between the peoples of Europe. But what the pilgrims were really looking for with their humble and penitent attitude was that testimony of faith to which I referred earlier: the Christian faith that seems to ooze from the stones of Compostela with which the Basilica of the Saint is built, that Christian and Catholic faith that constitutes the identity of the Spanish people. At the end of my pastoral visit to Spain, here, near the shrine of the Apostle James, I invite you to reflect on our faith, and try to reconnect with the apostolic origins of your Christian tradition.[55]

That same decade, Spain joined the European Community, and in October 1987 the Camino de Santiago was named the first of the Council of Europe's Cultural Routes. The shell used as a route marker was now yellow against a blue background, echoing the colours of the European flag. Membership of the European Community had a transformative effect on Santiago de Compostela and the Camino, with annual pilgrim numbers soaring from the hundreds into the thousands.

The pilgrimage to the shrine of St James in Galicia has become one of the most important and famous in the world. The old city itself was designated a UNESCO World Heritage Site for its symbolic value as a focus for the struggle of Spanish Christians against Islam and for its medieval pilgrimage heritage. In recent years international pilgrimage has grown exponentially, with pilgrims coming from all over the world. South Koreans visit in particularly large numbers, accounting for a quarter of the total of foreign pilgrims in 2010. The diversity of religions in South Korea, their protection in its constitution, and the journeys along the Camino of such famous figures as the members of the K-pop group g.o.d., may account for the visit of so many Koreans.[56] More generally, the growth in numbers is at least partially explained by the popularity of the Camino for secular walkers and for pilgrimages of well-being, which see hundreds of thousands undertake the journey to Santiago each year.

The Model Pilgrimage?

Many myths and misconceptions have sprung up surrounding St James, Santiago de Compostela and its pilgrimage routes. One common belief is that the German writer Johann Wolfgang von Goethe (1749–1832), author of *Faust*, claimed that 'Europe was made on the pilgrim road to Compostela.'[57] Goethe did write about pilgrimage and the birth of Europe but did not mention Santiago. However, the pilgrimage has become so popular over the last half a century that many simply accept this assertion because it so neatly encapsulates what a lot of people believe to be true.

But those looking for a definition or explanation of the significance of Santiago de Compostela as a pilgrimage destination should instead look to the work of Dante Alighieri, Italian poet extraordinaire. Dante believed that Santiago was set apart from all other pilgrimage destinations and that going there was the definition of pilgrimage. 'In a general sense a pilgrim is anyone who is out of his own country,' he wrote in *La Vita Nuova* in the early 1290s. 'In a limited sense,' he continued, 'pilgrim means only one who travels to or returns from the house of St James … they are called pilgrims who journey to the house of Galicia, because the tomb of St James is farther away from his own country than any other apostle.'[58] Pilgrims to Rome were *romei*, while those who went to Jerusalem were *palmieri* (palmers). Only pilgrims to Santiago de Compostela had earned the right to be called *pellegrini* – pilgrims.

NOTES

Introduction: A World of Pilgrimage

1 Kathryn Hurlock, *Medieval Welsh Pilgrimage, c.1100–1500* (New York: Palgrave, 2018), 179–81.

2 'Adolf Hitler Replaces Częstochowa's Madonna', *Catholic Bulletin of Foreign News*, 26 December 1942, 4.

3 'China Bans Haj for Muslims Who Fail Patriotism Test', *The Times* 14 October 2020.

1. Tai Shan, China

1 Tom F. Liao and Cuntong Wang, 'The Changing Face of Money: Forging Collective Memory with Chinese Banknote Designs', *China Review* 18 (2018), 87–120.

2 Xinping Zhuo, *Religious Faith of the Chinese* (Singapore: Springer, 2018), 36–7.

3 Susan Naquin, *Gods of Mount Tai: Familiarity and the Material Culture of North China, 1000–2000* (Leiden: Brill, 2022), 40.

4 Henri Maspero, *Taoism and Chinese Religion,* trans. Frank A. Kierman Jr (Amherst: University of Massachusetts Press, 1981), 102–104; Vincent Goossaert, 'Taishan', in *Encyclopedia of Taoism, I–II*, ed. Fabrizio Pregadio (London: Routledge, 2008), 947.

5 Brian R. Dott, *Identity Reflections: Pilgrimages to Mount Tai in Late Imperial China* (Cambridge, MA: Harvard University Press, 2004), 111, 114, 115, 122.

6 The Surveillance Commissioner of the Mongol Yuan Dynasty, quoted in Wilt L. Idema, 'The Pilgrimage to Taishan in the Dramatic Literature of the Thirteenth and Fourteenth Centuries', *Chinese Literature: Essays, Articles, Reviews (CLEAR)*, 19 (1997), 23–4.

7 Pei-yi Wu, 'An Ambivalent Pilgrim to T'ai Shan: Some Pages from a Seventeenth Century Novel', in *Pilgrims and Sacred Sites in China*, ed. Susan Naquin and Chun-Fang Yu (Berkeley, CA: University of California Press, 1992), 69.
8 Naquin, *Gods of Mount Tai*, 182.
9 Dott, *Identity Reflections*, 109; Marcus Bingenheimer, 'Pilgrimage in China', in *International Perspectives on Pilgrimage Studies: Itineraries, Gaps, and Obstacles*, ed. D. Albera and J. Eade (London: Routledge, 2015), 350–51; Edwin Bernbaum, *Sacred Mountains of the World*, 2nd edn (Cambridge: Cambridge University Press, 2022), 65.
10 Pei-yi Wu, 'An Ambivalent Pilgrim to T'ai Shan', 72–4, 76–7.
11 Ibid., 77.
12 Dott, *Identity Reflections*, 118.
13 Bingenheimer, 'Pilgrimage in China', 18.
14 Édouard Chavannes, *Le T'ai Chan: Essai de Monographie d'un Culte Chinois* (Paris: Ernest Leroux, 1910), 3.
15 Dott, *Identity Reflections*, 1, 115.
16 Bernbaum, *Sacred Mountains,* 56; Susan Naquin and Chun-Fang Yu, 'Introduction: Pilgrimage in China', in *Pilgrims and Sacred Sites in China*, 14.
17 Dott, *Identity Reflections,* 115.
18 Pei-yi Wu, 'An Ambivalent Pilgrim to T'ai Shan', 79.
19 Huang Liuhong, *A Complete Book Concerning Happiness and Benevolence*, trans. Djang Chu (Tucson, AZ: University of Arizona Press, 1984), 608.
20 Susan L. Mann, *Gender and Sexuality in Modern Chinese History* (Cambridge: Cambridge University Press, 2011), 36.
21 Mark C. Elliott, *Emperor Qianlong: Son of Heaven, Man of the World* (New York: Longman, 2009), 78; John Clements, *The First Emperor of China* (Stroud: Sutton, 2006), 113–17.
22 Bernbaum, *Sacred Mountains*, 54.
23 Sima Qian, *The First Emperor: Selections from the Historical Records*, K. E. Brashier, trans. Raymond Dawson (Oxford: Oxford University Press, 2007), 65, 96, 99.
24 Ibid., 54.

25 Michael Loewe, *Ways to Paradise: The Chinese Quest for Immortality* (London: George Allen & Unwin, 1979), 97, 200.
26 'Record of the Feng and Shan Rites', in Stephen Bokencamp, 'Record of the Feng and Shan Sacrifices', in *Religions of China in Practice*, ed. Donald S. Lopez Jr (Princeton: Princeton University Press, 1996), 254–60.
27 Howard J. Wechsler, *Offerings of Jade and Silk: Ritual and Symbol in the Legitimation of the T'ang Dynasty* (New Haven: Yale University Press, 1985), 170–211.
28 Jonathan Karam Skaff, *Sui-Tang China and Its Turko-Mongol Neighbors: Culture, Power, and Connections, 580–800* (Oxford: Oxford University Press, 2012), 146; X. L. Woo, *Empress Wu the Great* (New York: Algora, 2008), 86.
29 Dott, *Identity Reflections*, 153.
30 N. Harry Rothschild, *Empress Wu Zhao and Her Pantheon of Devis, Divinities, and Dynastic Mothers* (New York: Columbia University Press, 2015), 115–16, 170.
31 Wechsler, *Offerings of Jade and Silk*, 184.
32 Skaff, *Sui-Tang China*, 146.
33 Bingenheimer, 'Pilgrimage in China', 349.
34 Ibid., 353.
35 Han Lifeng, 'Communicating Civilization through Rituals: Mount Tai Pilgrimages in Song China, 960–1279', *Journal of Chinese Humanities*, 1 (2015), 335–62.
36 Michael G. Chang, *A Court on Horseback: Imperial Touring & the Construction of Qing Rule, 1680–1785* (Cambridge, MA: Harvard University Press, 2007), 79–80.
37 Dott, *Identity Reflections*, 159, 16.
38 Naquin, *Gods of Mount Tai*, 260.
39 Dott, *Identity Reflections*, 165–6.
40 Naquin, *Gods of Mount Tai*, 260.
41 Dott, *Identity Reflections*, 175; Jimmy Yu, *Sanctity and Self-Inflicted Violence in Chinese Religions, 1500–1700* (Oxford: Oxford University Press, 2012), 168, n. 9.
42 Dott, *Identity Reflections*, 175; Naquin, *Gods of Mount Tai*, 198.
43 Dott, *Identity Reflections*, 159.

44 Dott, *Identity Reflections*, 166.
45 Ibid., 160; Bernbaum, *Sacred Mountains*, 55.
46 Naquin, *Gods of Mount Tai*, 261; Dott, *Identity Reflections*, 150.
47 Kristina Kleutghen, *Imperial Illusions: Crossing Pictorial Boundaries in the Qing Palace* (Seattle: University of Washington Press, 2015), 111; Elliott, *Emperor Qianlong*, 41–3.
48 Norman Kutcher, 'The Death of the Xiaoxian Empress: Bureaucratic Betrayals and the Crises of Eighteenth-Century Chinese Rule', *Journal of Asian Studies*, 56 (1997), 708–25.
49 Alexander Woodside, 'The Ch'ien-lung Reign', in *Cambridge History of China: Volume 9, The Ch'ing Dynasty to 1800, Part 1* (Cambridge: Cambridge University Press, 2008), 234–5; Mark C. Elliott, 'Introduction: The Qianlong Emperor and His Age', in *The Emperor's Private Paradise: Treasures from the Forbidden City*, ed. Nancy Berliner (New Haven: Yale University Press, 2010), 40.
50 Robert E. Harrist, *The Landscape of Words: Stone Inscriptions from Early and Medieval China* (Seattle: University of Washington Press, 2008), 246.
51 William T. Rowe, *China's Last Empire: The Great Qing* (Cambridge, MA: Belknap Press of Harvard University Press, 2009).

2. The Ganges, India

1 Ruth A. Freed and Stanley A. Freed, *Rites of Passage of the Shanti Nagar* (New York: American Museum of Natural History, 1980), 349.
2 Vidya Dehejia, *Art of the Imperial Cholas* (New York: Columbia University Press, 1990), 79.
3 Steven G. Darian, *The Ganges in Myth and History* (Delhi: Motilal Banarsidass Publishers, 1978), 11.
4 Fanny Parks, *Wanderings of a Pilgrim, in Search of the Picturesque* (London: Richardson, 1850), 260.
5 Vikash Singh and Sangeeta Parashar, 'Hardwar: Spirit, Place, Politics', *Religions*, 10 (2019), 10.
6 Knut A. Jacobson, 'Pilgrimage', in *Hindu Law: A New History of Dharmaśāstra*, ed. Patrick Olivelle and Donald R. David Jr (Oxford: Oxford University Press, 2018), 335.
7 Christopher Bayly, 'From Ritual to Ceremony: Death, Ritual and

Society in North India since 1600', in J. Whaley, ed., *Mirrors of Mortality: Studies in the Social History of Death* (London: Europa Publications, 1981), 163.

8 Samuel Purchas, *Purchas his Pilgrimage* (London, 1626), 509.

9 Jean de Thévenot, *The travels of Monsieur de Thevenot into the Levant* (London: J. Clark, 1687), 66.

10 John Matheson, *England to Delhi: A Narrative of Indian Travel* (London: Longmans Green, 1835), 315.

11 Abdur Rasheed, *The Travellers' Companion: containing a brief description of places of pilgrimage and important towns in India* (Calcutta: Superintendent Government Printing, 1907), 20, 29, 30, 34, 39, 55, 80, 96, 123, 129, 235.

12 Jadunath Sarkar, *India of Aurangzib compared with the India of Akbar, with extracts from the Khulastatu-t-Tawarikh* (Calcutta: Bose Brothers, 1901), 19.

13 R. V. Raper, 'Narrative of a Survey for the Purpose of Discovering the Source of the Ganges', *Asiatick Researches*, 11 (1810), 452; James H. Lochtefeld, *God's Gateway: identity and meaning in Hindu Pilgrimage Place* (Oxford: Oxford University Press, 2010), 49–50.

14 *System of University Geography Founded on the Works of Malte-Brun and Balbi* (Edinburgh: Adam and Charles Black, 1842), 720.

15 *Kumbh Mela: Mapping the Ephemeral Megacity*, ed. Rahul Mehrotra and Felipe Vera (Allahabad: Noiyogi Books, 2015), 11.

16 Kama MacLean, *Pilgrimage and Power: The Kumbh Mela in Allahabad, 1765–1954* (Oxford: Oxford University Press, 2008), pp. 88–9.

17 David Arnold, 'The Ecology and Cosmology of Disease in the Banaras Region', in *Culture and Power in Banaras: Community, Performance and Environment, 1800–1980*, ed. Sandria B. Freitag (Berkeley: University of California Press, 1989), 255–6.

18 'Incidence and Spread of Cholera in India', *British Medical Journal*, 1 (1926), 785.

19 'Spread of Infection from Pilgrim Centres', *Tribune* 25 May 1917.

20 *Report of the Committee appointed by the Uttar Pradesh Government to enquire into the mishap which occurred in the Kumbh Mela at Prayaga on the 3rd February 1954* (Allahabad: Government of India, 1954), 6, 23, 60,

84–5; Dilip Kumar Roy and Indira Devi, *Kumbha: India's Ageless Festival* (Bombay: Bharatiya Vidya Bhavan, 1955), 4.

21 Arnold, 'Ecology', 231.

22 Robert B. Minturn, *From New York to New Delhi by way of Rio de Janeiro, Australia, and China* (New York: D. Appleton & Co., 1858), 137.

23 Diana L. Eck, *Banaras: City of Light* (New York: Alfred A. Knopf, 1982), 21.

24 H. R. Nevill, *Allahabad: A Gazetteer* vol. 23 (Allahabad: Government Press, 1911), 68–9.

25 Christopher Justice, *Dying the Good Death: The Pilgrimage to Die in India's Holy City* (New York: SUNY Press, 1997), 20.

26 L. P. Vidyarthi, *The Sacred Complex of Kashi: A Microcosm of Indian Civilization* (New Delhi: Concept, 2005), 129.

27 *The Great Tang Dynasty Record of the Western Regions*, trans. Li Rongxi (Ann Arbor: University of Michigan Press, 1996), 109.

28 Sudipta Sen, *Ganges: The Many Pasts of an Indian River* (Yale: Yale University Press, 2019), 3–4.

29 *The Travels of Ibn Battuta in Asia and Africa, 1325–1354*, trans. H. A. R. Gibb (New York: Augustus M. Kelley, 1969), 193.

30 Burjor Avari, *India: The Ancient Past, A History of the Indian Subcontinent from c.7000 BC to AD 1200* (London: Routledge, 2007), 18.

31 *Sarojini Naidu: Great Women of Modern India*, ed. Verinder Grover and Ranjana Arora (New Delhi: Deep & Deep Publications, 1993), 230.

32 Maclean, *Pilgrimage and Power*, 11; Harriette Ashmore, *Narrative of a Three Months March in India* (London: R. Hastings, 1841), 199–200.

33 MacLean, *Pilgrimage and Power*, 61.

34 Parks, *Wanderings*, 162.

35 Caleb Wright, *Lectures on India* (Boston: Caleb Wright, 1848), 7. See also Nancy Gardner Cassels, *Religion and Pilgrim Tax under the Company Raj* (Riverdale, MD: Riverdale Company, 1988).

36 Rasheed, *The Travellers' Companion*, preface; *Report of the Committee*, 27, 83.

37 Sarkar, *India of Aurangzib*, 20.

38 'Notes from India', *The Lancet* 2 September (1911), 731.

39 Eric Newby, *Slowly Down the Ganges* (London: Hodder & Stoughton, 1989), xvi.

40 Payal Sampat, 'The River Ganges' Long Decline', *World Watch*, 9.4 (1996).
41 Ellen Wohl, *A World of Rivers: Environmental Change of Ten of the World's Great Rivers* (Chicago; University of Chcago Press, 2010), 158–9.
42 Justin Rowlett, 'India's dying mother', *BBC News Online* 12 May 2016 https://www.bbc.co.uk/news/resources/idt-aad46fca-734a-45f9-8721-61404cc12a39

3. Delphi, Greece

1 Oracle of Delphi: King Aigeus in front of the Pythia: Antikensammlung Berlin, Altes Museum, F 2538.
2 'To Apollo', in *Homeric Hymns, Homeric Apocrypha, Lives of Homer*, ed. and trans. Martin L. West (Cambridge, MA: Harvard University Press, 2003), 109.
3 Michael Scott, *Delphi: A History at the Center of the World* (Princeton: Princeton University Press, 2014), 1.
4 Matthew Dillon, *Pilgrims and Pilgrimage in Ancient Greece* (Abingdon: Routledge, 1997), 29; Hugh Bowden, 'Delphi: Historical Overview', in Michael Gagarin, *Oxford Encyclopedia of Ancient Greece and Rome*, vol. 1 (Oxford: Oxford University Press, 2009), 17.
5 Scott, *Delphi*, 17.
6 Sarah Iles Johnston, *Ancient Greek Divination* (Oxford: Wiley Blackwell, 2008), 39.
7 Bowden, 'Delphi', 16.
8 Joan Breton Connelly, *Portrait of a Priestess: Women and Ritual in Ancient Greece* (Princeton: Princeton University Press, 2007), 43–4.
9 Johnston, *Ancient Greek Divination*, 40.
10 *Diodorus* Siculus, *Library of History*, 16.26, https://www.perseus.tufts.edu/hopper/text?doc=Diod.%2016.26&lang=original; Dillon, *Pilgrims*, 82.
11 Lucan, *Pharsalia*, 5.71, https://www.perseus.tufts.edu/hopper/text?doc=Perseus:text:1999.02.0134:book=5:card=71&highlight=de
12 Ibid., Scott, *Delphi*, 20; Joseph Fontenrose, *The Delphic Oracle: Its Responses and Operations* (Berkeley: University of California Press, 1978), 197, 204.
13 Bowden, 'Delphi', 17.

14 Ibid., 97.
15 James Longrigg, 'Death and Epidemic Disease in Classical Athens', in *Death and Disease in the Ancient City*, ed. Valerie M. Hope and Eireaan Marshall (London: Routledge, 2000), 64 n. 10.
16 Fontenrose, *The Delphic Oracle*, 249, 255, 263.
17 Ibid., 353.
18 Dillon, *Pilgrims*, 90.
19 Xenophon, *Hellenica*, trans. Carleton L. Brownson (Cambridge, MA: Harvard University Press, 1947), 349.
20 Thucydides, *History of the Peloponnesian War, Books III and IV*, trans. Charles Forster Smith (London: William Heinemann, 1920), 163–5; Dillon, *Pilgrims*, 88.
21 *Herodotus: The Histories*, trans. Aubrey de Selincourt (London: Penguin, 1963), 292–3.
22 Hugh Bowden, *Classical Athens and the Delphic Oracle: Divination and Democracy* (Cambridge: Cambridge University Press, 2005), 70.
23 Bowden, 'Delphi', 38.
24 Bowden, *Classical Athens*, 136–9.
25 Simon Price, 'Delphi and Divination', in *Greek Religion and Society,* ed. P. Easterling and J. Muir (Cambridge: Cambridge University Press, 1985), esp. 154. My thanks go to Dr Jason Crowley for his comments on this shift.
26 Fontenrose, *Delphic Oracle*, 259.
27 *The Geography of Strabo*, trans. Horace Leonard Jones (Cambridge, MA: Harvard University Press, 1927), iv, 348–49.
28 *Pausanias's Description of Greece Volume 1; Translation*, ed. James George Frazer (Cambridge: Cambridge University Press, 1898, reprinted 2012), 508.
29 Scott, *Delphi*, 81.
30 Pierre Bonnechere, 'Divination', in *A Companion to Greek Religion*, ed. Daniel Ogden (Oxford: Blackwell, 2010), 158.
31 Michael Scott, 'The Oracle at Delphi: Unknowability at the Heart of the Ancient Greek Word', *Social Research: an International Quarterly*, 87 (2020), 59–60.
32 Ibid., 61–3.

4. Jerusalem, Israel/Palestine

1 Amikan Elad, *Medieval Jerusalem and Islamic Worship: Holy Places, Ceremonies, Pilgrimage* (Leiden Brill, 1999), 79.

2 Jack Feldman, 'La circulation de la Tora: Les pèlerinages au second Temple', in *La société Juive à travers l'histoire,* ed. Shmuel Trigano, 4 vols (Paris: Fayard, 1993), iv, 161–78.

3 *Flavius Josephus, Translation and Commentary: Volume 1b, Judean War 2*, ed. Steve Mason (Leiden: Brill, 2008), 362.

4 Susan Graham, 'Justinian and the Politics of Space', in *Constructions of Space II: The Biblical City and Other Imagined Spaces*, ed. Jon L. Berquist and Claudia V. Camp (New York: T. & T. Clark, 2008), 59–61.

5 *Of the Holy Places Visited by Antoninus Martyr (Circ. 530 A.D.)*, trans. Aubrey Stewart (London: Palestine Pilgrims' Text Society, 1887), 14. Antoninus of Piacenza was not actually the author of this account, who was the anonymous individual known simply as the Piacenza Pilgrim.

6 Febe Armanios, *Coptic Christianity in Ottoman Egypt* (Oxford: Oxford University Press, 2011), 95.

7 Denys Pringle, *Churches of the Crusader Kingdom of Jerusalem: A Corpus, Volume 3: the City of Jerusalem* (Cambridge: Cambridge University Press, 2007), 10.

8 Nasir-i Khusrū (Khusraw), *The Book of Travels*, ed. and trans. W. M. Thackston (Costa Mesa, CA: Mazda Publishers, 2001), 27.

9 Adrian J. Boas, 'The Crusader Period', in *Routledge Handbook on Jerusalem*, ed. Suleiman A. Mourad, Naomi Koltun-Fromm and Bedross Der Matossian (New York: Routledge, 2018), 95.

10 Helen Nicholson, *Women and the Crusades* (Oxford: Oxford University Press, 2023), 84–5.

11 Usama Munqidh, *The Book of Contemplation: Islam and the Crusades*, ed. and trans. P. M. Cobb (London: Penguin Books, 2008), 147.

12 *Jewish Travellers in the Middle Ages: 19 Firsthand Accounts*, ed. Elkan Nathan Adler (New York: Dover Publications, 1987), xii.

13 *Jewish Travellers in the Middle Ages*, 103–10, 115–29.

14 Suleiman A. Mourad, 'Jerusalem in Early Islam', in *Routledge Handbook on Jerusalem*, ed. Suleiman A. Mourad, Naomi Koltun-Fromm and Bedross Der Matossian (London: Routledge, 2018), 84.

15 *Guide-Book to Jerusalem,(Circ. A.D. 1350)*, trans. J. H. Bernard (London: Palestine Pilgrims' Text Society, 1894), 3.
16 Zayde Antrim, 'Jerusalem in Ayyubid and Mamluk Periods', in *Routledge Handbook on Jerusalem*, 105.
17 Armstrong, *The History of Jerusalem*, 319.
18 *Jewish Travellers in the Middle Ages*, 235.
19 *Felix Fabri (circa 1480–1483 A.D.), Vol. I, Part I*, trans., Aubrey Stewart (London: Palestine Pilgrims' Text Society, 1896), 48–9.
20 Oleg Grabar, 'Islamic Jerusalem or Jerusalem under Muslim Rule', in *The City in the Islamic World, Vol. 2*, ed. Salma Khadra Jayyusi, Renata Holod, Antillio Petruccioli and André Raymond (Leiden: Brill, 2008), 325.
21 Yuval Ben-Bassat and Johann Buessow, 'Ottoman Jerusalem, 1517–1918', in *Routledge Handbook on Jerusalem*, 114.
22 Uriel Heyd, *Ottoman Documents on Palestine, 1552–1615: A Study of the Firman according to the Mühimme Defteri* (Oxford: Clarendon Press, 1960), 87–8.
23 Aquilante Rocchetta, *Peregrinatione di Terra Santa e d'altre provincie di Don Aquilanta Roccetta Cavaliere del Santissimo Sepolcro* (Palermo: Alfonzo dell'Isola, 1630), 2.
24 François Laplanche, 'Through Travelogues in the Holy Land (XVI–XIX centuries): The Devout, The Curious, The Erudite', *Bulletin du Centre de Recherche Français à Jérusalem*, 7 (2000), 130.
25 Grabar, 'Islamic Jerusalem', 181–2.
26 Hunt Janin, *Four Paths to Jerusalem: Jewish, Christian, Muslim, and Secular Pilgrimages 100 BCE to 2001 CE* (London: McFarland, 2002), 25.
27 Jacob Barnai, *The Jews in Palestine in the Eighteenth Century*, trans. Naomi Goldblum (Tuscaloosa: University of Alabama Press, 1992), 27–9.
28 David Goldfrank, 'The Holy Sepulcher and the Origin of the Crimean War', in *The Military and Society in Russia, 1450–1917*, ed. Eric Lohr and Marshall Poe (Leiden: Brill, 2002), 491–505; 'Commons Chamber, Monday 20 February 1854', *Hansard*, https://hansard.parliament.uk/Commons/1854-02-20/debates/53ea0417-76e2-4398-84ae-c76403510d80/CommonsChamber
29 *The Jerusalem Miscellany: An Occasional Publication of the Jerusalem*

Agricultural Association, ed. A. M'Caul, 1 (January, 1855), 3; Mansurov, *Pravoslavnye poklonniki*, 11, in Elena Astafieva, 'Russian Orthodox Pilgrims in Jerusalem in the Second Half of the Nineteenth Century: Between the Old City and "New Jerusalem"', *Acta Slavica Iaponica* 40 (2020), 153; A. Gravin, 'B. P. Mansurov and the creation of the Russian Palestine (1857–1864)', *Tambov University Review: Series Humanities* (2019), no pagination.

30 Roberto Mazza, *Jerusalem: From the Ottomans to the British* (London: I. B. Taurus, 2009), 78.

31 Mark Twain, *The Innocents Abroad: or, The New Pilgrims' Progress* (Hartford, CT: American Publishing Company, 1869)

32 Janin, *Four Paths to Jerusalem*, 166.

33 Ruth Kark, 'Geopietism and Pilgrimage/Tourism to the Holy Land/ Palestine (1850–1918), and the case of Thomas Cook', in *Nineteenth Century European Pilgrimages: A New Golden Age*, ed. Antón M. Pazos (Abingdon: Routledge, 2020), 68–70; Naomi Shephard, *The Zealous Intruders: The Western Discovery of Palestine* (London: Harper & Row, 1987), 173–5.

34 David Klatzker, 'American Catholic Travellers to the Holy Land, 1861–1929', *Catholic Historical Review*, 74 (1988), 55–74; James Pfeiffer, *First American Catholic Pilgrimage to Palestine, 1889* (Cincinnati: Jos. Berning and Company, 1892).

35 Pontifical Institute Notre Dame of Jerusalem Center, www.notredamecenter.org

36 Elzear O. B. Horn., *Ichnographiae Monumentum Terrae Sanctae 1724–1744* (Jerusalem: Franciscan Press, 1962), 183–4.

37 Thomas Hummel, 'Russian Pilgrims: A Peasant Army Invades Jerusalem', *Jerusalem Quarterly*, 44 (2010), 39.

38 Irina Mironenko-Marenkova and Kirill Vakh, 'An Institution, Its People and Its Documents: the Russian Consulate in Jerusalem through the Foreign Policy Archive of the Russian Empire, 1858–1914', in *Ordinary Jerusalem, 1840–1940: opening new archives, revisiting a global city*, ed. Angelos Dalachanis and Vincent Lamire (Leiden: Brill, 2018), 200, 204, 206 n. 18.

39 Thomas Hummel, 'Russian Pilgrims', 40.

40 Mazza, *Jerusalem*, 53.

41 Valentina Izmirlieva, 'Christian Hajjis – the Other Orthodox Pilgrims to Jerusalem', *Slavic Review*, 73.2 (Summer 2014), 322–5.

42 Matthew Hughes, *Allenby and British Strategy in the Middle East, 1917–1919* (London: Frank Cass, 1999), 41.

43 Luke McKernan, '"The Supreme Moment of the War": General Allenby's Entry into Jerusalem', *Historical Journal of Film, Radio, and Television*, 13 (1993), 169–80.

44 Dom Bede Camm, 'A Soldier's Pilgrimage to Jerusalem', *Downside Review* (1919), 17.

45 Matthew P. FitzPatrick, *The Kaiser and the Colonies: Monarchy in the Age of Empire* (Oxford: Oxford University Press, 2022), 78–81.

46 Simon Goldhill, 'Jerusalem', in *Cities of God: The Bible and Archaeology in Nineteenth Century Britain*, ed. David Gange and Michael Ledger-Lomas (Cambridge: Cambridge University Press, 2013), 108.

47 Kobi Cohen-Hattab, 'Religion and Nationalism in Jewish Pilgrimage and Holy Sites: the Western Wall and Rachel's Tomb as Case Studies', in *Religious Pilgrimage in the Mediterranean World*, ed. Antón M. Pazos (London: Routledge, 2023), 132–5.

48 Ibid., 129.

49 Gideon Bar, 'Reconstructing the Past: the Creation of Jewish Sacred Space in the State of Israel', *Israel Studies*, 13 (2008), 1–21; Doron Bar, 'Re-creating Jewish Sanctity in Jerusalem: Mount Zion and David's Tomb, 1948–67', *Journal of Israeli History*, 23 (2004), 260–78.

50 Uri Bialer, *Cross on the Star of David: The Christian World in Israel's Foreign Policy, 1948–1967* (Bloomington: Indiana University Press, 2005), 187–9.

51 Cohen-Hattab, 'Religion and Nationalism', 129.

52 Ibid., 135.

5. Mecca, Saudi Arabia

1 Farhad Daftary, *The Ismāʿilis: Their History and Doctrines* (Cambridge: Cambridge University Press, 2007), 205.

2 W. M. Watt, A. J. Wensinck, C. E. Bosworth and R. B. Winder, 'Mecca (Makka)', in *Historic Cities of the Islamic World*, ed. C. Edmund Bosworth (Leiden: Brill, 2007), 344–5.

3 John Slight, *The British Empire and the Hajj, 1865–1956* (Cambridge, MA: Harvard University Press, 2015), 325, n. 1.

4 L'Atlas Catalan, http://expositions.bnf.fr/ciel/catalan/index.htm

5 R. M. Eaton, 'From Bidar to Timbuktu: views from the edge of the 15th century Muslim world', *Medieval History Journal*, 14 (2011), 1–20; Michael A. Gomez, *African Dominion: A New History of Empire in Early and Medieval West Africa* (Princeton: Princeton University Press, 2018), 113–22.

6 Adrian Hastings, *The Church in Africa: 1450–1950* (Oxford: Clarendon Press, 1994), 61.

7 Michael Naylor Pearson, *Pious Passengers: The Hajj in Earlier Times* (London: Hurst, 1994), 174.

8 Quoted in Francis E. Peters, *Mecca: A Literary History of the Muslim Holy Land* (Princeton: Princeton University Press, 1994), 21.

9 Mai Yamani, *Cradle of Islam: The Hijaz and the Quest for Identity in Saudi Arabia* (London: I. B. Taurus, 2009), 42–4.

10 *The Travels of Ibn Jubayr*, trans. R. J. C. Broadhurst (London: Jonathan Cape, 1952), 116–17.

11 *One Thousand Roads to Mecca: ten centuries of travellers writing about Muslim Pilgrimage*, ed. Michael Wolfe (New York: Grove Press, 1997), 43.

12 Ludovico di Varthema, *The Travels of Ludovico di Varthema* (London: The Hakluyt Society, 2022), 35.

13 Guy Barak, 'Between Istanbul and Gujarat: Descriptions of Mecca in the Sixteenth-Century Indian Ocean', *Murqarnas*, 34 (2017), 311–15.

14 Joseph Pitts, *A True and Faithful Account of the Religion & Manners of the Mohametans, in which is a Particular Relations of their Pilgrimage to Mecca* (Exeter, 1717), 70.

15 *The Red Sea and Adjacent Countries at the Close of the Seventeenth Century*, ed. William Foster (London: Hakluyt Society, 1949), 25.

16 E. Kane, *Russian Hajj: Empire and the Pilgrimage to Mecca* (Ithaca, NY: Cornell University Press, 2015), 1–2.

17 *The Nawab Sikandar, Begum of Bhopal: A Pilgrimage to Mecca*, trans. and ed. Mrs Willoughby-Osborne (London: W. H. Allen, 1870), 9, 42.

18 *The Travels of Ibn Jubayr*, 91.

19 Arthur J. B. Wavell, *A Modern Pilgrim in Mecca and A Siege in Sanaa* (London: Constable, 1913), 68.
20 Ibid., 56, 58.
21 Ibid., 76.
22 Mirza Mohammad Hosayn Farahani, *A Shi'ite Pilgrimage to Mecca, 1885–86*, ed. and trans. Hafez Farmayan and Elton L. Daniel (Austin: University of Texas Press, 1990), 70.
23 Saurabh Misra, *Pilgrimage, Politics, and Pestilence: The Haj from the Indian Subcontinent, 1860–1920* (New Delhi: Oxford University Press, 2011).
24 Slight, *The British Empire and the Hajj*, 41, 64, 99.
25 Michael Christopher Low, '"The Infidel Piloting the True Believer": Thomas Cook and the Business of the Colonial Hajj', in *The Hajj and Europe in the Age of Empire*, ed. Umar Ryad (Leiden: Brill, 2017), 47–8.
26 Jonathan Miran, "Stealing the Way" to Mecca: West African Pilgrims and Illicit Red Sea Passages', *Journal of African History*, 56 (2015), 391.
27 For the date, Mahlik Dahlan, *The Hijaz: The First Islamic State* (Oxford: Oxford University Press, 2018) xv.
28 Eldon Rutter, *The Holy Cities of Arabia*, vol. I (London: G. P. Putnam's Sons, Ltd, 1928), 173.
29 Dahlan, *The Hijaz*, 113.
30 Saud al-Sarhan, 'The Saudis as Managers of the Hajj', in *The Hajj: Pilgrimage in Islam*, ed. E. Tagliocozzo and Shawkat M. Toorawa (Cambridge: Cambridge University Press, 2016), 201.
31 Rutter, *The Holy Cities of Arabia*, 174.
32 Madawi al-Rasheed, *A History of Saudi Arabia*, 2nd edn (Cambridge: Cambridge University Press, 2010), 89.
33 Toby Craig Jones, *Desert Kingdom: How Oil and Water Forged Modern Saudi Arabia* (Cambridge, MA: Harvard University Press, 2010), 28, 256.
34 For a description of the city at the time, see Rutter, *The Holy Cities of Arabia*, vol 1, 124–40.
35 Adam J. Silverstein, *Islamic History: A Very Short Introduction* (Oxford: Oxford University Press, 2010), 49.
36 Malcolm X, *The Autobiography of Malcolm X: As Told to Alex Haley* (New York: Ballantine Press, 1973), 346.
37 Joan Catherine Henderson, 'Religious Tourism and Its Management:

The Hajj in Saudi Arabia', *International Journal of Tourism Research*, 13 (2011), 541–52; Jonathan Bucks, 'The Hajj Crush: "It was the closest thing to hell on earth"', *Guardian,* 23 December 2015, https://www.theguardian.com/news/2015/dec/23/hajj-crush-pilgrimage-mecca-stampede-saudi-arabia-mina-valley#:~:text=Alone%20and%20unable%20to%20speak,thing%20to%20hell%20on%20earth.%E2%80%9D

6. Rome, Italy

1 Joseph Gill, *The Council of Florence* (Cambridge: University of Cambridge Press, 1959), 321–7.; Sam Kennerley, 'Ethiopian Christians in Rome, *c.*1400–*c.*1700', in *A Companion to Religious Minorities in Early Modern Rome*, ed. M. C. Wainwright and E. Nicholson (Leiden: Brill, 2020), 144–5.

2 Robert Glass, 'Filarete's Renovation of the Porta Argentea at Old Saint Peter's', in *Old St Peter's Rome*, ed. R. McKitterick, J. Osborne, C. M. Richardson and J. Story (Cambridge: Cambridge University Press, 2013), 349–52.

3 *The Chronicle of Adam of Usk, 1377–1421*, ed. and trans. C. Given-Wilson (Oxford: Clarendon Press, 1997) 189.

4 Eusebius, *Life of Constantine*, trans. and commentary by A. Cameron and S. G. Hall (Oxford: Clarendon Press, 1999), II, 21, 28, 40; III, 1.6.

5 *The Book of Pontiffs (Liber Pontificalis): The Ancient Biographies of the First Ninety Roman Bishops to AD 715*, trans. Raymond Davis (Liverpool: Liverpool University Press, 1989) 29, 212; J. Curran, *Pagan City and Christian Capital: Rome in the Fourth Century* (Oxford: Clarendon Press, 2000), 152–5.

6 Norbert D. Brockman, 'Marian Pilgrimage and Shrines', *Marian Studies*, 51 (2000), 99.

7 Alan Thacker, 'Rome: the pilgrims' city in the seventh century', in *England and Rome in the Early Middle Ages: Pilgrimage, Art, and Politics*, ed. Francesca Tinti (Turnhout: Brepols, 2014), 117–18.

8 Alan Thacker, 'Rome of the Martyr Saints, Cults and Relics, Fourth to Seventh Centuries', in *Roma Felix: Formation and Reflections of Medieval Rome*, ed. Éamonn Ó Carragáin, Carol Neumann de Vegvar (London: Routledge, 2007) 33.

9 Gillian Mackie, *Early Christian Chapels in the West: Decoration, Function and Patronage* (Toronto: University of Toronto Press, 2003), 72, 195, 235–6; *The Book of Pontiffs (Liber Pontificalis)*, I, 261–2.

10 N. Miedema, 'Following in the Footsteps of Christ: Pilgrimage and Passion Devotion', in *The Broken Body: Passion Devotion in Late-Medieval Culture*, ed. A. A. MacDonald, H. N. B. Ridderbos, and R. M. Schlusemann (Groningen: Egbert Forsten, 1998), 80.

11 Bede, *The Ecclesiastical History of the English People* (Oxford: Oxford University Press, 1999), x–xi, 244–5, 339; Bede, 'Lives of the Abbots of Wearmouth and Jarrow', in *The Age of Bede*, ed. and trans. D. H. Farmer (Harmondsworth: Penguin, 1965), 192–3, 196.

12 Margaret Meserve, *Papal Bull: Print, Politics, and Propaganda in Renaissance Rome* (Baltimore: Johns Hopkins University Press, 2021), 171.

13 Ibid., 162.

14 *Chronicon Astense,* in Ferdinand Gregorious, *History of the City of Rome in the Middle Ages, Volume V, Part II*, trans. Annie Hamilton (London: George Bell, 1906), 560.

15 Jessica Maier, *The Eternal City: A History of Rome in Maps* (Chicago: University of Chicago Press, 2020), 108.

16 R. J. B. Bosworth, *Whispering City: Rome and Its Histories* (New Haven: Yale University Press, 2011), 104.

17 Arthur White, *Plague and Pleasure: The Renaissance World of Pius II* (Catholic University of America Press, 2014), 30.

18 Christopher Hibbert, *Rome: The Biography of a City* (London: Penguin, 2001), 116–17.

19 Charles Stinger, *The Renaissance in Rome* (Bloomington: Indiana University Press, 1985), 31.

20 Ernest Hatch Wilkins, *Life of Petrarch* (Chicago: University of Chicago Press, 1961), 2.

21 Carol M. Richardson, *Reclaiming Rome: Cardinals in the Fifteenth Century* (Leiden: Brill, 2009), 147.

22 White, *Plague and Pleasure*, 94, 260; Hibbert, *Rome*, 116; Bosworth, *Whispering City*, 62.

23 Eleanor Clark, *Rome and a Villa* (New York: HarperCollins, 1992), 214.

24 Rosamund McKitterick, 'The representation of Old Saint Peter's basilica in the *Liber Pontificalis*', in *Old Saint Peter's Rome*, 99–100.
25 Hibbert, *Rome*, 76.
26 Ibid.
27 Yolande Lammerant, 'Les Pèlerins des Pays-Bas méridionaux à Saint-Julien des-Flamands à Rome au XVIIème et XVIIIème siècle' in *Pèlerins et Pèlerinage dans l'Europe moderne: actes de la table ronde organisée par le Département d'Histoire et Civilisation de l'Institut Universitaire Européen de Florence et l'École Française de Rome* (Rome, 4–5 June 1993), 271–306.
28 Loren Partridge, *The Renaissance in Rome, 1400–1600* (London: Weidenfeld & Nicolson, 1996), 23.
29 *Luther's Works, Vol. 44: The Christian in Society I*, ed. Hartmut T. Lehmann and James Atkinson (Philadelphia: Fortress, 1966), 171; Matthew R. Anderson, 'Luther and the Trajectories of Western Pilgrimage', *International Journal of Religious Tourism and Pilgrimage*, 7 (2019), 52–61.
30 Catherine Fletcher, *The Beauty and the Terror* (Oxford: Oxford University Press, 2020), 125–9.
31 Partridge, *Renaissance in Rome*, 25; Jill E. Blondin, 'Power Made Visible: Pope Sixtus IV as "Urbis Restaurateur" in Quattrocento Rome', *Catholic Historical Review*, 91 (2005), 1–25; Peter Partner, *Renaissance Rome, 1500–1559: a portrait of a society* (Berkeley: University of California Press, 1976), 19.
32 Barbara Wisch, 'The Matrix: "Le Sette Chiese di Roma" of 1575 and the Image of Pilgrimage', *Memoirs of the American Academy in Rome*, 56/57 (2011/2012), 271; Mario Romani, *Pellegrini e viaggiatori nell'economia di Roma dal XIV al XVII secolo (*Milan: Vita e Pensiero, 1948), 16–17.
33 Pastor, quoted in Stephen F. Ostrow, 'The Counter-Reformation and the End of the Century', in *Rome*, ed. Marcia Hall (Cambridge: Cambridge University Press, 2005), 281.
34 Partridge, *Renaissance in Rome*, 32.
35 Ostrow, 'The Counter-Reformation', 282–3.
36 Anna Blennow and Stefano Fogelberg Rota, 'Introduction', in *Rome and the Guidebook Tradition: From the Middle Ages to the 20th Century*, ed.

Anna Blennow and Stefano Fogelberg Rota (Berlin: De Gruyter, 2019), 25.

37 Gregory Martin, *Roma Sacra (1581)*, ed. George Bruner Parks (Rome, 1969).

38 Maier, *The Eternal City*, 109–110.

39 Ibid., 109.

40 Ibid., 113.

41 Minoru Ozawa, 'Why did a Viking King Meet a Pope? Cnut's Imperial Politics, Scandinavian Commercial Networks, and the Journey to Rome in 1027', in *Communicating Papal Authority in the Middle Ages*, ed. Minoru Ozawa, Thomas W. Smith and Georg Strack (London: Routledge, 2023), 131–44.

42 W. B. Bartlett, *King Cnut and the Viking Conquest of England* (Stroud: Amberley, 2016), 44.

43 *Pall Mall Gazette* 1 March 1877; J. Nolan, *History of the Irish National Pilgrimage to Rome; or, Notes on the Way* (London, 1893).

44 E. O'L. 'A Pilgrim's Notes of the Irish National Pilgrimage to Rome: October, 1908', *Irish Monthly*, 37 (1909), 136.

45 Francisco Javier Ramón Solans, '"A most select gathering": Mexican National Pilgrimages to Rome during the papacy of Leo XIII', *Religions*, 12 (2021), 1–18.

46 Brian Brennan, 'Visiting "Peter in Chains": French Pilgrimage to Rome, 1873–1893', *Journal of Ecclesiastical History* 51 (2000), 741–65.

47 Christopher Duggan, 'Political Cults in liberal Italy, 1861–1922', in *The Cult of the Duce: Mussolini and the Italians*, ed. Stephen Gundle, Christopher Duggan and Giuliana Peri (Manchester: Manchester University Press, 2013) 15.

48 Aristotle Kallis, *The Third Rome, 1922–1943: The Making of a Fascist Capital* (Basingstoke: Palgrave, 2014), 107.

49 *Weekly Dispatch (London)*, 28 October 1923, 1.

50 Bosworth, *Whispering City*, 163.

51 Ibid., 164.

52 David I. Kertzer, *The Pope and Mussolini: The Secret History of Pius XI and the Rise of Fascism in Europe* (Oxford: Oxford University Press, 2014), 217.

53 Georgiana Ţăranu, 'Romanians Visiting Mussolini's Italy: interwar

ideological pilgrimages as efficient propaganda tools', *Annals of the Ovidius University of Constanța*, 6 (2017), 49.

54 Kallis, *Third Rome,* 235.

55 Ibid., 236, 238.

56 Paul Koudounaris, *Heavenly Bodies: cult treasures and spectacular saints from the catacombs* (London: W. W. Norton 2013).

57 Kirstin Noreen, 'Sacred Memory and Confraternal Space: The Insignia of the Confraternity of Santissimo Salvatore (Rome)', in *Roma Felix*, 181.

7. Istanbul, Turkey

1 Wendy Mayer and Pauline Allen, *John Chrysostom* (London: Routledge, 2000), 86.

2 Michael Angold, 'Church and Society: Iconoclasm and After', in *A Social History of Byzantium*, ed. John Haldon (Oxford: Wiley Blackwell, 2008), 246.

3 M. M. Mango, 'Pilgrimage', in *Oxford History of Byzantium*, ed. C. Mango (Oxford: Oxford University Press, 2002), 118; Rene Pfeilschifter, 'Always in Second Place: Constantinople as an Imperial and Religious Center in Late Antiquity', in *City of Caesar, City of God: Constantinople and Jerusalem in Late Antiquity*, ed. Konstantin M. Klein and Johannes Wienand (Berlin: De Gruyter, 2022), 51. The earliest text referring to the translations is Jerome's *Chronicon*, xxxv, 19 and 20, https://www.tertullian.org/fathers/jerome_chronicle_03_part2.htm; Paulinus of Nola, *The Poems of Paulinus of Nola*, trans. P. G. Walsh (New York: Newman Press, 1974), 142.

4 Charles Freeman, *Holy Bones, Holy Dust: How Relics Shaped the History of Medieval Europe* (New Haven: Yale University Press, 2011), 38.

5 Sozemenus, 'The Ecclesiastical History of Sozomen', in *Nicene and Post-Nicene Fathers*, ed. Philip Schaff (Peabody, MA: Hendrickson, 2004), ii, 391.

6 Paul Stephenson, *New Rome: The Empire in the East AD 395–700* (London: Profile, 2022), 120.

7 *Three Byzantine Saints: Contemporary Biographies of St. Daniel the Stylite, St. Theodore of Sykeon and St. John the Almsgiver*, trans. Elizabeth Dawes, with Norman H. Baynes (Oxford: Blackwell, 1948), 13; *Life of St*

Daniel (BHG 486), *The Cult of Saints in Late Antiquity*, http://csla.history.ox.ac.uk/record.php?recid=E04560

8 Stephanos Efthymiadis and Vincent Déroche, 'Greek Hagiography in Late Antiquity (Fourth–Seventh Century)', in *The Ashgate Research Companion to Byzantine Hagiography, Volume 1: Periods and Places*, ed. Stephanos Efthymiadis (London: Routledge, 2011), 65–6.

9 Edward N. Luttwak, *The Grand Strategy of the Byzantine Empire* (Cambridge, MA: Harvard University Press, 2009), 115.

10 *The Buildings of Procopius*, ed. and trans. H. B. Dewing, Loeb Classical Library (Cambridge, MA: Harvard University Press, 1940), 27.

11 Timothy Gabashvili, *Pilgrimage to Mount Athos, Constantinople, and Jerusalem, 1755–1759*, trans. Mzia Ebanoidze and John Wilkinson (London: Routledge, 2013), 116.

12 Holger A. Klein, 'Sacred Relics and Imperial Ceremonies at the Great Palace of Constantinople', in *Visualisierungen von Herrschaft*, ed. Franz Alto Bauer (Istanbul: Ege Yayınları, 2006), 80, 91–2.

13 Bryan Ward-Perkins, 'Old and New Rome Compared: The Rise of Constantinople', in *Two Romes: Rome and Constantinople in Late Antiquity*, ed. Lucy Grig and Gavin Kelly (Oxford: Oxford University Press, 2012), 62.

14 Annemarie Weyl Carr, 'Threads of Authority: The Virgin Mary's Veil in the Middle Ages', in *Robes and Honor: The Medieval World of Investiture*, ed. Stewart Gordon (Basingstoke: Palgrave, 2001), 59–94; Vasiliki Limberis, *Divine Heiress: The Virgin Mary and the Creation of Constantinople* (London: Routledge, 2012), 57–8; Alexander the Clerk, 'On Constantinople', in *Russian Travellers to Constantinople*, ed. George P. Majeska (Washinghton: Dumbarton Oaks, 1984), 160.

15 *The Miracles of St Artemios: A Collection of Miracle Stories by an Anonymous Author of Seventh Century Byzantium*, trans. Virgil S. Crisafulli, with John W. Nesbitt (Brill: Leiden, 1997).

16 R. Janin, *La géographie ecclésiastique de l'empire byzantin. III Les églises et les monastères* (Paris, 1953), 233.

17 Alice-Mary Talbot, 'Pilgrimage to Healing Shrines: the Evidence of Miracle Accounts', *Dumbarton Oaks Papers*, 56 (2002), 162.

18 *Narrative of the Embassy of Ruy Gonzalez de Clavijo to the Court of Timor*

at Samarcand, A.D. 1403–6, trans. C. R. Markham (London: Hakluyt Society, 1859), 29–49.

19 Monica White, 'Relics and the Princely Clan in Rus', in *Byzantium and the Viking World*, ed. F. Androshchuk, J. Shepard and M. White (Uppsala: Acta Universitatis Upsaliensis, 2010), 391.

20 *The Russian Primary Chronicle: Laurentian Text*, trans. and ed. Samuel Hazzard Cross and Olgerd P. Sherbowitz-Wetzor (Cambridge, MA: Medieval Academy of America, 1953), 82.

21 Annemarie Weyl, Carr, 'Pilgrimage to Constantinople', in *Cambridge Companion to Constantinople*, ed. Sarah Bassett (Cambridge: Cambridge University Press, 2022), 312.

22 *The Pilgrimage of Etheria*, trans. M. L. McClure and C. L. Fletoe (New York: MacMillan, 1919), 44.

23 Charles H. Haskins, 'A Canterbury Monk at Constantinople', *English Historical Review*, 25 (1910), 294–5.

24 Fulcher of Chartres, *Chronicle of the First Crusade*, trans. Martha Evelyn McGinty (Philadelphia: University of Pennsylvania Press, 1941), 28.

25 John Kinnamos, *Deeds of John and Manuel Comnenus*, trans. Charles M. Brand (New York: Columbia University Press, 1976), 69.

26 George Majeska, 'Russian Pilgrims in Constantinople', *Dumbarton Oakes Papers*, 56 (2002), 94.

27 Robert of Clari, *The Conquest of Constantinople*, trans. Edgar Holmes McNeal (New York: Columbia University Press, 2005), 103.

28 David M. Perry, *Sacred Plunder: Venice and the Aftermath of the Fourth Crusade* (University Park: Pennsylvania University Press, 2015), 100, 149, 156.

29 Gunther of Pairis, *The Capture of Constantinople: The 'Hystoria Constantinopolitana' of Gunther of Pairis*, ed. and trans. Alfred J. Andrea (Philadelphia: University of Pennsylvania Press, 1997), 121–7.

30 *O City of Byzantium, Annals of Niketas Choniates*, trans. Harry J. Magoulias (Detroit: Wayne State University Press, 1984), 314–15.

31 *History of Mar Yahballaha and Rabban Sauma*, ed. and trans. Pier Giorgio Borbone (Hamburg: Verlag, 2021).

32 Alice-Mary M. Talbot, *Faith Healing in Late Byzantium: The Posthumous Miracles of the Patriarch Athanasios I of Constantinople by Theoktistos the Stoudite* (Brookline, MA: Hellenic College Press, 1983).

33 G .P. Majeska, *Russian Travelers to Constantinople in the Fourteenth and Fifteenth Centuries (*Washington DC: Dumbarton Oaks, 1984), 28.
34 Ibid., 18.
35 'The Journey of Ignatius of Smolensk', in Ibid., 76.
36 Nicholai N. Petro, 'The Novgorod Model: Creating a European Past in Russia', in *Cities after the Fall of Communism: Reshaping Cultural Landscapes and European Identity*, ed. J. J. Czaplicka et al. (Baltimore: Johns Hopkins University Press, 2009), 53–4.
37 *Narrative of the Embassy*, 29.
38 Ibid., 30–32.
39 Ibid., 33–49.
40 K. E. Fleming, 'Constantinople: From Christianity to Islam', *Classical World*, 97 (2003), 69.
41 Luttwak, *The Grand Strategy of the Byzantine Empire*, 115; Marc David Baer, *Honoured by the Glory of Islam: Conversion and Conquest in Ottoman Europe* (Oxford: Oxford University Press, 2008), 21–2.
42 Baer, *Honoured by the Glory of Islam*, 35.
43 Lâle Can, *Spiritual Subjects: Central Asian Pilgrims and the Ottoman Hajj at the End of Empire* (Redwood City, CA: Stanford University Press, 2020), 49.
44 Quoted in Philip Mansel, *Constantinople: City of the World's Desire, 1453–1924* (London: John Murray, 1995) 28.
45 Luca Patrizi, 'Relics of the Prophet', in *Muhammed in History, Thought, and Culture: An Encyclopedia of the Prophet of God*, ed. Coeli FitzPatrick and Adam Hani Walker (ABC-CLIO, 2014), 518; A. Hilâl Uğurlu, 'Philanthropy in the Form of a Hair Strand: Sacred Relics in Nineteenth Century Ottoman Lands', in *Philanthropy In Anatolia Through the Ages: The First International Suna & İnan Kiraç Symposium on Mediterranean Civilizations*, ed. Oğuz Tekin, Christopher H. Roosevelt and Engin Akyürek (Antalya: Koç Üniversitesi, 2020), 217.
46 Ibid., 215.
47 Robert R. Bianchi, *Guests of God: Pilgrimage and Politics in the Islamic World* (Oxford: Oxford University Press, 2004), 73.
48 'Vatican Returns Relics to Orthodox Church', *CBC News* 27 November 2004; 'Letter of John Paul II to the Ecumenical Patriarch of Constantinople His Holiness Bartholomew I (2004)', https://www.

vatican.va/content/john-paul-ii/en/letters/2004/documents/hf_jp-ii_let_20041127_consegna-reliquie.html

8. Iona, Scotland

1 Samuel Johnson and James Boswell, *Journey to the Hebrides: A Journey to the Western Isles of Scotland, The Journal of the Tour to the Hebrides*, ed. Ian McGowan (Edinburgh: Canongate, 1996), 131.

2 F. Marian McNeill, *An Iona Anthology* (Iona: Iona Community, 1990), 106.

3 Rowntree Harvey, 'Iona is the soul of Scotland', *Aberdeen Press and Journal* 15 June 1949, 2.

4 *Adomnán's Life of Columba*, ed. and trans. A. O. Anderson and M. O. Anderson, rev. edn (Oxford: Oxford University Press, 1991), 187.

5 *Bede's Ecclesiastical History of the English People*, ed. Bartram Colgrave and R. A. B. Mynors (Oxford: Clarendon Press, 1969), bk 3, iv, 223.

6 James E. Fraser, *From Caledonia to Pictland: Scotland to 795* (Edinburgh: Edinburgh University Press, 2009), 72.

7 *Adomnán's Life of Columba*, 271–3.

8 Ewan Campbell and Adrian Maldonado, 'A New Jerusalem "at the end of the Earth": Interpreting Charles Thomas's Excavations at Iona Abbey, 1956–63', *Antiquaries Journal*, 100 (2020), 57.

9 Gilbert Márkus, 'Four Blessings and a Funeral: Adomnán's theological map of Iona', *Innes Review*, 72 (2021), 1–26.

10 Daíbhí Ó Cróinín, *Early Medieval Ireland, 400–1200* (London: Routledge, 2017), 253.

11 Snorri Sturluson, *Heimskringla: History of the Kings of Norway*, trans. Lee M. Hollander (Austin: University of Texas Press, 1964), 675; Aidan McDonald, 'When Were St Columba's Corporeal Relics Enshrined?', *Hallel*, 23 (1998), 24–6.

12 Walafridus Strabo, 'Life of Blathmac', in *Early Sources of Scottish History, AD 500 to 1286*, trans. Alan Orr Anderson (Edinburgh: Oliver and Boyd, 1922), 264–5.

13 Máire Herbert, *Iona, Kells and Derry: The History and Hagiography of the Monastic Familia of Columba* (Dublin: Four Courts Press, 1996), 261.

14 *Adomnán's Life of Columba*, 16.

15 *Argyll: an inventory of the monuments, Volume 4: Iona* (Edinburgh:

Royal Commission on Ancient and Historical Monuments of Scotland, 1982), 279; F. Marian McNeill, *Iona: A History of the Island*, 7th edn (Moffat: Lochar, 1991), 72; Mairi MacArthur, *Iona: The Living Memory of a Crofting Community* (Edinburgh: Edinburgh University Press, 2007), 285.

16 Cindy Pavlinac, 'Circling Centre, Finding Our Way Home: Pilgrimages around Iona, Mount Tamalpais and Labyrinths', in *The Many Voices of Pilgrimage and Reconciliation*, ed. Ian S. McIntosh and Lesley D. Harman (Wallingford: CABI, 2017), 91.

17 Sturluson, *Heimskringla*, 675.

18 Peter Yeoman, *Pilgrimage in Medieval Scotland* (Edinburgh: Historic Scotland, 1999), 81–5.

19 Rosalind K. Marshall, *Columba's Iona: A New History* (Dingwall: Sandstone Press, 2013), ix.

20 *Calendar of Scottish Supplications to Rome, 1425–1428*, ed. Annie I. Dunlop (Edinburgh: T & A Constable, Ltd, 1956), 193.

21 Ron Ferguson, *George MacLeod: Founder of the Iona Community* (Glasgow: Wild Goose Publications, 1990), 155.

22 Jessica Christian and Charles Stiller, *Iona Portrayed: The Island through Artists' Eyes, 1760–1960* (Inverness: New Iona Press, 2000), 9.

23 John Keats, Letter to his brother Tom while travelling with Charles Brown, 23–26 July 1818, *The Letters of John Keats: Volume I, 1814–1818*, ed. H. E. Rollins (Cambridge: Cambridge University Press, 2012), 347.

24 John MacCulloch, *The Highlands and Western Isles of Scotland*, 4 vols (London: Longman, Hurst, Rees, Orme, Brown, and Green, 1824), iv, 182–3.

25 William Wordsworth, 'Iona' in *The Poems of William Wordsworth: Collected Reading Texts from the Cornell Wordsworth*, vol. 3, ed. Jared Curtis (Penrith: Humanities e-Books 2014), 503.

26 Ferguson, *George MacLeod*, 155.

27 James Drummond, 'Notice of One of the Supposed Burial Places of St Columba', in *Proceedings of the Society of Antiquaries of Scotland*, 10 (1870–72), 616; Canmore: National Record of the Historic Environment, https://canmore.org.uk/collection/377992

28 William F. Halloran, *The Life and Letters of William Sharp and 'Fiona*

Macleod' Volume 1: 1855–1894 (Cambridge: Open Book Publishers, 2018), 70, 532.

29 Duke of Argyll, *Iona* (London: Strahan, 1871); Alan MacQuarrie, *Iona Through the Ages* (Isle of Coll: Society of West Highland and Island Historical Research, 1983), 30; Ian Bradley, *Argyll: The Making of a Spiritual Landscape* (Edinburgh: St Andrew Press, 2015), 181–6.

30 'Catholic Pilgrimage to Iona', *Evening Telegraph (Dundee)* 11 May 1888, 2.

31 Katherine Haldane Grenier, '"Awakening the echoes of the ancient faith": the National Pilgrimages to Iona', *Northern Scotland*, 12 (2021), 132–54.

32 E. Mairi MacArthur, *Columba's Island: Iona from Past to Present* (Edinburgh: Edinburgh University Press, 1995), 250.

33 'The Roman Catholic Pilgrimage to Iona', *Dundee Evening Telegraph* 16 June 1897, 3.

34 Bernard Aspinwall, 'The formation of a British identity within Scottish Catholicism, 1830–1914', in *Religion and National Identity: Wales and Scotland,* c.*1700–2000*, ed. Robert Pope (Cardiff: University of Wales Press, 2001), 283.

35 'Scotland's Cradle of Christianity is Scene of High Mass', *Catholic News Service* 29 June 1936.

36 http://www.iona-cathedral.org.uk/

37 Ferguson, *George MacLeod*, 124.

38 Commons Chamber Debate, *Hansard* 10 March 1936; Lorn Macintyre, *Sir David Russell: A Biography* (Edinburgh: Canongate, 1994), 193–203.

39 Ferguson, *George MacLeod*, 306.

40 Ian Bradley, *Pilgrimage: A Spiritual and Cultural Journey* (Oxford: Lion Hudson, 2009), 124.

41 Ferguson, *George MacLeod*, 336.

42 Ibid., 401; 'Obituaries: Jack Glass', *The Times* 5 March 2004, 41.

43 P. Sheldrake, *Living Between Worlds: Place and Journey in Celtic Spirituality* (London: Darton, Longman, and Todd, 1995), 61.

44 *Adomnán's Life of Columba,* 279–81.

45 *The Annals of Ulster*, 238, 249: http://research.ucc.ie/celt/document/T100001A

46 *The Annals of Tigernach*, 341–2: http://research.ucc.ie/celt/document/T100002A

47 *The Annals of Tigernach*, 342: http://research.ucc.ie/celt/document/T100002A
48 William Shakespeare, *Macbeth: Third Series*, ed. Sandra Clark and Pamela Mason (London: Bloomsbury, 2015), 199.
49 'Anger grows as visitors flock to Smith grave', *Independent* 4 June, 1995https://www.independent.co.uk/news/uk/home-news/anger-grows-as-visitors-flock-to-smith-grave-1584918.html

9. Karbala, Iraq

1 John Robertson, *Iraq: A History* (London: Oneworld, 2015), 185–6.
2 Abu Mikhnaf, *Maqtal al-Husayn*, trans. Hamid Mavani, 170, https://moralsandethics.files.wordpress.com/2007/03/maqtal-by-abu-mikhnaf.pdf
3 Muhammad Muhammadi Rayshahri, *The Chronicles of the Martyrdom of Imam Husayn*, trans. Abbas Jaffer (London: ICAS Press, 2020), 604.
4 Philip K. Hitti, *History of the Arabs* (London: Macmillan, 1946), 191.
5 S. H. M. Jafri, *The Origins and Early Development of Shi'a Islam* (Oxford: Oxford University Press, 2000), 231.
6 Rayshahri, *Chronicles of the Martyrdom of Imam Husayn*, 901.
7 Mahmud Ayoub, 'Shi'i Literature', in *Shi'ism: Doctrines, Thought and Spirituality*, ed. Seyyed Hossein Nasr, Hamid Dabashi and Seyyed Vali Reza Nasr (New York: State University of New York Press, 1988), 314.
8 *Three Centuries of Travel Writing by Muslim Women*, ed. Siobhan Lambert-Hurley, Daniel Majchrowicz and Sunil Sharma (Bloomington: Indiana University Press, 2022), 75, 92, 123.
9 E. Szanto, 'Shi'a Islam in Practice', in *Handbook of Contemporary Islam and Muslim Lives*, ed. Ronal Lukens-Bull and Mark Woodward (Cham: Springer, 2021), 50.
10 Rayshahri, *Chronicles of the Martyrdom of Imam Husayn*, 871.
11 *Encyclopaedia Iranica*, ed. Ehsan Yarshater, vol. 12 (London: Routledge, 1982), 501.
12 https://www.aljazeera.com/gallery/2023/9/7/photos-arbaeen-worlds-largest-annual-pilgrimage-in-iraq
13 Ibn Qulawayh al-Qummi, *Kamil al-Ziyarat*, trans. Sayyid Mohsen al-Husayni al-Milani (Miami: Shiabook.ca Press, 2008), 64, 77.

14 Syed Akbar Hyder, *Reliving Karbala: Martyrdom in South Asian Memory* (Oxford: Oxford University Press, 2006), 18.
15 Juan Cole, *Sacred Space and Holy War: The Politics, Culture and History of Shi'ite Islam* (London: I. B. Taurus, 2001), 73.
16 Quoted in Josef W. Meri, *The Cult of Saints Among Muslims and Jews in Medieval Syria* (Oxford: Oxford University Press, 2002), 164.
17 Jacob N. Kinnard, *Places in Motion: The Fluid Identities of Temples, Images, and Pilgrims* (Oxford: Oxford University Press, 2014), 161.
18 Meir Litvak, *Shi'i Scholars of Nineteenth-Century Iraq: The 'Ulama' of Najaf and Karbala* (Cambridge: Cambridge University Press, 2002), 16.
19 Robertson, *Iraq: A History*, 212.
20 James H. Lindsay, *Daily Life in the Medieval Islamic World* (Cambridge: Hackett, 2005), 164.
21 Toby Matthiesen, *The Caliph and the Imam: The Making of Sunnism and Shiism* (Oxford: Oxford University Press, 2023), 87.
22 *The Travels of Ibn Battuta,* 325–26.
23 Zachary M. Heern, *The Emergence of Modern Shi'ism: Islamic Reform in Iraq and Iran* (London: Oneworld, 2015), 103.
24 Yitzhak Nakash, *The Shi'is of Iraq* (Princeton: Princeton University Press, 1994), 21–2.
25 Heern, *The Emergence of Modern Shi'ism*, 145.
26 Litvak, *Shi'i Scholars of Nineteenth-Century Iraq, 136.*
27 From Juan R. I. Cole and Moojan Momen, 'Mafia, Mob and Shiism in Iraq: the Rebellion of Ottoman Karbala, 1842–1842', *Past & Present*, 112 (1986), 124.
28 Litvak, *Shi'i Scholars of Nineteenth-Century Iraq*, 136.
29 Ibid., 143, 150–57.
30 Letter from Gertrude Bell to her stepmother, Dame Florence Bell, Gertrude Bell Archive (Newcastle University) GB/1/1/1/1/27/1.
31 Kamran Scot Ashaie, *The Martyrs of Karbala; Shi'i Symbols and Rituals in Modern Iran* (Washington DC: University of Washington Press, 2004), 60.
32 Marvin Zonis, *Majestic Failure: The Fall of the Shah* (Chicago: University of Chicago Press, 1991), 150–52.
33 M. J. Fischer, *Iran: From Religious Dispute to Revolution* (Cambridge,

MA: Harvard University Press, 2003), 213; V. Nasr, *The Shia Revival* (New York: W. W. Norton, 2007), 43.

34 Bill Rolston, 'When everywhere is Karbala: Murals, Martyrdom and propaganda in Iran', *Memory Studies*, 13 (2020), 3–23.

35 Robertson, *Iraq: A History*, 314.

36 Muhsin al-Musawi, *Reading Iraq: Culture and Power in Conflict* (London: I. B. Taurus, 2006), 51.

37 A. Nikjoo, Neda Razavizadeh and Michael A. Di Giovine, 'What draws Shia Muslims to an insecure pilgrimage? The Iranian journey to Arbaeen, Iraq during the presence of ISIS', *Journal of Tourism and Cultural Change*, 19 (2021), 606–27.

38 Heern, *The Emergence of Modern Shi'ism*, 31–2.

39 Cole and Momen, 'Mafia, Mob and Shiism in Iraq', 112–43.

40 Heern, *The Emergence of Modern Shi'ism*, 209.

41 Michael O'Sullivan, '"Indian money", Intra-Shi-i Polemics, and the Bohra and Khoja Pilgrimage Infrastructure in Iraq's Shrine Cities, 1897–1932', *Journal of the Royal Asiatic Society*, 32.1 (2022), 231, 234, 240.

42 Ibid., 213, 224.

43 Ira M. Lapidus, *A History of Islamic Societies* (Cambridge: Cambridge University Press, 1988), 302.

44 Heern, *The Emergence of Modern Shi'ism*, 131–2.

45 Nahash, *The Shi'is of Iraq*, 167.

10. Chichén Itzá, Mexico

1 T. A. Willard, *The City of the Sacred Well: Being a Narrative of the Discoveries of and Excavations of Edward Herbert Thompson in the Ancient City of Chi-Chen Itza with Some Discourse on the Culture and Development of the Mayan Civilization as Revealed by their Art and Architecture, here set down and illustrated from photographs* (New York: Century Co., 1926), frontispiece.

2 Edward Herbert Thompson, *People of the Serpent: Life and Adventure Among the Maya* (New York: Capricorn Books, 1960), 3–4.

3 Ibid., 274.

4 Alma M. Reed, *Peregrina: Love and Death in Mexico*, ed. Michael K. Schuessler (Houston: University of Texas Press, 2007), 201.

5 Reprinted as Alma Reed, 'The Well of the Maya's Human Sacrifice', *El Palacio*, 14 (1 June 1923), 160.
6 Reed, *Peregrina*, 65.
7 Channing Arnold and Frederick J. Tabor Frost, *The American Egypt: A Record of Travels in Yucatán* (London: Hutchinson & Co., 1909), 92–3.
8 Clemency Chase Coggins, *Cenote of Sacrifice: Maya Treasures from the Second Well at Chichén Itzá* (Austin: University of Texas Press, 1984), 179; 'Pre-Hispanic City of Chichén-Itzá', UNESCO: World Heritage Conservation, https://whc.unesco.org/en/list/483/
9 *Landa's Relación de las Cosas de Yucatán*, trans. Alfred M. Tozzer (Cambridge, MA: Peabody Museum Press, 1941), 109, 219.
10 Sylvanus Griswold Morley, 'Archaeological Investigations of the Carnegie Institution of Washington in the Maya Area of Middle America, during the Past Twenty-Eight Years', *Proceedings of the American Philosophical Society*, 86 (1943), 214; Sylvanus Griswold Morley, 'Chichén Itzá: An Ancient American Mecca', *National Geographic* (January 1925), 63–95.
11 T. Douglas Price, Vera Tiesler and Carolyn Freiwald, 'Place of Origins of the Sacrificial Victims in the sacred Cenote, Chichén Itzá, Mexico', *American Journal of Physical Anthropology*, 70 (2019), 100.
12 Nicholas P. Dunning, 'Life and Death from the Watery Underworld: ancient Maya interaction with caves and cenotes', in *Sacred Waters: A Cross-Cultural Compendium of Hallowed Springs and Holy Wells*, ed. Celeste Ray (London: Routledge, 2020), 51.
13 Luis Alberto Martos López, 'Underwater Archaeological Exploration of the Mayan Cenotes', *Museum International; Underwater Cultural Heritage*, LX (2008), 106.
14 David Webster, 'Maya Drought and Niche Inheritance', in *The Great Maya Droughts in Cultural Context*, ed. Gyles Iannone (Boulder: University Press of Colorado, 2014), 334, 356.
15 J. Eric Thompson, *Maya History and Religion* (Norman: University of Oklahoma Press, 1970, reprinted 1990), 204.
16 Reed, 'The Well of the Maya', 161.
17 Joel W. Palka, *Maya Pilgrimage to Ritual Landscapes: Insights from Archaeology, History and Ethnography* (Albuquerque: University of New Mexico Press, 2014), 56.

18 William M. Ringle, Tomás Gallareta Negrón and George J. Bey III, 'The Return of Quetzalcoatl: Evidence for the spread of a world religion during the Epiclassic period', *Ancient Mesoamerica*, 9 (1998), 183–232.
19 Robert J. Sharer and Loa P. Traxler, *The Ancient Maya*, 6th edn (Stanford: Stanford University Press, 2006), 619.
20 J. Gregory Smith and Tara M. Bond-Freeman, 'In the Shadow of Quetzalcoatl: How Small Communities in Northern Yucatán Responded to the Chichén Itzá Phenomenon', in *Landscapes of the Itza: Archaeology and Art History at Chichén Itzá and Neighboring Sites*, ed. Linnea Wren, Cynthia Kristan-Graham, Travis Nygard and Kaylee Spencer (Gainesville: University Press of Florida, 2018), 143.
21 Donald Ediger, *The Well of Sacrifice* (New York: Doubleday, 1971), 16.
22 Inga Clendinnen, *Ambivalent Conquests: Maya and Spaniard in Yucatán, 1517–1570* (Cambridge: Cambridge University Press, 2003), 95; *Landa's Relación* 180–81, 184.
23 Quoted in Ismael Arturo Montero García, 'Astronomy, Architecture and Caverns', in *The Role of Archeoastronomy in the Maya World: the Case Study of the Island of Cozumel* (Mexico City: UNESCO, 2020), 103–104.
24 Ralph L. Roys, *The Book of Chilam Balam of Chumayel* (Norman: University of Oklahoma Press, 1967), 173.
25 Kristin Romey, 'Watery tombs', *Archaeology*, 58 (2005), 49.
26 Price et al. 'Place of Origins', 98–115.
27 Traci Ardern, 'Empowered children in Classic Maya Sacrificial Rites', *Childhood in the Past*, 4 (2011), 133–45; Guillermo de Anda Alanis, 'Sacrifice and Ritual Mutilation in Postclassical Maya Society: Taphonomy of the Human Remains from Chichén Itzá's Cenote Sagrada', in *New Perspectives on Human Sacrifice and Ritual Body Treatments in Ancient Maya Society*, ed. Vera Tiesler and Andrea Cucina (New York: Springer, 2007), 190; Reed, 'The Well of the Maya', 160–61.
28 Anthony P. Andrews and Roberta Coletta, 'A Brief History of Underwater Archaeology in the Maya Area', *Ancient MesoAmerica*, 6 (1995), 103.
29 Pablo Bush Romero, 'The sacred well of Chichen-Itza', *Unesco Courier* (1972), 32.
30 Annabeth Headrick and John W. Hoopes, 'Foreign encounters: warfare,

trade, and status at Chichen Itza', in *3,000 Years of War and Peace in the Maya Lowlands*, ed. Geoffrey E. Braswell (Abingdon: Routledge, 2022), 279–83.

31 Coggins, *Cenote of Sacrifice*, 26, 111.

32 Disk G, A.D. 800–900. Mexico, Yucatan, Chichén Itzá, Sacred Cenote. Maya. Gold, 24 x 20 x 0.1 cm. Peabody Museum of Archaeology and Ethnology, Harvard University (10-71-20/C10067); Headrick and Hoopes, 'Foreign encounters', 279–83; Samuel Kirkland Lothrop, *Metals from the Cenote of Sacrifice, Chichen Itza, Yucatan* (Cambridge, MA: Peabody Museum Press, 1952), 51–2.

33 Reed, 'The Well of the Maya', 161.

34 Palka, *Maya Pilgrimage to Ritual Landscapes*, 81; Lothrop, *Metals from the Cenote of Sacrifice*, 3.

35 Lothrop, *Metals from the Cenote of Sacrifice*, 98; Cynthia Kristan-Graham and Linnea Wren, 'Introduction: Looking Backward, Looking Forward at Chichen Itza', in *Landscape of the Itzá: Archaeology and Art History at Chichen Itza and Neighboring Sites*, ed. Linnea Wren, Cynthia Kristan-Graham, Travis Nygard and Kaylee Spencer (Gainesville: University Press of Florida, 2018), 20.

36 Romey, 'Watery tombs', 49.

37 Quoted in Coggins, *Cenote of Sacrifice*, 23; John L. Stephens, *Incidents of Travel to Yucatan, in 2 Volumes* (Frankfurt am Main: GmbH, 2020), ii, 192.

38 John B. Carson, 'Pilgrimage and the Equinox "Serpent of Light and Shadow" Phenomenon at the Castillo, Chichén Itzá', *Archeoastronomy: the Journal of Astronomy and Culture*, xiv (1999), 136–9.

39 García, 'Astronomy, Architecture and Caverns', 85–6.

40 Alexandra Alper, 'UFO Lovers, light-seekers and lawyers await Maya end of days', *Reuters* 20 December 2012, https://www.reuters.com/article/maya-calendar/ufo-lovers-light-seekers-and-lawyers-await-maya-end-of-days-idUSL1E8NEDID20121220/

11. Muxima, Angola

1 Keith Augustus Burton, *The Blessing of Africa: The Bible and African Christianity* (Downers Grove, IL: IVP Academic, 2007), 199.

2 Bailier Wallys Diffie and George D. Winius, *Foundations of the*

Portuguese Empire, 1415–1580 (Minneapolis: University of Minnesota, 1977), 156–7; Mike Stead, Sean Rorison and Oscar Sacfidi, *Angola* (Chalfont St Peter: Brandt, 2009), 181.

3 Bengt Sundkler and Christopher Steed, *A History of the Church in Africa* (Cambridge: Cambridge University Press, 2000), 63.

4 Cecile Fromont, *The Art of Conversion: Christian Visual Culture in the Kingdom of Congo* (University of North Carolina Press, 2014), 190.

5 Klaas Ratelband, *Os holandeses no Brasil e na costa Africana: Angola, Kongo e São Tomé, 1600–1650* (Lisbon: Vega, 2003), 227; Antonio de Oliveira de Cadornega, *História geral das guerras Angolanas* (Lisbon: Agência-Geral do Ultramar, 1972), iii, 99.

6 Ratelband, *Os holandeses no Brasil*, 291; Cadornega, *História*, i, 458–77, iii, 11.

7 *Missione Evangelilone*, Book 2, Chapter 4: Cavazzi, Missione Evangelica | African American & Black Diaspora Studies (https://www.bu.edu/afam/people/faculty/john-thornton/cavazzi-missione-evangelica-2/book-2-chapter-4/

8 Linda M. Heywood, *Njinga of Angola: Africa's Warrior Queen* (Cambridge, MA: Harvard University Press, 2017), 238.

9 Daniel B. Domingues da Silva, *The Atlantic Slave Trade from West Central Africa, 1780–1867* (Cambridge: Cambridge University Press, 2017), 94.

10 Joseph C. Miller, 'The Slave Trade in Congo and Angola', in *The African Diaspora: Interpretative Essays*, 87–8.

11 *Missione Evangelilone*, Book 2, Chapter 4

12 Miller, 'The Slave Trade', 75.

13 Francisco Travassos Valdez, *Six Years of a Traveller's Life in South Africa* (London: Hurst and Blackett, 1861), 134.

14 Christoph Engels, *1000 Sacred Places: The World's Most Extraordinary Spiritual Sites* (Köln: H. F. Ullman, 2010), 789.

15 Gerald J. Bender, *Angola Under the Portuguese: The Myth and the Reality* (Berkeley: University of California Press, 1978), 15, n. 42.

16 Mary H. Kingsley, *West African Studies: with additional chapters* (London: MacMillan, 1901), 121.

17 Uanhenga Xitu, *The World of 'Mestre' Tamoda* (London: Readers International, 1988), 120.

18 José Millet, 'Aspectos da Religiosidad popular Angolana', *Revista do centro de Estudos Africanos*, 1–13 (1989/1990), 161.

19 Vanicléia Silva Santos, 'Africans, Afro-Brazilians and Afro-Portuguese in the Iberian Inquisition in the Seventeenth and Eighteenth Centuries', in *Rewriting the African Diaspora in Latin America and the Caribbean: Beyond Disciplinary and National Boundaries*, ed. Robert Lee Adams Jr (London: Routledge, 2013), 55.

20 João Figueiredo, 'The uncanniness of religious encounters in colonial Angola: A brief cultural history of the awkward emotion (18th and 19th centuries)', *Nordic Journal of Africa Studies*, 29 (2020), 12–13.

21 Didier Péclard, 'Religion and Politics in Angola: The Church, the Colonial State and the Emergence of Angolan Nationalism, 1940–1961', *Journal of Religion in Africa*, 29 (1998), 166.

22 Ibid., 166.

23 Joachim John Monteiro, *Angola and the River Congo, vol. 2* (London: MacMillan & Co., 1875), 123.

24 *Nautical Magazine and Naval Chronicle for 1854* (London: Simpkin Marshall and Co., 1854), 95; Consul du Verge, 'Trade and Customs of the River Quanza', *Reports from the Consuls of the United States on the Commerce, Manufactures, Etc.*, 31, July 1883 (Washington: Government Printing Office, 1883), 652.

25 David Birmingham, *Portugal and Africa* (New York: Palgrave MacMillan, 1999), 126.

26 Mabel Loomis Todd, 'Angola and the Eclipse', *Christian Union*, 31 October 1889, 533.

27 Fromont, *The Art of Conversion*, 54. The boat is now in the Museum in Porto, Portugal, inventory number 129; Santos Furtado, 'Uma imagem de Santo António em Angola (Santo António da Muxima): Breve estudo e apontamentos', *Boletim do Instituto de Angola*, 14 (July–December 1960), 41–51.

28 António Brásio, *Spiritana Monumenta Historica: Angola*, 5 vols (Pittsburgh: Duquesne University Press, 1966), v, 280.

29 John K. Thornton, *The Kongolese Saint Anthony: Dona Beatriz Kimpa Vita and the Antonian Movement, 1684–1706* (Cambridge: Cambridge University Press, 1998).

30 Samuel Coghe, *Population Politics in the Tropics: Demography, Health*

and Transimperialism in Colonial Angola (Cambridge: Cambridge University Press, 2022), 37.

31 Péclard, 'Religion and Politics in Angola', 166–7.

32 'Escritas num português pouco refinado', in Honório Ruiz de Arcaute, *Mil cartas a Mamã Muxima* (Luanda: Paulinas, 2010), 19.

33 Knut Rio, Michelle MacCarthy and Ruy Blanes, 'Introduction to Pentecostal Witchcraft and Spiritual Politics in Africa and Melanasia', in *Pentecostalism and Witchcraft: Spiritual Warfare in Africa and Melanesia*, ed. Knut Rio, Michelle MacCarthy and Ruy Blanes (London: Palgrave MacMillan, 2017), 1; Odílio Fernandes, 'Os azares de nossa Senhora da Muxima: Um percurso de trocas, movimenta ções milagrosas e intolerância', *Economica Informal*, 14 (2014), 41–57.

34 'Angola: Profanation du sanctuaire de Muxima', https://www.archivioradiovaticana.va/storico/2013/10/29/angola__profanation_du_sanctuaire_de_muxima/fr2-741908

35 David Birmingham, *Empire in Africa: Angola and Its Neighbours* (Athens: Ohio University Press, 2006), 148.

36 David Birmingham, 'Is "Nationalism" A Feature of Angola's Cultural Identity?', in *Sure Road? Nationalisms in Angola, Guinea-Bissau and Mozambique*, ed. Eric Morier-Genoud (Leiden: Brill, 2004), 224; David Birmingham, 'Angola 2006: a British Parliamentary Visit', *Lusotopie* xvi (2009), 221–43.

37 'Angola: Peregrinações movimentam Santuários da Muxima e do Monte', Radio Vaticano, https://www.archivioradiovaticana.va/storico/2017/08/04/angola_peregrina%C3%A7%C3%B5es_movimentam_santu%C3%A1rios_da_muxima_e_do_monte/pt-1328814

12. Bear Butte, South Dakota, USA

1 Helen H. Blish, with Amos Bad Heart Bull and Mari Sandoz, *A Pictographic History of the Oglala Sioux* (Lincoln: University of Nebraska Press, 1967), 289–90.

2 Linea Sundstrom, 'Heart of the Earth: A 1940s Lakota Map of the Black Hills Sacred Sites', *Great Plains Quarterly*, 41 (2021), 204.

3 Ibid., 209.

4 Pekka Hämäläinen, 'The Rise and Fall of Plains Indian Horse Cultures', *Journal of American History*, vol. 90, 3 (2003), 833–86, esp. 854, 857.

5 Chris Welsch, 'Bear Butte: Holy Mountain, Fragile Peace', *Star Tribune* 27 July 2003.
6 Linea Sundstrom, 'Mirror of Heaven: Cross-Cultural Transference of the Sacred Geography of the Black Hills', *World Archaeology*, 28 (1996), 177.
7 Ibid., 182, 185.
8 Charles Rambow, *Bear Butte: Journeys to the Sacred Mountain* (Sioux Falls: Pine Hill Press, 2006), 6.
9 Peter Rosen, *Pa-ha-sa-pah: or, The Black Hills of South Dakota. A Complete History of the Gold and Wonder-Land of the Dakotas, from the Remotest Date to the Present* (St Louis: Nixon-Jones Printing Co., 1895), 54.
10 Joel W. Martin, *The Land Looks After Us: A History of Native American Religion* (Oxford: Oxford University Press, 2000), 121.
11 K. Forbes-Boyte, 'Respecting Sacred Perspectives: the Lakotas, Bear Butte, and Land Management Strategies', *Public Historian* 18.4 (1996), 104.
12 David Martínez, 'The Soul of the Indian: Lakota Philosophy and the Vision Quest', *Wicazo Sa Review*, 19 (2004), 79–104.
13 Linea Sundstrom, *Storied Stone: Indian Rock Art in the Black Hills Country* (Norman: University of Oklahoma Press, 2004), 141.
14 Charlotte Black Elk, 'A Song from Sacred Mountain: Lakota-Dakota and Cheyenne Interviews', in *Readings in American Indian Law: Recalling the Rhythm of Survival*, ed. Jo Carillo (Philadelphia: Temple University Press, 1998), 105–106.
15 Quoted in K. Forbes-Boyte, 'Litigation, Mitigation, and American Indian Religious Freedom Act: The Bear Butte Example', *Great Plains Quarterly* (1999), 27; Susan L. Johnston, 'Native American Traditional and Alternative Medicine', *Annals of the American Academy of Political and Social Science* 583, Global Perspectives on Complementary and Alternative Medicine (2002), 195–213.
16 Mario Gonzalez, 'The Black Hills: the Sacred Land of the Lakota and Tsitsistas', in *Native American Voices: A Reader*, 3rd edn, ed. Susan Lobo, Steve Talbot and Traci L. Morris (London: Routledge, 2016), 118.
17 Bernbaum, *Sacred Mountains of the World*, 157.

18 Renate Schukies, Edward Red Hat, *Red Hat: Cheyenne Blue Sky Maker and Keeper of the Sacred Arrows* (Münster: Lit. Verlag, 1993), 288.
19 K. H. Schlesier, *The Wolves of Heaven: Cheyenne Shamanism, Ceremonies and Prehistoric Origins* (Norman: University of Oklahoma Press, 1987), 81, 95.
20 Richard Erdoes, *Lame Deer: Seeker of Visions* (New York: Pocket Books, 1994), xxii.
21 Peter Iverson, *The Plains Indians of the Twentieth Century* (Norman: University of Oklahoma Press, 1985), 250.
22 Thomas E. Odell, *Mato Paha: The Story of Bear Butte* (Spearfish, SD: privately printed, 1942), 25.
23 Forbes-Boyte, 'Respecting Sacred Perspectives', 104–06; Martínez, 'The Soul of the Indian', 79–104.
24 *Pilgrimage: From the Ganges to Graceland, An Encyclopedia,* 2 vols (Santa Barbara: ABC-CLIO, 2002), ii, 55.
25 K. Forbes-Boyte, 'Indigenous People, Land, and Space: the effects of law on sacred place, the Bear Butte example', unpublished PhD thesis, University of Nebraska-Lincoln (1997), 94–5.
26 Odell, *Mato Paha,* 21.
27 Todd Leahy and Nathan Wilson, *Historical Dictionary of Native American Movements* (Lanham, MD: Rowman & Littlefield, 2016), 217.
28 Martin, *The Land Looks After Us*, 121.
29 Vinson Brown, *Voices of Earth and Sky: Vision Search of the Native Americans* (Happy Camp, CA: Naturegraph, 1976), 143–4.
30 Kingsley M. Bray, *Crazy Horse: A Lakota Life* (Norman: University of Nebraska Press, 2006), 59; Rambow, *Bear Butte*, 43; Forbes-Boyte, 'Indigenous People, Land, and Space', 92.
31 Rambow, *Bear Butte*, 32.
32 Pekka Hämäläinen, 'Reconstructing the Great Plains: The Long Struggle for Sovereignty and Dominance in the Heart of the Continent', *Journal of the Civil War Era*, 6 (2016), 481–509.
33 Rambow, *Bear Butte*, 36.
34 Bernbaum, *Sacred Mountains of the World*, 213.
35 Rambow, *Bear Butte*, 38.
36 'Black Hills News', *Bismark Tribune* 9 July 1877, 2.
37 K. Tsianina Lomawaima and Jeffrey Ostler, 'Reconsidering Richard

Henry Pratt: Cultural Genocide and Native Liberation in an Era of Racial Oppression', *Journal of American Indian Education*, 57 (2018), 79–100.

38 Martin C. Loesch, 'The First Americans and the "Free" Exercise of Religion', *American Indian Law Review*, 18 (1993), 329.

39 Forbes-Boyte, 'Respecting Sacred Perspectives', 100–101.

40 Quoted in Philip M. White, 'Researching American Indian Revitalization Movements', *Journal of Religious and Theological Information*, 8 (2009), 155–63.

41 L. B. Palladino, *Indian and White in the Northwest* (Lancaster, PA: Wickersham Publishing Company, 1922), 112.

42 Sheldon E. Spotted Elk, 'Northern Cheyenne Tribe: Traditional Law and Constitutional Reform', *Tribal Law Journal*, 11 (2012), 11–12.

43 P. J. Powell, *Sweet Medicine: the continuing role of the sacred arrows, the sun dance, and the sacred buffalo hat in northern Cheyenne History* (Norman: University of Oklahoma Press, 1998), 414. Powell says grandfather but, given that Spotted Tail died in 1881, this is presumably a typographical error.

44 Ibid., 414.

45 Ibid.; Rambow, *Bear Butte*, 50.

46 Forbes-Boyte, 'Indigenous People, Land, and Space', 109.

47 Thomas E. Mails and Dallas Chief Eagle, *Fools Crow* (Lincoln: University of Nebraska Press, 1990), 148–9.

48 Walter R. Echo-Hawk, 'Native American Religious Liberty: Five Hundred Years after Columbus', *American Indian Culture and Research Journal*, 17 (1993), 37–8; Stephen L. Pevar, *The Rights of Indians and Tribes*, 4th edn (Oxford: Oxford University Press, 2012), 10–11.

49 Loesch, 'The First Americans', 331–2.

50 Powell, *Sweet Medicine*, 414.

51 *Rapid City Journal* 28 September 1939, in Odell, *Mata Paha*, 134–5.

52 Rambow, *Bear Butte*, 70.

53 Pechan, *Sturgis, South Dakota*, 103.

54 Powell, *Sweet Medicine*, 416.

55 Ibid., 417–20; John Stands in Timber and Margot Liberty, *Cheyenne Memories*, 2nd edn (Yale: Yale University Press, 1967), 89 n. 17, 90 n. 18.

56 *Northern Sun News*, November 1984, 6.

57 Mails and Chief Eagle, *Fools Crow*, 108.
58 Congressional Record at H6872 (18 July 1972), quoted in Echo-Hawk, 'Native American Religious Liberty', 40.
59 *Announcements: Native American Rights Fund* (Winter, 1979), 6, https://narf.org/nill/documents/nlr/nlr5-1.pdf
60 S. S. Harjo, 'It began with a vision in a sacred place', in *Past, Present, and Future: Challenges of the National Museum of the American Indian*, ed. NMAI (Washington DC: Smithsonian Institution, 2007), 32.
61 United States Senate Committee on Native Affairs, 108–1 *Hearing: Native American Sacred Places*, S-Hrg, 108–97, 18 June 2003, 78.
62 Gonzalez, 'The Black Hills', in *Native American Voices*, 114.
63 Loesch, 'The First Americans', 349–50.
64 Rambow, *Bear Butte*, 120.

13. Amritsar, Punjab, India

1 'Sikh Holy Books take a flight to Canada', *Times of India* 3 April 2004, https://timesofindia.indiatimes.com/city/chandigarh/sikh-holy-books-take-a-flight-to-canada/articleshow/598186.cms
2 'Morning Hymn', in Guru Nanak, *Poems from the Sikh Sacred Tradition*, trans. Nikky-Guninder Kaur Singh (Cambridge, MA: Harvard University Press, 2023), 11; R. S. Jutla, 'Understanding Sikh Pilgrimage', *Tourism Recreation Research* (2002), 68.
3 John Davidson, *A Treasury of Mystic Terms: Part III, Spiritual Experience & Practice* (New Delhi: Science of the Soul Research Centre, 2019), 88.
4 R. S. Jutla, 'The Evolution of the Golden Temple of Amritsar into a major Sikh Pilgrimage Center', *AIMS Geosciences* (2016), 266.
5 Ibid.
6 Andrea Marion Pinkney, 'What Are Sikhs Doing at "Historical Gurdwaras" if They're Not on Pilgrimage? Saints, Dust and Memorial Presence at Sikh Religious Places', in *Religious Journeys in India: Pilgrims, Tourists and Travelers*, ed. Andrea Marion Pinkney and John Whalen-Bridge (New York: Suny Press, 2018), 221, 226.
7 Khushwant Singh, *A History of the Sikhs: Volume 1, 1469–1838* (Delhi: Oxford University Press, 2004), 54.
8 J. S. Grewal, *The Sikhs: Ideology, Institutions, and Identity* (Oxford: Oxford University Press, 2009), 96.

9 Rudyard Kipling, *Kim* (Oxford: Oxford University Press, 2008), 57.
10 Eleanor M. Nesbitt, *Sikhism: A Very Short Introduction*, 2nd edn (Oxford: Oxford University Press, 2016), 40.
11 Ibid., 60.
12 Jutla, 'Understanding Sikh Pilgrimage', 67.
13 Singh, *A History of the Sikhs: Volume 1, 1469–1838*, 116.
14 Charles M. Townsend, 'The Darbar Sahib', in *Oxford Handbook of Sikh Studies*, ed. Pashaura Singh and Louis E. Fenech (Oxford: Oxford University Press, 2014), 432.
15 Ibid.
16 Singh, *A History of the Sikhs: Volume 2, 1839–1964* (Princeton: Princeton University Press, 1984), 123–4.
17 Quoted in Singh, *A History of the Sikhs: Volume 1*, 121.
18 Simon Coleman and John Elsner, *Pilgrimage: Past and Present in World Religions* (Cambridge, MA: Harvard University Press, 1995), 164.
19 Meredith L. Runion, *The History of Afghanistan*, 2nd edn (Santa Barbara, CA: ABC-CLIO, 2017), 69–71.
20 G. S. Chhabra, *Advanced Study in History of the Punjab, Volume 1 (1469–1799) (Guru and Post-Guru Period up to Ranjit Singh)* (Jullundur City: New Academic Publishing Co., 1971), 414.
21 Karamajit K. Malhotra, 'Emergence of the Golden Temple as the Premier Sikh Institution during the Eighteenth Century', *Proceedings of the Indian History Congress*, 76 (2015), 289–90.
22 A. H. Bingley, *Handbook for the Indian Army: Sikhs* (Simla: Government Central Printing Office, 1899), 14.
23 Chhabra, *Advanced Study in History of the Punjab*, 146.
24 Mohamed Sheikh, *The Emperor of the Five Rivers: The Life and Times of Maharajah Ranjit Singh* (London: I. B. Taurus, 2017), 36.
25 Susan Stronge, 'Maharaja Ranjit Singh and Artistic Patronage at the Sikh Court', *South Asian Studies*, 22 (2006), 95.
26 Rajinder Singh, *The Secular Maharaja: Maharaja Ranjit Singh* (Delhi: Dynamic Publications, 2008), 30–31.
27 Sheikh, *The Emperor of the Five Rivers*, 116; Madanjit Kaur, *Maharaja Ranjit Singh* (Chandigarh: Unistar, 2008), 24.
28 Ahmad Hasan Khan, *Census of India, 1931: Volume XVII. Punjab, Part 1* (Lahore: Civil and Military Gazette Press, 1933), 305.

29 K. C. Yadav, *Punjab: Colonial Challenge and Popular Response 1849–1947* (Haryana: Hope India, 2003), 28–9.
30 Chhanda Chaterjee, *The Sikh Minority and the Partition of the Punjab 1920–1947* (London: Routledge, 2010), 55.
31 Ian J. Kerr, 'British Relationships with the Golden Temple, 1849–90', *Indian Economic and Social History Review*, 21 (1984), 139–51.
32 Coleman and Elsner, *Pilgrimage: Past and Present*, 164.
33 'The Recent Riots in Bombay', *The Age* 18 August 1893, 6.
34 Chandrika Kaul, *Reporting the Raj: The British Press and India, c.1880–1922* (Manchester: Manchester University Press, 2003), 211.
35 'Seditious Publications', 24 August 2023, https://blogs.bl.uk/untoldlives/2023/08/seditious-publications.html
36 *Contemporary*, 23 (1979), 12.
37 Ian Talbot, 'A Tale of Two Cities: The Aftermath of Partition for Lahore and Amritsar', *Modern Asian Studies*, 1 (2007), 152.
38 J. Gordon Melton, 'Golden Temple', in *Religions of the World: A Comprehensive Encyclopedia of Beliefs and Practices*, ed. J. Gordon Melton and Martin Baumann (Santa Barbara, CA: ABC-CLIO, 2002), 1237.
39 Singh, *A History of the Sikhs: Volume 2*, 364.
40 Khushwant Singh, *Truth, Love, and a Little Malice: An Autobiography* (London: Penguin, 2002), 328.

14. Lourdes, France

1 Thérèse Taylor, *Bernadette of Lourdes: Her Life, Death and Visions* (London: Burns & Oates, 2003), 35–148; René Laurentin, *Bernadette of Lourdes: A Life Based on Authenticated Documents*, trans. John Drury (Minneapolis: Winston Press, 1978), 25–84; Patrick Marnham, *Lourdes: A Modern Pilgrimage* (Garden City, NY: Doubleday, 1982), 26–33.
2 Ruth Harris, *Lourdes: Body and Spirit in the Secular Age* (London: Viking, 1999), 9.
3 Emilie Garrigou-Kampton, 'Suffering and healing in the late nineteenth century: medical case studies from the Lourdes sanctuary', *Modern and Contemporary France*, 28 (2020), 442.
4 Marnham, *Lourdes,* 33.
5 Ibid.
6 Linda K. Davidson and David Gitlitz, *Pilgrimage From Ganges to*

Graceland, An Encyclopedia, vol. 1 (Santa Barbara: ABC-CLIO, 2002) 356–9.

7 Tine van Osselaer, 'Marian Piety and Gender: Marian Devotion and the "Feminization" of Religion', in *Oxford Handbook of Mary*, ed. Chris Maunder (Oxford: Oxford University Press, 2019), 583.

8 Marnham, *Lourdes,* 39.

9 Osselaer, 'Marian Piety and Gender', 596.

10 John Eade, 'Parish and Pilgrimage in a Changing Europe', in *Migration, Transnationalism and Catholicism: Global Perspectives*, ed. Dominic Pasure and Marta Bivand Erdal (London: Palgrave, 2016), 84.

11 Harris, *Lourdes*, 269, 313–14.

12 Bernard François, Esther M. Sternberg and Elizabeth Fee, 'The Lourdes Medical Cures Revisited', *Journal of the History of Medicine and Allied Sciences*, 69 (2012), 135–62.

13 'Meet Sister Bernadette, the most recently-cured person at Lourdes', https://www.catholicnewsagency.com/news/253153/meet-sister-bernadette-the-most-recently-cured-person-at-lourdes

14 Henry Lasserre, *Our Lady of Lourdes* (Lourdes: Notre-Dame de Lourdes, 1869).

15 Suzanne K. Kaufman, *Consuming Visions: Mass Culture and the Lourdes Shrine* (Ithaca, NY: Cornell University Press, 2005), 52.

16 Ibid., *passim.*

17 Suzanne K. Kaufman, 'Religion and Modernity: The Case of the Lourdes Shrine in Nineteenth-Century France', in *Disciplining Modernity*, ed. Pamela L. Caughie (Basingstoke: Palgrave, 2010), 103.

18 Elizabeth Emery, 'Modern Medieval Pilgrimages: The Nineteenth-Century Struggle for Lourdes', *Years' Work in Medievalism*, XV (1999), 155.

19 Émile Zola, *Lourdes*, trans. Ernest A. Vizetelly (New York: Prometheus Books, 2000), 293.

20 Harris, *Lourdes*, 173–5.

21 Arthur Matthews, *Well-Remembered Days: Eoin O'Ceallaigh's Memoir of a Twentieth-Century Catholic Life* (London: Macmillan, 2001), 146.

22 Joseph Demarteau, in Emery, 'Modern Medieval Pilgrimage', 194 n. 19.

23 Maria Warner, *Alone of All Her Sex: The Myth and the Cult of the Virgin Mary* (Oxford: Oxford University Press, 2013), 318.

24 Miri Rubin, *Mother of God: A History of the Virgin Mary* (London: Allen Lane, 2009), 414.
25 Marnham, *Lourdes*, 39.
26 Christian Sorrel, 'Politics of the Sacred: Lourdes, France, and Rome', in *Marian Devotions, Political Mobilization and Nationalism in Europe and America*, ed. Roberto di Stefano, Francisco Javier Ramón Solans (London: Palgrave, 2016), 60; *Tablet*, 12 October 1872, 1.
27 Emery, 'Modern Medieval Pilgrimages', 150, 152.
28 Angelique Christafis, 'Tourism miracle has turned water into profits', *Guardian* 9 February 2008, https://www.theguardian.com/world/2008/feb/09/france.catholicism
29 Annette Becker, *War and Faith: The Religious Imagination in France, 1914–1930*, trans. Helen McPhail (Oxford: Berg, 1998), 63–4.
30 Patrick H. Kelly, *Story of the Knights of Columbus Pilgrimage* (Philadelphia: Kelly Publishing Company, 1920).
31 'Back From Lourdes', *Birmingham Daily Gazette* 4 August 1923, 5; 'Lourdes Cure Creates Profound Effect in Liverpool', NCWC News Service September 1923; Paul Glynn, *Healing Fire of Christ: Reflections on Modern Miracles – Knock, Lourdes, Fatima* (San Francisco, Ignatius Press, 2003), 59–73; Patrick O'Connor, *I Met A Miracle: The Story of Jack Traynor* (London: Catholic Truth Society, 1943); 'Jack's Lourdes Cure Still Inspires Faith', *Sunday Mirror* 10 January 1982, 21; 'Lourdes Pilgrims', *Lancashire Evening Post* 13 July 1926, 4;
32 'Pilgrimage to Pray for Peace at Lourdes', *The Times* 25 August 1934, 6; *Western Daily Press,* 19 September 1934, 6; 'Le pèlerinage des ancient combattants à Lourdes', *L'Action Française*, 14 September 1936.
33 'Austria and Germany', *Catholic Standard* 7 September 1934, 20.
34 'An Arm of Peace for Lourdes', *Tablet* 18 April 1936, 505.
35 John M. Todd, 'The Work for World Peace', *Furrow*, 4 (1953), 28–9.
36 '100,000 Pilgrims Pay Homage at Lourdes', *Irish Weekly and Ulster Examiner* 14 September 1946, 1; Phyllis Jenkin, 'Pilgrimage to Lourdes', *Glasgow Herald* 13 September 1946, 3.
37 John Eade, 'Healing Social and Physical Bodies: Lourdes and Military Pilgrimage', in *Military Pilgrimage and Battlefield Tourism: Commemorating the Dead*, ed. John Eade and Mario Katič (Abingdon: Routledge, 2018), 15–33.

38 'Warriors to Lourdes', https://www.warriorstolourdes.com/en/index.html
39 Eade, 'Parish and Pilgrimage', 83.

15. Saintes-Maries-de-la-Mer, France

1 Friends, Families, & Travellers: Frequently Asked Questions: https://www.gypsy-traveller.org/about-us/frequently-asked-questions/#:~:text=It%20depends.,%27Gypsy%27%20to%20describe%20themselves. See Minority Rights Group, 'Language Matters: Representations of Gypsies and Travellers in British Media', https://minorityrights.org/language-matters-representation-of-gypsies-and-travellers-in-british-media/#:~:text=Alongside%20the%20above%2C%20it%20is,Travellers%20is%20an%20excellent%20start. for the need for capitalisation.
2 'Les Gitans ont invoque Ste Sara', *Compagnons de France* (1941), 9.
3 Mark, 16:1–8.
4 Ellen Badone, 'Pilgrimage, Tourism, and the da Vinci Code at Saintes-Maries-de-la-Mer, France', *Culture and Religion*, 9 (2008), 24; Marc Bordigoni, 'Sara aux Saintes-Maries-de-la-Mer. Métaphore de la présence gitane dans le monde des Gadjé', *Etudes Tsiganes*, 20 (2005), 12–34 ; Sophie Bergaglio, *L'Histoire du Pèlerinage des Saintes-Maries-de-la-Mer* (Aix-en-Provence: Édition des Lilas, 2016), 87–88; Pierre Causse, 'Les Saintes Maries de la Mer', *La Roulette*, 49 (1999), http://gitanseneglise.org/cultures-tsiganes.org/st_maries/deux_maries/deux_maries_p1.htm
5 M. de La Curne, 'Mémoire concernant la vie de Jean de Venette, avec la Notice de l'Histoire en vers des Trois Maries, dont il est l'auteur', in *Mémoires de Littérature, tirez des registres de L'Academie Royale des Inscriptions et Belles Lettres*, vol. 13 (Paris: De L'Imprimerie Royale, 1740), 521.
6 Annie Faugère, 'Le Pèlerinage de Hans von Waltheym en l'an 1474', *Provence Historique*, 166 (1991), 537.
7 Zina Peterson, 'Twisted Paths of Civilization: Saint Sara and the Romani', *Journal of Religion and Popular Culture*, 26.3 (2014), 313.
8 Marc Bordigioni, 'Le pèlerinage de Saintes-Maries-de-la-Mer : De la fête votive au pèlerinage des Gitans xixe–xxe siècles', in *Les Fêtes en Provence Autrefois et Aujourd'hui*, ed. Régis Bertrand et Laurent-Sébastien

Fournier (Aix-en-Provence: Presses Universitaires de Provence, 2014), 152.

9 A. Mazel, *Notes sur la Camargue et les Saintes-Maries-de-la-Mer* (Vaison la Romaine: Société de la Bonne Presse du Midi, 1935), 153–4.

10 *The Memoirs of Frédéric Mistral*, trans. George Wickes (Paris: Alyscamps Press, 1994), 196.

11 Peterson, 'Twisted Paths', 310.

12 Gaëlla Loiseau, 'Globalizing Romani Culture': the pilgrimage to the sea in Les-Saintes-Maries-de-la-Mer (France)', in *Locality Identities and Transnational Cults within Europe*, ed. F. Giacalone and K. Griffin (Wallingford: CABI, 2018), 62.

13 John Manson, 'A Provençal Pilgrimage', *Gentleman's Magazine*, 290 (1901), 347.

14 M. Dregni, *Gypsy Jazz: In Search of Django Reinhardt and Gypsy Swing* (New York: Oxford University Press, 2008), 134.

15 Peterson, 'Twisted Paths', 313.

16 Janne-Elisabeth McOwan, 'Ritual Purity: An Aspect of the Gypsy Pilgrimage to Stes-Maries-de-la-Mer', *Journal of the Gypsy Lore Society*, 4 (1994), 96; *Jacques Lefèvre D'Étaples and The Three Maries Debates: On Mary Magdalen, On Christ's Three Days in the Tomb, On the One Mary in Place of Three. A Discussion. On the Threefold and Single Magdalen. A Second Discussion*, ed. and trans. Sheila M. Porrer (Geneva: Librairie Drosz, 2009), 75.

17 McOwan, 'Ritual Purity', 96, citing Phillipon (1521).

18 Ronald Lee, 'The Romani Goddess Kali Sara' (2002). Retrieved from: http://kopachi.com/articles/the-romani-goddess-kali-sara-ronald-lee/

19 Bordigioni, 'Le "pèlerinage des Gitans"', 492.

20 *The Memoirs of Frédéric Mistral*, 197.

21 Marilyn Brown, *Gypsies and Other Bohemians: The Myth of the Artist in Nineteenth Century France* (Ann Arbor: UMI Research Press, 1985), 96.

22 McOwan, 'Ritual Purity', 105.

23 *The Memoirs of Frédéric Mistral*, 193.

24 Ibid., 197.

25 Brown, *Gypsies and Other Bohemians*, 22.

26 Eric Wiley, 'Romani Performance and heritage tourism: the pilgrimage

of the Gypsies at Les Saintes-Maries-de-la-Mer', *Drama Review*, 49 (2005), 135.

27 Report quoted in Dregni, *Gypsy Jazz*, 144.

28 Chris Pearson, *Scarred Landscapes: War and Nature in Vichy France* (Basingstoke: Palgrave, 2008), 78.

29 Pierre Causse, 'Le pèlerinage des Saintes-Maries: hier et aujourd'hui', *Monde Gitan*, 83 (1992), 33.

30 Angus Fraser, *The Gypsies* (London: Wiley, 1995), 313–15; Becky Taylor, *Another Darkness, Another Dawn: A History of Gypsies, Roma, and Travellers* (London: Reaktion Books, 2014), 229.

31 J. de Bariacli Levy, 'Gypsy Figures at the Fiesta of Les Saintes Maries, 1949', *Romani Studies* (1950), 115.

32 F. Courrier, 'Le mystère de Sara la noire', *Monde Gitan*, 2 (1967), 4–6.

33 Bordigioni, *L'Histoire du pèlerinage*, 494.

34 Causse, 'Le pèlerinage des Saintes-Maries', 34.

35 Ibid., 35.

36 Levy, 'Gypsy Figures', 116.

37 Pierre Causse, 'Un quart de siècle aux Saintes-Maries de la Mer', *Monde Gitan*, 46 (1978), 4.

38 Ibid., 1.

39 Ibid.

40 'Découvrez Les Saintes Maries de la Mer', https://www.camargue.fr/villes-villages/les-saintes-maries-de-la-mer

41 Causse, 'Les Saintes Maries de la Mer'.

42 Ibid.

43 Courrier, 'Le mystère de Sara la noire', 4–6.

44 Pierre Derlon, *Secrets of the Gypsies* (New York: Ballantine Books, 1977), 228–9.

45 Jean-Baptiste Humeau, *Tsiganes en France de l'assignation au droit d'habiter* (Paris: L'Harmattan, 1995), 196; Fraser, *The Gypsies*, 312–13.

46 Jean Aicard, *King of Camargue* (Philadelphia: Georgie Barrie & Son, 1901), 3, 13, 16.

47 Walter Starkie, *In Sara's Tents* (London: John Murray, 1953), 21–2.

48 Bordigioni, 'Le "pèlerinage des Gitans"', 493.

49 Causse, 'Les Saintes Maries de la Mer'.

50 McOwan, 'Ritual Purity', 98, 106.

51 Ruth A. Hawkins, *Unbelievable Happiness and Final Sorrow: The Hemingway–Pfeiffer Marriage* (Fayetteville: University of Arkansas Press, 2012), 78.
52 Wiley, 'Romani Performance', 152.
53 Falco de Baroncelli-Javon, *Les Bohémiens des Saintes-Maries-de-la-Mer* (Paris: Lemerre, 1910), 16–17.
54 Wiley, 'Romani Performance', 37, 150.
55 Garth Cartwright, 'Partying with the Gypsies in the Camargue', *Guardian* 26 March 2011, https://www.theguardian.com/travel/2011/mar/26/saintes-maires-gypsy-festival-camargue
56 Ellen Badone, 'Seduction in the "Gypsy Pilgrimage" at Les Saintes Maries de la Mer', in *The Seductions of Pilgrimage: Sacred Journeys Afar and Astray in the Western Religious Tradition*, ed. Michael A. Di Giovane and David Picard (London: Routledge, 2016), 174.
57 Badone, 'Pilgrimage, Tourism', 34; Loiseau, 'Globalizing Romani Culture', 61.
58 Badone, 'Pilgrimage, Tourism', 35–7; Dan Brown, *The Da Vinci Code* (London: Transworld, 2013), 339; Michael Baigent, Richard Leigh and Henry Lincoln, *The Holy Blood and the Holy Grail* (London: Jonathan Cape, 1982).
59 'Les Gitans ont invoque Ste Sara', *Compagnons de France* (1941), 9.

16. Rātana Pā, New Zealand

1 John Garett, *Footsteps in the Sea: Christianity in Oceania to World War II* (Suva: Fiji Institute of Pacific Studies, 1992), 134; Lindsay Cox, *Kotahitanga: The Search for Māori Political Unity* (Auckland, NZ: Oxford University Press, 1993), 117–18.
2 'Ratana, Tahupotiki Wiremu', *Encyclopedia of New Zealand* https, // teara.govt.nz/en/biographies/3r4/ratana-tahupotiki-wiremu 'Ratana . . . Maori Prophet Claims 400,000 cures', 26 August (1939), 18.
3 Marilyn Lashley, 'In our own way: the parallel development of culturally anchored self-help in African American and New Zealand Maori Communities in Historical Perspectives', in *Identity, Culture and the Politics of Community Development*, ed. Stacey-Ann Wilson (Cambridge: Cambridge Scholars Publishing, 2015), 110.
4 'The Wonder-Worker', *Northern Advocate* 8 December 1920, 6; Moana

Raureti, 'The Origins of the Ratana Movement', in *Te Ao Hurihuri: Aspects of Maoritanga*, ed. Michael King (Auckland: Raupo Publishing, 1992), 149.

5 'Ratana the Healer', *Hawke's Bay Tribune* 20 October 1921, 4.

6 'Mecca of the Maori', *Evening Star* 29 December 1921, 6; '"Lourdes" of New Zealand', *Harbinger of Light,* 1 March 1921, 272–3.

7 John Bell Condliffe, *Te Rangi Hiroa: The Life of Sir Peter Buck* (Melbourne: Whitcombe and Tombs, 1971), 142.

8 Clair Price, 'The Miracle Man of New Zealand', *New York Times*, 3 August 1924, 8

9 Ibid.

10 R. J. Walker, 'The Social Implications of Medical Practice Among Māoris', *Tu Tangata* 1 August 1982, 31.

11 'A Maori "miracle"', *Auckland Star* 12 January 1921, 7.

12 'Maori Faith Healer', *Daily Mercury* 19 November 1923, 4.

13 'Further Afield: Ratana in Morrinsville', *Evening Post* 2 April 1921, 8.

14 'Modern "Miracle Man" Found in New Zealand', *Manchester Guardian* 30 March 1921, 4.

15 '"Lourdes" of New Zealand', *Harbinger of Light,* 1 March 1921, 272–3.

16 Price, 'The Miracle Man', 8.

17 'Visiting Ratana', *Greymouth Evening Star* 27 January 1921, 5.

18 Wellcome Collection, London: MS 7712.

19 *Manchester Guardian* 2 March 1922, 14.

20 'Ratana, the Maori Healer: Story of a Cure', *Queanbeyan Age and Queanbeyan Reporter* 7 February 1922, 2.

21 'A Great Moment', *Taranaki Daily News* 25 February 1922, 11.

22 'Ratana at Home: the Mecca of the Maori', *Evening Post* 27 December 1921, 8.

23 'Maori Visionary: Visit to Japan', *Register* 17 January 1925, 11.

24 Arthur F. Williams, 'The Māori Miracle Man', *Waiapu Church Gazette*, XVI, 1 January 1921, 345.

25 'Maori King Wants Modern Conveniences', *Sun* 25 September 1938, 3; 'Cripples Left Crutches with Ratana', *Pix* 26 August 1926, 19–20.

26 Pieter H. de Bres, 'Religion in the Atene: Religious Associations and the Urban Maori', *Memoirs of the Polynesian Society*, 37 (1971), 41.

27 Raureti, 'Origins', 150; 'The Māori Prophet', *Manchester Guardian* 18 April 1927, 5.
28 Angela Ballara, 'Molo, Pita Te Tūruki Tāmati', *Dictionary of New Zealand Biography*, first published in 1998. Te Ara – the Encyclopedia of New Zealand, https://teara.nz/en/biographies/4m56/moko-pita-te-turuki-tamati (accessed 11 January 2024).
29 'Spiritual Healing', *Waiapu Church Gazette*, XII, 1 September 1921, 306.
30 De Bres, 'Religion in the Atene', 29.
31 Selwyn Muru, 'Ratana Birth Rebirth', *Tu Tangata* 1 August 1981, 27.
32 De Bres, 'Religion in the Atene', 40.
33 'Maori Visitors', *Daily Mail* 27 April 1924, 17; 'Ratana Remembered', *World's News* 20 May 1953, 31; 'Maoris Vote For Cult', *Herald* 30 November 1949, 12.
34 Pieter H. de Bres, 'The Contribution of Maori Religious Movements to Religion in New Zealand', *Exchange*, 8 (1979), 3.
35 Hans Mol, *The Fixed and the Fickle: Religion and Identity in New Zealand* (Dunedin: Pilgrims South Press, 2006), 34.
36 'Maoris Vote For Cult', *Herald*, 12.
37 G. V. Butterworth, 'A Rural Maori Renaissance? Māori Society and Politics 1920 to 1951', *Journal of Polynesian Society*, 81 (1972), 166.
38 'Maori Prophet Dies', *Sun* 18 September 1939, 8.
39 Waerete Norman, 'Taura', *Growing Up Māori*, ed. Witi Ihimaera (Auckland: Tandem Press, 1998), 123–4.
40 'Maoris Vote For Cult', *Herald*, 12.
41 Nigel Palethorpe, 'Where Labor is a Religion', *Sun* 4 December 1949, 24.
42 Raureti, 'Origins', 158; Cox, *Kotahitanga*, 121.
43 Butterworth, 'A Rural Maori Renaissance?', 179.
44 'Maoris Vote for Cult', *Herald*, 12.
45 Matt McCarten, 'The political pilgrimage our leaders fear to miss', *Herald on Sunday* 28 January 2012.
46 'Pilgrimage to Ratana Pa', *Otago Daily Times* 26 January 2012, https://www.odt.co.nz/opinion/editorial/pilgrimage-ratana-pa
47 Michelle Duff, *Jacinda Ardern: The Full Story of an Extraordinary Prime Minister* (Sydney: Allen & Unwin, 2023), 23.
48 'Editorial: Pilgrimage to Ratana Pa', *Otago Daily Times* 26 January 2023.

17. Buenos Aires, Argentina

1 'Commemorating Eva Peron', *Sphere* 2 August 1953, 192.

2 'Luck Runs Out For Eva Peron', *American Mercury*, January 1952, 34.

3 Donna J. Guy, *Creating Charismatic Bonds in Argentina: Letters to Juan and Eva Peron* (Albuquerque: University of New Mexico Press, 2016), 136.

4 'Argentina: Little Eva', *Time* 14 July 1947.

5 Quoted in Austen Ivereigh, *Catholicism and Politics in Argentina, 1810–1960* (New York: St Martin's Press, 1995), 160.

6 'Luck Runs Out', 34.

7 Ibid.

8 L. Ehrlich and S. Gayol, 'Las vias post mortem de Eva Peron: cuerpo, ausencia y biographias en las revistas de masas de Argentina', *Historia Critica*, 70 (2018), 111–31.

9 *La Gaceta*, 9 August 1952.

10 Susana Bianchi, 'Catolicismo y peronismo: La religion como campo de conflicto (Argentina, 1945–1955)', *Boletin Americanista*, 44 (1994), 25–37.

11 *Illustrated London News*, 221 (1952), 211.

12 'Argentina: In Mourning', *Time* 11 August 1952.

13 Bianchi, 'Catolicismo y peronismo', 31.

14 'Eva's Wake at the Ministry of Labour and Welfare' (fig. 10), in Iliana Cepero, 'Photographic Propaganda under Peronism, 1946–55: Selections from the Archivo General de la Nación Argentina', *History of Photography*, 40 (2016), 211.

15 Lucía Santos Lepera, 'Las manifestaciones colectivas de deulo frente a la muerte de Eva Perón', *Americanist Bulletin* (2013), 161–80.

16 *Newcastle Evening Chronicle* 9 August 1952, 5.

17 J. M. Taylor, *Eva Peron: The Myths of a Woman* (Chicago: Chicago University Press, 1979), 107.

18 Linda B. Hall, 'Evita and Maria: Religious Reverence and Political Resonance in Argentina', in *Mary, Mother, and Warrior: The Virgin in Spain and the Americas*, ed. Linda B. Hall (Austin: University of Texas Press, 2004), 226–7.

19 Taylor, *Eva Peron*, 170–71; Graciela Albornoz de Videla, *Libero de*

Lactura para Primero Grado Inferior (Buenos Aires, 1953), 10, https://librosperonistas.com/evita/paginas-10-11.html

20 *The Truth*, 7 November 1952, 489; *Newcastle Evening Chronicle* 9 August 1952, 5.

21 Ines San Martin, 'Argentine Union Wants a St Evita, Church says "not so fast"', *Tablet* 22 May 2019.

22 'Perón, Evita y Francisco: La Fe como fiesta popular y la fuerza de lucha', *AGN Prensa*, 6 July 2021, https://agnprensa.com/peron-evita-y-francisco-la-fe-como-fiesta-popular-y-la-fuerza-de-lucha/

23 Eduardo Montes-Bradley (director), *Evita*, Episode 2: 'Presencia de Eva Peron' (1953).

24 Edwin Murphy, *After the Funeral: The Posthumous Adventures of Famous Corpses* (New York: Barnes & Noble, 1998), 172.

25 Hall, 'Evita and Maria', 233.

26 Murphy, *After the Funeral*, 179.

27 María José Moyano, *Argentina's Lost Patrol; Armed Struggle, 1989–1979* (New Haven: Yale University Press, 1995), 58.

28 'Argentines Remember Eva Perón – In Pictures', *Guardian* 27 July 2022, https://www.theguardian.com/world/gallery/2022/jul/27/argentina-remembers-eva-peron-evita-in-pictures

29 Donna J. Guy, 'Life and the Commodification of Death in Argentina: Juan and Eva Person', in *Death, Dismemberment, and Memory: Body Politics in Latin America*, ed. Lyman L. Johnson (Albuquerque: University of New Mexico Press, 2004), 250.

30 'Otra estación para peregrinos: sudario de Eva, al Congreso', 25 August 2004, https://www.ambito.com/politica/otra-estacion-peregrinos-sudario-eva-al-congreso-n3287181

18. Shikoku, Japan

1 *The 1918 Shikoku Pilgrimage of Takamure Itsue: An English Translation of Musume Junreiki*, trans. Susan Tennant (Bowen Island, Canada: Bowen Publishing, 2010), 1–2.

2 Yasuko Sato, *Takamure Itsue, Japanese Antiquity, and Matricultural Paradigms that Address the Crisis of Modernity: A Woman from the Land on Fire* (Cham: Palgrave MacMillan, 2023), 44; E. Patricia Tsurumi,

'Feminism and Anarchism in Japan: Takamure Itsue, 1894–1964', *Bulletin of Concerned Asian Scholars*, 17 (1985), 4–5.

3 Ian Reader, 'Dead to the World: Pilgrims in Shikoku', in *Pilgrimage and Popular Culture*, ed. Ian Reader and Tony Walter (Basingstoke: Springer, 1993), 111.

4 Michael Pye, *Japanese Buddhist Pilgrimage* (Sheffield: Rambelli, 2014), 80; Reader, 'Dead to the World', 114.

5 Ian Reader, *Making Pilgrimages: Meaning and Practice in Shikoku* (Honolulu: University of Hawai'i Press, 2005), 119.

6 *Konjaku Monogatari*, quoted in Kenji Matsuo, *A History of Japanese Buddhism* (Leiden: Brill, 2007), 240; Reader, 'Dead to the World', 116.

7 *Four Japanese Travel Diaries of the Middle Ages*, trans. Herbert Plutschow and Hideichi Fukuda (Ithaca, NY: Cornell University, 1981), 15; William R. Lafleur, *Awesome Nightfall: The Life, Times and Poetry of Saigyō* (Boston: Wisdom Publications, 2003), 32.

8 H. E. Plutschow, 'Japanese Travel Diaries in the Middle Ages', *Oriens Extremus*, 29 (1982), 110.

9 Yung-Hee Kim, *Songs to Make the Dust Dance: The Ryōjin hishō of Twelfth-Century Japan* (Berkeley: University of California Press, 1994), 106.

10 Alfred Bohner, *Two on a Pilgrimage: The 88 Holy Places of Shikoku*, trans. Katharine Merrill, ed. David C. Moreton (Frankfurt: E & H Verlag, 2011), 76.

11 Reader, *Making Pilgrimages*, 128.

12 Natalie Kouamé, 'The daily life of the *henro* on the island of Shikoku during the Edo period: A mirror of Tokugawa society', in *Pilgrimages and Spiritual Quests in Japan*, ed. Maria Rodríguez del Alisal, Peter Ackermann and Dolores P. Martinez (London: Routledge, 2007), 40.

13 Reader, *Making Pilgrimages*, 112, 115, 116.

14 Constantine Nomikops Vaporis, *Breaking Barriers: Travel and the State in Early Modern Japan* (Cambridge, MA: Harvard University Press, 1994), 329.

15 Ian Reader, 'Legends, Miracles, and Faith in Kōbō Daishi and Shikoku Pilgrimage', in *Religions of Japan in Practice*, ed. George J. Tanabe Jr (Princeton: Princeton University Press, 1999), 362.

16 Reader, *Making Pilgrimages*, 127.

17 Ibid., 119; Bohner, *Two on a Pilgrimage*, 37.
18 Matsuo, *A History of Japanese Buddhism*, 242.
19 Reader, *Making Pilgrimages*, 119; Pye, *Japanese Buddhist Pilgrimage*, 81.
20 Reader, *Making Pilgrimages*, 121.
21 Kouame, 'Shikoku's Local Authorities', 415–18.
22 Bohner, *Two on a Pilgrimage*, 130–33.
23 Reader, 'Kōbō Saishi and Shikoku Pilgrimage', 364.
24 Oliver Statler, *Japanese Pilgrimage* (London: Picador, 1984), 218.
25 Henry Noël, *Karakoro – At Home in Japan* (Tokyo: Hokuseido Press, 1939), 193.
26 Teigo Yoshida, 'Strangers and Pilgrims in Village Japan', in *Pilgrimages and Spiritual Quests in Japan*, 55.
27 Bohner, *Two on a Pilgrimage*, 134–5.
28 Laura Nenzi, 'To Ise at All Costs: Religious and Economic Implications of Early Modern Mukemairi', *Japanese Journal of Religious Studies*, 33 (2006), 99.
29 Reader, 'Dead to the World', 124.
30 Reader, *Making Pilgrimages*, 121–3; Ian Reader and John Shultz, *Unending Pilgrimage in Shikoku* (Oxford: Oxford University Press, 2021), 44–7; Bohner, *Two on a Pilgrimage*, 198.
31 Statler, *Japanese Pilgrimage*, 205.
32 Reader, 'Dead to the World', 121.
33 Nathalie Kouamé, 'Shikoku's Local Authorities and *Henro* during the Golden Age of Pilgrimage', *Japanese Journal of Religious Studies*, 24 (1997), 413.
34 Nakayama Kazuhisa, 'La Dynamique de creation, replication et déclin des lieux de pèlerinage: le nouveau pèlerinage de Shikoku à Sasaguri', *Cahiers d'Extrême Asie*, 22 (2013), 274–5.
35 Reader and Shultz, *Unending Pilgrimage*, 148.
36 Ian Reader, 'Positively Promoting Pilgrimage: Media Representation of Pilgrimage in Japan', *Nova Religio* (2007), 15.
37 Chisato Hotta, 'Japan's Modernization and the Persecution of Buddhism', *HUE Journal of Humanities, Social and Natural Science*, 35 (2012), 61.
38 Statler, *Japanese Pilgrimage*, 244–5.

39 Sara Kang, 'Contested Pilgrimage: Shikoku Henro and Dark Tourism', *Asia-Pacific Journal*, 17 (2019), 7.
40 Reader, 'Dead to the World', 108.
41 M. Mori, 'Spatial Formation and change in the Henro pilgrimage in Modern Japan [in Japanese]', *Japanese Journal of Human Geography*, 54 (2002), 22; M. Mori, 'Mobilising Pilgrim Bodily Space: the contest between authentic and folk pilgrimage in the interwar period', in *Understanding Tourism Mobilities in Japan*, ed. Hideki Endo (London: Routledge, 2021), 172.
42 Murakami, quoted in Ibid., 176.
43 Bohner, *Two on a Pilgrimage*, 181, 196.
44 M. Mori, 'Contemporary Religious Meaning of the Pilgrimage Route [in Japanese]', *Japanese Journal of Human Geography*, 2 (2001), *abstract*, 173; Mori, 'Mobilising Pilgrim Bodily Space', 174–5; Kang, 'Contested Pilgrimage', 12.
45 Eiki Hoshino, 'Current Increase in Walking Pilgrims', in *Pilgrimages and Spiritual Quests in Japan*, ed. Rodríguez del Alisal, María Dolores, Peter Ackerman and D. P. Martinez (London: Routledge, 2007), 63.
46 David C. Moreton, 'A 100-year History of Foreigners and the Shikoku Pilgrimage – Part 2', *Awa Life*, 294 (2015), 4.
47 Kang, 'Contested Pilgrimage', 1–3.
48 Statler, *Japanese Pilgrimage*, 237–40.
49 Moreton, 'A 100-year History', 2.
50 Reader and Schultz, *Unending Pilgrimage*, 47.
51 Reader, 'Dead to the World', 119.
52 Ibid., 107.
53 Pye, *Japanese Buddhist Pilgrimage*, 82.
54 Mori, 'Contemporary Religious Meaning', 75.
55 'Camiño di Shikoku', https://museoperegrinacions.xunta.gal/gl/exposicions/camino-de-shikoku, 27 July 2017.
56 Kang, 'Contested Pilgrimage', 17.

19. Santiago de Compostela, Spain

1 Antón M. Pazos, 'Compostela, Rome and the Revival of the Pilgrimages to Santiago', in *Nineteenth-Century European Pilgrimages: A New Golden Age*, ed. Antón M. Pazos (Abingdon: Routledge, 2020), 101; Marilyn

Stokstad, *Santiago de Compostela in the Age of the Great Pilgrimages* (Norman: University of Oklahoma Press, 1978), 160.

2 S. D. Pack, 'Revival of the Pilgrimage to Santiago de Compostela: The Politics of Religious, National, and European Patrimony, 1879–1988', *Journal of Modern History*, 82 (2010), 345.

3 See *Translating the Relics of St James*, ed. Antón M. Pazos (London: Routledge, 2017).

4 Alberto Ferreiro, 'The Cult of Saints and Divine Patronage in Gallaecia before Santiago', in *The Pilgrimage to Compostela in the Middle Ages*, ed. Linda K. Davidson and Maryjane Dunn (London: Routledge, 2012), 3–22.

5 Ana María Carballeira Debasa, 'The Pilgrims' Way of St James and Islam: Pilgrimage, Politics and Militias', in *Pilgrims and Politics: Rediscovering the Power of the Pilgrimage*, ed. Antón M. Pazos (London: Routledge, 2012), 20–25.

6 R. A. Fletcher, *St James's Catapult: The Life and Times of Diego Gelmírez of Santiago de Compostela* (Oxford: Oxford University Press, 1984).

7 *Liber Sancti Jacobi 'Codex Calixtinus'*, eds A. Moralejo, C. Torres and J. Feo (Santiago de Compostela: Xunta de Galicia, 2004).

8 R. B. Tate, *Pilgrimage to St James of Compostela from the British Isles in the Middle Ages* (Liverpool: Liverpool University Press, 1990), Appendix I.

9 *The Ecclesiastical History of Orderic Vitalis*, ed. and trans. Marjorie J. Chibnall, 6 vols (Oxford: Clarendon Press, 1969–1980), vi, 480–82.

10 *Description de l'Afrique et de l'Espagne par Edrîsî*, ed. and trans. R. Dozy and M. J. de Goeje (Leiden: Brill, 1968); Debasa, 'The Pilgrims' Way of St James and Islam', 12.

11 Pāivi Salmesvuori, 'Brigitta of Sweden and her pilgrimage to Santiago de Compostela', in *Women and Pilgrimage in Late Medieval Galicia*, ed. Carlos Andrés González-Paz (London: Routledge, 2016), 117.

12 Denise Péricard-Méa, 'French Noblewomen on Pilgrimage to Compostela in the Middle Ages', in Ibid., 102.

13 Teofilo Ruiz, *Spain's Centuries of Crisis: 1300–1474* (Oxford: Blackwell, 2007), 61, 135.

14 William Wey, *The Itineraries of William Wey*, trans. and ed. Francis Davey (Oxford: Bodleian Library, 2010), 210–21.

15 Kathryn Hurlock, *Medieval Welsh Pilgrimage, c.1100–1500* (Cardiff: University of Wales Press, 2018), 155–6.
16 *The Book of Margery Kempe*, trans. Anthony Bale (Oxford: Oxford University Press, 2015), 97.
17 Diana Webb, ed., *Pilgrims and Pilgrimage in the Medieval West* (London: I. B. Taurus, 2001), 17.
18 *Relato del viaje por Europa del obipso armenio Martir (1489–1496),* ed. Ignatcio Iñarrea Las Herjas and Denise Péricard-Méa (Logroño: Universidad de la Rioja, 2009).
19 Jan van Herwaarden, *Between St James and Erasmus. Studies in Late Medieval Religious Life: Devotion and Pilgrimage in the Netherlands* (Leiden: Brill, 2003), 190; *Festival Sermons of Martin Luther: The Church Postils*, trans. Joel R. Baseley (Dearborn, MI: Mark V Publications, 2005), 123.
20 Henry Kamen, *Philip of Spain* (New Haven: Yale University Press, 1997), 56.
21 Ofelia Rey Castelao, 'Visiting the Apostle Santiago: Pilgrimages to Santiago de Compostela in the 16th to 19th centuries', in *Relics, Shrines and Pilgrimages: Sanctity in Europe from Late Antiquity*, ed. Antón M. Pazos (London: Routledge, 2020), 97.
22 Katrina B. Olds, 'The "False Chronicles", Cardinal Baronio, and Sacred History in Counter-Reformation Spain', *Catholic Historical Review*, 100 (2014), 13–14.
23 B. Graham and M. Murray, 'The Spiritual and the Profane: The pilgrimage to Santiago de Compostela', *Ecumene*, 4 (1997), 398.
24 Erin Kathleen Rowe, *Saint and Nation: Santiago, Teresa of Avila, and Plural Identities in Early Modern Spain* (University Park: Pennsylvania State University Press, 2011), 77–106, 222–24.
25 Diego de Guzman, *Le peregrinacion a Santiago de Diego de Guzman: diario ineditio de 1610*, ed. and trans. Julio Vazque Castro (Santiago de Compostela: Xunta de Galicia, 2014), 1–10.
26 Miguel Taín Guzmán, *A Medici Pilgrimage: The Devotional Journal of Cosimo III to Santiago de Compostela (1669)* (Turnhout: Brepols, 2019).
27 Georges Provost, 'Les pèlerins accueillis à l'Hospital Real de Saint-Jacques-de-Compostelle dans la seconde moitié du XVIIe siècle', in *Pèlerins et pèlerinages dans l'Europe moderne: actes de la table ronde*

organisée par le Département d'Histoire et Civilisation de l'Institut Universitaire Européen de Florence et l'École Française de Rome (Rome, 4–5 June 1993), (Rome: École Française de Rome, 2000), 127–50.

28 Maryjane Dunn and Linda Kay Davidson, 'Introduction: Bibliography of the Pilgrimage: the State of the Art', in *The Pilgrimage to Compostela in the Middle Ages,* xxviii.

29 Miguel Taín Guzmán, 'A Decade of Research', in *Religious Pilgrimages in the Mediterranean World*, ed. Antón M. Pazos (London: Routledge, 2023), 101.

30 The Exclaustration Act of 1835, see Stokstad, *Santiago de Compostela in the Age of the Great Pilgrimages*, 162; María Liňeira, 'Santiago de Compostela: Fact and Fetish' in *A Companion to Galician Culture*, ed. Helena Miguélez-Carballeira (Woodbridge: Boydell and Brewer, 2014), 55.

31 Guzmán, 'A Decade of Research', 104; for the text, see János Zádori, *Viaje a España*, ed. A. Pombo Rodríguez (Santiago de Compostela: Xunta de Galicia 2010), 356–77.

32 Pack, 'Revival of the Pilgrimage', 336.

33 Dunn and Davidson, 'Introduction', in *The Pilgrimage to Compostela in the Middle Ages*, xix.

34 Pack, 'Revival of the Pilgrimage', 384.

35 Bartolini (1885), 232, quoted in John Williams, 'The Tomb of St James: Coming to Terms with History and Tradition', in *Culture and Society in Medieval Galicia* (Leiden: Brill, 2015), 552.

36 *Leo XIII's 'Deus Omnipotens' Bull: On the Body of the Apostle Saint James*, Santiago de Compostela: Organizing Committee of the Holy Year, 1953.

37 Pack, 'Revival of the Pilgrimage', 349.

38 Rubén C. Lois-González, Xosé M. Santos and Pilar Taboada-de-Zúñiga Romero, 'The Camino de Santiago de Compostela: the most important historic pilgrimage way in Europe', in *Religious Pilgrimage Routes and Trails,* ed. D. H. Olsen and A. Trono (Wallingford: CABI, 2018), 73–4.

39 Katherine Lee Bates, *Spanish Highways and Byways* (New York: Chautauqua Press, 1905), 394, 424, 426.

40 Paul Preston, *Franco: A Biography* (London: HarperCollins, 1993), 283.

41 Robert Plötz, quoted in Xosé M. Santos, 'The Contemporary

Resurgence of the Pilgrimage to Santiago', in *Religious Pilgrimages in the Mediterranean World*, 115.
42 Pack, 'Revival of the Pilgrimage', 353–4.
43 Guzman, 'A Decade of Research', 115.
44 Liňeira, 'Santiago de Compostela: Fact and Fetish', 59.
45 Quoted in Pack, 'Revival of the Pilgrimage', 353.
46 Lynn Talbot, 'Revival of the Medieval Past: Francisco Franco and the Camino de Santiago', in *The Camino de Santiago in the 21st century: Interdisciplinary Perspectives and Global Views*, ed. Samuel Sánchez y Sánchez and Annie Hesp (London: Routledge, 2016), 46.
47 Liňeira, 'Santiago de Compostela: Fact and Fetish', 64.
48 'Camino de Santiago: la Peregrinación Moderna', https://www.sasua.net/estella/articulo.asp?f=santiago2
49 Anton M. Pazos, 'Recent Research on a Renewed Pilgrimage: The Way of St James in the Nineteenth and Twentieth Centuries', in *Religious Pilgrimages in the Mediterranean World*, 78.
50 Walter Starkie, *Road to Santiago* (New York: E. R. Dutton & Co., 1957), 152–3.
51 Santos, 'The Contemporary Resurgence', 113.
52 Lee Hoinacki, *El Camino: Walking to Santiago de Compostela* (University Park: Pennsylvania State University Press, 1996), 215; Starkie, *Road to Santiago*, 292–3.
53 Hoinacki, *El Camino*, 215.
54 Elías Valiña Sampedro, *Caminos a Compostela* (Vigo: Faro de Vigo, 1971); Elías Valiña Sampedro, *El Camino de Santiago: Guia del Peregrino* (León: Everest, 1985); Talbot, 'Revival of the Medieval Past', 50.
55 My translation, 'Homilia de Juan Pablo II', Santiago de Compostela, 9 Noviember 1982, Vatican, https://www.vatican.va/content/john-paul-ii/es/homilies/1982/documents/hf_jp-ii_hom_19821109_santiago-compostela.html
56 Park Jin-hai, 'G.O.D. Returns with Travel Variety Show', https://www.koreatimes.co.kr/www/art/2024/02/398_256969.html 14 October 2018.
57 Xacopedia: 'Goethe, Johann Wolfgang', https://xacopedia.com/Goethe_Johann_Wolfgang
58 Dante Alighieri, *La Vita Nuova*, trans. Mark Musa (Bloomington: Indiana University Press, 1962), 82.

ACKNOWLEDGEMENTS

Thanks should go first to the two other Catherines – Catherine Fletcher and my agent at Felicity Bryan, Catherine Clarke – for helping me conceive this book in the first place. To Owen Rees for bouncing around ideas and some frankly genius title ideas; Rosamund Oates, Jason Crowley, Gervase Phillips and Catherine Fletcher for reading all or part of the manuscript; Anne Bailey and Philip Booth for all kinds of discussions about pilgrimage by land, sea and air; and George Abram for offering to whip up an excellent cover design, probably involving dinosaurs (he's ten; maybe next time, kiddo).

Several of the ideas on pilgrimage in this book have been tested on engaging audiences at Christ Church College, Oxford; the DeMontfort University, Leicester; the University of Chester; and the Social History Society annual conference at Lancaster University. Some of the most helpful audiences have been the various local history groups I have discussed pilgrimage with over the past decade, as their questions have helped to refine my understanding of what people think pilgrimage is (or should be), the things they find surprising, and given me food for thought.

Heartfelt thanks to Cecily Gayford, my editor at Profile, for her patience in answering questions and shepherding me through, and to Georgina Difford and Jon Petre for help with pulling everything together. Further thanks go to Hugh Davis for the meticulous copy-editing – all remaining errors are, of course, entirely my own.

Biggest thanks and love go, as always, to Andy, Ada and George, for their willingness to tramp around Rome in the heat and, in Andy's case, walk to Santiago and take me to Iona. I couldn't do any of this without them.

BIBLIOGRAPHY

'100,000 Pilgrims Pay Homage at Lourdes', *Irish Weekly and Ulster Examiner* 14 September 1946.

'A Great Moment', *Taranaki Daily News* 25 February 1922.

'A Maori "miracle"', *Auckland Star*, 12 January 1921.

Abu Mikhnaf, *Maqtal al-Husayn*, trans. Hamid Mavani, https://moralsandethics.files.wordpress.com/2007/03/maqtal-by-abu-mikhnaf.pdf

'Adolf Hitler Replaces Częstochowa's Madonna', *Catholic Bulletin of Foreign News*, 26 December 1942.

Adomnán's Life of Columba, ed. and trans. A. O. Anderson and M. O. Anderson, rev. edn, Oxford Medieval Texts (Oxford: Oxford University Press, 1991)

Aghaie, Kamran Scot, *The Martyrs of Karbala; Shi'i Symbols and Rituals in Modern Iran* (Washington DC: University of Washington Press, 2004)

Aicard, Jean, *King of Camargue* (Philadelphia: Georgie Barrie & Son, 1901)

al-Musawi, Muhsin, *Reading Iraq: Culture and Power in Conflict* (London: I.B. Taurus, 2006)

Alper, Alexandra, 'UFO Lovers, light-seekers and lawyers await Maya end of days', *Reuters* 20 December 2012 https://www.reuters.com/article/maya-calendar/ufo-lovers-light-seekers-and-lawyers-await-maya-end-of-days-idUSL1E8NEDID20121220/

al-Qummi, Ibn Qulawayh, *Kamil al-Ziyarat*, trans. Sayyid Mohsen al-Husayni al-Milani (Miami: Shiabook.ca Press, 2008)

al-Rasheed, Madawi, *A History of Saudi Arabia*, 2nd edn (Cambridge: Cambridge University Press, 2010)

al-Sarhan, Saud, 'The Saudis as Managers of the Hajj', in *The Hajj: Pilgrimage in Islam*, ed. E Tagliocozzo and Shawkat M. Toorawa (Cambridge: Cambridge University Press, 2016), 196–212.

'An Arm of Peace for Lourdes', *Tablet* 18 April 1936.

Anda Alanis, Guillermo de, 'Sacrifice and Ritual Mutilation in Postclassical Maya Society: Taphonomy of the Human Remains from Chichén Itza's Cenote Sagrada', in *New Perspectives on Human Sacrifice and Ritual Body Treatments in Ancient Maya Society*, ed. Vera Tiesler and Andrea Cucina (New York: Springer, 2007), 190–208.

Anderson, Matthew R., 'Luther and the Trajectories of Western Pilgrimage', *International Journal of Religious Tourism and Pilgrimage* 7 (2019), 52–61.

Andrews, Anthony P. and Roberta Coletta, 'A Brief History of Underwater Archaeology in the Maya Area', *Ancient MesoAmerica* 6 (1995), 101–17.

'Anger grows as visitors flock to Smith grave', *Independent* 4 June 1995, https://www.independent.co.uk/news/uk/home-news/anger-grows-as-visitors-flock-to-smith-grave-1584918.html

'Angola: Peregrinações movimentam Santuários da Muxima e do Monte', Radio Vaticano, https://www.archivioradiovaticana.va/storico/2017/08/04/angola_peregrina%C3%A7%C3%B5es_movimentam_santu%C3%A1rios_da_muxima_e_do_monte/pt-1328814

'Angola: Profanation du sanctuaire de Muxima', https://www.archivioradiovaticana.va/storico/2013/10/29/angola__profanation_du_sanctuaire_de_muxima/fr2-741908

Angold, Michael, 'Church and Society: Iconoclasm and After', in *A Social History of Byzantium*, ed. John Haldon (Oxford: Wiley Blackwell, 2008), 233–56.

The Annals of Ireland by Friar John Clyn, ed. Richard Butler (Dublin: Irish Archaeological Society, 1849)

The Annals of Tigernach, http://research.ucc.ie/celt/document/T100002A

The Annals of Ulster, http://research.ucc.ie/celt/document/T100001A

Announcements: Native American Rights Fund (Winter, 1979), https://narf.org/nill/documents/nlr/nlr5-1.pdf

Antrim, Zayde, 'Jerusalem in Ayyubid and Mamluk Periods', in *Routledge Handbook on Jerusalem*, ed. Suleiman A. Mourad, Naomi Koltun-Fromm and Bedross Der Matossian (New York: Routledge, 2018), 102–109.

Arcaute, Honório Ruiz de, *Mil cartas a Mamã Muxima* (Luanda: Paulinas, 2010)
Ardern, Traci, 'Empowered children in Classic Maya Sacrificial Rites', *Childhood in the Past* 4 (2011), 133–45.
'Argentina: In Mourning', *Time* 11 August 1952.
'Argentina: Little Eva', *Time* 14 July 1947.
'Argentines Remember Eva Perón – In Pictures', *Guardian* 27 July 2022, https://www.theguardian.com/world/gallery/2022/jul/27/argentina-remembers-eva-peron-evita-in-pictures
Argyll, Duke of, *Iona* (London: Strahan, 1871)
Argyll: an inventory of the monuments, vol. 4: Iona (Edinburgh: The Royal Commission on Ancient and Historical Monuments of Scotland, 1982)
Armanios, Febe, *Coptic Christianity in Ottoman Egypt* (Oxford: Oxford University Press, 2011)
Armstrong, Karen, *The History of Jerusalem* (London: HarperCollins, 1997)
Arnold, Channing and Frederick J. Tabor Frost, *The American Egypt: A Record of Travels in Yucatán* (London: Hutchinson & Co., 1909)
Arnold, David, 'The Ecology and Cosmology of Disease in the Banaras Region', in *Culture and Power in Banaras: Community, Performance and Environment, 1800–1980*, ed. Sandria B. Freitag (Berkeley: University of California Press, 1989), 246–68.
Arnush, Michael, 'Pilgrimage to the Oracle of Apollo at Delphi: Patterns of Public and Private Consultation', in *Pilgrimage in Graeco-Roman and Early Christianity: Seeing the Gods*, ed. Jas Elner and Ian Rutherford (Oxford: Oxford University Press, 2005), 97–110.
Ashley, James R., *The Macedonian Empire: The Era of Warfare Under Philip II and Alexander the Great, 359–323 B.C.* (Jefferson: McFarland & Company, 1998)
Ashmore, Harriette, *Narrative of a Three Months' March in India* (London: R. Hastings, 1841)
Aspinwall, Bernard, 'The formation of a British identity within Scottish Catholicism, 1830–1914', in *Religion and National Identity: Wales and Scotland, c.1700–2000*, ed. Robert Pope (Cardiff: University of Wales Press, 2001), 268–305.
Astafieva, Elena, 'Russian Orthodox Pilgrims in Jerusalem in the Second

Half of the Nineteenth Century: Between the Old City and "New Jerusalem"', *Acta Slavica Iaponica* 40 (2020), 149–68.

'Austria and Germany', *Catholic Standard* 7 September 1934.

Avari, Burjor, *India: The Ancient Past, A History of the Indian Subcontinent from* c.*7000 BC to AD 1200* (London: Routledge, 2007)

Ayoub, Mahmud, 'Shi'i Literature', in *Shi'ism: Doctrines, Thought and Spirituality*, ed. Seyyed Hossein Nasr, Hamid Dabashi and Seyyed Vali Reza Nasr (New York: State University of New York Press, 1988), 312–29.

'Back From Lourdes', *Birmingham Daily Gazette* 4 August 1923.

Badone, Ellen, 'Pilgrimage, Tourism, and the da Vinci Code at Saintes-Maries-de-la-Mer, France', *Culture and Religion* 9 (2008), 23–44.

Badone, Ellen, 'Seduction in the "Gypsy Pilgrimage" at Les Saintes-Maries-de-la-Mer', in *The Seductions of Pilgrimage: Sacred Journeys Afar and Astray in the Western Religious Tradition*, ed. Michael A. Di Giovane and David Picard (London: Routledge, 2016), 169–86.

Baer, Marc David, *Honoured by the Glory of Islam: Conversion and Conquest in Ottoman Europe* (Oxford: Oxford University Press, 2008)

Baigent, Michael, Richard Leigh and Henry Lincoln, *The Holy Blood and the Holy Grail* (London: Jonathan Cape, 1982)

Ballara, Angela, 'Molo, Pita Te Tūruki Tāmati', *Dictionary of New Zealand Biography,* first published in 1998. Te Ara – the Encyclopedia of New Zealand, https://teara.nz/en/biographies/4m56/moko-pita-te-turuki-tamati (accessed 11 January 2024)

Bar, Doron, 'Re-creating Jewish Sanctity in Jerusalem: Mount Zion and David's Tomb, 1948–67', *Journal of Israeli History* 23 (2004), 260–78.

Bar, Gideon, 'Reconstructing the Past: the Creation of Jewish Sacred Space in the State of Israel', *Israel Studies* 13 (2008), 1–21.

Barak, Guy, 'Between Istanbul and Gujarat: Descriptions of Mecca in the Sixteenth-Century Indian Ocean', *Murqarnas* 34 (2017), 287–320.

Barnai, Jacob, *The Jews in Palestine in the Eighteenth Century*, trans. Naomi Goldblum (Tuscaloosa: University of Alabama Press, 1992)

Baroncelli-Javon, Falco de, *Les Bohémiens des Saintes-Maries-de-la-Mer* (Paris: Lemerre, 1910)

Bartlett, W.B., *King Cnut and the Viking Conquest of England* (Stroud: Amberley, 2016)

Bates, Katherine Lee, *Spanish Highways and Byways* (New York: Chautauqua Press, 1905)

Bayly, Christopher, 'From Ritual to Ceremony: Death, Ritual and Society in North India since 1600', in *Mirrors of Mortality: Studies in the Social History of Death*, ed. J. Whaley (London: Europa Publications, 1981), 154–86.

Becker, Annette, *War and Faith: The Religious Imagination in France, 1914–1930*, trans. Helen McPhail (Oxford: Berg, 1998)

Bede, '*Lives of the Abbots of Wearmouth and Jarrow*', in *The Age of Bede*, ed. and trans. D. H. Farmer (Harmondsworth: Penguin, 1965), 185–208.

Bede, *The Ecclesiastical History of the English People* (Oxford: Oxford University Press, 1999)

Bede's Ecclesiastical History of the English People, ed. Bartram Colgrave and R. A. B. Mynors (Oxford: Clarendon Press, 1969)

Ben-Bassat, Yuval and Johann Buessow, 'Ottoman Jerusalem, 1517–1918', in *Routledge Handbook on Jerusalem*, ed. Suleiman A. Mourad, Naomi Koltun-Fromm and Bedross Der Matossian (New York: Routledge, 2018), 113–21.

Bender, Gerald J., *Angola Under the Portuguese: the Myth and the Reality* (Berkeley: University of California Press, 1978)

Benedictow, Ole J., *The Black Death, 1346–1353: The Complete History* (Woodbridge: Boydell, 2004), 35–215.

Bergaglio, Sophie, *L'Histoire du Pèlerinage des Saintes-Maries-de-la-Mer* (Aix-en-Provence: Édition des Lilas, 2016)

Bernbaum, Edwin, *Sacred Mountains of the World*, 2nd edn (Cambridge: Cambridge University Press, 2022)

Bialer, Uri, *Cross on the Star of David: The Christian World in Israel's Foreign Policy, 1948–1967* (Bloomington: Indiana University Press, 2005)

Bianchi, Robert R., *Guests of God: Pilgrimage and Politics in the Islamic World* (Oxford: Oxford University Press, 2004)

Bianchi, Susana, 'Catolicismo y peronismo: La religion como campo de conflicto (Argentina, 1945–1955)', *Boletin Americanista* 44 (1994), 25–37.

Bingenheimer, Marcus, 'Pilgrimage in China', in *New Pathways in Pilgrimage Studies*, ed. Dionigi Albera and John Eade (London: Routledge, 2016), 18–35.

Bingley, A. H., *Handbook for the Indian Army: Sikhs* (Simla: Government Central Printing Office, 1899)

Birmingham, David, 'Is "Nationalism" a Feature of Angola's Cultural Identity?', in *Sure Road? Nationalisms in Angola, Guinea-Bissau and Mozambique*, ed. Eric Morier-Genoud (Leiden: Brill, 2004), 217–30.

Birmingham, David, 'Angola 2006: a British Parliamentary Visit', *Lusotopie* xvi (2009), 221–43.

Birmingham, David, *Empire in Africa: Angola and Its Neighbours* (Athens: Ohio University Press, 2006)

Birmingham, David, *Portugal and Africa* (New York: Palgrave MacMillan, 1999)

Black Elk, Charlotte, 'A Song from Sacred Mountain: Lakota-Dakota and Cheyenne Interviews', in *Readings in American Indian Law: Recalling the Rhythm of Survival,* ed. Jo Carillo (Philadelphia: Temple University Press, 1998), 105–07.

'Black Hills News', *Bismark Tribune* 9 July 1877.

Blennow, Anna and Stefano Fogelberg Rota, 'Introduction', in *Rome and the Guidebook Tradition: From the Middle Ages to the 20th Century*, ed. Anna Blennow and Stefano Fogelberg Rota (Berlin: De Gruyter, 2019), 2–32.

Blish, Helen H., with Amos Bad Heart Bull and Mari Sandoz, *A Pictographic History of the Oglala Sioux* (Lincoln: University of Nebraska Press, 1967)

Blondin, Jill E., 'Power Made Visible: Pope Sixtus IV as "Urbis Restaurateur" in Quattrocento Rome', *Catholic Historical Review* 91 (2005), 1–25.

Boas, Adrian J., 'The Crusader Period', in *Routledge Handbook on Jerusalem*, ed. Suleiman A. Mourad, Naomi Koltun-Fromm and Bedross Der Matossian (New York: Routledge, 2018), 90–101.

Bohner, Alfred, *Two on a Pilgrimage: The 88 Holy Places of Shikoku*, trans. Katharine Merrill, ed. David C. Moreton (Frankfurt: E & H Verlag, 2011)

Bokencamp, Stephen, 'Record of the Feng and Shan Sacrifices', in *Religions of China in Practice*, ed. Donald S. Lopez Jr (Princeton: Princeton University Press, 1996), 254–60.

Bonnechere, Pierre 'Divination', in *A Companion to Greek Religion*, ed. Daniel Ogden (Oxford: Blackwell, 2010), 145–60.

The Book of Margery Kempe, trans. Anthony Bale (Oxford: Oxford University Press, 2015)

The Book of Pontiffs (Liber Pontificalis): the Ancient Biographies of the First Ninety Roman Bishops to AD 715, trans. Raymond Davis (Liverpool: Liverpool University Press, 1989)

Bordigoni, Marc, 'Le pèlerinage de Saintes-Maries-de-la-Mer: De la fête votive au pèlerinage des Gitans XIXe–XXe siècles', in *Les Fêtes en Provence Autrefois et Aujourd'hui*, ed. Régis Bertrand and Laurent-Sébastien Fournier (Aix-en-Provence: Presses Universitaires de Provence, 2014), 151–61.

Bordigoni, Marc, 'Sara aux Saintes-Maries-de-la-Mer. Métaphore de la présence gitane dans le «monde des Gadjé»', *Etudes Tsiganes*, 20 (2005), 12–34.

Bosworth, R. J. B., *Whispering City: Rome and Its Histories* (New Haven: Yale University Press, 2011)

Bowden, Hugh, 'Delphi: Historical Overview', in *Oxford Encyclopedia of Ancient Greece and Rome Vol. 1*, ed. Michael Gagarin (Oxford: Oxford University Press, 2009), 382–4.

Bowden, Hugh, *Classical Athens and the Delphic Oracle: Divination and Democracy* (Cambridge: Cambridge University Press, 2005)

Bradley, Ian, *Argyll: the Making of a Spiritual Landscape* (Edinburgh: St Andrew Press, 2015)

Bradley, Ian, *Pilgrimage: A Spiritual and Cultural Journey* (Oxford: Lion Hudson, 2009)

Brásio, António, *Spiritana Monumenta Historica*: *Angola*, 5 vols (Pittsburgh: Duquesne University Press, 1966)

Bray, Kingsley M., *Crazy Horse: a Lakota Life* (Norman: University of Nebraska Press, 2006)

Brennan, Brian, 'Visiting "Peter in Chains": French Pilgrimage to Rome, 1873–1893', *Journal of Ecclesiastical History* 51 (2000), 741–65.

Brockman, Norbert D., 'Marian Pilgrimage and Shrines', *Marian Studies* 51 (2000), 96–111.

Brown, Dan, *The Da Vinci Code* (London: Transworld, 2013)

Brown, Marilyn, *Gypsies and Other Bohemians: the Myth of the Artist in Nineteenth Century France* (Ann Arbor: UMI Research Press, 1985)

Brown, Vinson, *Voices of Earth and Sky: Vision Search of the Native Americans* (Happy Camp: Naturegraph, 1976)

Bucks, Jonathan, 'The Hajj Crush: "It was the closest thing to hell on earth"',

Guardian 23 December 2015, https://www.theguardian.com/news/2015/dec/23/hajj-crush-pilgrimage-mecca-stampede-saudi-arabia-mina-valley#:~:text=Alone%20and%20unable%20to%20speak,thing%20to%20hell%20on%20earth.%E2%80%9D

The Buildings of Procopius, ed. and trans. H. B. Dewing, Loeb Classical Library (Cambridge, MA: Harvard University Press, 1940)

Burton, Keith Augustus, *The Blessing of Africa: The Bible and African Christianity* (Downers Grove, IL: IVP Academic, 2007)

Butterworth, G. V., 'A Rural Māori Renaissance? Mabāori Society and Politics 1920 to 1951', *Journal of Polynesian Society* 81 (1972), 160–95.

Cadornega, Antonio de Oliveira de, *História geral das guerras Angolanas* (Lisbon: Agência-Geral do Ultramar, 1972)

Calendar of Scottish Supplications to Rome, 1425–1428, ed. Annie I. Dunlop (Edinburgh: T & A Constable, Ltd, 1956)

'Camino de Santiago: la Peregrinación Moderna', 27 July 2017, https://www.sasua.net/estella/articulo.asp?f=santiago2

'Camiño di Shikoku', https://museoperegrinacions.xunta.gal/gl/exposicions/camino-de-shikoku

Camm, Dom Bede, 'A Soldier's Pilgrimage to Jerusalem', *Downside Review* (1919), 17–38.

Campbell, Ewan and Adrian Maldonado, 'A New Jerusalem "at the end of the Earth": Interpreting Charles Thomas's Excavations at Iona Abbey, 1956–63', *Antiquaries Journal* 100 (2020), 33–85.

Can, Lâle, *Spiritual Subjects: Central Asian Pilgrims and the Ottoman Hajj at the End of Empire* (Redwood City: Stanford University Press, 2020)

Canmore: National Record of the Historic Environment, https://canmore.org.uk/collection/377992

Carlson, J. B., 'Pilgrimage and the Equinox: Serpent of Light and Shadow Phenomenon at the Castillo, Chichén Itzá, Yucatán' *Astroastronomy* (1999), 136–52.

Carr, Annemarie Weyl, 'Pilgrimage to Constantinople', in *Cambridge Companion to Constantinople*, ed. Sarah Bassett (Cambridge: Cambridge University Press, 2022), 310–23.

Carr, Annemarie Weyl, 'Threads of Authority: The Virgin Mary's Veil in the Middle Ages', in *Robes and Honor: The Medieval World of Investiture*, ed. Stewart Gordon (Basingstoke: Palgrave, 2001), 59–94.

Carson, John B., 'Pilgrimage and the Equinox "Serpent of Light and Shadow" Phenomenon at the Castillo, Chichen Itza', *Archeoastronomy: the Journal of Astronomy and Culture* xiv (1999), 136–52.

Cartright, Garth, 'Partying with the Gypsies in the Camargue', *Guardian* 26 March 2011 https://www.theguardian.com/travel/2011/mar/26/saintes-maires-gypsy-festival-camargue

Cassels, Nancy Gardner, *Religion and Pilgrim Tax under the Company Raj* (Riverdale, MD: Riverdale Company, 1988)

Castelao, Ofelia Rey, 'Visiting the Apostle Santiago: Pilgrimages to Santiago de Compostela in the 16th to 19th centuries', in *Relics, Shrines and Pilgrimages: Sanctity in Europe from Late Antiquity*, ed. Antón M. Pazos (London: Routledge, 2020), 92–108.

'Catholic Pilgrimage to Iona', *Evening Telegraph (Dundee),* 11 May 1888.

Causse, Pierre, 'Le pèlerinage des Saintes-Maries: hier et aujourd'hui', *Monde Gitan* 83 (1992), 33–42.

Causse, Pierre, 'Les Saintes-Maries-de-la-Mer', *La Roulette* 49 (1999), http://gitanseneglise.org/cultures-tsiganes.org/st_maries/deux_maries/deux_maries_p1.htm

Causse, Pierre, 'Un quart de siècle aux Saintes-Maries-de-la-Mer', *Monde Gitan* 46 (1978), 1–9.

Cavazzi, Giovanni, *Descrição histórica dos três reinos Congo, Angola e Matamba,* ed. and trans. Graziano Saccardo, 2 vols (Lisbon: Agência Geral do Ultramar, 1965)

Cepero, Iliana, 'Photographic Propaganda under Peronism, 1946–55: Selections from the Archivo General de la Nación Argentina', *History of Photography* 40 (2016), 193–214.

Chang, Michael G., *A Court on Horseback: Imperial Touring & the Construction of Qing Rule, 1680–1785* (Cambridge, MA: Harvard University Press, 2007)

Charles, Freeman, *Holy Bones, Holy Dust: How Relics Shaped the History of Medieval Europe (*New Haven: Yale University Press, 2011)

Chaterjee, Chhanda, *The Sikh Minority and the Participation of the Punjab 1920–1947* (London: Routledge, 2010)

Chavannes, Édouard, *Le T'ai Chan: Essai de Monographie d'un Culte Chinois* (Paris: Ernest Leroux, 1910)

Chhabra, G. S., *Advanced Study in History of the Punjab, Vol. 1 (1469–1799)*

Guru and Post-Guru Period Up to Ranjit Singh (Jullundur City: New Academic Publishing Co., 1971)

'China Bans Haj for Muslims Who Fail Patriotism Test', *The Times* 14 October 2020.

Christafis, Angelique, 'Tourism miracle has turned water into profits', *Guardian* 9 February 2008, https://www.theguardian.com/world/2008/feb/09/france.catholicism

Christian, Jessica and Charles Stiller, *Iona Portrayed: The Island through Artists' Eyes, 1760–1960* (Inverness: New Iona Press, 2000)

The Chronicle of Adam of Usk, 1377–1421, ed. and trans. C. Given-Wilson (Oxford: Clarendon Press, 1997)

Clark, Eleanor, *Rome and a Villa* (New York: Harper Collins, 1992)

Clements, John, *The First Emperor of China* (Stroud: Sutton, 2006)

Clendinnen, Inga, *Ambivalent Conquests: Maya and Spaniard in Yucatán, 1517–1570* (Cambridge: Cambridge University Press, 2003)

Coggins, Clemency Chase, *Cenote of Sacrifice: Maya Treasures from the Second Well at Chichén Itzá* (Austin: University of Texas Press, 1984)

Coghe, Samuel, *Population Politics in the Tropics: Demography, Health and Transimperialism in Colonial Angola* (Cambridge: Cambridge University Press, 2022)

Cohen-Hattab, Kobi, 'Religion and Nationalism in Jewish Pilgrimage and Holy Sites: the Western Wall and Rachel's Tomb as Case Studies', in *Religious Pilgrimage in the Mediterranean World*, ed. Antón M. Pazos (London: Routledge, 2023), 128–44.

Cole, Juan R. I. and Moojan Momen, 'Mafia, Mob and Shiism in Iraq: the Rebellion of Ottoman Karbala, 1842–1842', *Past & Present* 112 (1986), 112–43.

Cole, Juan, *Sacred Space and Holy War: The Politics, Culture and History of Shi'ite Islam* (London: I.B. Taurus, 2001)

Coleman, Simon and John Elsner, *Pilgrimage: Past and Present in World Religions* (Cambridge, MA: Harvard University Press, 1995)

'Commemorating Eva Peron', *Sphere* 2 August 1953.

Commons Chamber Debate, *Hansard* 10 March 1936, https://hansard.parliament.uk/Commons/1936-03-10/debates/53284081-d17f-4ee2-870a-8f6dfofodea5/CommonsChamber

Commons Chamber, *Hansard* Monday 20 February 1854, https://hansard.

parliament.uk/Commons/1854-02-20/debates/53ea0417-76e2-4398-84ae-c76403510d80/CommonsChamber

Condliffe, John Bell, *Te Rangi Hiroa: the Life of Sir Peter Buck* (Melbourne: Whitcombe and Tombs, 1971)

Connelly, Joan Breton, *Portrait of a Priestess: Women and Ritual in Ancient Greece* (Princeton: Princeton University Press, 2007)

Consul du Verge, *Reports from the Consuls of the United States on the Commerce, Manufactures, Etc., No 31, July 1883* (Washington: Government Printing Office, 1883)

Cornelius Nepos, trans. John C. Wolfe (Cambridge, MA: Harvard University Press, 1984)

Courrier, F., 'Le mystère de Sara la noire', *Monde Gitan* 2 (1967), 4–6.

Cox, Lindsay, *Kotahitanga: the Search for Māori Political Unity* (Auckland, NZ: Oxford University Press, 1993)

'Cripples Left Crutches with Ratana', *Pix* 26 August 1926.

Curne, M. de La, 'Mémoire concernant la vie de Jean de Venette, avec la Notice de l'Histoire en vers des Trois Maries, dont il est l'auteur', in *Mémoires de Littérature, tirez des registres de L'Academie Royale des Inscriptions et Belles Lettres, Vol. 13* (Paris: De L'Imprimerie Royale, 1740), 520–33.

Curran, J., *Pagan City and Christian Capital: Rome in the Fourth Century* (Oxford: Clarendon Press, 2000)

Daftary, Farhad, *The Ismāʿilis: their History and Doctrines* (Cambridge: Cambridge University Press, 2007)

Dahlan, Malik, *The Hijaz: the First Islamic State* (Oxford: Oxford University Press, 2018)

Dante Alighieri, *La Vita Nuova*, trans. Mark Musa (Bloomington: Indiana University Press, 1962)

Darian, Steven G., *The Ganges in Myth and History* (Delhi: Motilal Banarsidass Publishers, 1978)

Davidson, John, *A Treasury of Mystic Terms: Part III, Spiritual Experience & Practice* (New Delhi: Science of the Soul Research Centre, 2019)

Davidson, Linda K. and David Gitlitz, *Pilgrimage From Ganges to Graceland, An Encyclopedia*, vol. 1 (Santa Barbara; ABC-CLIO, 2002)

de Bres, Pieter H., 'Religion in the Atene: Religious Associations and the Urban Maori', *Memoirs of the Polynesian Society* 37 (1971), 1–50.

de Bres, Pieter H., 'The contribution of Māori Religious Movements to Religion in New Zealand', *Exchange* 8 (1979), 1–36.
Debasa, Ana María Carballeira, 'The Pilgrims' way of St James and Islam: Pilgrimage, Politics and Militias', in *Pilgrims and Politics: Rediscovering the Power of the Pilgrimage*, ed. Antón M. Pazos (London: Routledge, 2012), 9–28.
'Découvrez Les Saintes-Maries-de-la-Mer', https://www.camargue.fr/villes-villages/les-saintes-maries-de-la-mer
Dehejia, Vidya, *Art of the Imperial Cholas* (New York: Columbia University Press, 1990)
Denig, Edwin, *Five Indian Tribes of the Upper Missouri: Sioux, Aricharas, Assiniboines, Crees, Crows* (Norman: University of Oklahoma Press, 1854, repr. 1961)
Derlon, Pierre, *Secrets of the Gypsies* (New York: Ballantine Books, 1977)
di Varthema, Ludovico, *The Travels of Ludovico di Varthema* (London, The Hakluyt Society, 2022)
Diffie, Bailier Wallys and George D. Winius, *Foundations of the Portuguese Empire, 1415–1580* (Minneapolis: University of Minnesota, 1977)
Dillon, Matthew, *Pilgrims and Pilgrimage in Ancient Greece* (Abingdon: Routledge, 1997)
Diodorus Siculus, *Library of History* 16.26, https://www.perseus.tufts.edu/hopper/text?doc=Diod.%2016.26&lang=original
Disk G, A.D. 800–900. Mexico, Yucatán, Chichén Itzá, Sacred Cenote. Maya. Gold, 24 x 20 x 0.1 cm (9 7/16 x 7 7/8 x 1/16 in.). Peabody Museum of Archaeology and Ethnology, Harvard University (10-71-20/C10067)
Dodge, Richard I., *The Black Hills* (New York: James Miller, 1875)
Domingues da Silva, Daniel B., *The Atlantic Slave Trade from West Central Africa, 1780–1867* (Cambridge: Cambridge University Press, 2017)
Sarojini Naidu: Great Women of Modern India, ed. Verinder Grover and Ranjana Arora (New Delhi: Deep & Deep Publications, 1993)
Dott, Brian R., *Identity Reflections: Pilgrimages to Mount Tai in Late Imperial China* (Cambridge, MA: Harvard University Press, 2004)
Dregni, M., *Gypsy Jazz: In Search of Django Reinhardt and Gypsy Swing* (New York: Oxford University Press, 2008)
Drummond, James, 'Notice of One of the Supposed Burial Places of St

Columba', in *Proceedings of the Society of Antiquaries of Scotland* 10 (1870–72), 613–17.

Duff, Michelle, *Jacinda Ardern: the Full Story of an Extraordinary Prime Minister* (Sydney: Allen & Unwin, 2023)

Duggan, Christopher, 'Political Cults in Liberal Italy, 1861–1922', in *The Cult of the Duce: Mussolini and the Italians,* ed. Stephen Gundle, Christopher Duggan and Giuliana Peri (Manchester: Manchester University Press, 2013), 11–26.

Dunlop, Anne, 'Pinturicchio and the Pilgrims: Devotion and the Past at Santa Maria Del Popolo', *Papers of the British School at Rome* 71 (2003), 259–85.

Dunn, Maryjane and Linda Kay Davidson, 'Introduction: Bibliography of the Pilgrimage: the State of the Art', in *The Pilgrimage to Compostela in the Middle Ages: A Book of Essays*, ed. Maryjane Dunn and Linda Kay Davidson (London: Routledge, 1996), xxiii–xlviii.

Dunning, Nicholas P., 'Life and Death from the Watery Underworld: ancient Maya interaction with caves and cenotes', in *Sacred Waters: A Cross-Cultural Compendium of Hallowed Springs and Holy Wells*, ed. Celeste Ray (London: Routledge, 2020), 50–58.

E. O'L. 'A Pilgrim's Notes of the Irish National Pilgrimage to Rome: October, 1908', *Irish Monthly* 37 (1909), 127–45.

Eade, John, 'Healing Social and Physical Bodies: Lourdes and Military Pilgrimage', in *Military Pilgrimage and Battlefield Tourism: Commemorating the Dead*, ed. John Eade and Mario Katič (Abingdon: Routledge, 2018), 15–33.

Eade, John, 'Parish and Pilgrimage in a Changing Europe', in *Migration, Transnationalism and Catholicism: Global Perspectives*, ed. Dominic Pasure and Marta Bivand Erdal (London: Palgrave, 2016), 75–92.

Eaton, R. M., 'From Bidar to Timbuktu: views from the edge of the 15th century Muslim world', *Medieval History Journal* 14 (2011), 1–20.

The Ecclesiastical History of Orderic Vitalis, ed. and trans. Marjorie J. Chibnall, 6 vols (Oxford: Clarendon Press, 1969–80)

Echo-Hawk, Walter R., 'Native American Religious Liberty: Five Hundred Years after Columbus', *American Indian Culture and Research Journal* 17 (1993), 33–52.

Eck, Diana L., *Banaras: City of Light* (New York: Alfred A. Knopf, 1982)

Ediger, Donald, *The Well of Sacrifice* (New York: Doubleday, 1971)
'Editorial: Pilgrimage to Ratana Pa', *Otago Daily Times* 26 January 2023.
Edmonson, Munro S., trans., *The Ancient Future of the Itza: The Book of Chilam Balam of Tizimin* (Houston: University of Texas Press, 1982)
Efthmiadis, Stephanos and Vincent Déroche, 'Greek Hagiography in Late Antiquity (Fourth–Seventh Century)', in *The Ashgate Research Companion to Byzantine Hagiography, Volume 1: Periods and Places,* ed. Stephanos Efthymiadis (London: Routledge, 2011), 35–94.
Ehrlich, L. and S. Gayol, 'Las vias post mortem de Eva Peron: cuerpo, ausencia y biographias en las revistas de masas de Argentina', *Historia Critica*, 70 (2018), 111–31.
El Chronicon Iriense, ed. Manuel Rubén Garcío Álvarez (Madrid, 1963)
Elad, Amikan, *Medieval Jerusalem and Islamic Worship: Holy Places, Ceremonies, Pilgrimage* (Leiden Brill, 1999)
Elliott, Mark C., 'Introduction: the Qianlong Emperor and His Age', in *The Emperor's Private Paradise: Treasures from the Forbidden City*, ed. Nancy Berliner (New Haven: Yale University Press, 2010), 32–45.
Elliott, Mark C., *Emperor Qianlong: Son of Heaven, Man of the World* (London: Longman, 2009)
Emery, Elizabeth, 'Modern Medieval Pilgrimages: The Nineteenth-Century Struggle for Lourdes', *Years' Work in Medievalism*, XV (1999), 149–68.
Encyclopaedia Iranica, ed. Ehsan Yarshater, vol. 12 (London: Routledge, 1982)
Engels, Christoph, *1000 Sacred Places: the World's Most Extraordinary Spiritual Sites* (Köln: H. F. Ullman, 2010)
Erdoes, Richard, *Lame Deer: Seeker of Visions* (New York: Pocket Books, 1994)
Eusebius, *Life of Constantine*, trans. and commentary by A. Cameron and S. G. Hall (Oxford: Clarendon Press, 1999)
Farahani, Mirza Mohammad Hosayn, *A Shi'ite Pilgrimage to Mecca, 1885–86*, ed. and trans Hafez Farmayan and Elton L. Daniel (Austin: University of Texas Press, 1990)
Faugère, Annie, 'Le Pèlerinage de Hans von Waltheym en l'an 1474', *Provence Historique* 166 (1991), 465–91.
Feldman, Jack, 'La circulation de la Tora. Les pèlerinages au second Temple', in *La société Juive à travers l'histoire*, ed. Shmuel Trigano, 4 vols (Paris: Fayard, 1993), iv, 161–78.

Felix Fabri (circa 1480–1483 A.D.), Vol. I, Part I, trans. Aubrey Stewart (London: Palestine Pilgrims' Text Society, 1896)

Ferguson, Ron, *George MacLeod: Founder of the Iona Community* (Glasgow: Wild Goose Publications, 1990)

Fernandes, Odílio, 'Os azares de nossa Senhora da Muxima: Um percurso de trocas, movimenta ções milagrosas e intolerância', *Economica Informal*, 14 (2014), 41–57.

Ferreiro, Alberto, 'The Cult of Saints and Divine Patronage in Gallaecia before Santiago', in *The Pilgrimage to Compostela in the Middle Ages: A Book of Essays*, ed. Linda K. Davidson and Maryjane Dunn (London: Routledge, 2012), 3–22.

Festival Sermons of Martin Luther: The Church Postils, trans. Joel R. Baseley (Dearborn, MI: Mark V Publications, 2005)

Figueiredo, João, 'The uncanniness of religious encounters in colonial Angola: A brief cultural history of the awkward emotion (18th and 19th centuries)', *Nordic Journal of Africa Studies* 29 (2020), 1–26.

Fischer, M. J., *Iran: From Religious Dispute to Revolution* (Cambridge, MA: Harvard University Press, 2003)

FitzPatrick, Matthew P., *The Kaiser and the Colonies: Monarchy in the Age of Empire* (Oxford: Oxford University Press, 2022)

Flavius Josephus, Translation and Commentary: Volume 1b, Judean War 2, ed. Steve Mason (Leiden: Brill, 2008)

Fleming, K. E., 'Constantinople: From Christianity to Islam', *Classical World*, 97 (2003), 69–78.

Fletcher, Catherine, *The Beauty and the Terror* (Oxford: Oxford University Press, 2020)

Fletcher, R. A., *St James's Catapult: The Life and Times of Diego Gelmírez of Santiago de Compostela* (Oxford: Oxford University Press, 1984)

Fontenrose, Joseph, *The Delphic Oracle: Its Responses and Operations* (Berkeley: University of California Press, 1978)

Forbes-Boyte, K., 'Respecting Sacred Perspectives: the Lakotas, Bear Butte, and Land Management Strategies', *Public Historian*, 18.4 (1996), 99–117.

Forbes-Boyte, K, 'Indigenous People, Land, and Space: the effects of law on sacred place, the Bear Butte example', unpublished PhD thesis, University of Nebraska-Lincoln (1997)

Forbes-Boyte, K., 'Litigation, Mitigation, and American Indian Religious

Freedom Act: The Bear Butte Example', *Great Plains Quarterly* (1999), 23–34.
Four Japanese Travel Diaries of the Middle Ages, trans. Herbert Plutschow and Hideichi Fukuda (Ithaca, NY: Cornell University, 1981)
François, Bernard, Esther M. Sternberg and Elizabeth Fee, 'The Lourdes Medical Cures Revisited', *Journal of the History of Medicine and Allied Sciences*, 69 (2012), 135–62.
Fraser, Angus, *The Gypsies* (London: Wiley, 1995)
Fraser, James E., *From Caledonia to Pictland: Scotland to 795* (Edinburgh: Edinburgh University Press, 2009)
Freed, Ruth A. and Stanley A. Freed, *Rites of Passage of the Shanti Nagar* (New York: American Museum of Natural History, 1980)
Fromont, Cecile, *The Art of Conversion: Christian Visual Culture in the Kingdom of Congo* (University of North Carolina Press, 2014)
Fulcher of Chartres, *Chronicle of the First Crusade,* trans. Martha Evelyn McGinty (Philadelphia: University of Pennsylvania Press, 1941)
Furtado, Santos, 'Uma imagem de Santo António em Angola (Santo António da Muxima): Breve estudo e apontamentos,' *Boletim do Instituto de Angola,* 14 (July–December 1960), 41–51.
'Further Afield: Ratana in Morrinsville', *Evening Post*, 2 April 1921.
Gabashvili, Timothy, *Pilgrimage to Mount Athos, Constantinople, and Jerusalem, 1755–1759*, trans. Mzia Ebanoidze and John Wilkinson (London: Routledge, 2013)
García, Ismael Arturo Montero, 'Astronomy, Architecture and Caverns', in *The Role of Archeoastronomy in the Maya World: the Case Study of the Island of Cozumel* (Mexico City: UNESCO, 2020), 85–109
Garett, John, *Footsteps in the Sea: Christianity in Oceania to World War II* (Suva: Fiji Institute of Pacific Studies, 1992)
Garrigou-Kampton, Emilie, 'Suffering and Healing in the late nineteenth century: medical case studies from the Lourdes sanctuary', *Modern & Contemporary France*, 28 (2020), 442–55.
The Geography of Strabo, trans. Horace Leonard Jones (Cambridge, MA: Harvard University Press, 1927)
Gill, Joseph, *The Council of Florence* (Cambridge: University of Cambridge Press, 1959)
Glass, Robert, 'Filarete's Renovation of the Porta Argentea at Old Saint

Peter's', in *Old St Peter's Rome*, ed. R. McKitterick, J. Osborne, C. M. Richardson and J. Story (Cambridge: Cambridge University Press, 2013), 349–52.

Glynn, Paul, *Healing Fire of Christ: Reflections on Modern Miracles – Knock, Lourdes, Fatima* (San Francisco, Ignatius Press, 2003)

Goldfrank, David, 'The Holy Sepulcher and the Origin of the Crimean War', in *The Military and Society in Russia, 1450–1917*, ed. Eric Lohr and Marshall Poe (Leiden: Brill, 2002), 491–505.

Goldhill, Simon, 'Jerusalem', in *Cities of God: the Bible and Archaeology in Nineteenth Century Britain*, ed. David Gange and Michael Ledger-Lomas (Cambridge: Cambridge University Press, 2013), 71–110.

Gomez, Michael A., *African Dominion: A New History of Empire in Early and Medieval West Africa* (Princeton: Princeton University Press, 2018)

Gonzalez, Mario, 'The Black Hills: the Sacred Land of the Lakota and Tsitsistas', in *Native American Voices: A Reader*, 3rd edn, ed. Susan Lobo, Steve Talbot and Traci L. Morris (London: Routledge, 2016), 113–19.

Goossaert, Vincent, 'Taishan', in *Encyclopedia of Taoism, I–II*, ed. Fabrizio Pregadio (London: Routledge, 2008), 947.

Grabar, Oleg, 'Islamic Jerusalem under Muslim Rule', in *The City in the Islamic World, Vol. 2* (Leiden: Brill, 2008), 317–28.

Graham, B., and M. Murray, 'The Spiritual and the Profane: the pilgrimage to Santiago de Compostela', *Ecumene*, 4 (1997), 389–409.

Graham, Susan, 'Justinian and the Politics of Space', in *Constructions of Space II: The Biblical City and Other Imagined Spaces*, ed. Jon L. Berquist and Claudia V. Camp (New York: T. & T. Clark, 2008), 53–77.

Gravin A., 'B. P. Mansurov and the creation of the Russian Palestine (1857–1864)', *Tambov University Review: Series Humanities* (2019), no pagination.

The Great Tang Dynasty Record of the Western Regions, trans. Li Rongxi (Ann Arbor: University of Michigan Press, 1996)

Gregorious, Ferdinand, *History of the City of Rome in the Middle Ages, Vol. V, Part II*, trans. Annie Hamilton (London: George Bell, 1906)

Grenier, Katherine Haldane, '"Awakening the echoes of the ancient faith"': the National Pilgrimages to Iona', *Northern Scotland* 12 (2021), 132–54.

Grewal, J. S., *The Sikhs: Ideology, Institutions, and Identity* (Oxford: Oxford University Press, 2009)

Guide-Book to Jerusalem (Circ. A.D. 1350), trans. J. H. Bernard (London: Palestine Pilgrims' Text Society, 1894)
Gunther of Pairis, *The Capture of Constantinople: the 'Hystoria Constantinopolitana' of Gunther of Pairis*, ed. and trans. Alfred J. Andrea (Philadelphia: University of Pennsylvania Press, 1997)
Guy, Donna J., 'Life and the Commodification of Death in Argentina: Juan and Eva Peron', in *Death, Dismemberment, and Memory: Body Politics in Latin America*, ed. Lyman L. Johnson (Albuquerque: University of New Mexico Press, 2004), 245–72.
Guy, Donna J., *Creating Charismatic Bonds in Argentina: Letters to Juan and Eva Peron* (Albuquerque: University of New Mexico Press, 2016)
Guzman, Diego de, *Le peregrinacion a Santiago de Diego de Guzman: diario ineditio de 1610*, ed. and trans. Julio Vazque Castro (Santiago de Compostela: Xunta de Galicia, 2014)
Guzmán, Miguel Taín, 'A Decade of Research', in *Religious Pilgrimages in the Mediterranean World*, ed. Antón M. Pazos (London: Routledge, 2023), 89–112.
Guzmán, Miguel Taín, *A Medici Pilgrimage: The Devotional Journal of Cosimo III to Santiago de Compostela (1669)* (Turnhout: Brepols, 2019)
Gwynn, David M., 'The Council of Chalcedon and the Definition of Christian Tradition', in *Chalcedon in Context: Church Councils, 400–700*, ed. Richard Price and Mary Whitby (Liverpool: Liverpool University Press, 2009), 7–26.
'Hajj in the shadow of coronavirus', *Aljazeera* 30 July 2020, https://www.aljazeera.com/gallery/2020/7/30/in-pictures-hajj-in-the-shadow-of-coronavirus
Hall, Linda B., 'Evita and Maria: Religious Reverence and Political Resonance in Argentina', in *Mary, Mother, and Warrior: the Virgin in Spain and the Americas*, ed. Linda B. Hall (Austin: University of Texas Press, 2004), 207–42.
Halloran, William F., *The Life and Letters of William Sharpe and 'Fiona MacLeod' Volume 1: 1855–1894* (Cambridge: Open Book Publishers, 2018)
Hämäläinen, Pekka, 'Reconstructing the Great Plains: The Long Struggle for Sovereignty and Dominance in the Heart of the Continent', *Journal of the Civil War Era* 6 (2016), 481–509.

Hämäläinen, Pekka, 'The Rise and Fall of Plains Indian Horse Cultures', *Journal of American History*, Vol. 90, 3 (2003), 833–86.
Harjo, S. S., 'It began with a vision in a sacred place', in *Past, Present, and Future: Challenges of the National Museum of the American Indian*, ed. NMAI (Washington DC: Smithsonian Institution, 2007), 25–52.
Harris, Ruth, *Lourdes: Body and Spirit in the Secular Age* (London: Viking, 1999)
Harrist, Robert E., *The Landscape of Words: Stone Inscriptions from Early and Medieval China* (Seattle: University of Washington Press, 2008)
Harvey, George Rowntree, 'Iona is the soul of Scotland', *Aberdeen Press and Journal*, 15 June 1949, 2.
Haskins, Charles H., 'A Canterbury Monk at Constantinople', *English Historical Review*, 25 (1910), 293–5.
Hastings, Adrian, *The Church in Africa: 1450–1950* (Oxford: Clarendon Press, 1994)
Hawkins, Ruth A., *Unbelievable Happiness and Final Sorrow: The Hemingway–Pfeiffer Marriage* (Fayetteville: University of Arkansas Press, 2012)
Headrick, Annabeth and John W. Hoopes, 'Foreign encounters: warfare, trade, and status at Chichen Itza', in *3,000 Years of War and Peace in the Maya Lowlands*, ed. Geoffrey E. Braswell (Abingdon: Routledge, 2022), 256–303.
Heber, Reginald, *Narrative of a Journey Through the Upper Provinces of India, from Calcutta to Bombay, 1824–1825*, 2 vols (Philadelphia: Carey, Lea & Casey, 1829)
Heern, Zachary M., *The Emergence of Modern Shi'ism: Islamic Reform in Iraq and Iran* (London: Oneworld, 2015)
Henderson, Joan Catherine, 'Religious Tourism and Its Management: The Hajj in Saudi Arabia', *International Journal of Tourism Research*, 13 (2011), 541–52.
Herbert, Máire, *Iona, Kells and Derry: The History and Hagiography of the Monastic Familia of Columba* (Dublin: Four Courts Press, 1996)
Herodotus: The Histories, trans. Aubrey de Selincourt (London: Penguin, 1963)
Herwaarden, Jan van, *Between St James and Erasmus. Studies in Late*

Medieval Religious Life: Devotion and Pilgrimage in the Netherlands (Leiden: Brill, 2003)
Heyd, Uriel, *Ottoman Documents on Palestine, 1552–1615: A Study of the Firman according to the Mühimme Defteri* (Oxford: Clarendon Press, 1960)
Heywood, Linda M., *Njinga of Angola: Africa's Warrior Queen* (Cambridge, MA: Harvard University Press, 2017)
Heywood, Linda M., John K. Thornton, *Central Africans, Atlantic Creoles, and the Foundation of the Americas, 1585–1660* (Cambridge: Cambridge University Press, 2007)
Hibbert, Christopher, *Rome: The Biography of a City* (London: Penguin, 2001)
History of Mar Yahballaha and Rabban Sauma, ed. and trans. Pier Giorgio Borbone (Hamburg: Verlag Tredition, 2021)
Hitti, Philip K., *History of the Arabs* (London: Macmillan, 1946)
Hoinacki, Lee, *El Camino: Walking to Santiago de Compostela* (University Park: Pennsylvania State University Press, 1996)
Homeric Hymns, Homeric Apocrypha, Lives of Homer, ed. and trans. Martin L. West (Cambridge, MA: Harvard University Press, 2003).
'Homilia de Juan Pablo II', Santiago de Compostela, 9 November 1982, Vatican, https://www.vatican.va/content/john-paul-ii/es/homilies/1982/documents/hf_jp-ii_hom_19821109_santiago-compostela.html
Horn, Elzear, O. B., *Ichnographiae Monumentum Terrae Sanctae 1724–1744* (Jerusalem: Franciscan Press, 1962)
Hoshino, Eiki, 'Current Increase in Walking Pilgrims', in *Pilgrimages and Spiritual Quests in Japan*, eds María Rodriguez del Alisal, Peter Ackermann and Dolores P. Martinez (London: Routledge, 2007), 63–88.
Hotta, Chisato, 'Japan's Modernization and the Persecution of Buddhism', *HUE Journal of Humanities, Social and Natural Science*, 35 (2012), 61–73.
http://www.iona-cathedral.org.uk/
https://www.aljazeera.com/gallery/2023/9/7/photos-arbaeen-worlds-largest-annual-pilgrimage-in-iraq
Huan, Ma, *Ying-Yai Sheng-Lan: 'The Overall Survey of the Ocean's Shores'*, trans. J. V. G. Mills (Cambridge: Cambridge University Press, 1970)

Hughes, Matthew, *Allenby and British Strategy in the Middle East, 1917–1919* (London: Frank Cass, 1997)

Humeau, Jean-Baptiste, *Tsiganes en France de l'assignation au droit d'habiter* (Paris: L'Harmattan, 1995)

Hummel, Thomas, 'Russian Pilgrims: A Peasant Army Invades Jerusalem', *Jerusalem Quarterly*, 44 (2010), 39–44.

Hurlock, Kathryn, *Medieval Welsh Pilgrimage*, c.*1100–1500* (Cardiff: University of Wales Press, 2018)

Hyder, Syed Akbar, *Reliving Karbala: Martyrdom in South Asian Memory* (Oxford: Oxford University Press, 2006)

ibn Munqidh, Usama, *The Book of Contemplation: Islam and the Crusades*, ed. and trans. P. M. Cobb (London: Penguin Books, 2008)

Idema, Wilt L., 'The Pilgrimage to Taishan in the Dramatic Literature of the Thirteenth and Fourteenth Centuries', *Chinese Literature: Essays, Articles, Reviews (CLEAR)*, 19 (1997), 23–57.

Illustrated London News, 221 (1952)

'Incidence and Spread of Cholera in India', *British Medical Journal* 1 (1926), 784–5.

Inscribed Landscapes: Travel Writing in Imperial China, trans. Richard E. Strassberg (Berkeley: University of California Press, 1994)

Itinerary from Bordeaux to Jerusalem: 'the Bordeaux Pilgrim' (333 A.D.), trans. Aubrey Stewart (London: Palestine Pilgrims' Text Society, 1887)

Ivereigh, Austen, *Catholicism and Politics in Argentina, 1810–1960* (New York: St Martin's Press, 1995)

Iverson, Peter, *The Plains Indians of the Twentieth Century* (Norman: University of Oklahoma Press, 1985)

Izmirlieva, Valentina, 'Christian Hajjis – the Other Orthodox Pilgrims to Jerusalem', *Slavic Review* 73.2 (Summer 2014), 322–46.

'Jack's Lourdes Cure Still Inspires Faith', *Sunday Mirror* 10 January 1982.

Jacobson, Knut A., 'Pilgrimage', in *Hindu Law: A New History of Dharmaśāstra*, ed. Patrick Olivelle and Donald R. David Jr (Oxford: Oxford University Press, 2018), 335–46.

Jacques Lefèvre D'Étaples and The Three Maries Debates: on Mary Magdalen, On Christ's Three Days in the Tomb, On the One Mary in Place of Three. A Discussion. On the Threefold and Single Magdelen. A Second Discussion, ed. and trans. Sheila M. Porrer (Geneva: Librairie Drosz, 2009)

Jafri, S. H. M., *The Origins and Early Development of Shi'a Islam* (Oxford: Oxford University Press, 2000)
Janin, Hunt, *Four Paths to Jerusalem: Jewish, Christian, Muslim, and Secular Pilgrimages 100 BCE to 2001 CE* (London: McFarland, 2002)
Janin, R., *La géographie ecclésiastique de l'empire byzantin. III Les églises et les monastères* (Paris, 1953)
Jenkin, Phyllis, 'Pilgrimage to Lourdes', *Glasgow Herald* 13 September 1946, 3.
Jerome's *Chronicon,* xxxv 19 and 20, https://www.tertullian.org/fathers/jerome_chronicle_03_part2.htm
The Jerusalem Miscellany: An Occasional Publication of the Jerusalem Agricultural Association, ed. A. M'Caul, 1 (January, 1855)
Jewish Travellers in the Middle Ages: 19 Firsthand Accounts, ed. Elkan Nathan Adler (New York: Dover Publications, 1987)
Johnson, Samuel and James Boswell, *Journey to the Hebrides: A Journey to the Western Isles of Scotland, The Journal of the Tour to the Hebrides*, ed. Ian McGowan (Edinburgh: Canongate, 1996)
Johnston, Sarah Iles, *Ancient Greek Divination* (Oxford: Wiley Blackwell, 2008)
Johnston, Susan L., 'Native American Traditional and Alternative Medicine', *Annals of the American Academy of Political and Social Science*, 583.
Jones, Toby Craig, *Desert Kingdom: How Oil and Water Forged Modern Saudi Arabia* (Cambridge, MA: Harvard University Press, 2010)
Justice, Christopher, *Dying the Good Death: The Pilgrimage to Die in India's Holy City* (New York: SUNY Press, 1997)
Jutla, R. S., 'The Evolution of the Golden Temple of Amritsar into a major Sikh Pilgrimage Center', *AIMS Geosciences* 2 (2016), 259–72.
Jutla, R. S., 'Understanding Sikh Pilgrimage', *Tourism Recreation Research* 27 (2002), 65–72.
Kallis, Aristotle, *The Third Rome, 1922–1943: The Making of a Fascist Capital* (Basingstoke: Palgrave, 2014)
Kamen, Henry, *Philip of Spain* (New Haven: Yale University Press, 1997)
Kane, E., *Russian Hajj: Empire and the Pilgrimage to Mecca* (Ithaca, NY: Cornell University Press, 2015)
Kang, Sara, 'Contested Pilgrimage: Shikoku Henro and Dark Tourism', *Asia-Pacific Journal*, 17 (2019), 1–20.
Kark, Ruth, 'Geopietism and Pilgrimage/Tourism to the Holy Land/

Palestine (1850–1918), and the case of Thomas Cook', in *Nineteenth Century European Pilgrimages: A New Golden Age*, ed. Antón M. Pazos (Abingdon: Routledge, 2020), 65–81.

Kaufman, Suzanne K., 'Religion and Modernity: the Case of the Lourdes Shrine in Nineteenth-Century France', in *Disciplining Modernity*, ed. Pamela L. Caughie (Basingstoke: Palgrave, 2010), 92–108.

Kaufman, Suzanne K., *Consuming Visions: Mass Culture and the Lourdes Shrine* (Ithaca, NY: Cornell University Press, 2005)

Kaul, Chandrika, *Reporting the Raj: The British Press and India, c.1880–1922* (Manchester: Manchester University Press, 2003)

Kaur, Madanjit, *Maharaja Ranjit Singh* (Chandigarh: Unistar, 2008)

Kazuhisa, Nakayama, 'La Dynamique de creation, replication et déclin des lieux de pèlerinage: le nouveau pèlerinage de Shikoku à Sasaguri', *Cahiers d'Extrême Asie*, 22 (2013), 269–350.

Keats, John, *The Letters of John Keats: Volume I, 1814–1818*, ed. H. E. Rollins (Cambridge: Cambridge University Press, 2012)

Kelly, Patrick H., *Story of the Knights of Columbus Pilgrimage* (Philadelphia: Kelly Publishing Company, 1920)

Kennerley, Sam, 'Ethiopian Christians in Rome, *c.*1400–*c.*1700', in *A Companion to Religious Minorities in Early Modern Rome*, ed. M. C. Wainwright and E. Nicholson (Leiden: Brill, 2020), 142–68.

Kerr, Ian J., 'British Relationships with the Golden Temple, 1849–90', *Indian Economic and Social History Review*, 21 (1984), 139–51.

Kertzer, David I., *The Pope and Mussolini: The Secret History of Pius XI and the Rise of Fascism in Europe* (Oxford: Oxford University Press, 2014)

Khan, Ahmad Hasan, *Census of India, 1931: Volume XVII. Punjab, Part 1* (Lahore: Civil and Military Gazette Press, 1933)

Kim, Yung-Hee, *Songs to Make the Dust Dance: The Ryōjin hishō of Twelfth-Century Japan* (Berkeley: University of California Press, 1994)

Kingsley, Mary H., *West African Studies: with additional chapters* (London: MacMillan, 1901)

Kinnamos, John, *Deeds of John and Manuel Comnenus*, trans. Charles M. Brand (New York: Columbia University Press, 1976)

Kinnard, Jacob N., *Places in Motion: the Fluid Identities of Temples, Images, and Pilgrims* (Oxford: Oxford University Press, 2014)

Kipling, Rudyard, *Kim* (Oxford: Oxford University Press, 2008)

Klatzker, David, 'American Catholic Travellers to the Holy Land, 1861–1929', *Catholic Historical Review*, 74 (1988), 55–74.

Klein, Holger A., 'Sacred Relics and Imperial Ceremonies at the Great Palace of Constantinople', in *Visualisierungen von Herrschaft*, ed. Franz Alto Bauer (Istanbul: Ege Yayınları, 2006), 79–99.

Kleutghen, Kristina, *Imperial Illusions: Crossing Pictorial Boundaries in the Qing Palace* (Seattle: University of Washington Press, 2015)

Kouamé, Nathalie, 'The daily life of the *henro* on the island of Shikoku during the Edo period: A mirror of Tokugawa society', in *Pilgrimages and Spiritual Quests in Japan*, ed. María Rodriguez del Alisal, Peter Ackermann and Dolores P. Martinez (London: Routledge, 2007), 37–46.

Kouamé, Nathalie, 'Shikoku's Local Authorities and *Henro* during the Golden Age of Pilgrimage', *Japanese Journal of Religious Studies*, 24 (1997), 413–25.

Koudounaris, Paul, *Heavenly Bodies: cult treasures and spectacular saints from the catacombs* (London: W. W. Norton, 2013)

Kumbh Mela: Mapping the Ephemeral Megacity, ed. Rahul Mehrotra and Felipe Vera (Allahabad: Noiyogi Books, 2015)

Kristan-Graham, Cynthia, and Linnea Wren, 'Introduction: Looking Backward, Looking Forward at Chichen Itza', in *Landscape of the Itzá: Archaeology and Art History at Chichén Itzá and Neighboring Sites*, ed. Linnea Wren, Cynthia Kristan-Graham, Travis Nygard and Kaylee Spencer (Gainesville: University Press of Florida, 2018), 1–27.

Kutcher, Norman, 'The death of the Xiaoxian Empress: Bureaucratic Betrayals and the Crises of Eighteenth-Century Chinese Rule', *Journal of Asian Studies* 56 (1997), 708–25.

L'Atlas Catalan, http://expositions.bnf.fr/ciel/catalan/index.htm

La Gaceta, San Miguel de Tucumán, Argentina, 9 August 1952.

Lafleur, William R., *Awesome Nightfall: The Life, Times and Poetry of Saigyō* (Boston: Wisdom Publications, 2003)

Lammerant, Yolande, 'Les Pèlerins des Pays-Bas méridionaux a Saint-Julien des-Flamands à Rome au XVIIème et XVIIIème siècle' in *Pèlerins et Pèlerinages dans l'Europe moderne: actes de la table ronde organisée par le Département d'Histoire et Civilisation de l'Institut Universitaire Européen de Florence et l'École Française de Rome* (Rome, 4–5 June 1993), 271–306.

Landa's Relación de las Cosas de Yucatán, trans. Alfred M. Tozzer (Cambridge, MA: Peabody Museum Press, 1941)

Lapidus, Ira M., *A History of Islamic Societies* (Cambridge: Cambridge University Press, 1988)

Laplanche, François, 'Through Travelogues in the Holy Land (XVI–XIX centuries): The Devout, The Curious, The Erudite', *Bulletin du Centre de Recherche Français à Jérusalem* 7 (2000), 129–35.

Lashley, Marilyn, 'In our own way: the parallel development of culturally anchored self-help in African American and New Zealand Maori Communities in Historical Perspectives', in *Identity, Culture and the Politics of Community Development*, ed. Stacey-Ann Wilson (Cambridge: Cambridge Scholars Publishing, 2015), 100–126.

Lasserre, Henry, *Our Lady of Lourdes* (Lourdes: Notre-Dame de Lourdes, 1869)

Laurentin, René, *Bernadette of Lourdes: A Life Based on Authenticated Documents*, trans. John Drury (Minneapolis: Winston Press, 1978), 25–84.

'Le pèlerinage des ancient combattants à Lourdes', *L'Action Française*, 14 Septembre 1936.

Leahy, Todd and Nathan Wilson, *Historical Dictionary of Native American Movements* (Lanham: Roman & Littlefield, 2016)

Lee, Ronald, 'The Romani Goddess Kali Sara' (2002), retrieved from, http://kopachi.com/articles/the-romani-goddess-kali-sara-ronald-lee/

*Leo XIII's 'Deus Omnipotens' Bull: On the Body of the apostle Saint James (*Santiago de Compostela: Organizing Committee of the Holy Year, 1953)

Lepera, Lucía Santos, 'Las manifestaciones colectivas de deulo frente a la muerte de Eva Perón', *Americanist Bulletin* (2013), 161–80.

Letter from Gertrude Bell to her stepmother, Dame Florence Bell, Gertrude Bell Archive (Newcastle University) GB/1/1/1/1/27/1.

'Letter of John Paul II to the Ecumenical Patriarch of Constantinople His Holiness Bartholomew I (2004)', https://www.vatican.va/content/john-paul-ii/en/letters/2004/documents/hf_jp-ii_let_20041127_consegna-reliquie.html

Levy, J. de Bariacli, 'Gypsy Figures at the Fiesta of Les Saintes Maries, 1949', *Romani Studies* (1950), 115–23.

Liao, Tom F. and Cuntong Wang, 'The Changing Face of Money: Forging Collective Memory with Chinese Banknote Designs', *China Review* 18 (2018), 87–120.

Liber Sancti Jacobi 'Codex Calixtinus', eds A. Moralejo, C. Torres and J. Feo (Santiago de Compostela: Xunta de Galicia, 2004)

Life of St Daniel (BHG 486), *The Cult of Saints in Late Antiquity*, http://csla.history.ox.ac.uk/record.php?recid=E04560

Lifeng, Han, 'Communicating Civilization through Rituals: Mount Tai Pilgrimages in Song China, 960–1279', *Journal of Chinese Humanities* 1 (2015), 335–62.

Limberis, Vasiliki, *Divine Heiress: the Virgin Mary and the Creation of Constantinople* (London: Routledge, 2012)

Lindsay, James H., *Daily Life in the Medieval Islamic World* (Cambridge: Hackett, 2005)

Liñeira, María, 'Santiago de Compostela: Fact and Fetish', in *A Companion to Galician Culture*, ed. Helena Miguélez-Carballeira (Woodbridge: Boydell and Brewer, 2014), 53–71.

Litvak, Meir, *Shi'i Scholars of Nineteenth-Century Iraq: The 'Ulama' of Najaf and Karbala* (Cambridge: Cambridge University Press, 2002)

Liuhong, Huang, *A Complete Book Concerning Happiness and Benevolence*, trans. Djang Chu (Tucson: University of Arizona Press, 1984)

Lochtefeld, James H., *God's Gateway: identity and meaning in a Hindu Pilgrimage Place* (Oxford: Oxford University Press, 2010)

Loesch, Martin C., 'The First Americans and the "Free" Exercise of Religion', *American Indian Law Review*, 18 (1993), 313–77.

Loewe, Michael, *Ways to Paradise: The Chinese Quest for Immortality* (London: George Allen & Unwin, 1979)

Loiseau, Gaëlla, 'Globalizing Romani Culture: the pilgrimage to the sea in Les-Saintes-Maries-de-la-Mer (France)', in *Locality Identities and Transnational Cults within Europe*, ed. F. Giacalone and K. Griffin (Wallingford: CABI, 2018), 58–68.

Lois-González, Rubén C., Xosé M. Santos and Pilar Taboada-de-Zúñiga Romero, 'The Camino de Santiago de Compostela: the most important historic pilgrimage way in Europe', in *Religious Pilgrimage Routes and Trails,* ed. D. H. Olsen and A. Trono (Wallingford: CABI, 2018), 72–87.

Lomawaima, K. Tsianina and Jeffrey Ostler, 'Reconsidering Richard Henry

Pratt: Cultural Genocide and Native Liberation in an Era of Racial Oppression', *Journal of American Indian Education*, 57 (2018), 79–100.

Longrigg, James, 'Death and Epidemic Disease in Classical Athens', in *Death and Disease in the Ancient City*, ed. Valerie M. Hope and Eireaan Marshall (London: Routledge, 2000), 67–76.

López, Luis Alberto Martos, 'Underwater Archaeological Exploration of the Mayan Cenotes', *Museum International; Underwater Cultural Heritage*, LX (2008), 100–110.

Lothrop, Samuel Kirkland, *Metals from the Cenote of Sacrifice, Chichen Itza, Yucatán* (Cambridge, MA: Peabody Museum Press, 1952)

'Lourdes Cure Creates Profound Effect in Liverpool', NCWC News Service September 1923.

'Lourdes of New Zealand', *Harbinger of Light* 1 March 1921.

'Lourdes Pilgrims', *Lancashire Evening Post* 13 July 1926.

Low, Michael Christopher, '"The Infidel Piloting the True Believer": Thomas Cook and the Business of the Colonial Hajj', in *The Hajj and Europe in the Age of Empire*, ed. Umar Ryad (Leiden: Brill, 2017), 47–80.

Lucan, *Pharsalia* 5.71, https://www.perseus.tufts.edu/hopper/text?doc=Perseus:text:1999.02.0134:book=5:card=71&highlight=de

'Luck Runs Out For Eva Peron', *American Mercury* January 1952.

Luther's Works, Vol. 44: The Christian in Society I, ed. Hartmut T. Lehmann and James Atkinson (Philadelphia: Fortress, 1966)

Luttwak, Edward N., *The Grand Strategy of the Byzantine Empire* (Cambridge, MA: Harvard University Press, 2009)

MacArthur, E. Mairi, *Columba's Island: Iona from past to present* (Edinburgh: Edinburgh University Press, 1995)

MacArthur, Mairi, *Iona. The Living Memory of a Crofting Community* (Edinburgh: Edinburgh University Press, 2007)

MacCulloch, John, *The Highlands and Western Isles of Scotland*, 4 vols (London: Longman, Hurst, Rees, Orme, Brown, and Green, 1824)

Macintyre, Lorn, *Sir David Russell: A Biography* (Edinburgh: Canongate, 1994)

Mackie, Gillian, *Early Christian Chapels in the West: Decoration, Function and Patronage* (Toronto: University of Toronto Press, 2003)

MacLean, Kama, *Pilgrimage and Power: the Kumbh Mela in Allahabad* (Oxford: Oxford University Press, 2008)

MacQuarrie, Alan, *Iona Through The Ages* (Isle of Coll: Society of West Highland and Island Historical Research, 1983)
Maier, Jessica, *The Eternal City: A History of Rome in Maps* (Chicago: University of Chicago Press, 2020)
Mails, Thomas E. and Dallas Chief Eagle, *Fools Crow* (Lincoln: University of Nebraska Press, 1990)
Majeska, G. P., *Russian Travelers to Constantinople in the Fourteenth and Fifteenth Centuries* (Washington DC: Dumbarton Oaks, 1984)
Majeska, George, 'Russian Pilgrims in Constantinople', *Dumbarton Oaks Papers* 56 (2002), 93–108.
Malcolm X, *The Autobiography of Malcolm X: As Told to Alex Haley* (New York: Ballantine Press, 1973)
Malhotra, Karamajit K., 'Emergence of the Golden Temple as the Premier Sikh Institution during the Eighteenth Century', *Proceedings of the Indian History Congress* 76 (2015), 287–93.
Manchester Guardian 2 March 1922.
Mango, M. M., 'Pilgrimage', in *Oxford History of Byzantium*, ed. C. Mango (Oxford: Oxford University Press, 2002), 115–50.
Mann, Susan L., *Gender and Sexuality in Modern Chinese History* (Cambridge: Cambridge University Press, 2011)
Mansel, Philip, *Constantinople: City of the World's Desire, 1453–1924* (London: John Murray, 1995)
Manson, John, 'A Provençal Pilgrimage', *Gentleman's Magazine* 290 (1901), 347.
'Maori Faith Healer', *Daily Mercury* 19 November 1923, 4.
'Maori King Wants Modern Conveniences', *Sun* 25 September 1938.
'The Māori Prophet', *Manchester Guardian*, 18 April 1927.
'Maori Prophet Dies', *Sun* 18 September 1939.
'Maori Visionary: Visit to Japan', *Register* 17 January 1925.
'Maori Visitors', *Daily Mail* 27 April 1924.
'Maoris Vote For Cult', *Herald* 30 November 1949.
Márkus, Gilbert, 'Four Blessings and a Funeral: Adomnán's theological map of Iona', *Innes Review*, 72 (2021), 1–26.
Marnham, Patrick, *Lourdes: A Modern Pilgrimage* (Garden City, NY: Doubleday, 1982)

Marshall, Rosalind K., *Columba's Iona: A New History* (Dingwall: Sandstone Press, 2013)

Martin, Gregory, *Roma Sacra (1581)*, ed. George Bruner Parks (Rome, 1969)

Martin, Joel W., *The Land Looks After Us: A History of Native American Religion* (Oxford: Oxford University Press, 2000)

Martínez, David, 'The Soul of the Indian: Lakota Philosophy and the Vision Quest', *Wicazo Sa Review*, 19 (2004), 79–104.

Maskarinec, Maya, *City of Saints: Rebuilding Rome in the Early Middle Ages* (Philadelphia: University of Pennsylvania Press, 2018)

Maspero, Henri, *Taoism and Chinese Religion*, trans. Frank A. Kierman Jr (Amherst: University of Massachusetts Press, 1981)

Matheson, John, *England to Delhi: A Narrative of Indian Travel* (London: Longmans Green, 1835)

Matsuo, Kenji, *A History of Japanese Buddhism* (Leiden: Brill, 2007)

Matthews, Arthur, *Well-Remembered Days: Eoin O'Ceallaigh's Memoir of a Twentieth-Century Catholic Life* (London: Macmillan, 2001)

Matthiesen, Toby, *The Caliph and the Imam: The Making of Sunnism and Shiism* (Oxford: Oxford University Press, 2023)

Mayer, Wendy and Pauline Allen, *John Chrysostom* (London: Routledge, 2000)

Mazel, A., *Notes sur la Camargue et les Saintes-Maries-de-la-Mer* (Vaison-la-Romaine: Société de la Bonne Presse du Midi, 1935)

Mazza, Roberto, *Jerusalem: from the Ottomans to the British* (London: I.B. Taurus, 2009)

McCarten, Matt, 'The political pilgrimage our leaders fear to miss', *Herald on Sunday* 28 January 2012, https://www.nzherald.co.nz/kahu/matt-mccarten-the-political-pilgrimage-our-leaders-fear-to-miss/NDKFDPXPRK4S3NXIYJJZYOQ7AI/

McDonald, Aidan, 'When were St Columba's Corporeal Relics Enshrined?', *Hallel*, 23 (1998), 20–30.

McKernan, Luke, '"The Supreme Moment of the War": General Allenby's Entry into Jerusalem', *Historical Journal of Film, Radio, and Television*, 13 (1993), 169–80.

McKitterick, Rosamund, 'The representation of Old Saint Peter's basilica in the *Liber Pontificalis*', in *Old St Peter's Rome*, ed. R. McKitterick, J.

Osborne, C. M. Richardson and J. Story (Cambridge: Cambridge University Press, 2013), 95–118.

McNally, Michael D., *Defend the Sacred: Native American Religious Freedom Beyond the First Amendment* (Princeton: Princeton University Press, 2020)

McNeill, F. Marian, *An Iona Anthology* (Iona: Iona Community, 1990)

McNeill, F. Marian, *Iona. A History of the Island*, 7th edn (Moffat: Lochar, 1991)

McOwan, Janne-Elisabeth, 'Ritual Purity: An Aspect of the Gypsy Pilgrimage to Stes-Maries-de-la-Mer', *Journal of the Gypsy Lore Society* 4 (1994), 95–109.

'Mecca of the Maori', *Evening Star* 29 December 1921.

'Meet Sister Bernadette, the most recently-cured person at Lourdes', https://www.catholicnewsagency.com/news/253153/meet-sister-bernadette-the-most-recently-cured-person-at-lourdes

Melton, J. Gordon, 'Golden Temple', in *Religions of the World: A Comprehensive Encyclopedia of Beliefs and Practices*, ed. J. Gordon Melton and Martin Baumann (Santa Barbara: ABC-CLIO, 2002), 1237–8.

The Memoirs of Frederic Mistral, trans. George Wickes (Paris: Alyscamps Press, 1994)

Meri, Josef W., *The Cult of Saints Among Muslims and Jews in Medieval Syria* (Oxford: Oxford University Press, 2002)

Meserve, Margaret, *Papal Bull: Print, Politics, and Propaganda in Renaissance Rome* (Baltimore: Johns Hopkins University Press, 2021)

Miedema, N., 'Following in the Footsteps of Christ: Pilgrimage and Passion Devotion', in *The Broken Body: Passion Devotion in Late-Medieval Culture,* ed. A. A. MacDonald, H. N. B. Ridderbos and R. M. Schlusemann (Groningen: Egbert Forsten, 1998), 73–92.

Miller, Joseph C., 'The Slave Trade in Congo and Angola', in *The African Diaspora: Interpretative Essays*, ed. Martin L. Kilson and Robert I. Rotberg (Cambridge, MA: Harvard University Press, 1976), 75–113.

Millet, José, 'Aspectos da Religiosidad popular Angolana', *Revista do centro de Estudos Africanos*, 1–13 (1989/1990)

Minturn, Robert B., *From New York to New Delhi by way of Rio de Janeiro, Australia, and China* (New York: D. Appleton & Co., 1858)

The Miracles of St Artemios: A Collection of Miracle Stories by an Anonymous

Author of Seventh Century Byzantium, trans. Virgil S. Crisafulli, with John W. Nesbitt (Brill: Leiden, 1997)

Miran, Jonathan, '"Stealing the Way" to Mecca: West African Pilgrims and Illicit Red Sea Passages', *Journal of African History*, 56 (2015), 389–408.

Mironenko-Marenkova, Irina and Kirill Vakh, 'An Institution, Its People and Its Documents: the Russian Consulate in Jerusalem through the Foreign Policy Archive of the Russian Empire, 1858–1914', in *Ordinary Jerusalem, 1840–1940: opening new archives, revisiting a global city*, ed. Angelos Dalachanis and Vincent Lamire (Leiden: Brill, 2018), 200–22.

Misra, Saurabh, *Pilgrimage, Politics, and Pestilence: the Haj from the Indian Subcontinent, 1860–1920* (New Delhi: Oxford University Press, 2011)

Missione Evangelilone Bk 2, Ch. 4, https://www.bu.edu/afam/people/faculty/john-thornton/cavazzi-missione-evangelica-2/

'Modern "Miracle Man" Found in New Zealand', *Manchester Guardian*, 30 March 1921

Mol, Hans, *The Fixed and the Fickle: Religion and Identity in New Zealand* (Dunedin: Pilgrims South Press, 2006)

Monteiro, Joachim John, *Angola and the River Congo, Volume 2* (London: MacMillan & Co., 1875)

Montes-Bradley, Eduardo (director) *Evita*, Episode 2: 'Presencia de Eva Peron', documentary film (1953)

Moreton, David C., 'A 100-year History of Foreigners and the Shikoku Pilgrimage – Part 2', *Awa Life* 294 (2015), 4.

Mori, M. 'Modernity and Materiality in the Henro Pilgrimage in Japan' [in Japanese], *Research Center for the Shikoku Henro and Pilgrimages of the World*, 27–36, https://henro.ll.ehime-u.ac.jp/wp-content/uploads/2013/03/6feb9fb7e635f33a75c29cb1a8ec3a67.pdf

Mori, M., 'Contemporary Religious Meaning of the Pilgrimage Route' [in Japanese], *Japanese Journal of Human Geography*, 2 (2001), 173–89.

Mori, M. 'Spatial Formation and change in the Henro pilgrimage in Modern Japan' [in Japanese], *Japanese Journal of Human Geography*, 54 (2002), 535–56.

Mori, M., 'Mobilising Pilgrim Bodily Space: the contest between authentic and folk pilgrimage in the interwar period', in *Understanding Tourism Mobilities in Japan*, ed. Hideki Endo (London: Routledge, 2021), 170–81.

Morley, Sylvanus Griswold, 'Archaeological Investigations of the Carnegie Institution of Washington in the Maya Area of Middle America, during the Past Twenty-Eight Years', *Proceedings of the American Philosophical Society* 86 (1943), 205–19.

Morley, Sylvanus Griswold, 'Chichén Itzá: An Ancient American Mecca', *National Geographic* (January 1925), 63–95.

Mourad, Suleiman A., 'Jerusalem in Early Islam: the Making of the Muslims' Holy City', in *Routledge Handbook on Jerusalem*, ed. Suleiman A. Mourad, Naomi Koltun-Fromm and Bedross Der Matossian (London: Routledge, 2018), 77–89.

Moyano, María José, *Argentina's Lost Patrol; Armed Struggle, 1989–1979* (New Haven: Yale University Press, 1995)

Muisit, Gilles le, *Annales*, ed. H. Lemaitre (Paris: Libraire Renouard, 1966)

Murphy, Edwin, *After the Funeral: the Posthumous Adventures of Famous Corpses* (New York: Barnes & Noble, 1998)

Muru, Selwyn, 'Ratana Birth Rebirth', *Tu Tangata* 1 August 1981.

Nakash, Yitzhak, *The Shi'is of Iraq* (Princeton: Princeton University Press, 1994)

Naquin, Susan, and Chün-Fang Yü, 'Introduction: Pilgrimage in China', in *Pilgrims and Sacred Sites in China*, ed. Susan Naquin and Chun-Fang Yu (Berkeley: University of California Press, 1992), 1–28.

Naquin, Susan, *Gods of Mount Tai: Familiarity and the Material Culture of North China, 1000–2000* (Leiden: Brill, 2022)

Narrative of the Embassy of Ruy Gonzalez de Clavijo to the Court of Timor at Samarcand, A.D. 1403–6, trans. C. R. Markham (London: Hakluyt Society, 1859)

Nasir-i Khusrū (Khusraw), *The Book of Travels,* ed. and trans. W. M. Thackston (Costa Mesa, CA: Mazda Publishers, 2001)

Nasr, V., *The Shia Revival* (New York: W. W. Norton, 2007)

Nautical Magazine and Naval Chronicle for 1854 (London: Simpkin Marshall and Co., 1854)

The Nawab Sikandar, Begum of Bhopal. A Pilgrimage to Mecca, ed. and trans. Mrs Willoughby-Osborne (London: W. H. Allen, 1870)

'Nearly 50 injured as devotees clash with police at Pakistan shrine closed due to Covid-19', *Hindu Times* 2 April 2021, https://www.thehindu.com/

news/international/devotees-clash-with-police-at-pakistan-shrine/article34223755.ece

Nenzi, Laura, 'To Ise at All Costs: Religious and Economic Implications of Early Modern Mukemairi', *Japanese Journal of Religious Studies*, 33 (2006), 75–114.

Nesbitt, Eleanor M. Nesbitt, *Sikhism: A Very Short Introduction*, 2nd edn (Oxford: Oxford University Press, 2016)

Nevill, H. R., *Allahabad: A Gazetteer*, vol. 23 (Allahabad: Government Press, 1911)

Newby, Eric, *Slowly Down the Ganges* (London: Hodder & Stoughton, 1989)

Newcastle Evening Chronicle 9 August 1952.

Nicholson, Helen, *Women and the Crusades* (Oxford: Oxford University Press, 2023)

Niebuhr, M., *Travels Through Arabia and Other Countries in the East, Volume 2*, trans. Robert Heron (Edinburgh: R. Morison and Son, 1792)

Nikjoo, A. Neda Razavizadeh and Michael A. Di Giovine, 'What draws Shia Muslims to an insecure pilgrimage? The Iranian journey to Arbaeen, Iraq during the presence of ISIS', *Journal of Tourism and Cultural Change* 19 (2021) 606–27.

Noël, Henry, *Karakoro – At Home in Japan* (Tokyo: Hokuseido Press, 1939)

Nolan, J., *History of the Irish National Pilgrimage to Rome; or, Notes on the Way* (London, 1893)

Noreen, Kirstin, 'Sacred Memory and Confraternal Space: The Insignia of the Confraternity of Santissimo Salvatore (Rome)', in *Roma Felix: Formation and Reflections of Medieval Rome*, ed. Éamonn Ó Carragáin and Carol Neumann de Vegvar (London: Routledge, 2007) 6–19.

Norman, Waerete, 'Taura', *Growing Up Māori*, ed. Witi Ihimaera (Auckland: Tandem Press, 1998), 110–32.

Northern Sun News November 1984.

O City of Byzantium, Annals of Niketas Choniates, trans. Harry J. Magoulias (Detroit: Wayne State University Press, 1984)

Ó Cróinín, Daíbhí, *Early Medieval Ireland, 400–1200* (London: Routledge, 2017)

O'Connor, Patrick, *I Met A Miracle: the Story of Jack Traynor* (London: Catholic Truth Society, 1943)

O'Sullivan, Michael, '"Indian money", Intra-Shi-i Polemics, and the Bohra

and Khoja Pilgrimage Infrastructure in Iraq's Shrine Cities, 1897–1932', *Journal of the Royal Asiatic Society*, 32.1 (2022), 213–50.
'Obituaries: Jack Glass', *The Times* 5 March 2004.
Odell, Thomas E., *Mato Paha: the Story of Bear Butte* (Spearfish, SD: privately printed, 1942)
Of the Holy Places Visited by Antoninus Martyr (Circ. 530 A.D.), trans. Aubrey Stewart (London: Palestine Pilgrims' Text Society, 1887)
Olds, Katrina B., 'The "False Chronicles", Cardinal Baronio, and Sacred History in Counter-Reformation Spain', *Catholic Historical Review*, 100 (2014), 1–26.
One Thousand Roads to Mecca: ten centuries of travellers writing about Muslim Pilgrimage, ed. Michael Wolfe (New York: Grove Press, 1997)
Oracle of Delphi: King Aigeus in front of the Pythia: Antikensammlung Berlin, Altes Museum, F 2538.
Osselaer, Tine van, 'Marian Piety and Gender: Marian Devotion and the "Feminization" of Religion', in *Oxford Handbook of Mary*, ed. Chris Maunder (Oxford: Oxford University Press, 2019), 579–91.
Ostrow, Stephen F., 'The Counter-Reformation and the End of the Century', in *Rome: Artistic Centres of the Italian Renaissance*, ed. Marcia Hall (Cambridge: Cambridge University Press, 2005), 246–320.
'Otra estación para peregrinos: sudario de Eva, al Congreso', 25 August 2004, https://www.ambito.com/politica/otra-estacion-peregrinos-sudario-eva-al-congreso-n3287181
Ozawa, Minoru, 'Why did a Viking King Meet a Pope? Cnut's Imperial Politics, Scandinavian Commercial Networks, and the Journey to Rome in 1027', in *Communicating Papal Authority in the Middle Ages*, ed. Minoru Ozawa, Thomas W. Smith and Georg Strack (London: Routledge, 2023), 131–44.
Pack, S. D., 'Revival of the Pilgrimage to Santiago de Compostela: the Politics of Religious, National, and European Patrimony, 1879–1988', *Journal of Modern History* 82 (2010), 335–67.
Pain, Crispin, 'Sikh Pilgrimage: A Study in Ambiguity', *International Journal of Punjab Studies*, 10 (2003), 143–62.
Palethorpe, Nigel, 'Where Labor is a Religion', *Sun* 4 December 1949.
Palka, Joel W., *Maya Pilgrimage to Ritual Landscapes: Insights from*

Archaeology, History and Ethnography (Albuquerque: University of New Mexico Press, 2014)

Pall Mall Gazette 1 March 1877.

Palladino, L.B., *Indian and White in the Northwest* (Lancaster, PA: Wickersham Publishing Company, 1922.

Park Jin-hai, 'G.O.D. Returns with Travel Variety Show', 14 October 2018, https://www.koreatimes.co.kr/www/art/2024/02/398_256969.html.

Parks, Fanny, *Wanderings of a Pilgrim, in Search of the Picturesque* (London: Richardson, 1850)

Partner, Peter, *Renaissance Rome, 1500–1559: a portrait of a society* (Berkeley: University of California Press, 1976)

Partridge, Loren, *The Renaissance in Rome, 1400–1600* (London: Weidenfeld & Nicolson, 1996)

Patrizi, Luca, 'Relics of the Prophet', in *Muhammed in History, Thought, and Culture: An Encyclopedia of the Prophet of God*, ed. Coeli FitzPatrick and Adam Hani Walker (ABC-CLIO, 2014), 518–19.

Paulinus of Nola, *The Poems of Paulinus of Nola*, trans. P. G. Walsh (New York: Newman Press, 1974)

Pausanias's Description of Greece Volume 1; Translation, ed. James George Frazer (Cambridge: Cambridge University Press, 1898, reprinted 2012)

Pavlinac, Cindy, 'Circling Centre, Finding Our Way Home: Pilgrimages around Iona, Mount Tamalpais and Labyrinths', in *The Many Voices of Pilgrimage and Reconciliation*, ed. Ian S. McIntosh and Lesley D. Harman (Wallingford: CABI, 2017), 79–93.

Pazos, Antón M., 'Compostela, Rome and the Revival of the Pilgrimages to Santiago', in *Nineteenth-Century European Pilgrimages: A New Golden Age*, ed. Antón M. Pazos (Abingdon: Routledge, 2020), 101–118.

Pazos, Antón M., 'Recent Research on a Renewed Pilgrimage: the Way of St James in the Nineteenth and Twentieth Centuries', in *Religious Pilgrimages in the Mediterranean World*, ed. Antón M. Pazos (London: Routledge, 2023), 67–88.

Pearson, Chris, *Scarred Landscapes: War and Nature in Vichy France* (Basingstoke: Palgrave, 2008)

Pearson, Michael Naylor, *Pious Passengers: the Hajj in Earlier Times* (London: Hurst, 1994)

Pechan, Bev, *Sturgis, South Dakota 1878–1960* (Charleston, SC: Arcadia, 2003)

Péclard, Didier, 'Religion and Politics in Angola: The Church, the Colonial State and the Emergence of Angolan Nationalism, 1940–1961', *Journal of Religion in Africa*, 29 (1998), 160–86.

Peggs, James, 'India's Cries to British Humanity', *Calcutta Review*, X (1848), 404–36.

Perciaccente, Antonio et al. 'Saint Roch and Social Distancing During Pandemics: Lessons to be Remembered', *Journal of Religion & Health*, 60 (2021), 2324–30.

Péricard-Méa, Denise, 'French Noblewomen on Pilgrimage to Compostela in the Middle Ages', in *Women and Pilgrimage in Late Medieval Galicia*, ed. Carlos Andrés González-Paz (London: Routledge, 2016), 93–112.

'Perón, Evita y Francisco: La Fe como fiesta popular y la fuerza de lucha', *AGN Prensa*, 6 July 2021, https://agnprensa.com/peron-evita-y-francisco-la-fe-como-fiesta-popular-y-la-fuerza-de-lucha/

Perry, David M., *Sacred Plunder: Venice and the Aftermath of the Fourth Crusade* (University Park: Pennsylvania University Press, 2015)

Peters, Francis E. *Mecca: A Literary History of the Muslim Holy Land* (Princeton: Princeton University Press, 1994)

Peterson, Zina, 'Twisted Paths of Civilization: Saint Sara and the Romani', *Journal of Religion and Popular Culture*, 26.3 (2014), 310–22.

Petro, Nicholai N., 'The Novgorod Model: Creating a European Past in Russia', in *Cities after the Fall of Communism: Reshaping Cultural Landscapes and European Identity*, ed. J. J. Czaplicka et al. (Baltimore: Johns Hopkins University Press, 2009), 53–74.

Pevar, Stephen L., *The Rights of Indians and Tribes*, 4th edn (Oxford: Oxford University Press, 2012)

Pfeiffer, James, *First American Catholic Pilgrimage to Palestine, 1889* (Cincinnati: Jos. Berning and Company, 1892)

Pfeilschifter, Rene, 'Always in Second Place: Constantinople as an Imperial and Religious Center in Late Antiquity', in *City of Caesar, City of God: Constantinople and Jerusalem in Late Antiquity*, ed. Konstantin M. Klein and Johannes Wienand (Berlin: De Gruyter, 2022), 39–67.

The Pilgrimage of Etheria trans. M. L. McClure and C. L. Fletoe (New York: MacMillan, 1919)

'Pilgrimage to Pray for Peace at Lourdes', *The Times* 25 August 1934.
'Pilgrimage to Ratana Pa', *Otago Daily Times* 26 January 2012, https://www.odt.co.nz/opinion/editorial/pilgrimage-ratana-pa
Pilgrimage: from the Ganges to Graceland, An Encyclopedia, 2 vols (Santa Barbara: ABC-CLIO, 2002)
Pinkney, Andrea Marion, 'What Are Sikhs Doing at "Historical Gurdwaras" if They're Not on Pilgrimage? Saints, Dust and Memorial Presence at Sikh Religious Places', in *Religious Journeys in India: Pilgrims, Tourists and Travelers*, ed. Andrea Marion Pinkney and John Whalen-Bridge (New York: Suny Press, 2018), 221–51.
Pitts, Joseph, *A True and Faithful Account of the Religion & Manners of the Mohametans, in which is a Particular Relations of their Pilgrimage to Mecca* (Exeter, 1717)
Pliny, *Natural History*, trans. H. Rackham, Loeb Classical Library (Cambridge, MA: Harvard University Press, 1961)
Plutschow, H. E., 'Japanese Travel Diaries in the Middle Ages', *Oriens Extremus* 29 (1982), 1–136.
Poems from the Sikh Sacred Tradition, trans. Nikky-Guninder Kaur Singh (Cambridge, MA: Harvard University Press, 2023)
Pontifical Institute Notre Dame of Jerusalem Center, www.notredamecenter.org
Powell, P. J., *Sweet Medicine: the continuing role of the sacred arrows, the sun dance, and the sacred buffalo hat in northern Cheyenne history* (Norman: University of Oklahoma Press, 1998)
'Pre-Hispanic City of Chichén-Itzá', UNESCO: World Heritage Conservation, https://whc.unesco.org/en/list/483/
Preston, Paul, *Franco: A Biography* (London: HarperCollins, 1993)
Price, Clair, 'The Miracle Man of New Zealand', *New York Times*, 3 August 1924, 8
Price, Simon, 'Delphi and Divination', in *Greek Religion and Society*, ed. P. Easterling and J. Muir (Cambridge: Cambridge University Press, 1985), 128–54.
Price, T. Douglas, Vera Tiesler and Carolyn Freiwald, 'Place of Origins of the Sacrificial Victims in the sacred Cenote, Chichén Itzá, Mexico', *American Journal of Physical Anthropology*, 70 (2019), 98–115.
Pringle, Denys, *Churches of the Crusader Kingdom of Jerusalem, A Corpus,*

Volume 3: the City of Jerusalem (Cambridge: Cambridge University Press, 2007)

Proskouriakoff, Tatiana, *Jades from the Cenote of Sacrifice Chichén Itzá, Yucatán* (Cambridge, MA: Peabody Museum Press, 1974)

Provost, Georges, 'Les pèlerins accueillis à l'Hospital Real de Saint-Jacques-de-Compostelle dans la seconde moitié du XVIIe siècle', in *Pèlerins et pèlerinages dans l'Europe moderne: actes de la table ronde organisée par le Département d'Histoire et Civilisation de l'Institut Universitaire Européen de Florence et l'École Française de Rome (Rome, 4–5 Juin 1993)*, (Rome: École Française de Rome, 2000), 127–50.

Purchas, Samuel, *Purchas his Pilgrimage* (London, 1626)

Pye, Michael, *Japanese Buddhist Pilgrimage* (Sheffield: Rambelli, 2014)

Qian, Sima, *The First Emperor: Selections from the Historical Records*, ed. K. E. Brashier, trans. Raymond Dawson (Oxford: Oxford University Press, 2007)

Rambow, Charles, *Bear Butte: Journeys to the Sacred Mountain* (Sioux Falls: Pine Hill Press, 2006)

Raper, R. V., '*Narrative of a Survey for the Purpose of Discovering the Source of the Ganges*', *Asiatick Researches*, 11 (1810), 446–564.

Rasheed, Abdur, *The Travellers' Companion: containing a brief description of places of pilgrimage and important towns in India* (Calcutta: Superintendent Government Printing, 1907)

'Ratana at Home: the Mecca of the Maori', *Evening Post* 27 December 1921.

'Ratana Remembered', *World's News* 20 May 1953.

'Ratana, Tahupotiki Wiremu', *Encyclopedia of New Zealand,* https://teara.govt.nz/en/biographies/3r4/ratana-tahupotiki-wiremu

'Ratana the Healer', *Hawke's Bay Tribune* 20 October 1921.

'Ratana, the Maori Healer: Story of a Cure', *Queanbeyan Age and Queanbeyan Reporter* 7 February 1922.

Ratelband, Klaas, *Os holandeses no Brasil e na costa Africana: Angola, Kongo e São Tomé, 1600–1650* (Lisbon: Vega, 2003)

Raureti, Moana, 'The Origins of the Ratana Movement', in *Te Ao Hurihuri: Aspects of Maoritanga*, ed. Michael King (Auckland: Raupo Publishing, 1992), 144–61.

Rayshahri, Muhammad Muhammadi, *The Chronicles of the Martyrdom of Imam Husayn,* trans. Abbas Jaffer (London: ICAS Press, 2020)

Reader, Ian, 'Dead to the World: Pilgrims in Shikoku', in *Pilgrimage and Popular Culture*, ed. Ian Reader and Tony Walter (Basingstoke: Springer, 1993), 107–36.

Reader, Ian, 'Legends, Miracles, and Faith in Kōbō Daishi and Shikoku Pilgrimage', in *Religions of Japan in Practice*, ed. George J. Tanabe Jr (Princeton: Princeton University Press, 1999), 360–69.

Reader, Ian, *Making Pilgrimages: Meaning and Practice in Shikoku* (Honolulu: University of Hawai'i Press, 2005)

Reader, Ian, 'Positively Promoting Pilgrimage: Media Representation of Pilgrimage in Japan', *Nova Religio* (2007), 13–31.

Reader, Ian, and John Shultz, *Unending Pilgrimage in Shikoku* (Oxford: Oxford University Press, 2021)

'The Recent Riots in Bombay', *The Age* 18 August 1893.

The Red Sea and Adjacent Countries at the Close of the Seventeenth Century, ed. William Foster (London: Hakluyt Society, 1949)

Reed, Alma, 'The Well of the Maya's Human Sacrifice', *El Palacio*, 14 (1 June 1923)

Reed, Alma M., *Peregrina: Love and Death in Mexico*, ed. Michael K. Schuessler (Houston: University of Texas Press, 2007)

Relato del viaje por Europa del obipso armenio Martir (1489–1496), ed. Ignatcio Iñarrea Las Herjas and Denise Péricard-Méa (Logroño: Universidad de la Rioja, 2009)

Report of the Committee appointed by the Uttar Pradesh Government to enquire into the mishap which occurred in the Kumbh Mela at Prayaga on the 3rd February 1954 (Allahabad: Government of India, 1954)

Richardson, Carol M., *Reclaiming Rome: Cardinals in the Fifteenth Century* (Leiden: Brill, 2009)

Ringle, William M., Tomás Gallareta Negrón and George J. Bey III, 'The Return of Quetzalcoatl: Evidence for the spread of a world religion during the Epiclassic period', *Ancient Mesoamerica* 9 (1998), 183–232.

Rio, Knut, Michelle MacCarthy and Ruy Blanes, 'Introduction to Pentecostal Witchcraft and Spiritual Politics in Africa and Melanasia', in *Pentecostalism and Witchcraft: Spiritual Warfare in Africa and Melanesia*, ed. Knut Rio, Michelle MacCarthy and Ruy Blanes (London: Palgrave MacMillan, 2017), 1–36.

Robert of Clari, *The Conquest of Constantinople*, trans. Edgar Holmes McNeal (New York: Columbia University Press, 2005)

Robertson, John, *Iraq: A History* (London: Oneworld, 2015)

Rocchetta, Aquilante, *Peregrinatione di Terra Santa e d'altre provincie di Don Aquilanta Roccetta Cavaliere del Santissimo Sepolcro* (Palermo: Alfonzo dell'Isola, 1630)

Rolston, Bill, 'When Everywhere is Karbala: Murals, Martyrdom and Propaganda in Iran', *Memory Studies* 13 (2020), 3–23.

'The Roman Catholic Pilgrimage to Iona', *Dundee Evening Telegraph* 16 June 1897.

Romani, Mario, *Pellegrini e viaggiatori nell'economia di Roma dal XIV al XVII secolo (*Milan: Vita e Pensiero, 1948)

Romero, Pablo Bush, 'The sacred well of Chichén Itzá', *Unesco Courier* (1972), 32.

Romey, Kristin, 'Watery Tombs', *Archaeology*, 58 (2005), 42–9.

Rosen, Peter, *Pa-ha-sa-pah: or, The Black Hills of South Dakota. A Complete History of the Gold and Wonder-Land of the Dakotas, from the Remotest Date to the Present* (St Louis: Nixon-Jones Printing Co., 1895)

Rothschild, Harry N., *Empress Wu Zhao and Her Pantheon of Devis, Divinities, and Dynastic Mothers* (New York: Columbia University Press, 2015)

Rowe, Erin Kathleen, *Saint and Nation: Santiago, Teresa of Avila, and Plural Identities in Early Modern Spain* (University Park: Pennsylvania State University Press, 2011)

Rowe, William T., *China's Last Empire: the Great Qing* (Cambridge, MA: Belknap Press of Harvard University Press, 2009)

Rowlett, Justin, 'India's dying mother', *BBC News Online* 12 May 2016, https://www.bbc.co.uk/news/resources/idt-aad46fca-734a-45f9-8721-61404cc12a39

Roy, Dilip Kumar and Indira Devi, *Kumbha: India's Ageless Festival* (Bombay: Bharatiya Vidya Bhavan, 1955)

Roys, Ralph L., *The Book of Chilam Balam of Chumayel* (Norman: University of Oklahoma Press, 1967)

Rubin, Miri, *Mother of God: A History of the Virgin Mary* (London: Allen Lane, 2009)

Ruiz, Teófilo, *Spain's Centuries of Crisis: 1300–1474* (Oxford: Blackwell, 2007)

The Russian Primary Chronicle: Laurentian Text, ed. and trans. Samuel Hazzard Cross and Olgerd P. Sherbowitz-Wetzor (Cambridge, MA: Medieval Academy of America, 1953)

Runion, Meredith L., *The History of Afghanistan*, 2nd edn (Santa Barbara: ABC-CLIO, 2017)

Russian Travellers to Constantinople, ed. George P. Majeska (Washington: Dumbarton Oaks, 1984)

Rutter, Eldon, *The Holy Cities of Arabia*, vol. I (London: G. P. Putnam's Sons, Ltd, 1928)

Ryley, J. Horton, *Ralph Fitch: England's Pioneer to India and Burma* (London: T. Fisher Unwin, 1899)

Salmesvuori, Pāivi, 'Brigitta of Sweden and her pilgrimage to Santiago de Compostela,' in *Women and Pilgrimage in Late Medieval Galicia*, ed. Carlos Andrés González-Paz (London: Routledge, 2016), 113–21.

Sampat, Payal, 'The River Ganges' Long Decline', *World Watch* 9.4 (1996)

Sampedro, Elías Valiña, *Caminos a Compostela* (Vigo: Faro de Vigo, 1971)

Sampedro, Elías Valiña, *El Camino de Santiago: Guia del Peregrino* (León: Everest, 1985)

San Martin, Ines, 'Argentine Union Wants a St Evita, Church says "not so fast"', *Tablet*, 22 May 2019.

Santos, Vanicléia Silva, 'Africans, Afro-Brazilians and Afro-Portuguese in the Iberian Inquisition in the Seventeenth and Eighteenth Centuries', in *Rewriting the African Diaspora in Latin America and the Caribbean: Beyond Disciplinary and National Boundaries*, ed. Robert Lee Adams Jr (London: Routledge, 2013), 46–60.

Santos, Xosé M., 'The Contemporary Resurgence of the Pilgrimage to Santiago', in *Religious Pilgrimages in the Mediterranean World*, ed. Antón M. Pazos (London: Routledge, 2023), 113–27.

Sarkar, Jadunath, *India of Aurangzib compared with the India of Akbar, with extracts from the Khulastatu-t-Tawarikh* (Calcutta: Bose Brothers, 1901)

Sarojini Naidu: Great Women of Modern India, ed. Verinder Grover and Ranjana Arora (New Delhi: Deep & Deep Publications, 1993)

Sato, Yasuko, *Takamure Itsue, Japanese Antiquity, and Matricultural*

Paradigms that Address the Crisis of Modernity: A Woman from the Land on Fire (Cham: Palgrave MacMillan, 2023)

Schlesier, K. H., *The Wolves of Heaven: Cheyenne Shamanism, Ceremonies and Prehistoric Origins* (Norman: University of Oklahoma Press, 1987)

Schukies, Renate, and Edward Red Hat, *Red Hat: Cheyenne Blue Sky Maker and Keeper of the Sacred Arrows* (Münster: Lit. Verlag, 1993)

'Scotland's Cradle of Christianity is Scene of High Mass', *Catholic News Service* 29 June 1936.

Scott, Michael, 'The Oracle at Delphi: Unknowability at the Heart of the Ancient Greek Word', *Social Research: an International Quarterly*, 87 (2020), 51–74.

Scott, Michael, *Delphi: A History at the Center of the World* (Princeton: Princeton University Press, 2014)

'Seditious Publications', 24 August 2023, https://blogs.bl.uk/untoldlives/2023/08/seditious-publications.html

Sen, Sudipta, *Ganges: the Many Pasts of an Indian River* (Yale: Yale University Press, 2019)

Shakespeare, William, *Macbeth: Third Series*, ed. Sandra Clark and Pamela Mason (London: Bloomsbury, 2015)

Sharer, Robert J. and Loa P. Traxler, *The Ancient Maya*, 6th edn (Stanford: Stanford University Press, 2006)

Sheikh, Mohamed, *The Emperor of the Five Rivers: the life and times of Maharajah Ranjit Singh* (London: I. B. Taurus, 2017)

Sheldrake, P., *Living Between Worlds: Place and Journey in Celtic Spirituality* (London: Darton, Longman, and Todd, 1995)

Shephard, Naomi, *The Zealous Intruders: the Western Discovery of Palestine* (London: Harper & Row, 1987)

'Shrine Culture Suffers Under Covid', *Express Tribune* 3 August 2021, https://tribune.com.pk/story/2313593/shrine-culture-suffers-under-covid

'Sikh Holy Books take a flight to Canada', *Times of India* 3 April 2004, https://timesofindia.indiatimes.com/city/chandigarh/sikh-holy-books-take-a-flight-to-canada/articleshow/598186.cms

Silverstein, Adam J., *Islamic History: A Very Short Introduction* (Oxford: Oxford University Press, 2010)

Singh, Khushwant, *A History of the Sikhs: Volume 1, 1469–1838* (Delhi: Oxford University Press, 2004)

Singh, Khushwant, *A History of the Sikhs: Volume 2, 1839–1964* (Princeton: Princeton University Press, 1984)

Singh, Khushwant, *Truth, Love, and a Little Malice: An Autobiography* (London: Penguin, 2002)

Singh, Rajinder, *The Secular Maharaja: Maharaja Ranjit Singh* (Delhi: Dynamic Publications, 2008)

Singh, Vikash and Sangeeta Parashar, 'Hardwar: Spirit, Place, Politics', *Religions*, 10 (2019), 1–14.

Skaff, Jonathan Karam, *Sui-Tan China and Its Turko-Mongol Neighbors: Culture, Power, and Connections, 580–800* (Oxford: Oxford University Press, 2012)

Slight, John, *The British Empire and the Hajj, 1865–1956* (Cambridge, MA: Harvard University Press, 2015)

Smith, J. Gregory and Tara M. Bond-Freeman, 'In the Shadow of Quetzalcoatl: How Small Communities in Northern Yucatán Responded to the Chichén Itzá Phenomenon', in *Landscapes of the Itza: Archaeology and Art History at Chichén Itza and Neighboring Sites*, ed. Linnea Wren, Cynthia Kristan-Graham, Travis Nygard and Kaylee Spencer (Gainesville: University Press of Florida, 2018), 138–70.

Solans, Francisco Javier Ramón, '"A most select gathering": Mexican National Pilgrimages to Rome during the papacy of Leo XIII', *Religions*, 12 (2021), 1–18.

Sorrel, Christian, 'Politics of the Sacred: Lourdes, France, and Rome', in *Marian Devotions, Political Mobilization & Nationalism in Europe and America*, ed. Roberto di Stefano and Francisco Javier Ramón Solans (London: Palgrave, 2016), 57–82.

Sozemenus, 'The Ecclesiastical History of Sozomen', in *Nicene and Post-Nicene Fathers*, ed. Philip Schaff (Peabody, MA: Hendrickson, 2004)

'Spiritual Healing', *Waiapu Church Gazette*, XII, 1 September 1921.

Spotted Elk, Sheldon E., 'Northern Cheyenne Tribe: Traditional Law and Constitutional Reform', *Tribal Law Journal*, 11 (2012), 1–18.

'Spread of Infection from Pilgrim Centres', *Tribune* 25 May 1917.

Stands in Timber, John, and Margot Liberty, *Cheyenne Memories*, 2nd edn (Yale: Yale University Press, 1967)

Starkie, Walter, *In Sara's Tents* (London: John Murray, 1953)
Starkie, Walter, *Road to Santiago* (New York: E. R. Dutton & Co., 1957)
Statler, Oliver, *Japanese Pilgrimage* (London: Picador, 1984)
Stead, Mike, Sean Rorison and Oscar Sacfidi, *Angola* (Chalfont St Peter: Brandt, 2009)
Stephens, John L., *Incidents of Travel to Yucatán, in 2 Volumes* (Frankfurt am Main: Verlag GmbH, 2020)
Stephenson, Paul, *New Rome: the Empire in the East AD 395–700* (London: Profile, 2022)
Stinger, Charles, *The Renaissance in Rome* (Bloomington: Indiana University Press, 1985)
Stokstad, Marilyn, *Santiago de Compostela in the Age of the Great Pilgrimages* (Norman, University of Oklahoma Press, 1978)
Stronge, Susan, 'Maharaja Ranjit Singh and Artistic Patronage at the Sikh Court', *South Asian Studies*, 22 (2006), 89–101.
Sturluson, Snorri, *Heimskringla: History of the Kings of Norway*, trans. Lee M. Hollander (Austin: University of Texas Press, 1964)
Sundkler, Bengt, and Christopher Steed, *A History of the Church in Africa* (Cambridge: Cambridge University Press, 2000)
Sundstrom, Linea, 'Mirror of Heaven: Cross-Cultural Transference of the Sacred Geography of the Black Hills', *World Archaeology*, 28 (1996), 177–89.
Sundstrom, Linea, *Storied Stone: Indian Rock Art in the Black Hills Country* (Norman: University of Oklahoma Press, 2004)
Sundstrom, Linea, 'Heart of the Earth: A 1940s Lakota Map of the Black Hills Sacred Sites', *Great Plains Quarterly*, 41 (2021), 195–223.
System of University Geography Founded on the Works of Malte-Brun and Balbi (Edinburgh: Adam and Charles Black, 1842)
Szanto, E., 'Shi'a Islam in Practice', in *Handbook of Contemporary Islam and Muslim Lives*, ed. Ronal Lukens-Bull and Mark Woodward (Cham: Springer, 2021), 39–54.
Tablet, 12 October 1872.
Talbot, Alice-Mary M., *Faith Healing in Late Byzantium: the Posthumous Miracles of the Patriarch Athanasios I of Constantinople by Theoktistos the Stoudite* (Brookline, MA: Hellenic College Press, 1983)

Talbot, Alice-Mary, 'Pilgrimage to Healing Shrines: the Evidence of Miracle Accounts', *Dumbarton Oaks Papers*, 56 (2002), 153–73.
Talbot, Ian, 'A Tale of Two Cities: The Aftermath of Partition for Lahore and Amritsar', *Modern Asian Studies*, 1 (2007), 151–85.
Talbot, Lynn, 'Revival of the Medieval Past: Francisco Franco and the Camino de Santiago', in *The Camino de Santiago in the 21st century: Interdisciplinary Perspectives and Global Views*, ed. Samuel Sánchez y Sánchez and Annie Hesp (London: Routledge, 2016), 36–56.
Țăranu, Georgiana, 'Romanians Visiting Mussolini's Italy: interwar ideological pilgrimages as efficient propaganda tools', *Annals of the Ovidius University of Constanța*, 6 (2017), 35–59.
Tate, R. B., *Pilgrimage to St James of Compostela from the British Isles in the Middle Ages* (Liverpool: Liverpool University Press, 1990)
Taylor, Becky, *Another Darkness, Another Dawn: A History of Gypsies, Roma, and Travellers* (London: Reaktion Books, 2014)
Taylor, J. M., *Eva Peron: the Myths of a Woman* (Chicago: Chicago University Press, 1979)
Taylor, Thérèse, *Bernadette of Lourdes: her life, death and visions* (London: Burns & Oates, 2003)
Thacker, Alan, 'Rome of the Martyr Saints, Cults and Relics, Fourth to Seventh Centuries', in *Roma Felix: Formation and Reflections of Medieval Rome*, ed. Éamonn Ó Carragáin, Carol Neumann de Vegvar (London: Routledge, 2007), 13–50.
Thacker, Alan, 'Rome: the pilgrims' city in the seventh century', in *England and Rome in the Early Middle Ages: Pilgrimage, Art, and Politics*, ed. Francesca Tinti (Turnhout: Brepols, 2014), 89–139.
The 1918 Shikoku Pilgrimage of Takamure Itsue: An English Translation of Musume Junreiki, trans. Susan Tennant (Bowen Island, Canada: Bowen Publishing, 2010)
The Truth 7 November 1952.
Thévenot, Jean de, *The Travels of Monsieur de Thevenot into the Levant* (London: J. Clark, 1687)
Thompson, Edward Herbert, *People of the Serpent: Life and Adventure Among the Maya* (New York: Capricorn Books, 1960)
Thompson, J. Eric, *Maya History and Religion* (Norman: University of Oklahoma Press, 1970, reprinted 1990)

Thornton, John K., *The Kongolese Saint Anthony: Dona Beatriz Kimpa Vita and the Antonian Movement, 1684–1706* (Cambridge: Cambridge University Press, 1998)

Three Byzantine Saints: Contemporary Biographies of St. Daniel the Stylite, St. Theodore of Sykeon and St. John the Almsgiver, trans. Elizabeth Dawes, with Norman H. Baynes (Oxford: Blackwell, 1948)

Three Centuries of Travel Writing by Muslim Women, ed. Siobhan Lambert-Hurley, Daniel Majchrowicz and Sunil Sharma (Bloomington: Indiana University Press, 2022)

Thucydides, *History of the Peloponnesian War, Books III and IV*, trans. Charles Forster Smith (London: William Heinemann, 1920)

Thurstan, Herbert, *The Roman Jubilee: History and Ceremonial* (London: Sands, 1925)

Todd, John M., 'The Work for World Peace', *Furrow*, 4 (1953), 28–32.

Todd, Mabel Loomis, 'Angola and the Eclipse', *Christian Union* 31 October 1889, 533.

Townsend, Charles M., 'The Darbar Sahib', in *Oxford Handbook of Sikh Studies*, ed. Pashaura Singh and Louis E. Fenech (Oxford: Oxford University Press, 2014), 430–40.

Translating the Relics of St James, ed. Antón M. Pazos (London: Routledge, 2017)

The Travels of Ibn Battuta, A.D. 1325–1354, vol. 2, H. A. R. Gibb (Cambridge: Cambridge University Press for the Hakluyt Society, 1962)

The Travels of Ibn Jubayr, trans. R. J. C. Broadhurst (London: Jonathan Cape, 1952)

Travassos Valdez, Francisco, *Six Years of a Traveller's Life in South Africa* (London: Hurst and Blackett, 1861)

Tsurumi, E. Patricia, 'Feminism and Anarchism in Japan: Takamure Itsue, 1894–1964', *Bulletin of Concerned Asian Scholars*, 17 (1985), 2–19.

Uğurlu, A. Hilâl, 'Philanthropy in the Form of a Hair Strand: Sacred Relics in Nineteenth Century Ottoman Lands', in *Philanthropy in Anatolia Through the Ages: The First International Suna and İnan Kiraç Symposium on Mediterranean Civilizations*, ed. Oğuz Tekin, Christopher H. Roosevelt and Engin Akyürek (Antalya: Koç Üniversitesi, 2020), 215–25.

United States Senate Committee on Native Affairs, 108–1 *Hearing: Native American Sacred Places*, S-Hrg, 108–97, 18 June 2003.

Vaporis, Constantine Nomikops, *Breaking Barriers: Travel and the State in Early Modern Japan* (Cambridge, MA: Harvard University Press, 1994)

'Vatican Returns Relics to Orthodox Church', *CBC News* 27 November 2004.

Videla, Graciela Albornoz de, *Evita: Libro de Lectura para Primer Grado Inferior* (Buenos Aires: Editorial Lasserre, 1953)

Vidyarthi, L. P., *The Sacred Complex of Kashi: A Microcosm of Indian Civilization* (New Delhi: Concept, 2005)

'Visiting Ratana', *Greymouth Evening Star* 27 January 1921.

Walafridus Strabo, 'Life of Blathmac', in *Early Sources of Scottish History, AD 500 to 1286*, trans. Alan Orr Anderson (Edinburgh: Oliver and Boyd, 1922), 263–65.

Walker, R. J., 'The Social Implications of Medical Practice Among Māoris', *Tu Tangata*, 1 August 1982, 31–32.

Ward-Perkins, Bryan, 'Old and New Rome Compared: The Rise of Constantinople', in *Two Romes: Rome and Constantinople in Late Antiquity*, ed. Lucy Grig and Gavin Kelly (Oxford: Oxford University Press, 2012), 53–80.

Warner, Maria, *Alone of All Her Sex: The Myth and the Cult of the Virgin Mary* (Oxford: Oxford University Press, 2013)

'Warriors to Lourdes', https://www.warriorstolourdes.com/en/index.html

Watt, W. M., A. J. Wensinck, C. E. Bosworth and R. B. Winder, 'Mecca (Makka)', in *Historic Cities of the Islamic World*, ed. C. Edmund Bosworth (Leiden: Brill, 2007), 342–79.

Wavell, Arthur J. B., *A Modern Pilgrim in Mecca and a Siege in Sanaa* (London: Constable, 1913)

Webb, Diana, ed., *Pilgrims and Pilgrimage in the Medieval West* (London: I. B. Taurus, 2001)

Webb, Diana, *Medieval European Pilgrimage, c.700–c.1500* (Basingstoke: Palgrave, 2002)

Webster, David, 'Maya Drought and Niche Inheritance', in *The Great Maya Droughts in Cultural Context*, ed. Gyles Iannone (Boulder: University Press of Colorado, 2014), 333–57.

Wechsler, Howard J., *Offerings of Jade and Silk: Ritual and Symbol in the*

Legitimation of the T'ang Dynasty (New Haven: Yale University Press, 1985)
Weekly Dispatch (London) 28 October 1923.
Wellcome Collection, London: MS 7712.
Welsch, Chris, 'Bear Butte: Holy Mountain, Fragile Peace', *Star Tribune* 27 July 2003.
Western Daily Press 19 September 1934.
Wey, William, *The Itineraries of William Wey*, trans. and ed. Francis Davey (Oxford: Bodleian Library, 2010)
White, Arthur, *Plague and Pleasure: the Renaissance World of Pius II* (Catholic University of America Press, 2014)
White, Monica, 'Relics and the Princely Clan in Rus', in *Byzantium and the Viking World*, ed. F. Androshchuk, J. Shepard and M. White (Uppsala: Acta Universitatis Upsaliensis, 2010), 391–408.
White, Philip M., 'Researching American Indian Revitalization Movements', *Journal of Religious and Theological Information*, 8 (2009), 155–63.
Wiley, Eric, 'Romani Performance and Heritage Tourism: the Pilgrimage of the Gypsies at Les Saintes-Maries-de-la-Mer', *Drama Review*, 49 (2005), 135–58.
Wilkins, Ernest Hatch, *Life of Petrarch* (Chicago: University of Chicago Press, 1961)
Willard, T. A., *The City of the Sacred Well: Being a Narrative of the Discoveries of and Excavations of Edward Herbert Thompson in the Ancient City of Chi-Chen Itza with Some Discourse on the Culture and Development of the Mayan Civilization as Revealed by their Art and Architecture, here set down and illustrated from photographs* (New York: Century Co., 1926)
Williams, Arthur F., 'The Māori Miracle Man', *Waiapu Church Gazette*, XVI, 1 January 1921, 345.
Williams, John, 'The Tomb of St James: Coming to terms with History and Tradition', in *Culture and Society in Medieval Galicia*, ed. James D'Emilio (Leiden: Brill, 2015), 543–72.
Wisch, Barbara, 'The Matrix: "Le Sette Chiese di Roma" of 1575 and the Image of Pilgrimage', *Memoirs of the American Academy in Rome* 56/57 (2011/2012), 271–303.
Wohl, Ellen, *A World of Rivers: Environmental Change of Ten of the World's Great Rivers* (Chicago: University of Chicago Press, 2010)

'The Wonder-Worker', *Northern Advocate* 8 December 1920.
Woo, X. L., *Empress Wu the Great* (New York: Algora, 2008)
Woodside, Alexander, 'The Ch'ien-lung Reign', in *Cambridge History of China: Volume 9, The Ch'ing Dynasty to 1800, Part 1* (Cambridge: Cambridge University Press, 2008), 230–309.
Wordsworth, William, 'Iona', in *The Poems of William Wordsworth: Collected Reading Texts from the Cornell Wordsworth*, vol. 3, ed. Jared Curtis (Penrith: Humanities e-Books 2014)
Wright, Caleb, *Lectures on India* (Boston: Caleb Wright, 1848)
Wu, Pei-yi, 'An Ambivalent Pilgrim to T'ai Shan: Some Pages from a Seventeenth Century Novel', in *Pilgrims and Sacred Sites in China*, ed. Susan Naquin and Chun-Fang Yu (Berkeley, CA: University of California Press, 1992), 65–88.
Xacopedia: 'Goethe, Johann Wolfgang', https://xacopedia.com/Goethe_Johann_Wolfgang
Xenophon, *Hellenica*, trans. Carleton L. Brownson (Cambridge, MA: Harvard University Press, 1947)
Xitu, Uanhenga, *The World of 'Mestre' Tamoda* (London: Readers International, 1988)
Yadav, K. C., *Punjab: Colonial Challenge and Popular Response 1849–1947* (Haryana: Hope India, 2003)
Yamani, Mai, *Cradle of Islam: The Hijaz and the Quest for Identity in Saudi Arabia* (London: I. B. Taurus, 2009)
Yeoman, Peter, *Pilgrimage in Medieval Scotland* (Edinburgh: Historic Scotland, 1999)
Yoshida, Teigo, 'Strangers and Pilgrims in Village Japan', in *Pilgrimages and Spiritual Quests in Japan*, ed. Maria Rodríguez del Alisal, Peter Ackermann and Dolores P. Martinez (London: Routledge, 2007), 47–60.
Yu, Jimmy, *Sanctity and Self-Inflicted Violence in Chinese Religions, 1500–1700* (Oxford: Oxford University Press, 2012)
Zádori, János, *Viaje a España*, ed. A. Pombo Rodríguez (Santiago de Compostela: Xunta de Galicia, 2010)
Zhuo, Xinping, *Religious Faith of the Chinese* (Singapore: Springer, 2018)
Zola, Émile, *Lourdes*, trans. Ernest A. Vizetelly (New York: Prometheus Books, 2000)
Zonis, Marvin, *Majestic Failure: The Fall of the Shah* (Chicago: University of Chicago Press, 1991)

INDEX

Individuals whose surnames are known are listed by that name. When an individual is instead known by a geographical or other distinction, they are listed by first name. Italicised numbers in entries refer to images in the text.

A

Abd al-Malik, caliph, develops Jerusalem, 68
Abdul Rahman al-Saud, 99–100
Abdülhamid I, pilgrimage to tomb of, 143
Abdülmecid I, building work of, 142
Abraham, 68, 87
Abu Fadhl al-Abbas, shrine of (Karbala), 161
Access, arguments over, 75
Acre, fall of (1291), 72
Adomnán, abbot of Iona, 146, 147, 148
Aelia Eudoxia, empress, 124
Afghanistan, 35, 222, 251
Africa, conversion to Christianity in, 195–6
Agesipolis, king of Sparta, 54
Ahmad Durrani, founder of Afghanistan, 226
Akbar, Mughal emperor, 28, 220
Al-Asqa Mosque, Jerusalem, 68, 71
Alcaeus, poet, 47
Alea, citizens of, 53–4
Alexander the Great, 58
Alexandria, 128
Alighieri, Dante, 327–8
Alfonso II, king of Asturias, 311, 312
Alfonso III, king of Asturias, 311, 314
Alfonso XI, king of Castile, 316
Alfonso XII, king of Spain, 320
Al-Hakim, caliph, 69
Ali Reza Pasha, pilgrimage of, 170
Ali, king of Sudan, 91
Al-Idrisi, description of Santiago de Compostela of, 315
Allahabad, *see* Prayag
Allenby, Gen. Edmund H, 80
Al-Mansur, Umayyad caliph of Cordoba, 312
Amalfi, acquisition of St Andrew by, 135
American Civil War, 208
American Indian Religious Freedom Act, 215
Americans, travel to Jerusalem of, 77
Amlaíb Cuará, Norse king, pilgrimage of, 158
Amos Bad Hear Bull, 202

Amritsar (India), 7, 44, 166, 217–32
  attacks on, 219, 221, 223, 225–6, 231
  British rule in, 228–32
  centrality to Sikh faith of, 221–2, 226
  communal kitchen (Guru Ka Langar) at, 220
  decline of pilgrimage to, 224–6, 228
  foundation of, 218, 219–24
  holy tank of, 218, 219, 220, 225–6
Amritsar, Massacre (1919), 230–1
Ancestor worship, 11
André le Breton, Compostela of, 324
Angola, Christianisation of, 190, 192–3
  civil war in (1975–2002), 200
  colonisation of, 191, 192–3, 197
  disease in, 199
  independence of, 199
Anthony of Novrogod, pilgrimage of, 134
Antioch, 128
Apollo, Greek god, 46, 47, 48, 50, 51, 52, 53, 54, 55, 56, 60
  oracle at Didyma of, 58
Appius Claudius, pilgrimage to Delphi of, 50–1
Aquilante Rocchetta, journey of, 75
Arab-Israeli War, 83
Arba'in, annual Karbala pilgrimage of, 165, 166
Arcadius, emperor, 124–5, 128
Arch of Titus, 65
Ardern, Jacinda, prime minister of New Zealand, 277–8
Arepa, saintly identity of, 274
Argentina, 238, 285
Argentinan Congress, 291
Argos, 54, 253, 256, 258
Arles (France), 252, 253, 255, 256, 258, 324
Armaburu, president of Argentina, 288
Artgal, king of Connacht (Ireland), pilgrimage of, 158
Association for Protecting Japanese Pilgrimage, 305
Assumptionist Fathers, 78, 245
Astypalaia (Greece), island of, 54
Atene (New Zealand), 272–3
Athens (Greece), pilgrims from, 52, 56
Atlantis, lost city of, 177, 263
Australia, pilgrims from, 247, 269
Avignon Papacy, 112
Aymeric Picaud, 314
Ayyub al-Ansari, shrine of, 140–1

B

Baba Buddha, first *granthi,* 222
Baba Deep Singh, shrine to, 221
Baba Ram Singh, 229
Babylonians, 64
Baghdad (Iraq), 89
Bahrain, pilgrims from, 173
Bakongo, religion of the, 196
Baldwin II, Latin emperor, 136, 139
Balkans, pilgrims from, 76
Bandukpur (India), pilgrimage to, 31
Bangladesh, 222
Baronelli-Javon, Marquis Falco de, 261, 263
Basil I, emperor, 132
Bathélémy, André, 259, 260
Battle of Chaeronea, 58
  of Clavijo, 312
  of Cúl Dreinne, 146

of Karbala, 160–61, 165
of Rio Salado, 316
of Salamis, 56
Battos, 55
Bayonne (France), archbishop of, 244
Bear Butte (USA), 7, 44, 202–16, *204*, 266
and vision quests, 206–7, 208–9, 211
contact with the Creator on, 206, 207
death and, 205
law and, 205, 215–16
Native American identity and, 205
orientation of structures towards, 206
sacred objects from, 203, 204
Sun Dance and, 203
threats to, 207–9, 212–14, 215
tourist behaviour at, 213
tribal council held at (1857), 208
Bear Butte Company, 213
Bear Butte State Park, 213
Beatriz Kimpa Vita, prophetess, 199
Bedouins, attacks on pilgrims of, 74–5
Begum Sarbuland, pilgrimage to Karbala of, 164–5
Belgium, pilgrims from, 119, 237
Bellarmine, Robert, cardinal, 319
Benares (see Varanasi)
Benedictines, 80, 135, 151, 156
Benoit, bishop of Saint-Pol-de-Léon (Brittany), 253
Bernadette (Marie-Bernard Soubirous), 233–5, 237, 238, 241
Bernini, Gianlorenzo, 115–16
Bhai Mani Singh, *granthi,* 224–5
Bhim Goda Weir (India), 40
Bixia Juanun, 12, 16, 23
Blachernai palace (Constaantinople), 134
Black Death, spread by pilgrims of, 97
Black Hills (USA), discovery of gold in, 208, 209
Black Stone, 87, 90
Bohner, Alfred, 304, 306
Bordeaux Pilgrim, 66
Bosphorus (Turkey), 125
Boswell, John, 145
Boucher, Jean, 75
Brahmins, on the Ganges, 37–8, 42
Brancardiers (Lourdes), 239
Brazil, 194, 198, 238
Bridge of Sant-Angelo (Rome), 113, 114
Bristol (England), 316
British rule, impact on Amritsar of, 228
Brown, Dan, novelist, 265–6
Brunete (Spain), 321
Buchenwald (Germany), 251
Buddhism, 157, 296
Buenos Aires (Argentina), 8, 61, 279–91
Bukkai, twenty-one pilgrimages of, 299
Bureau de Contestations Médicales (Lourdes Medical Bureau), 239–40
Burial, pilgrimage sites and, 141, 158–59, 166–7, 300

C

Cairo (Egypt), 72, 90
Camargue (France), 254, 263
Cambrai (France), diocese of, 237

Camino de Santiago (Spain), 310, 313, 323, 325–6
Camino Francés, 8, 313, 316
Canada, 203, 217, 237, 271
Canterbury cathedral (England), 2
Cão, Diogo, navigator, 190
Capuchin friars, 193, 194
Carfin (Scotland), 239
Carmen Polo, pilgrimages of, 322
Carroll, Lewis, 61
Casablanca (Morocco), 87
Castalian Spring (Delphi), 48
Catacombs (Rome), 106–7, 123
Celtic Christianity, 145, 153
Cenote Sagrado (Mexico), 176–7, *179*, 181
  decline of pilgrimage to, 188
  human sacrifice at, 176–8, 185
  offerings in, 181, 185–8, *186*
Centre of the World, 37, 47, 63
Cesare Borgia, 112
Chang Tai, pilgrimage of, 14
Chapel of Reconciliation (Lourdes), 238
Chapel of the Virgin of the Pharos (Istanbul), 130
Charlemagne, Holy Roman Emperor, 314
Charles Spotted Elk, pilgrimage of, 212
Charlotte Black Elk, 205
Cheyenne, reservations of the, 206
Chichén Itzá (Mexico), 7, 176–89
  and comparison with major pilgrimage sites, 178–9
  and equinox pilgrimage, 188–9
  origins and development of, 178–81
Chile, 288
Chimayó (USA), 239
China, sacred mountains of, 11–12
  travellers from, 136
Chita Hantō (Japan), pilgrimage circuit at, 302
Chocarne, Victor, 245–6
Cholera, spread by pilgrims, 35, 97–8
Chōzen, pilgrimage of, 297
Christ the Redeemer (Brazil), 279
Christ, relics of, 130, 139
  tomb of, 253
Christians, protections for, 66
Church of Panagia Blachernai (Istanbul), 131
  of the Holy Apostles (Istanbul), 125
  of the Holy Sepulchre (Jerusalem), 66, *67*, 69, 75, 83, 84,
  of the Vivifying Source (Istanbul), 239
Churchill, Winston, 89
Clark, Eleanor, 113
Cluniacs, 313
Cnut, king of England, 118–19, 123
Code of Indian Offences (1883), 210
Coimbra, conquest of (Portugal), 312
Colonialism, in the New World, 183
  pilgrimage and, 176, 190, 191–94, 228–32
  use of religion in, 191, 187
Communism, pilgrimage and, 10
Congo, enslaved people from, 195
Constantine II, emperor, 126–7
Constantine I the Great, 60, 66–7, 106, 125, 126
Constantinople (Turkey) (*see also* Istanbul)
Constantinople (Turkey), 60, 125–6, 166
  alternative names for, 125, 128–9, 143

Islamic pilgrimage to, 139–44
Muslim attacks on, 132
pilgrimage sites converted to Islamic use, 140–1
relics in, 126–7, 144
reputation as a Christian city, 130
rivalry with Jerusalem of, 129, 131
sack of (1204), 108, 134, 135, 136
seizure by Ottomans of (1453), 139–40
Cordoba (Spain), 312
Corinth (Greece), 47
Cosimo de Medici, pilgrimage of, 319
Coste, Msgr, archbishop of Aix, 261
Council of Florence (1438–42), 105–6
of Trent, 115
Counter-Reformation, impact on pilgrimage of, 115–16, 118
Couve, Henry, artist, 264–5
Cozumel (Mexico), Mayan pilgrimage to, 178
Crazy Horse, 208, 209
Crimean War, 76, 78
Croatia, pilgrims from, 251
Croesus, king of Lydia, 55–6
Cross, tour of Argentina of, 284
Crown of Thorns, 130, 132, 135, 136, 321
Crucifixion relics, 126, 131–2, 134, 139, 321
Crusades, 69, 70, 72, 108, 133–4
Cuba, 321
Curly Hair, *see* Crazy Horse
Custer, George A., Colonel, 209
Cyriacus of Ancona, 61
Częstochowa (Poland), Black Madonna's shrine at, 6

D
Dachau (Germany), 251
Daigo, emperor of Japan, 293
Damascus (Syria), 72, 90, 96, 128, 163, 165
David Deafy, 213
David, king, 64
Dawes Act (1887), 210
Deadwood, 209
Death, pilgrimage and, 16, 23–4, 25, 26, 38, 111, 158–9, 182, 300–2
de Landa, Diego, Spanish bishop, 178, 183–5
Delphi (Greece), 7, *59*, 45–62
decline of, 46, 58–60
looting of, 59–60
origins of, 47–51
rebuilding of, 60
rediscovery of, 61
control of, 56, 58
Delphi, treasury at, 53
Delphic Amphictyony, 56
Delphic Oracle, modern politics and the, 61–2
Descamisados, Argentinian poor called, 282
Didyma (Greece), oracle at, 58
Disease, spread of pilgrims, 97, 111, 166–7
Divination, 48
Dodona (Greece), oracle at, 56
Dōhan, pilgrimage of, 295
Dome of the Rock (Jerusalem), 68, 71, 74
Donald, lord of the Isles,151
Dos Santos, José Eduardo, president of Angola, pilgrimage of, 200
Dragonfly, Lakota artist, 202
Drought, 182, 211

Drypia (Constantinople), translation of relics to, 124–5
Dukh Bhanjani Tree (Amritsar), 221
Dunster (England), pilgrims from, 316
Dutch, in Angola, 193
Dyer, Colonel Reginald, 230–1

E

East India Company, 39–42
Egeria, in Constantinople, 133
Egypt, sultan of, 90
El Castillo, Chichén Itzá (Mexico), 182, 188–9
End of the World, pilgrimage and, 189
England, pilgrims from 108, 118–19, 314
English Hospice (Rome), 113
Episcopalians, pilgrimages of, 157
Erasmus, Desiderius, 317
Ethiopia, pilgrims from, 105–6, 113
Eudocia, empress, 128, 131
European Community, impact on pilgrimage of, 326
Exhibition of the Fascist Revolution (Rome), 121
Eyüp Sultan Mosque (Istanbul), politicisation of, 140–1

F

Famine, impact on pilgrimage of, 300
Fascism, pilgrimage and, 121–2, 321–3
Father Horn, criticism of, 78
Fatima, daughter of the Prophet Muhammad, 160
Felix Fabri, pilgrimage of, 73–4
Feng and *shan* sacrifice, 19–20, 21, 26
Ferdinand the Great, king of Leon, 312, 313
Fertility, pilgrimage and, 16–17, 28
Filarete (Antonio di Pietro Averlino), 105, 123
Filial piety and duty, pilgrimages of, 15–17, 24, 25
First Gulf War (1991), 172
First Peloponnesian War, 56
First Temple (Jerusalem), 64
First World War, 80, 98, 171, 211, 213, 237, 246–7, 247–8, 249, 268, 306
Flagellation, on pilgrimage, 165
Fleury, Jean, 259, 260
Flood, biblical, 203–4
Floral Games (Spain), 322
Florence (Italy), 243
Fools Crow v. Gullet, 215–6
Fools Crow, 211, 213, 215
Fort Laramie, Treaty of, 209, 215
Fould, Achille, French minister of finance, 236–7
Four Sacred Arrows, 205–6
France, Nazi defeat of, 245
  pilgrims from, 119, 120, 260, 313
Francis Drake, 317
Franciscans, 73, 284
Francisco Franco, ruler of Spain, 321–4
Franco-Prussian War, 245
Fraser, Peter Fraser, prime minister of New Zealand, 276
Frederich Wilhlem of Prussia, 45
French Revolution (1789), 254
French, atonement for capture of Rome of, 120

G
Galician Regional Exhibition, 321
Ganga, goddess, 27–8, 37, 44
Ganges Canal (India), 40
Ganges River (India), 7, 27–44, 257
  water, transport of, 28, *29*
  as a purifier, 44
  as a symbol of India, 39, 40, 44
  baptism in, 39
  control of, 40
  cremation on, 38, 39, 43
  origins of pilgrimage to, 29–30
  pilgrimage cities of, 30–9
  pollution of, 43–4
Gangotri glacier (India), 27, 43
Gaozong, Chinese Emperor (ruled 649–83 CE), 20
Gelmírez, Diego, bishop of Santiago de Compostela, 313, 314–15
General Soleimani, images of, 172
Genroku culture, impact on pilgrimage of, 298
George V, king of England, 272
George, duke of Argyll, 153–5
George, Lloyd, prime minster of Great Britain, 80
Germany, 249, 288
  pilgrims from, 237–8, 251, 260, 321
Ghandi, Indira, Indian prime minister, 231–2
Ghat, 32, *33*, 36–7, 38
Ghost Dance, prohibition of, 210
Giovanni Maggi, map of, 117
Gipsy Kings, 259
Goethe, Johann Wolfgang von Goethe, 327
Gold, offerings of, 186–7
Golden Horn (Istanbul), 129
Golden Temple (Amritsar), *221*, 227, 228, 230, 231, 232
  massacre at (1984), 231–2
  see also Harmandir
Granada (Spain), conquest of, 318–19
Grand Tour, 118
Grand Trunk Road, 222
Great Depression, 276
Great German Pilgrimage (1064), 69
Great Mosque (Mecca), 88, 84, 88, 100
Greek City States, 52–3, 54, 57
Greek Orthodox, 75, 79
  pilgrims, domestic status of, 79–80
Grinnos, king of Thera, 55
Grotto Fathers, 236, 238, 242, 245
Guangwu, Chinese emperor, 20
Guidebooks for pilgrims, 72, 76, 92, 97, 108, 116–17, 167, 174, 240, 241, 297–8, 305, 320, 325
Guru Ajan Dev, 220, 222–3
  Amar Das, 219, 220
  Gobind Singh, 223–4
  Granth Sahib, 217–18, 219, 222, 224–7
  Har Krishan, 223
  Har Rai, 223
  Hargobind, militancy of, 223
  Nanak, 218–19
  Ram Das, 219–20
  Tegh Bahadur, 223
Gyges, king of Lydia, 54
Gypsies, 3, 265, *264*
  control of, 252, 257
  exoticism of, 263
  pilgrims, 252, 257–8, 259, 261–2, 265

H

Hadrian, emperor, 65–6
Hagia Sofia (Constantinople/Istanbul), 124, 125, *127*, 129–30, 131, 134, 137
  converted into a museum, 143
  converted to a mosque, 140
Hajj, 89, 175, 99, 98
  as a requirement for all Muslims, 86
  as fifth pillar of Islam, 163
  special clothing for, 89
Hanbalis, reconstruction of Karbala's shrines by, 167–8
Hannibal of Carthage, 58
Haridwar (India), 30, 32, 35, 40
Harmandir (Amritsar), 220–1, 218, 222
  damage of, 225, 226, 232
  gold covering applied to, 227
Hawaii, pilgrimage restrictions on, 215
Heinrich Bünting of Magdeburg, 63
Hejaz, 98–9
Helena, mother of Constantine, 126, 130
Henro, *see* Shikoku
Henro-Dogyaki, interest group, 303
Henry II, king of England, 1–2
Henry of Blois, bishop of Winchester, pilgrimage of, 314
Heraclea, 54
Heresy, 199
Herod I, king, 64–5
Herrera, José Martin, cardinal archbishop, 321
Himalayas, 27
Hindu pilgrimage, 27, 28, 29, 37, 157
Hitler, Adolf, German chancellor, 122, 249
Holy Redeemer Church (Jerusalem), 81
Holy Spirit, 267
Holy years, 84, 310, 318, 320, 321, 322, 324,
Homestead Act (1862), 208–9
Honshu (Japan), island of, 298
Hosoda Shūei, map-maker, 299
Human sacrifice, 178, 183–5, 186–7
Husayn Ibn Ali, martyrdom of, 160, 161, 165
  shrine of (Karbala), 161, *162*, 167, 168, 172, 173
Hussein, Saddam, president of Iraq, 172

I

Iberian Peninsula, Muslim attacks on, 310, 312, 314, 316
Ibn Battuta, Muslim writer, 38–9, 168
Ibn Jubayr, 92–3, 94
Ignatius of Smolensk, 138
Imbangala, work with slavers of, 194
Immigration, impact on pilgrimage of, 153
Immortality, nectar of, 219
Imperial pilgrimage, 17–26
Incense, and importance in China, 14–15
India, British rule in, 228–32
  holy rivers, of, 29
  Independence, 36, 230
  partition of, 231
  pilgrims from, 97, 164, 165, 189, 173–4
Indian money, 173–4
Indian Reorganization Act, 212

Indonesia, pilgrims from, 100
Indulgences, 108, 110, 112, 114, 115, 151, 254, 318
Institute of Spain, 322
Iona (Scotland), 7, 145–59, *150*
 and writers visiting, 152, 153
 circular pilgrimage route on, 149
 compared to Jerusalem 147
 crosses on, 149, 156
 decline of, 151, 152–3
 isolation of, 146–7, 149, 156
 nunnery on, 151
 origins of, 145–7
 pilgrimage chapel on, 151
 restoration of the abbey on, 154
 revival of pilgrimage to, 152–7
 Scottish identity and, 145–6
 Viking raids on, 148
Iona Community, 156–57
Iran, pilgrims from, 172
 shrines of, 4
 see also Persia
Iraq, 161, 169, 171, 172, 251
Ireland, journey from, 1
 pilgrims from, 119–20, 238
Isabel of Portugal, pilgrimage of, 315
Islamic State, and attacks on pilgrims, 172
Islamic World Conference, 99
Israel, creation of alternative pilgrimage sites in, 83–4
Istanbul, 7, 124–44
 Islamification of, 143
 secularisation of, 143
 see also Constantinople
Italy, 288
 pilgrims from, 76, 238, 260

J
Jade Maiden Pool (Tai Shan), 13
Jade, offerings of, 187–8
Jaffa Gate (Jerusalem), 80, 81
Jakuhon, guidebook of, 295, 298
Jallianwala Bagh (Amritsar), 230–1
James II, king of England, 154
János Zádori, pilgrimage of, 319
Japan, modernisation of, 302–3
Jason of Pherai, 53
Jean de Thévenot, explorer, 30
Jean de Tournai, pilgrimage of, 316
Jean de Venette, 257
Jerusalem (Israel), 7, 9, 63–85, 155, 284, 316, 321
 access to for pilgrims, 68–9, 71
 and importance to Islam, 68, 72
 and life of Christ, 63–4
 Babylonian attack on, 64
 British in, 80–1, 83
 Christian pilgrims first come to, 66
 Christian settlement in, 68
 foreign development of, 78–9
 Jewish pilgrimage to, 71, 75–6
 Jewish settlement in, 76
 loss of, 68, 69, 70, 108
 Mamluks and, 72–3
 Ottoman control of 74–80
 rebuilding of, 65–6, 70
 removal of relics from, 131
 rioting in, 82
 split control of, 83–5
Jesuit, 5, 30, 113, 155, 191, 195, 210
Jews, Diaspora of, 66
 Jerusalem and, 64, 66, 76
 pilgrimages of, 63, 64–6, 71, 73, 75–6, 82, 157
Jimena, wife of Alfonso III, pilgrimage of 311

Jinin, pilgrimage of, 302
John Black Wolf, pilgrimage of, 212
Johnson, Samuel, 145, 152
Jubilee years, 110–12, 113, 117, 321, 324,
Jubilee years, critics of, 111–12
Judah Halevi, pilgrimage of, 71
Judgement Day, 147
Julian the Apostate, 60
Jupiter, altar dedicated to, 311
Justinian I the Great, 67, 127, 129, 131

K

Kaaba (Mecca), 87, 89, 98
Kabul (Afghanistan), 222
Kali, Hindu goddess, 257
Kanpur (India), pollution from, 43
Kanwar Mela, 29
Karachi (India/Pakistan), pilgrimage hall in, 174
Karbala (Iraq), 7, 160–75
  and lawlessness, 170
  and Shia identity, 163, 173, 175
  as symbol of rebellion, 171–2
  attack on, 167–8, 170, 172
  decline of, 170–1
  flight of Shia from, 170
  sacred soil of, 166–7
  Shia rebuilding of, 169
Kartarpur (India/Pakistan), 218
Katherine Lee Bates, pilgrimage of, 321
Keats, John, on Iona, 152
Kempe, Margery, pilgrimage of, 316
Key, John , prime minister of New Zealand, 277
Kibeho (Rwanda), 239
Kievan Rus, pilgrims from, 132–33, 124
Kipling, Rudyard, 222
King Aigeus (mythical), 46
Kirra (Greece), port of, 48, 56
Kiswa, covering of the Kaaba, 87
Knights of St Columba, 247
Knights of St John of Jerusalem (Hospitallers), 70
Knock (Ireland), 237, 239, 262
Kōbō Daishi, 293, *294*, 302
  legends of, 295
  pilgrimage in honour of, 298
Kongo (Africa), kingdom of, 190
Korea, pilgrims from, 327, 305
Koyoto (Japan), 297
Kukai, *see* Kōbō Daishi
Kumbh Mela, pilgrimage festival, 31–5, 36, 42
Kwanza River (Angola), 190, 194, 185
Kyrene (Libya), city of, 55
Kyushu (Japan), pilgrimage circuit on, 302

L

La Coruña (Spain), port of, 308, 316, 317, 319
Lafreri, Antonio, *The Seven Churches of Rome*, 116, *117*
La Planta (Argentina), renamed after Eva Perón, 285
La Reconquista, 312
La Salette (France), 233, 237
Lach Ber, tree of (Amritsar), 221
Lame Deer Reservation (Montana), 206
Languedoc (France), pilgrims from, 258
Las Lajas (South America), 239
Last Supper, relics from, 135, 139
Lateran Baptisty and Palace (Rome), 107, 115

Lateran Treaty (1929), 119
Lenin, Vladimir, Russian leader, pilgrimage to tomb of, 281
Lindisfarne (England), bishop of, 147
Lion's Cave (Jerusalem), promotion of as a pilgrimage site, 84
Little Bighorn, Battle of (1876), 209
Liverpool (England), pilgrim from, 249
Lopez Ferrerio, Antonio, 308
Louis IX, king of France, 136
Louis VII, king of France, 134
Lourdes (France), 8, *234*, 233–51, 268
  criticism of vulgarity of, 243–4
  cures of pilgrims to, 236
  French national pilgrimage to, 245
  growth of town of, 235–7, 239, 243
  pilgrimages of reconciliation to, 246, 249
  politics and, 244–5
  revival of, 250
  sites likened to, 238–9
  spring at, 235, 242
war and, 246–51
Luanda (Angola), 192, 193–4, 195, 198
Lucknow (India), pilgrims from, 173
Luther, Martin, 114, 317

M

Magaret of Austria, queen of Spain, pilgrimage of, 318
Magnus Barelegs, king of Norway, pilgrimage of, 150–1
Mahmud Khan, pilgrimage of, 168
Malaya, pilgrims from, 100
Malcolm X, pilgrimage of, 102
Mama Muxima, *see* Our Lady of Muxima
Manipura (India), pilgrimage to, 28–9
Mansa Musa, king of Mali, pilgrimage of, 91, *92*
Manukarnika Ghat (Varanasi), 37, 38
Māori Party, 277
Māori, 267, 269
  impact of Spanish flu on, 268
Mappa Mundi, 63
Maradona, Diego 291
Margaret of Anjou, queen of England, 254
Margaret of Beverley, 70
Maria II, queen of Portugal, 197
Martín García Island, 288
Martir, bishop of Arzendjan (Turkey), pilgrimage of, 316
Martyrs, cults of, 106–7
Mary I, queen of England, 317
Mary Jacobe, 253, 257
Mary Magdalene, 253, 266
Mary Salome, 253, 257
Mashhad, pilgrimage to, 171
Massabielle Grotto (Lourdes), 233
Massangano (Angola), 194
Mata Sundari, 224
Mato Paha (USA), *see* Bear Butte
Mattoso, Álvaro de Carvalho, slave trader, 195
Maya, 176, 177,
  decline of, 181
  settlements of, 179–80
Mecca (Saudi Arabia), 6, 7, 44, 68, 72, *88*, 86–104, 162–3, 171, 268
  capture of by, 99
  control of as a sign of power, 89
  development of, 88, 89, 90–1, 93, 101
  economy of, 91–3, 95

growth of pilgrimage to, 100
Hashemite revolt in, 98
modernisation of, 101–2
prayer facing, 87
sharifs of, 89, 90, 94
Medina (Saudi Arabia), 72, 87, 88–9, 92, 94, 96, 160, 163
Megara (Greece), city of, 53
Mehmed II, Ottoman sultan, 139–40, 141
Mehrmah Khanom, princess, pilgrimages of, 164
Melisende, queen of Jerusalem, 70
Mere Rikiriki, 273–74
Merkez Efendi, holy well of, 141
Mexico, pilgrimages from, 120
Michael III, emperor, 130
Michaelangelo, 115
Miguel Payá Rico, cardinal archbishop of Santiago de Compostela, 208, 320
Milan (Italy), 106
Military pilgrimage, to Lourdes, 246, 249, 251
Ministry of Health (Argentina), 282
Ministry of Labour (Argentina), 282, 284, 287
Miracles, 129, 240
Montmartre (Paris, France), 120
Morais, Vincente de, 196
Mormonism, 4–5, 277
Mount Arafat (Turkey), 201
Mount Kōya (Japan), 294
Mount Libredon (Spain), 311
Mount of Olives (Jerusalem), 67–8
Mount Parnassus (Greece), 46, 56
Mount Zion (Jerusalem), 67, 83, 84
Mountains, importance in China, 14–15
Mourning, pilgrimage and, 163–7, 172
Muffel, Nichols, pilgrimage of, 108
Muhammad Ibn Hasan al-Mahdi, the twelfth imam, 162
Muhammad Reza, shah of Iran, pilgrimages of, 171
Mullikin, Mary, pilgrimage of, 14
Murad IV, Ottoman sultan, 175
Murakami Nagando, 304
Muslims, British empire's responsibility for, 89–90
Mussolini, Benito, Italian dictator, politicised pilgrimage and, 121
Muxima (Angola), 7, 190–201
and enslaved people at, 195
church at, 190–91, *192*, 198–9
decline of, 198, 199
fort at, 191, 193, 194
growth of pilgrimage to, 198
use of charms at, 196–7
Muxima Quitangombe, Quissama chief, 191

N

N'Gola kingdom, 191
Najaf (Iraq), city of, 169, 175
Nakasukasa Mōhei, 282 pilgrimages of, 301
Nantes (France), 244
Naples (Italy), 106
Napoleon III, president of France, 237, 244
Napoleonic Wars, 319
Napot Xiu, assassination of, 182
Narendra Modi, Indian prime minister, 43–4
Nasir Khrushaw, 69, 86
National hostels, 113

National League of Ex-Combatant Priests, pilgrimages of, 247
National Library of Argentina, 290
National pilgrimages, 119–21
Native American land, European threats to, 207–9, 210
Native American nations, appeal of Bear Butte to, 203
Native Americans, 3, 44, 203, 210–211
  law to protect religion of, 211–12
  respect for sacred places of, 214–15
Ndongo, queen of Kongo, 193
Nea (New) Church, Jerusalem, 67
Nectar, 31, 32, 33
Nehru, Jawaharlal , Indian prime minister, 39
Nelson (New Zealand), 271
Nelson Medicine Bird, pilgrimage of, 212
Nevers (France, 235
New Zealand First, 277
New Zealand Labour Party, 276
New Zealand, 267–78
  pilgrims from, 247
Nizinga, king of Kongo, 190
Njinga, queen of the Matamba, 194
Noah's Ark, 203
North Africa, pilgrims from, 76
Nossa Senhora da Assunção (Angola), 191–2
Notre Dame de France (Jerusalem), 78
Noulette (France), sanctuary of, 246
Novgorod (Russia), 137–8
Nzambi, Angolan deity, 196

O

O Cebreiro (Spain), development of, 325
Obelisks (Rome), 115
Oglala Lakota, 202, 203
Oil, discovery of, 101
Old Crazy Horse, visions of, 207–8
Olga, princess of Kiev, 132
Oliver Statler, pilgrimages of, 305
Olympia (Greece), 48
Omeka, illness and death of, 267–8, 274
Operation Blue Star (Amritsar), 232
Oracle at Delphi, *see* Pythia
Oracles, prohibition of, 60
Orthodox Christians, pilgrimages of, 136–7, 157
Osaka (Japan), 297, 298, 303
Ottoman Empire, 76, 98, 143
  control of Mecca by, 89, 93–4
Oudh Bequest (1849), 173
Our Lady of Hope, Macarena (Seville), 282
  of Lujan (Argentina), pilgrimage and, 285, 286
  of Muxima (Angola), as defender, 192, 193, 199–200
  of the Gypsies, 260
  of the Immaculate Conception, at Muxima, 190–1
  see also Virgin Mary
Oviedo (Spain), cathedral at, 321

P

Padma River (see Ganges)
Padua (Italy), 135
Paio, hermit, 311
Pairis Abbey (France), acquisition of relics by, 135
Palestine, Britain withdraws from, 83
Pantheon (Rome), 107, 121

Pantocrator complex (Constantinople), 137
Papacy, corruption of, 114–15
Paris (France), 233, 235, 279
Paryatak Mitra, 37
Passion of Christ, relics from the, 130, 136
Pau (France), 236
Pax Christi, 250
Pax Romana, pilgrimages of, 247
Peace of Nicias (421 BCE), 56
Pedro Ara, doctor, 287
Peláe, Diego, bishop of Santiago de Compostela, 313
Perón, Eva and Juan, joint reverence of, 286
Perón, Eva, Argentinian first lady, 272–91
  'kidnap' of remains of, 287
  alleged martyrdom of, 283–6
  anniversary commemoration of, 286
  as Spiritual Leader of the Nation, 283
  burial of, 288, 289–90
  death of, 281, 283
  display of shroud of, 291
  embalming of, 287
  funeral of, 284–85
  healing touch of, 282
  identity as a saint of, 280, 281–3, 286
  image of, *280*, 283, 285
  likened to Jesus Christ, 284
  likened to the Virgin Mary, 285
  mourning for, 283–4
  pilgrimages in honour of, 280, 288–91, 290–1
  planned memorial for, 279
  political role of, 282
  prayers to, 285
  remains of, 279–80, 284, 287–8
Perón, Isabel, 288, 289
Perón, Juan, president of Argentina, 281, 286, 287, 288,
Persia, *see also* Iran
Persia, 35, 56, 174–5
Persian Wars (499–449 BCE), 56
Pétain, Marshal, leader of Vichy France, 245
Petrarch, 111
Philanthropos monastery (Istanbul), 131
Philip II, king of Spain, 317
Philip III, king of Spain, 318
Philip IV, king of Spain, patronage of, 318–19
Philipp II, king of Macedonia, 58
Phocians, take over Delphi, 56
Phoebe, a Titan, 47
Piacenza Pilgrim, 68
Pierre Causse, 260
Pilgrim, definitions of, 328
Pilgrimage, 'Caminoisation' of, 310
  alternative forms of, 216
  ancestral power and, 181
  as a unifier, 22–3, 39, 102, 205, 220–1, 250–1, 253, 258–9, 266, 273, 274
  as heritage practice, 303, 304
  British rule in India and, 35, 40, 42
  business and, 28
  by proxy, 218, 300
  caste distinctions and, 174
  colonialism and, 5, 54, 55, 228–32
  comforts of, 77, 78
  commercialisation of, 241–3, 252–3
  dangers of, 74, 76, 90, 95, 96, 110, 172, 200, 210, 224–6, 261, 296, 316, 319
  disappointments of, 73–4

economic impact of, 5, 14, 31, 32, 34, 64–5, 70, 73, 75, 76, 84, 91–3, 94, 100–1, 111–12, 163, 168, 169, 171, 173, 175, 182, 198, 240–4, 265, 293, 301, 322
famine and, 300
peace and, 5, 6, 249
hardships of, 303
healing and, 28, 129, 131, 137, 141, 178, 199, 220, 236, 238–40, 247–8, 254, 258, 268–71, 299–300
homecoming and, 205
identity and, 212, 296
importance of landscape to, 203–7
law and, 299, 319
motives for, 2–3, 25, 28, 40, 46, 51–4, 86, 118, 149–50, 158, 163, 181, 198, 229, 245, 253, 258, 292–3, 300–1
organisation of, 73, 77, 97, 100, 296, 303–4
politics and, 2, 3, 12, 17, 19–21, 22–3, 24, 46, 52, 57, 58, 61–2, 91, 100, 105–6, 128, 130, 144, 159, 169–71, 181, 200–1, 206, 228, 237, 244–6, 250, 268, 276–8, 287, 311, 315–16,
politics and, in Rome, 118–22
post-war trauma and, 155
power and, 44–1, 21, 143, 167–8, 181–2
prohibition of, 6, 71, 167, 209–12, 215, 235, 260–1, 302, 306, 319
promotion of, 48, 297–8
provisions for, 64–5, 70, 74, 73, 80, 81, 84, 96, 100–1, 112, 165–6, 174, 220, 239, 297, 298, 299, 320
reconciliation and, 246, 250–1
regulation of, 5, 30, 103
secret conduct of, 211
secular, 152, 279–81, 327
Sikh opinion of, 218, 219
soldiers on, 80–1
spreading knowledge and, 91, 102
war and, 36, 46, 52, 54–7, 76, 84, 187, 211, 213, 226, 235, 242, 245–51, 306, 312, 319, 322
Pilgrims, accommodation for, 29, 67, 77, 78, 81, 95, 101, 111, 153, 166, 240, 254, 304, 313, 323
attacks on, 32, 69, 70, 230, 232
behaviour of, 12, 102, 262–3 293
control of, 36, 39–43, 57, 81–2, 103, 131, 170, 203, 215–16, 257, 298, 301, 302
criticism of, 174, 302–3, 304, 305
deaths of, 71, 114, 295, 314, 316
dress of, 2, 165
journeys of, 70, 73, 76–7, 91, 126, 165, 182, 187, 222, 238, 242–3, 252, 270–1, 293–4
permanent, 299–300
protection of, 74–5, 94, 95–6
records of, 113
sickness and, 299
status of, 12–13, 295–6, 315, 319
tolerance of, 71, 72–3
Pits, Joseph, 94–5
Plague, impact of, 317
Plains of Arafat (Saudi Arabia), 101
Plutarch, 51
Poland, pilgrims from, 238
Pontius Pilate, Roman governor, 257
Poor Fellow-Soldiers of Christ and the Temple of Solomon (Templars), 70, 71
Pope Alexander VII, construction of St Peter's plaza by, 115–16
Benedict XVI, pilgrimage to Lourdes of, 245–46

Boniface IX, 111–12
Boniface VIII, 110
Damasus, 107
Eugenius IV, 105
Francis, 286
Gregory XIII, 115
Innocent III, 108
John Paul II, 144, 326
John Paul XXIII, 256
Nicholas III
Nicholas V, 110
Pelagius I, 112
Pius IX, defeat and imprisonment, 119
Pius VI, imprisonment of, 118
Pius VII, imprisonment of, 118
Pius XII, 84, 113
Sixtus V, major building plans of, 115
Symmachus, 107, 112
Urban V, 111
Urban VIII, reform of, 115
Porta Argentea (Rome), 105
Ports, ethic mixing in, 97
Portugal, 5, 190, 312, 310
Prayag (India), 30, 32–5, 36, 40, 41, 42
Presley, Elvis, pilgrimage to home of (USA), 281
Prince of Wales, 272
Print, growth of, 297
Prisoners of war, pilgrimages of, 251
Prophet Muhammad, 68, 87, 88, 160, 166
Night Journey of, 64
as founder of Islam, 87–8
relics of, 141–3
Pucheria, empress, 128, 130
Purchas, Samuel, 30
Pythia (Delphi), 45, *46*, 49, 50, 54, 58, 60
access to, 48, 52
and Roman interest, 58
causes of visions of, 61
confusing advice of, 55–6
favouritism of, 56
madness of, 49–51
responses of, 52, 54, 55–7
Pythian Games (Delphi), 48, 53, 59–60

Q

Qianlong, Chinese emperor, 25–6
Qin Shi Huang, Chinese emperor, 17–19
Qom (Iran), pilgrimage to, 171
Quetzalcoatl, Aztec god, pilgrimage in honour of, 181, 182

R

Rabbi Jacob, pilgrimage of, 71
Rabbi Obadiah de Bertinoro, travels of, 73
Rabbi Samuel Ben Samson, pilgrimage of, 71
Railway, criticisms of use by pilgrims of, 242–3
impact on pilgrimage caravans of, 96–7
moral risks of, 97
pilgrim use of, 42–3, 77, 81, 96, 236–7, 252, 268, 269, 304–5, 320, 321
religious services onboard the, 243
special provisions for pilgrims on, 78, 239, 242–3, 321
Raja Bhakt Singh of Alwar, pilgrimage of, 40

Rajendra the Great, 28
Ramdaspur (India), 220
Ramiro I, king of Asturias, 312
Ranjit Singh, Maharaja, 226–7, 228
Rātana Pā, 8, 61, 267–78, *270*
access to, 271
anniversary pilgrimages to, 273, 274–5, 276–7
Rātanaism, hierarchy of, 274
MPs representative of, 276, 277
spread of, 272–6
Recoleta Cemetery (Buenos Aires), 288, *289*–90
Reconquista, 322
Red Cloud, 208, 209
Red Sea, 98
Reformation, impact on pilgrimage of, 4, 75, 114, 116, 151, 317–21
Reincarnation, 38
Reinhardt, Django, 259
René, duke of Anjou, 254
Rewiti Te Whena, 275
Rhône, river (France), 253
Rhys ap Gruffydd, Welsh prince, 1
Richard Two Dogs, 205
Rio de Janiero (Brazil), 279
Robert of Clari, relic list of, 135
Robert Yellow Nose, pilgrimage of, 212
Roger II, king of Sicily, 315
Roman ruins, Christianisation of, 115
Romani, *see,* Gypsy
Romania, pilgrimages from, 122
Rome (Italy), 1, 7, 9, 77, 105–23, 128, 235, 243, 316
decline of pilgrimage to, 118
decline of, 106
impact of loss of Jerusalem on, 108
rebuilding of, 112, 115
sack of (410), 106
spiritual renewal of, 115
Roosevelt, Franklin D., president of the USA, 211
Rosary Basilica (Lourdes), 237, 240
Roxelana, patronage of, 74
Russia, 35, 76
subsidises pilgrimage to Mecca, 95
pilgrims from, 76–9 137–38
Rutter, Eldon, pilgrimage of, 99–100
Ruy González de Clavijo, accidental pilgrimage of, 138–9
Ryōnzenji (Shikoku), temple of, 297

S

Saigoku, pilgrimage to, 292, 303
Saigyō, pilgrimage of, 295
Sainte Chapelle (Paris), 136
Saintes Maries, grave of, 254
processions of statues of, 254–6, *255*, 257
relics of, 254, 255–6, 257
Saintes-Maries de la Mer (France),
night time vigil at, 258
altar stone at, 254
growth of pilgrimage to, 260
renaming of, 254
Sakineh, wife of the Shah of Iran, 164
Saladin, sultan, 70, 71
Salazar, António de Oliveira, Catholicism of, 199
Sampedro, Elias Valiña , 325–6
San Lorenzo (Rome), 112
San Stefano (Rome), 113
Sancha, wife of Ferdinand the Great, pilgrimage of, 312
Santa Maria dell Anima (Rome), 113
Santiago de Compostela, 8, 9, 253, 308–28
association with Shikoku of, 307

attacks on, 312, 313, 319
building in, 311, 317, 322–3
cathedral in, 308, *309*, 313
decline of, 316, 317–18, 319–20, 324
donations and payments to, 319, 322
internationalisation of, 313, 323, 324–7
origins of, 311
popularity of, 310
royal patronage of, 311
Sara la Kali, St Sara's identity as, 257
Saraswati River (India), 33
Sarkozy, Nicolas, French president, religiosity of, 246
Saronjini Naidu, 39
Sasaguri (Japan), pilgrimage circuit at, 302
Satellite pilgrimage sites, 22, 28
Saxony (Germany), pilgrim from, 254
Scallop shell, colours of, 326
symbol of Santiago de Compostela pilgrimage, 315, 323, 325
Scott, Walter, 152
Second Sacred War, 56
Second Temple (Jerusalem), 64, 65
Second World War, 5–6, 101, 120, 213, 238, 250, 251, 259, 260, 306
Secular pilgrimages, 6, 77, 121
Selmin the Grim, sultan, 94
Seven Churches of Rome, 116, 117
Sex, pilgrimage and, 17
Shah Safi, pilgrimage to Karbala of, 168-
Shi'ites, expulsion from Mecca of Persians by, 94
Shikoku (Japan), 8, 9, 166, 292–307
association with Santiago de Compostela of, 307
circuit of, 293–5
criticisms of, 304–5
decline of pilgrimage on, 302
development of route around, 297, 307
exile to, 295
growth of pilgrimage to, 296
imitation of, 302
internationalisation of pilgrimage to, 305–6
Japanese culture linked to, 303
national symbol of Japan of, 296
pilgrim numbers to, 306–7
repeat pilgrimage around, 301
revival of pilgrimage on, 303
temples on, 293–4, 297, 298, 303
Shikoku Henro Ezu, 299
Shikoku Henro, international recognition of, 307
Shingon Buddhism, 293
Shinnen-bō, publisher, 298
Shinnyo Shinnō, prince, pilgrimage of, 295
Shinto priests, forced conversion of, 302–3
Shinzei, pilgrimage of, 295
Shiva, god of destruction, 27, 28, 29, 32, 37
Shōdoshima (Japan), pilgrimage circuit at, 302
Shogan Tsunayoshi, laws of, 296–7
Shroud of Turin (Italy), 122
Sikander Begum, her concern for pilgrims, 95
Sikhs, pilgrimages of, 44, 157, 217–32
Sitting Bull, 208, 209
Six Day War (1967), 84
Slavery, Angola and, 194–9
Smith, John, politician, 159

Solomon, biblical king, 64
Somerled, king of the Isles, 151
South America, pilgrims from, 187
Souvenirs, 240–1, 254
Spain, pilgrims from, 238, 260
Spanish flu, 268
Sparta (Greece), 48
 pilgrims from, 52, 54
Sri Akal Takht Sahib (Amritsar), throne, 223
Saint Acacius, 125
 Andrew, relics of, 127, 135
 Anne, head of, 135
 Anthony (Muxima), 198–99
 Artemios, relics of, 129, 131
 Athanasio I, shrine of, 137
 Athanasius, relics of, 308, 320
 Barnabas, 129
 Blathmac, martyrdom and burial of (Iona), 148–49
 Bridget of Sweden, pilgrimage of, 315
 Brigid, 150
 Ceathan's Well (Iona), 149–50
 Columba, 145, 146–148, 149, 153, 157–9
 Cosmas, relics of, 129
 Damian, relics of, 129
 Daniel, 129
 Francis Solano, 284
 Gennaro, 318
 Helena, relics of, 135
 Hippolytus of Rome, relics of, 254
 James the Great, 253, 310–11
  as *miles Christi,* 312
  as patron saint of Spain, 311, 318
  as symbol of Spain, 319, 320
  as victor over the Moors, 312
  attack on Spanish links of, 319
  concealment of relics of, 318
  discovery of the grave of, 311
  fascist promotion of, 322
  portraits of Franco and, 322
  relics of, 308, 310, 311, 312, 317, 320
  tomb of, 314, 318–19
 John Chrysostom, 49, 124–5
  relics of, 125, 144
 John Lateran (Rome), 107
 John of Oxeia (Istanbul), 131
 John Prodromos (Istanbul), 128
 John the Baptist, church of (Istanbul), 129
  relics of, 123 128, 130, 135, 137, 139
 John the Evangelist, 149, 308
 Joseph, 128, 318
 Lawrence, 107
 Lucia, relics of, 135
 Luke the Evangelist, 131
  relics of, 127, 135
  image of the Virgin by, 137
 Margaret of Scotland, patronage on Iona of, 150
 Mark, relics of, 135
 Matthew, Gospel of, 129
 Michael, archangel, 267, 318
 Mokios, 125
 Paul the New Martyr, relics of, 135
 Paul, 126
  relics of, 107, 126–7
 Peter, 107, 126
 Philip Neri, 117
 Phocas, relics of, 128
 Sara, 252, 256, 261,
  Catholicisation of, 259–60
  origins and identity of, 253, 256–7, 263, 265–6
  procession of statue of, 257, 261, 263

reliquary of, 256
Stephen the Protomartyr, relics of, 128
Symeon Stylites, 129–30
Teresa of Ávila, patron of Spain, 318
Theodore, relics of, 308, 320
Thomas Becket, 2
Thomas the Apostle, 124
Timothy, relics of, 126–7
Zachariah, relics of, 128
St Andrews, bishop of (Scotland), 155
St George, cathedral of (Constantinople), 144
St Peter's (Rome), 105, 106, 112, 113
St Winefride's well (Wales), 239, 262
St Mary's chapel (Iona), 149
St Mary's, Mount Zion, 72
St Michael's Chapel (Iona), 151
St Justinian's Bay (Wales), 1
St Oran, chapel of (Iona), 149, 157
St David's cathedral (Wales), 1–2
Stalin, Russian leader, 323
Starkie, Walter, pilgrimages of, 262, 324
Statue of Liberty (USA), 279
Status Quo of the Holy Places (1929), 82
Status Quo, edict (1757), 75
Stephen of Novgorod, 137
Stevenson, Robert Louis, 152
St-Jean-Pied-de-Port (France), 314
Straits of Gibraltar, 316
Suez Canal, 97
Suicide, pilgrimage and, 23–4, 38–9
Suleiman the Magnificent, 74, 82, 168, 170
Sun Dance, 203, 206, 210, 213
Sweden, pilgrims from, 315
Sweet Medicine, 205–6
Switzerland, pilgrims from, 238
Syracuse (Sicily), 54

T

Tada Emon, pilgrimage of, 301
Tahupōtiki Wiremu Rātana, 267–8, 269–70, 271, 272–3
Tai Shan (China), 7, 10–26,
ascent of, 12–13, 23
imagery of, 10, *11*, *18*
inscriptions on, 19, 25–6
Taizong, Chinese Emperor, 20–1
Takamure Itsue, pilgrimage of, 292
Takeda Tokuemon, pilgrimage of, 301
Tarbes (France), 236, 238
Tarn Taran (India), pool of, 220
Tax, pilgrimage and, 39, 40, 41, 42, 56, 70, 100–1, 175, 225
Te Kehupūkoro, pilgrimage of, 268
Tehran (Iran), 172
Temple Mount (Jerusalem), 83
Tennyson, Alfred, Lord, 61
The Holy Blood and the Holy Grail, 265
Théas, bishop of Tarbes, 250, 251
Themis, daughter of Gaia, 46, 47
Themistocles, general, 56
Theodemir, bishop of Iria, 311
Theodosius I, emperor, 67, 127–8
Theodosius II, emperor, 128, 131
Thomas Cook and Son, 77, 97–8
Thompson, Edward Herbert, 176–7
Thourioi (Italy), pilgrims from, 53
Timur the Lame, Turco-Mongol conqueror, 32, 138
Tirtha, 32, 38
Tōkaidō road (Japan), travel on the, 297

Tokouru, MP, 276
Tokyo (Japan), 297, 303
Topkapi Palace (Constantinople), relics and the, 141–42
Toulouse (France), 239
Tourism, pilgrimage and, 143–4, 241, 263–65, 303, 321, 323
Transport of pilgrims, 2140, 42, 47–8, 81, 101, 90, 137, 238, 325
  by air, 81
  by bus, 324
  by horse, 314
  by motorcar, 305, 325
  on foot, 165, 306, 310, 314, 315, 323–4
  by sea, 76, 81, 304, 316
  see also Railway
Traynor, Jack, pilgrimage of, 247–9
Treaty of Waitangi (1840), 272, 275
True Cross, 123, 130, 135, 139, 321
  discovery by Helena, 126
  relic of, acquired by Bromholm Priory, Norfolk (England), 135
Tucamán (Argentina), 284
Tuki Shortland, pilgrimage of, 269
Tup, cure of, 269–70
Tupu tai-Ngakawa, 275
Turkey, pilgrims from, 76, 165
Twain, Mark, 77
Twelver Shi'ism, 162

U

Udall, Morris, 214–15
UNESCO, pilgrimage sites and, 13, 307, 326–7
United States of America, pilgrims from, 237, 247, 251
Unzué Palace (Buenos Aires), pilgrimage to, 284, 290
Upanishads, 27–28
Uruguay, 288
Usama Ibn Munqidh, pilgrimage of, 71
Uyghurs, limits on pilgrimage to Mecca for, 103

V

van Gogh, Vincent, 158
Varanasi (India), 30, 36–9, 43
Vatican City, 107, 119, 286
Venezuela, pilgrims from, 238
Venice (Italy), 73, 77, 135
Veronica (Rome), 108, *109*, 110, 123, 130
Veterans, pilgrimages to Lourdes of, 247–8, 249, 250
Via Alexandria (Rome), 115
Via Crucis (Lourdes), 237
Via del Pellegrino (Rome), 113
Via Dolorosa (Jerusalem), 64, 108, 147
Via Giulia (Rome), 115
Via Sistina (Rome), 115
Via Tiburtina (Italy), 107
Victor Emmanuel, king of Italy, 120–1
Victoria, queen of England, 89
Victoria Cross, pilgrimage by holders of, 249
Virgin Mary, 8, 113, 190, 191, 253, 325
  French devotion to, 244
  Immaculate Conception, 235
  on Iona, 147
  relics of, 130–31, 134, 135
  visions of, 233–5, 238
  see also, Our Lady
Vision quests, 206

W
Waerete Norman, pilgrimage of, 275
Wahhabi Sunnis, 169, 174
Wang Shizhen, pilgrimage of, 13
Water, importance to Mayan
  cosmology of, 180
  pilgrimage in honour of, 180
  to Karbala, 169
Wavell, Arthur, pilgrimage of, 316
Way of St James (Spain), *see* Camino
  de Santiago
Weeping, pilgrimage and, 163–64
Western (wailing) Wall (Jerusalem),
  65, 66, *82*, 83, 84–5
Whistling Elk, pilgrimage of, 211
White Buffalo Woman, 205
Wilhelm II, German kaiser, 81
William X, duke of Aquitaine,
  pilgrimage of, 314
Williams, Thomas, archbishop of
  Birmingham, 249
Women, criticism of pilgrimage of,
  17, 237
  pilgrimage and, 77, 292, 300, 321
Wordsworth, William, 152
Wu, Chinese Emperor, 19, 20–1

X
Xipe Totec, god, pilgrimage in
  honour of, 181
Xuanzang, Buddhist writer, 38

Y
Yamuna River (India), 32
Yangtze River (China), 10
Yazid I, caliph, 160, 163
Yuben Shinnen, guidebook of, 297
Yucatán Peninsula (Mexico), 176, 177,
  179, 180

Z
Zeus, king of the gods, 47
  oracle of, 56
Zhenzong, Chinese Emperor, 21–2
Zionism, 76, 83
Zola, Émile, novel by, 242
Zoödochos Pege (Istanbul), 131